Dancing Mestizo Modernisms

Dancing Mestizo Modernisms

Choreographing Postcolonial and Postrevolutionary Mexico

JOSÉ LUIS REYNOSO

OXFORD
UNIVERSITY PRESS

Oxford University Press is a department of the University of Oxford. It furthers
the University's objective of excellence in research, scholarship, and education
by publishing worldwide. Oxford is a registered trade mark of Oxford University
Press in the UK and certain other countries.

Published in the United States of America by Oxford University Press
198 Madison Avenue, New York, NY 10016, United States of America.

© Oxford University Press 2024

All rights reserved. No part of this publication may be reproduced, stored in
a retrieval system, or transmitted, in any form or by any means, without the
prior permission in writing of Oxford University Press, or as expressly permitted
by law, by license, or under terms agreed with the appropriate reproduction
rights organization. Inquiries concerning reproduction outside the scope of the
above should be sent to the Rights Department, Oxford University Press, at the
address above.

You must not circulate this work in any other form
and you must impose this same condition on any acquirer.

Library of Congress Control Number: 2023945035

ISBN 978–0–19–762256–8 (pbk.)
ISBN 978–0–19–762255–1 (hbk.)

DOI: 10.1093/oso/9780197622551.001.0001

Paperback printed by Marquis Book Printing, Canada
Hardback printed by Bridgeport National Bindery, Inc., United States of America

*Dedico this book
a mi familia
y to all undocumented inmigrantes in the world
¡Animo!*

Contents

Acknowledgments	ix
Introduction: Dancing Embodied Mestizo Modernisms, Choreographing Transnational Nationalisms	1
1. Mexico City's Ambivalent Spatial *Mestizaje*: Bodies in Motion from Independence to Dictatorship	34
2. Choreographing the Indigenous Body in the Independence Centennial: From Dictatorship to Revolution	80
3. Embracing the Indigenous while Establishing a Mestizo Nation: *Forjando* a Revolutionary *Patria*	118
4. The Making of a Postrevolutionary Modern Dance Form: Debating National and International Politics and Aesthetics (1930s–1940)	168
Coda: Contemporary Mestizo Modernisms and Transnational Nationalisms in the United States	230
Bibliography	251
Index	265

Acknowledgments

This book is as much the direct product of my experiences as a scholar and choreographer as it is of my experiences growing up in Guadalajara, Mexico, as a brown, working-class teenager who eventually migrated to the United States. The book is a product of the many situations and people who have influenced me along this trajectory. I feel the need to go as far back as I can remember to thank people with whom I shared ordinary life experiences that motivate my thinking about some of the main topics in this book: colonial legacies of racialization and socialization, Mexican history, identity formation, migration, and the role that dance plays in these processes. How can I account for all who have contributed, directly and indirectly, to the life of this book—family, relatives, friends, colleagues, mentors, and institutions—both in Mexico and the United States, without missing anyone? Unable to do so, I offer my best effort here before submitting the book to the press. However, I am grateful to everyone named and not named whose influence and support have made this book possible.

I will start by thanking those whose labor and expertise contributed in many ways to shaping the content and production of this book. I am deeply grateful to Norm Hirschy, Oxford University Press (OUP) editor, for his patience, generous support, and for leading his production team in bringing this book to light. I am grateful for the enthusiasm and critical feedback two OUP anonymous readers provided. Thank you to those who read and shared comments on a short portion of the manuscript at different stages of development (in Mexico and the United States): Manuel R. Cuellar, Susan L. Foster, Imani Kai Johnson, Anthea Kraut, Jorge N. Leal, Dolores (Lolita) Ponce, Cristina F. Rosa, and Margarita Tortajada Quiroz. Big thanks to Adrián Félix for his leadership in facilitating the UC Riverside interdisciplinary Latino Studies Working Group, which funded a manuscript workshop that benefited my book's development enormously. I am grateful to workshop members and colleagues Xóchitl C. Chávez (Music), Claudia Holguín Mendoza (Hispanic Studies), and Jorge N. Leal (History), who provided feedback during the discussion, and to Iván E. Aguirre Darancou (Hispanic Studies) and Adrián Félix (Ethnic Studies), who also shared written comments throughout the manuscript. Immense gratitude to the workshop's primary guest reader-respondent, Dr. Mary K. Coffey (Art History, Dartmouth College), whose generous participation during the discussion and detailed written feedback proved crucial in my process of developing the work.

Conversations with and/or inspiring works by colleagues interested in dance, Mexico, and Latin America have also informed the development of this book. I thank Juan Manuel Aldape Muñoz, Melissa Blanco Borelli, María Eugenia Cadús, Manuel R. Cuellar, Victoria Fortuna, Anita Gonzalez, Ellie Guerrero, Ruth Hellier-Tinoco, Ana Paula Höfling, Hannah Kosstrin, Cristina F. Rosa, Elizabeth Schwall, Paul A. Scolieri, K. Mitchell Snow, and Lester Tomé, among others cited in the text, including many of the dance historians at the CENIDID-Danza in Mexico City. I am also grateful to Primera Generación Dance Collective members Alfonso (Fonzy) Cervera, Irvin Manuel González, Patricia (Patty) Huerta, and Rosa Rodríguez Fraizer for their inspiring work (which I discuss in the book's coda), feedback, and friendship. I am indebted to Jessica Hinds-Bond for editing work on an earlier draft of the manuscript and to Shannon Wray for her enthusiastic support while copyediting the manuscript and sharing other feedback twice in the process. Thanks for your kindness, Shannon! Gracias también a Eunice Anahi Romero Ayala for editing assistance and organizing images in my personal archive. I am grateful to every single person for the extent to which they indirectly inspired and/or directly impacted the book's content and production development. Whatever strengths the book has are the reflection of their labor and expertise. I was ultimately the person who decided the theoretical orientation of the work and its content, and thus I am solely responsible for its weaknesses, imprecisions, and omissions.

Generous funding and other forms of support from various institutions and people allowed me to conduct archival research in Mexico City and develop the writing at different stages in the process. My gratitude to the University of California Institute for Mexico and the United States (UC-MEXUS) for two Small Grants (2009, 2010, UC-MEXUS Associate Director Dr. Andrea Kaus) and a UC-MEXUS-CONACYT Postdoctoral Research Fellowship (UC-MEXUS and Mexico's National Council for Science and Technology, CONACYT) for a research residency at the Centro Nacional de Investigación, Difusión e Información de la Danza José Limón (CENIDID-Danza) in Mexico City, where I drafted portions of the book (January–December 2017, UC-MEXUS Associate Director Dr. Wendy DeBoer); the Committee on Research of the Riverside Division of the Academic Senate for a Regents Faculty Fellowship (2019–2020); the UC Riverside Hellman Fellowship Program for a Hellman Fellowship (2016–2017); and the Andrew W. Mellon Dance Studies in/and the Humanities program for a Postdoctoral Fellowship in Dance Studies at Northwestern University (2012–2014).

I am grateful to the following institutions and people for giving me access to do research in their archives and/or processing my requests and granting permission to reproduce images in this book: at the Biblioteca Miguel Lerdo de Tejada, agradecimiento to Mtra. Adriana Castillo Román (Directora General de Promoción Cultural y Acervo Patrimonial) for granting permission, and to Dr. Porfirio Tamez Avantes (Director de Bibliotecas) and Lic. Angel Aurelio González Amozorrutia (Jefe de Atención a Usuarios) for their assistance in different aspects of the process; gracias to all the staff at the biblioteca, including Antonio Rosas and especially Mario Rebollo Alatorre who was often the person facilitating archival materials and patiently waited for me as I was usually the last person leaving the library, minutes after it had already closed to the public. At the Escuela Nacional de Danza Nellie y Gloria Campobello, agradecimiento to Mtra. Jessica Adriana Lezama Escalona (Directora) for granting permission and Dafne Domínguez Vázquez for her generous help in the process regarding research and images; gracias also to Mtro. Fernando Aragón Monroy who was the school director when I conducted research there more than a decade earlier. At the Instituto Nacional de Antropología e Historia (INAH), agradecimiento to Lic. María del Perpetuo Socorro Villarreal Escárrega (Coordinadora Nacional) for granting permission and to the INAH's extensive team for assisting me at different stages in the process. For two images of Anna Sokolow and Frances Hellman, thank you to the family of Edward J. and Frances H. Bauman, especially Ms. Nina Bauman de Fels (a daughter of Frances Hellman) for granting permission and to Lauren Naslund (Associate Artistic Director of the Sokolow Theater Dance Ensemble) and Francesca Todesco (Isadora Duncan Archive) for their crucial assistance in the process. I am grateful to all these people for making possible my access to archival materials and facilitating the use of images that provide visual support and context for the stories I tell in this book.

My gratitude to colleagues and mentors, past and present, whose work, collegiality, and mentorship have inspired me and served as role models as I developed many of the ideas that led to this book. To my colleagues at UC Riverside Department of Dance, professors María Regina Firmino-Castillo, Imani Kai Johnson, Anusha Kedhar, Anthea Kraut, Luis Lara Malvacías, Joel Mejia Smith, taisha paggett, Wendy Rogers (Emerita), Jacqueline Shea Murphy, Linda J. Tomko (Emerita), Sage Ni'Ja Whitson; continuing lecturers Brandon J., Kelli King, Clydean (Makeda Kumasi) Parker, and the many talented guest artists and scholars who have taught in the department as well as the staff who help to keep our department operating, especial thanks to Reasey Heang, Katrina Oskie, Lily Chan Szeto, and more recently Marcelina Rose Ryneal for providing me administrative assistance in departmental and research related activities. During the last year of writing for this book, I organized an online writing group; thank you to my colleagues Anusha, Imani, and María, as well as doctoral students Xiomara Forbez and Lindsay Rapport, for being such great writing partners when they made it to our writing sessions. Especial thanks to Lindsay for being such a committed writing buddy from beginning to end in our group!

Gratitude also to my professors at UCLA for the MFA and PhD programs: Cheng-Chieh Yu, Donald Cosentino, Dan Froot, David Gere, Angelia Leung, Victoria Marks, Judy Mitoma, Allen Roberts, and David Roussève, as well as Maria Gillespie and many other talented lecturers. Gracias to Professor Marta Savigliano, who had a special impact on my development of a Latin Americanist critical perspective, and for her enthusiastic support!

When I sent an email with this request, "Dear Professor Susan Leigh Foster, I would appreciate it if you will consider being my MFA committee chair," she responded, "Yes, but only and only if you call me Susan." I am profoundly and forever grateful to Susan for her groundbreaking and inspiring scholarship and for her patience, care, trust, and mentorship during and after the completion of my MFA and PhD degrees under her guidance. For everything that I know, and for all that I do not know you have done for me, Thank you, Susan! I feel so fortunate to have had you as a mentor in one of the most formative phases of my adult life.

I thank professors Anurima Banerji, Guillermo Gomez-Peña, Janet O'Shea, Lionel Popkin, and Peter Sellars for being such great role models while I was a TA in their classes. Gratitude to my graduate-student colleagues and friends—in my cohort and those with whom my graduate career overlapped—whose work inspired me during the completion of my two degrees: in the MFA track, Rebecca Alson-Milkman, Amy "Catfox" Campion, I Nyoman Cerita (in memoriam), Kate Foley, taisha paggett, Jin-Sook Yang, and Ana María Álvarez, Esther Baker-Tarpaga, Liam Clancy, Sheetal Gandhi, d. Sabela grimes, Krenly Guzman, Arianne Hoffmann, Nicole Klaymoon (previously Smith) Sarah Leddy, Cinthya Lee, Meena Murugesan, Nguyen Nguyen, Cid Pearlman, Iddi Saaka, Michael Sakamoto, Alexandra Shilling, Joe Small, Hannah Van der Kolk, Sara Wookey, Jia Jia Wu, and Allison Wyper; in the PhD track, Feriyal Aslam, Eva Aymami Rene, Rosemary Candelario, Ana Paula Höfling, Angeline Shaka, Šara Stranovsky, and Lorena Alvarado, Jacinta Arthur, Harmony Bench, Claudia Brazzale, I-Wen Chang, Jenna Delgado, César García-Alvarez, Cindy García, Doran George (in memoriam), Mana Hayakawa, Neelima Jeychandran, Olive Mckeon, Leonard Melchor, Damola (Adedamola) Osinulu, Lorenzo Perillo, Cedar Bough Saeji, Mathew Sandoval, Cristina Rosa, Carolina San Juan, Yehuda Sharim, Brynn Shiovitz, Sangita Shresthova, Annie Tucker, Giavanni Washington, Sarah Wilbur, Alessandra Williams, Kathleen (Kat) Williams, and Sarah Wolf. Thanks to all the staff who made my stay at UCLA's department of World Arts and Cultures/Dance a very rewarding experience: Arsenio Apillanes, Eveline Chang, Ginger Holguin, Sam Jones, Daniel Millner, Mimi Moorhead, Carl Patrick (in memoriam), Wendy Temple, Silvily Thomas, and Lillian Wu.

Many others have been crucial in my development and the direction I have taken toward dance studies and dance practice. I am forever grateful to Susan

Manning for her brilliant and influential work as a scholar and advocate for the field, and more especially for her caring mentorship while I was an Andrew Mellon Dance Studies postdoctoral fellow at Northwestern University. Thank you, Susan! Thanks to all my inspiring peers at the various events organized by the Andrew Mellon Dance Studies in/and the Humanities initiative led by Susan Manning, Rebecca Schneider, and Janice Ross and my colleagues at the Dance Studies Organization.

Margarita Toratajada Quiroz's prolific work and generous support since I first met her in 2009 enabled me to cultivate a relationship not only with the CENIDID-Danza scholars but also with her as a colleague and friend. Gracias Margarita por tu generosidad!

Thanks to Professor Judith Hamera, who introduced me to dance studies when I began exploring dance theory while a graduate student in psychology (and a dancer with Hae Kyung Lee) at CSULA. Hae pushed me physically in ways that helped me make so many discoveries about my (dancing) body as her student and company dancer. Thank you, both! Thanks to Hae's dancers, Miguel Olvera and Claudia Lopez, for embracing me from the start when I took their dance classes at CSULA. Much gratitude to all the dancers and dance makers from whom I have learned, danced with, and co-created over the years. To all the undergraduate and graduate students with whom I have worked as a TA and professor at UCLA, Northwestern University, and UC Riverside, thank you for sharing your life experiences, inspiring me with your research interests, and challenging me with your questions.

I have a special place in my heart for the working-class, primarily Mexican immigrant and Mexican American community of Boyle Heights in East Los Angeles, where I lived for many years and which I mention in the coda of this book. My life experiences and interpersonal relationships there profoundly shaped my orientation to scholarship and creative practice. I am grateful to everyone in the barrio who taught me how to survive and how to thrive. I am deeply grateful to my teachers in the ESL program I attended, especially Mses. Gloria, Indie, and Linda (who taught the upper levels), and Mr. Galarze (who insisted on teaching us lessons other teachers thought we were not ready for), and in the high school programs for adults, especially Mr. Fong and Mr. Mackie who encouraged me to go to a community college. Throughout the years, I volunteered in various social programs at local churches, public libraries, and other contexts. The people I worked with and the people "I served" taught me the meaning of collectivity and community. Thanks to all my friends, who became my family in the United States and supported and influenced me in more ways than I can name here: mi compadre y comadre Carlos y Toñis, her daughters, my ahijadas Carlita y Jasmine; Toni, Leopoldo (Jay, Sopita), Miguel, Luciano, Carlos, Vero, Ricardo, Julio, Carmen, Armando, Hector, Susy, Olivia, Heriberto, Wendy, Carmen,

Migue ("Pedrito Fernandez"), Don Gil y doña Chave, Gil y Norma, Lupe y Gary, Uriel, Rigo y su esposa, Monse y doña Soco, Sr. Maria (en memoria), la familia Gonzalez, Padre Lorenzo (en memoria), Pety, y todes mis neighbors.

My gratitude to Katsumi Imoto, my construction boss, whose flexibility enabled me to miss work whenever I fell behind on school homework. You have done more for me than you can imagine Katz, gracias!!!! Gracias a mis construction coworkers: Miguel, Tony, David, Layo, y Nacho. And to my dearest father figure, Harry Okamoto, "the nicest person you could ever meet," as a community award he received stated, and who went by "Kiku, The Oriental Mystifier" as a magician and musician (in memoriam). He set the bar so high as to what it means to be kind to every single person, familiar and stranger, always with a smile or joyful laughter. I can only aspire to his seemingly unattainable level of kindness. I miss you dearly, Harry! Thank you for your presence in my life. Margarita, a mother figure, has been equally kind along the way, supporting me and sharing her wisdom. ¡Gracias Margarita! Thanks to Dr. Moriel for helping me in the process of regaining my footing!

To an equally influential group of people, in another working-class barrio but in Guadalajara, Mexico, where I grew up. Gracias to my dearest friends whose friendship was vital during some of my most formative years as a little boy and teenager: a mis grandes amigos Litos (¡Manueeeeel!) y Concho, Lalo, Chagui, Gusillo, Polka, Lorena, Lupe y Don Alfonso, Cuatra, Mono, Chili, Doña Cuca y Don Toño, Bros, Fer Orion, Jorge Fonseca, Palomo, Gordo, Rolis, Justo, Chel, Isra, Liz, Vero, Titi, Tere, Luisa, Gamaliel, Hippie, Topete, Chava, Fernando, George, Canay Juan, Canay Ricardo, Calzon, Takechi, Adriana, Joel, Alex, Willie, Justo, Doña Anita, Gustavo, Pepe Coco, Licho, doña Celia, Hugo, Cayos, Rata, Laura, Gustavo, Jesús, Chino, Cabe, Judith, Silvia, doña Adela y don Isaias, Roman, Carlos, Ricky, doña Carmelita, don Roman y su mama, y muchos otros amiges y vecines. Gratitude to my closest coworkers and friends in the textile factory where I worked as a teenager (all of them much older than me), Pancho (en memoria), Sergio, Fausto (en memoria), Arturo, y el Pato. Gracias don Cheo (en memoria), another father figure, porque su gran confianza en mí me inspiró a comenzar el proceso de aprender a confiar en mí mismo.

My extended family have always been loving. Gracias a mi tía Vira y mi tío Chava siempre tan amorosos como otra mamá y papá para mí; a mis muy querides primos-hermanos Gera, con quien emigré a EU, el Chino, Tavio, y mi hermanita Kary. Tía Licho, como otra mamá, gracias por todo su cariño antes, durante y después del tiempo que nos tuvo mientras Gera y yo dábamos el brinco al otro lado. Gracias a mis primas Abi, Geny, Mary, y Yoly. Gracias a mi tío Rigo, siempre generoso haciendo por toda la familia, incluyendo la mía. Por su influencia, gracias a mis tías Betty, Carmelita, Lily (en memoria), Lety, Ofe (en memoria) y a mis tíos Toño (en memoria), Chuy (en memoria), y Panchito. A mis abuelita/os, Reyna y Toño, Balbi, y Pancho (todes en memoria).

And my familia who have been so influential in the way I learned to experience the world. Con todo mi corazón, gracias a mi beloved late mami cuyo amor sentí siempre, in any situation we went through. ¡Te amo y te extraño mucho mami Noy! A mi papi, José Luis cuya inteligencia le permitió enseñarse a sí mismo la Ley Federal del Trabajo y la Ley del Seguro Social para en su capacidad de líder sindical luchar tanto por los trabajadores en la fábrica de Atemajac y muchos otros lugares; ¡Te quiero y te admiro papi, heredé muchos de tus dones, gracias! Con amor a mi hermano Hugo, el talentoso artista que me inspira; a Fran, mi carnalito quien modela cómo se ama a una familia; a mi hermanita Eri con quien jugaba luchitas cuando era una nenita antes que yo emigrara a EU; a mi preciosa sobrina Gaby; a mi precioso sobrino Nathan; a mis querides sobrines Paulina, Danny, Karen and their beautiful children.

Finally, gracias Kiku for taking me into the fascinating space of interspecies affect, cariño, and mutual care, a different sense of time and space, a world within the world.

Gracias Maye, por el amor, cariño, y compañia cercana—aún en la distancia—durante este proceso a veces arduo, pero siempre fascinante, de caminar por la vida.

Introduction
Dancing Embodied Mestizo Modernisms, Choreographing Transnational Nationalisms

Little more than a month after they arrived in Mexico City in late January 1919, the famous Russian ballet dancer Anna Pavlova and her company began performing Mexican dances in their shows. Based on primary sources and other materials chronicling Pavlova's visit to the Mexican capital, the following describes her dancing from the perspective of someone who witnessed Pavlova performing the iconic *Jarabe Tapatío* (sources included in footnotes). The vignette provides a glimpse into what might have been the experience of a person watching the performance at the Plaza el Toreo, an outdoor bullfight ring where thousands of people from all social classes enthusiastically applauded the internationally acclaimed ballerina. The passage intends to stir up one's kinesthetic imagination while beginning to suggest the dance's political implications:

> *Expressing an attitude of playful reluctance, the china poblana's balleticized body comes in and out of physical proximity to her charro dancing partner.*[1] *She engages in this dance of seduction while constantly moving across the space on the tip of her toes with grace and lightness. She pauses occasionally, grounding her heels on the floor and curling her arms to hold her skirt to the sides as she looks at her pursuant lover from a distance. At each pause, she elongates her torso and neck while turning her shy face slightly away from the gallant charro. All the while, she keeps him in sight from the corner of her eyes. As she coquettishly entices him, she sometimes seems to give in to his romantic advances. Their bodies and faces near each other so close before veering apart once more. Towards the end of the*

---

[1] The two characters have long been associated with the *Jarabe Tapatío*. The *china poblana*, a symbol of *mestiza* docile femininity, wears variations of a shawl, ribbons interlaced through her braids, and a traditional long skirt with colorful embroidery, typically including the green, white, and red of the Mexican flag. The *charro*, established as a referent of a Mexican cowboy's (hyper)masculinity, wears tight pants, a jacket with shiny accents and buttons, and a bow tie on his chest. His distinctive wide-brim sombrero (hat) has given the dance its name outside of Mexico (i.e., the Mexican Hat Dance). For discussions on the development of the *china poblana* and the *charro*, see María Del Carmen Vázquez Mantecón, "La china mexicana, mejor conocida como china poblana" 22, no. 77 (México, DF: Anales del Instituto de Investigaciones Estéticas, 2000): 123–50; and Tania Carreño King, *El charro, La construcción de un estereotipo nacional (1920-1940)* (México, DF: INEHRM, Federación Mexicana de la Charrería, 2000).

dance, Mr. Pianowsky chases Madam Pavlowa[2] around the brim of his sombrero (hat), by now lying on the ground (Figure I.1). She holds up her skirt right below her knees as her china poblana braids sway from side to side in response to the motions of intricate footwork she performs to the music on the tip of her refined arching feet. In the end, Madam Pavlowa succumbs to the charro's insistence, and they consummate their relationship with a veiled kiss hidden behind his sombrero. The audience, rich and poor, erupts in euphoric approval. "Many men [hurl] their own hats onto the stage, hoping that [Madam Pavlowa] would dance on them."[3] It is very emotional to see one of the most famous ballerinas in the world dancing our Jarabe Tapatío on her "Russian and celestial" pointe ballet shoes. Her dancing has just made the "heart of our race palpitate" forcibly and our "blood precipitate in a wild uncontrollable torrent"[4] as we all join in yelling out bravos, hurrahs, and increasingly louder Viva México! Viva México! Viva México![5]

This imaginative dance reconstruction represents a writing strategy employed by dance scholars to comment on the challenges and possibilities in the processes of reconstructing history—especially dancing bodies' histories—from archival fragments.[6] The vignette also illustrates the focus of *Dancing Mestizo Modernisms: Choreographing Postcolonial and Postrevolutionary Mexico*. This book argues that dance has contributed to reproducing and resisting colonial ideas about race and social status in forming individual and collective identities within Mexico's nation-building projects. In so doing, it emphasizes the transnational flow of dancers from various countries who participated in forging ideas

---

[2] Many primary sources in Spanish consulted for this book spell "Pavlova" as "Pavlowa."

[3] Keith Money, *Anna Pavlova: Her Life and Art* (New York: Alfred A. Knopf, 1982), 273.

[4] These three phrases within quotation marks are from Gabriel Fernández Ledesma, *El universal ilustrado*, Mexico, July 31, 1919, 7. Unless otherwise noted, all translations from Spanish throughout the book are my own.

[5] The celebratory phrase *Viva México* has been recurrent in Mexican history as an expression of Mexican pride, including in response to performances of dances like the *Jarabe Tapatío*; see Gabriel Saldívar, *El Jarabe: Baile popular mexicano* (México, DF: Talleres Gráficos de la Nación, 1937), 9.

[6] I suggest here that reconstructing Pavlova's dance and any other dancers' performance of Mexican (historical) dances presents similar challenges and possibilities when reconstructing—on stage and on the written page—any form of "Western theater dance" or "the staging of ancient Greek tragedy or Shakespearean drama." Susan Manning, "Modern Dance in the Third Reich: Six Positions and a Coda," in *Choreographing History*, ed. Susan L. Foster (Indianapolis: Indiana University Press, 1995), 175. For an expanded version of this vignette, see Jose L. Reynoso, "Choreographing Modern Mexico: Anna Pavlova in Mexico City (1919)," ed. Carrie J. Preston, *Modernist Cultures* 9, no. 1 (May 2014): 80–98. For other examples of dance scholars who have devised imaginative means to reconstruct and theorize dance and other cultural, historical, and kinesthetic encounters, see Marta E. Savigliano, *Tango and the Political Economy of Passion* (Boulder, CO: Westview Press, 1995); Susan L. Foster, "Choreographing History," in *Choreographing History*, ed. Susan L. Foster (Bloomington: University of Indiana Press, 1995), 3–21; Priya Srinivasan, "The Bodies beneath the Smoke or What's behind the Cigarette Poster: Unearthing Kinesthetic Connections in American Dance History," *Discourses in Dance* 4, no. 1 (Summer 2007): 7–47.

Figure I.1 Anna Pavlova and Mieczyslaw Pianowsky dancing *El Jarabe Tapatío*. Roberto El Diablo, "Después de medio siglo," *Revista de revistas*, Crónicas Teatrales, March 30, 1919, 20. Public Domain, Courtesy of Biblioteca Miguel Lerdo de Tejada de la Secretaría de Hacienda y Crédito Público.

of the Mexican nation and ideas about what it meant to be aligned with or opposed to this imagined national collective.[7]

This brief example begins to show how collaborations between national and international artists constantly crossing multiple borders have played a crucial role in the formation of a country. Pavlova was one of many European artists touring across the Americas, partly prompted by the effects of World War I (1914–1918). Arriving in Mexico only nine years after the onset of the Mexican Revolution (1910–1920), she and her dancers experienced the fervent nationalism fostered by the rising revolutionary nation. She watched popular artistic productions like the *Jarabe Tapatío* at venues catering to the working classes. The ballet star learned the "raw" dance steps from a performer in one such space and "refined" them with her ballet technique. Pavlova's rechoreographed Mexican Pavlova's "refinement" of the dance was also the product of collaborations with

---

[7] For a discussion on the nation as an imagined community, see Benedict Anderson, *Imagined Communities: Reflections on the Origin and Spread of Nationalism* (London: Verso, 2006).

Mexican artists educated in Mexico and Europe, where they lived in exile during the bloodiest phase of their country's revolution. As all these various actors crossed social, aesthetic, and geographical borders, their efforts contributed to restructuring the nation socially and culturally.

Pavlova's white, Russian body and her ballet technique added a new layer of *mestizaje* to an already mestizo dance that incorporated historical elements of the colonial encounter between indigenous Mesoamerican and European peoples.[8] Pavlova and her *charro*'s hybridized movement vocabularies, playful spatial dynamics, and coquettish interactions resembled bodily mixings, the yielding and resisting, adulations and ambivalence that white and non-white people have historically negotiated during Mexico's formation as a nation. Dance representations combining multiple cultural elements aligned with the revolutionary government's efforts to consolidate *mestizaje* as a dominant racial and cultural ideology, reimagining Mexico as an inclusive and modern country (chapter 3). As a *china poblana*, her braids swaying from side to side in response to the motion of her pointe shoes tapping on Mexican soil, Pavlova spoke in unique ways to people of different social and racial backgrounds in a crucial time of national and global reconstruction.

Opening this introduction with a brief description and analysis of Pavlova's historical performance also centers dance as both subject and method of critical inquiry in this book. By foregrounding dance, *Dancing Mestizo Modernisms* extends current understandings of the arts' role in developing Mexico's cultural and political histories. It is well known that Mexican muralists such as Diego Rivera, José Clemente Orozco, and David Alfaro Siqueiros, among many others, played a foundational role in (re)imaging Mexico as a modern nation after its Revolution.[9] Also informed by transnational experiences, musicians like Carlos

---

[8] Traditionally, *mestizo* in the Mexican context refers to bodies and cultures resulting from the willing and forced colonial encounters between Indigenous people and Europeans (particularly Spaniards) starting at the turn of the sixteenth century. *Mestizaje* refers to variations of such processes of biological and cultural intermixing. As a discursive construct in this book, *mestizaje* encompasses influences by diverse bodies and cultures from Mexico, France, Spain, Russia, the United States, and other countries. I discuss mestizo and *mestizaje* further in the rest of this introduction. Also, I am aware that my use of *mestizo* (rather than the feminine form, *mestiza*) in this book risks naturalizing the masculine form of *mestizaje*. I follow this usage solely for practical reasons. For theoretical conceptualizations of the *mestiza* and queer *mestizaje*, see Gloria Anzaldúa, *Borderlands/La Frontera: The New Mestiza* (San Francisco: Aunt Little Books, 1987); and Alicia Arrizón, *Queering Mestizaje: Transculturation and Performance* (Ann Arbor: University of Michigan Press, 2006), respectively.

[9] Mary K. Coffey, *How a Revolutionary Art Became Official Culture: Murals, Museums, and the Mexican State* (Durham, NC: Duke University Press, 2012); Desmond Rochfort, *Mexican Muralists* (San Francisco: Chronicle Books, 1998). For the work of female artists painting in "the shadow of the big three" Mexican muralists, see essays by Sarah M. Lowe, Adriana Zavala, and James Oles on Frida Kahlo, María Izquierdo, and Marion and Grace Greenwood, respectively, in *The Eagle and the Virgin: Nation and Cultural Revolution in Mexico 1920–1940*, ed. Mary Kay Vaughan and Stephen E. Lewis (Durham NC: Duke University Press, 2006), 58–94.

INTRODUCTION 5

Chávez, Julián Carrillo, Manuel M. Ponce, and Silvestre Revueltas combined European-inspired techniques with elements of Mexican indigenous cultures to create a new *mestizo* identity that appealed to nationalistic and cosmopolitan values.[10] Alongside these muralists and musicians, Mexican writers and poets drew upon national and international literary traditions to create works that aligned with and resisted official efforts to forge a cohesive national identity.[11]

Less widely known is that national and international choreographers and dancers also played an equally pivotal role in creating divergent conceptualizations of the nation by combining techniques and elements from different cultures. To examine how these mestizo dance practices reproduced and resisted colonial ideas about race and social formations crucial to the development of Mexican history, *Dancing Mestizo Modernisms* analyzes dancers' distinctive dance practices, intercultural collaborations, and specific choreographic works. A set of interrelated questions guides this analysis: How did indigenous cultures coexist with mestizo desires to embrace Western modernity as part of becoming an independent country and then a revolutionary nation? To what extent did transnational cultural, political, and economic forces shape these nation-building processes? How did race, social class, gender, and sexuality influence the development of individual and collective identities? How did dance participate in shaping these identities? Moreover, how did the work of local and international dance artists influence ideas about what Mexico should be as a modern nation?

To illustrate how the book addresses these questions, I will first define key concepts and elaborate on its central argument. While doing so, I will begin delineating the book's contributions to dance and other fields of study. Then, a discussion about racial and social formations in colonial Mexico will serve as context for analyses of case studies in subsequent chapters. A section problematizing some of the book's propositions will precede further notes on methodologies, contributions, and chapter descriptions.

---

[10] Alejandro L. Madrid, *Sounds of the Modern Nation: Music, Culture, and Ideas in Post-Revolutionary Mexico* (Philadelphia: Temple University Press, 2008), and *Music in Mexico: Experiencing Music, Expressing Culture* (New York: Oxford University Press, 2013); Leonora Saavedra, "Carlos Chávez's Polysemic Style: Constructing the National, Seeking the Cosmopolitan," *Journal of the American Musicological Society* 68, no. 1 (2015) 99–149, and her edited volume, *Carlos Chávez and His World* (Princeton, NJ: Princeton University Press, 2015); Marco Velazquez and Mary Kay Vaughan, "Mestizaje and Musical Nationalism in Mexico," in *The Eagle and the Virgin*, 95–118.

[11] Mariano Azuela, *Los de abajo* (El Paso, Texas, *Folletín de El Paso del Norte*, 1915); Martín Luis Guzmán, *El águila y la serpiente* (Madrid, Compañía Ibero-Americana de Publicaciones S.A., Librería Fernando Fe, 1928); Nellie Campobello, *Cartucho* (México: Ediciones Integrales, 1931); Germán List Arzubide, *El movimiento estridentista* (Jalapa: Ediciones de Horizonte, 1927); Luis Mario Schneider, *El estridentismo: México 1921-1927* (México, DF: Universidad Autónoma de México, 1985); Guillermo Sheridan, *Los contemporáneos ayer* (México, DF: Fondo de Cultura Económica, 2015).

The Argument, Key Concepts, and Contributions

This book contributes a unique perspective to an emerging body of literature that has addressed some of the preceding questions from various disciplinary positions. Some works focus on artistic collaborations shaping notions of Mexican modernity between the 1920s and 1950s[12] and the 1920s and 1960s.[13] Others highlight how folkloric dance, featured as festive performances in massive events and films, represented competing ideas about Mexican nationalism between 1910 and the 1940s.[14] *Dancing Mestizo Modernisms* attends to these artistic interactions and aesthetic developments to historicize contrasting notions of Mexico as a postrevolutionary nation. However, the book centers dance also to demonstrate the unique ways dances, choreographers, and dancing bodies create meaning and what they reveal about the normalization of racial and social hierarchies before and after the revolution.

The study asserts that dances, choreographers, and dancing bodies do not merely *reflect* societal values but are cultural agents capable of creating meaning in particular ways. As Pavlova's case begins to illuminate, dances and dance artists actively *produce* social values with political implications—expressed, perceived, and experienced through storytelling, abstract representation, and affective sensations. Analyses of case studies in this book assume that these unique ways of signifying are not limited exclusively to producing, conveying, and receiving an easily graspable conceptual idea, story, and message. These embodied ways of creating and conveying "meaning" can contrast or coexist with various levels of abstraction. That is, different ways of dancing and composing dances elicit diverse affective reactions, feelings, emotions, and other subtle bodily sensations in dancers and viewers. These responses develop according to people's histories of associations (embodied and imagined) with specific dance practices, settings, and personal backgrounds (i.e., gender, class, race, ethnicity, etc.). This book contends that this set of simultaneous operations, mobilized by the act of dancing and viewing others dance, contributes unique ways to understand the formation of people's sense of who they and others are, as they also debate divergent approaches to dance-making.[15]

---

[12] Ellie Guerrero, *Dance and the Arts in Mexico, 1920–1950* (Cham, Switzerland: Palgrave Macmillan), 2018.

[13] K. Mitchell Snow, *A Revolution in Movement: Dancers, Painters, and the Image of Modern Mexico* (Gainesville: University Press of Florida, 2020).

[14] Manuel R. Cuellar, *Choreographing Mexico: Festive Performances and Dancing Histories of a Nation* (Austin: University of Texas Press, 2022).

[15] Dance theorist Susan L. Foster argues that choreographers theorize corporeality while scholars theorize what dance is in "Dance Theory?," in *Teaching Dance Studies*, ed. Judith Chazin-Bennahum (New York: Routledge, 2005), 31. I would emphasize that dance artists and scholars theorize *what they think* corporeality and dance *are* and *do* from their specific social, racial, gender, historical, and geopolitical positionalities. Thus, my work as a working-class, cisgender, brown Mexican

This way of looking at dances and dancing bodies provides ways to understand how people in general move within diverse spaces while activating multiple symbols, meanings, and histories.[16] Thus, it facilitates an appreciation of how dancing and quotidian bodies have participated in producing and challenging nationalist ideologies and the rhetoric of modernity. The book examines the development of these power dynamics, aesthetic ideologies, and identity formations during three crucial historical moments: the period immediately after the Mexican War of Independence against Spain (1821–1876), the dictatorship of Porfirio Díaz (1876–1911), and the postrevolutionary period from 1919 to 1940. By covering a more extended time period, this story adds to historical accounts that have concentrated on postrevolutionary Mexico.[17]

To understand the unique role that dance, as well as dancing and pedestrian bodies, played within nation-building projects in postcolonial and postrevolutionary Mexico, the book theorizes two interrelated concepts—*embodied mestizo modernisms* and *transnational nationalisms*. The former refers to the combination of indigenous, folkloric, ballet, and modern dance elements in performances choreographed by national and international artists from various racial, cultural, and social backgrounds. I argue that these modernist *mestizo* dance practices contributed vitally to constructing *transnational nationalisms*—the idea that notions of the nation result in response to local and international forces. In other words, mestizo modernist dance works—choreographed collaboratively by Mexican and foreign dancers traveling within transnational circuits—have been crucial to Mexico's formation as a nation.

Embodied mestizo modernisms is a concept that centers dance alongside other forms of embodiment to understand the development of distinctive identities. Some authors have combined varied notions of *mestizaje* and modernity in

---

immigrant choreographer, performer, and dance scholar informs the theoretical and methodological approaches employed to articulate the arguments offered in this book and the story it tells.

[16] I elaborate this claim further relative to choreography as an analytical methodology later in the introduction.

[17] Anita González and Ruth Hellier-Tinoco analyze dance practices in more contemporary time. González provides a vitally important analysis of the Africanist presence in Mexican dance, primarily among indigenous and rural communities, in *Afro-Mexico: Dancing between Myth and Reality* (Austin: University of Texas Press, 2010). Hellier-Tinoco discusses *The Dance of the Old Men* alongside the *Night of the Dead* festivity relative to the tourist industry and nationalism in *Embodying Mexico: Tourism, Nationalism & Performance* (New York: Oxford University Press, 2011). Hanna Kosstrin analyzes some of Anna Sokolow's works in postrevolutionary Mexico after 1939 in *Honest Bodies: Revolutionary Modernism in the Dances of Anna Sokolow* (New York: Oxford University Press, 2017). Paul A. Scolieri examines dance's centrality to postconquest fifteenth- and sixteenth-century Aztec life in *Dancing the New World: Aztecs, Spaniards, and the Choreography of Conquest* (Austin: University of Texas Press, 2013). A vast body of literature in Spanish has explored the expansive cultural and political landscapes of dance practices in Mexican history. Some of this scholarship, cited throughout the chapters, has provided the basis for formulating critical analyses and theoretical propositions this book offers.

titles that frame their studies on the formation of identities in postrevolutionary Mexico and twentieth-century Latin America, more broadly.[18] However, while they analyze intersections between technology, science, and a wide range of expressive cultures—literature, painting, film, and muralism—these authors pay no attention to dance. Dance scholars have addressed modernity and *mestizaje* within concert dance during periods of nation-building in Mexico[19] and other Latin American countries.[20] These works, like this book, expand on dance studies scholarship focused primarily on social, popular, and ritual dance forms in the region. Resonating with this literature, *Dancing Mestizo Modernisms* asserts that Mexico, like other places in Latin America, developed forms of being modern that were not (entirely) imitative of European and US notions of modernity. However, this book uses the concept of embodied mestizo modernisms to emphasize that ideas about Mexican modernity directly resulted from the *multiple* forms in which colonial legacies of racialization and socialization have shaped Mexico's history.

As a concept and practice, embodied mestizo modernisms imply a corporeality of multiplicity that indexes Mexico's contentious histories of racial and cultural *mestizaje*. In this case, corporeality references a sense of reality and identity resulting from bodily activities while navigating quotidian life within a web of sociopolitical, economic, and cultural forces. This position assumes that negotiating these influences through the dancing and pedestrian body within specific historical contexts is central to constructing a sense of self and others as racial, social, gendered, and sexual subjects. As a form of physical activity, dance participates in these formative processes. That is, the unique ways through which dances, dance makers, and dancing bodies create meaning contribute to producing social values that characterize the cultural and historical contexts in which dances and identities are created and performed. A mestizo corporeality of multiplicity signals embodied forces simultaneously at play in corporeal processes of subjectification and signification within Mexico's specific racial, ethnic, and cultural histories.[21]

---

[18] David S. Dalton, *Mestizo Modernity: Race, Technology, and the Body in Postrevolutionary Mexico* (Gainesville: University of Florida Press, 2018); Tace Hedrick, *Mestizo Modernism: Race, Nation, and Identity in Latin American Culture, 1900–1940* (New Brunswick, NJ: Rutgers University Press, 2003).
[19] Kosstrin, *Honest Bodies*; Guerrero, *Dance and the Arts*; Snow, *A Revolution*.
[20] Cristina F. Rosa, *Brazilian Bodies and their Choreographies of Identification: Swing Nation* (Houndmills: Palgrave Macmillan, 2015); Ana Paula Höfling, *Staging Brazil: Choreographies of Capoeira* (Middletown, CT: Wesleyan University Press, 2019); Elizabeth B. Schwall, *Dancing with the Revolution: Power, Politics, and Privilege in Cuba* (Chapel Hill: University of North Carolina Press, 2021); (with less emphasis on *mestizaje*) Victoria Fortuna, *Moving Otherwise: Dance, Violence, and Memory in Buenos Aires* (New York: Oxford University Press, 2019).
[21] The idea of a mestizo corporeality of multiplicity has resonances with two sources. First, I re-adapt the concept of corporeality as formulated collectively by dance theorists Susan Foster et al. in "Introduction," in *Corporealities: Dancing, Knowledge, Culture, and Power*, ed. Susan L. Foster (London: Routledge, 1996), xi–xvii. They posit that *Corporealities* "seeks to vivify the study of bodies through a consideration of bodily reality, not as natural or absolute given but as a tangible

By studying embodied mestizo modernisms as a corporeality of multiplicity, this book challenges essentialist notions about biological factors forming identities (i.e., that there is something in people's "blood" that makes them Mexican). It opts instead for a focus on the exchange and integration of cultural factors—processes contextualized by historical power relations—in the formation of individual and collective identities.[22] This form of de-essentialized *mestizaje* helps explain why Pavlova's constructed mestizo corporeality of multiplicity could be perceived as "deeply Mexican." How can a ballet-trained, white Russian dancer donning *china poblana* attire, swaying her braids in response to her modernizing arching feet tiptoeing the traditional *Jarabe Tapatío*, be able, as a Mexican critic put it, to "decipher the secret of our ancestral soul"?[23] As I respond to this question in detail in chapter 3, famous international artists like Pavlova embodied multiple histories of colonization that enabled their talented dancing bodies to be perceived as universal representatives of humanity, even if through an embodied representation of Mexicanness. Thus, embodied mestizo modernisms refer to a unique form of corporeality cultivated by contrasting cultural sources in the development of distinctive racial and social formations stemming from legacies of colonialism. Before elaborating this claim further, I will explain the second concept that drives this study.

Transnational nationalisms holds that the nation is neither formed exclusively by its natives nor produced solely by regional politics. Instead, notions of the nation result from the *interaction* between domestic and foreign affairs. Transnational forces interact with and shape local cultural specificities, economic interests, and political ideologies. As this study demonstrates, the confluence of internal and external power dynamics ultimately enables the development of competing national imaginaries. In this context, the concept of transnational nationalisms serves as an analytical tool. It attends to how the

---

and substantial category of cultural experience" (ibid., xi). They suggest that in "approaching physicality as a site of meaning-making [we can gain] greater precision to our understanding of the reality of embodiment [and of] the corporeal play that is vital to cultural production and to theoretical formulations of cultural processes" (ibid., xi). Second, the concept *corporeality of multiplicity* also resonates with Randy Martin's conceptualization of the *composite body*, which accounts for the "motion of cultural processes that emanate from different sources and never fully come to rest. It is a body that is not one but multiple. [. . . It is] a heuristic for thinking [through] the physical constitution of complex social relations" that arise in both the symbolic and the performative spheres; *Critical Moves: Dance Studies in Theory and Politics* (Durham, NC: Duke University Press, 1998), 110.

[22] In the rest of this book, I refer to this idea as "de-essentialized *mestizaje*" in reference to a unique *mestizo* corporeality (of multiplicity) and forms of *mestizo* cultural production created by artists with different national, racial, ethnic, and aesthetic backgrounds. The use of this idea accounts for the frictions and unequal power dynamics implicit in these identity formation processes.

[23] Luis A. Rodríguez, "La Fantasía Mexicana," *El universal ilustrado*, March 28, 1919, 10.

rhetoric of modernity influenced histories of domination and resistance in countries constructing national identities while negotiating transnational forces.[24]

The concept of transnational nationalisms also helps to understand the formation of diasporic communities and their influence in shaping the places where they live. That is, people who live in a foreign country, from months to a few years or for the rest of their lives, become agents of change in their adopted localities. In Mexico, Spaniards remained an influential force in the country's economic and cultural development after its (official) independence from Spain. France also became a major actor in shaping the new republic. At various historical moments, the United States, the Soviet Union, and other countries established transformative alliances with Mexico. Throughout Mexican history, people from all these countries forming distinct diasporic communities shaped the nation's political, economic, and cultural life.

As this book illustrates, collaborations among visiting international dance artists, diasporic communities established in the country, and other groups of Mexican people created varied embodied mestizo modernisms that contributed to fashioning notions of the nation, from the post/colonial[25] to the postrevolutionary periods. For instance, French dance artists such as Andrés Susano Pautret Chapalber arrived to stay in the emerging nation where he choreographed a ballet celebrating the country's independence achieved only three years before he arrived in 1824 (chapter 1). He and his wife devoted the rest of their lives to developing new approaches to concert dance performance and education in Mexico. Their students, and those they influenced, performed ballet, Spanish dances, and stylized Mexican dances like the *Jarabe Tapatío* to keep concert dance alive during the tumultuous post-independence wars and the Porfiriato.[26] Pavlova herself, as well as Spanish-born Carmen Tórtola Valencia

---

[24] I have applied this concept of *transnational nationalisms* to a call for a more expanded and inclusive international map of dance studies histories, not only dance practices, specifically in Mexico City. See Reynoso, "Towards a Critical Globalized Humanities: Dance Research in Mexico City at the CENIDID," in *The Futures of Dance Studies*, ed. Susan Manning, Janice Ross, and Rebecca Schneider (Madison: University of Wisconsin Press, 2020), 523–540. My term *transnational nationalisms* builds from scholarship in dance and transnationalism. Gabriele Klein argues that "the history of dance is the history of globalization and transnationalism" in "Toward a Theory of Cultural Translation in Dance," in *New German Dance Studies*, ed. Susan Manning and Lucia Ruprecht (Urbana: University of Illinois Press, 2012), 247. Lok C. D. Siu contends that citizenship results from "transnational as well as national and local forces" in *Memories of a Future Home: Diasporic Citizenship of Chinese in Panama* (Stanford, CA: Stanford University Press, 2005), 8. Laura Briggs, Gladys McCormick, and J. T. Way view transnationalism as a category of analysis that is useful "as a strategy for identifying the ideological work of the nation" in constructions of the "national" in "Transnationalism: A Category of Analysis," *American Quarterly* 60, no. 3 (September 2008): 637. While applying transnationalism as an analytical methodology, this book resonates with Kosstrin's approach to studying Sokolow's work in the United States, Mexico, and Israel (*Honest Bodies*).

[25] The composite term *post/colonial* in this book acknowledges that legacies of neocolonial logic continued to operate long after Mexico achieved official independence from its colonizers.

[26] *Porfiriato* refers to the period under Porfirio Díaz's dictatorial rule (1876–1911).

and Swedish-Italian violinist Norka Rouskaya, collaborated with members of diasporic and other local communities to produce different postrevolutionary embodied mestizo modernisms during their visits to Mexico City between 1917 and the mid-1920s (chapter 3). During the 1920s, sisters Gloria and Nellie Campobello trained with Letti Carroll, who migrated permanently from the United States to Mexico City in 1910 to work primarily with upper-class members of diasporic communities from Europe and the United States. The Campobello sisters produced a new form of embodied mestizo modernism that resonated with transnational calls for a global socialist revolution while shaping dance education in the 1930s (chapter 4). In the early 1940s, students they trained worked with two US choreographers, Anna Sokolow, who traveled to the country periodically, and Waldeen Falkenstein, who stayed in Mexico for the rest of her life. These choreographers collaborated with Mexican and Spanish artists and benefactors—some established in the country for generations, and others recently arrived after fleeing Francisco Franco's dictatorship in the late 1930s. They proposed distinctive approaches to creating a Mexican modern dance form that resonated with local and transnational political and aesthetic debates (chapter 4). The book concludes by gesturing to how the diasporic aspect of transnational nationalisms illuminates the impact that Mexican immigrants and Mexican Americans, including dancers, have in the twenty-first-century United States.

By centering dance as subject and method of study, this book theorizes the concepts of embodied mestizo modernisms and transnational nationalisms while contributing to current debates about dance, modernism, nationalism, and transnationalism. It highlights how racial and social formations intersect within and between these areas of study. The following is not an exhaustive history of colonial Mexico. However, the discussion provides a context to understand the development of notions about race, racism, and social status as sociocultural constructs embraced and contested by dancers and their collaborators throughout Mexican history.

Embodied Legacies of Colonial Racial and Social Formations

As I introduced above, the complex interaction between the concepts of embodied mestizo modernisms and transnational nationalisms illustrates processes through which people develop a sense of self and Other. In other words, while people engage in quotidian movement practices (i.e., social mannerisms and domestic routines) and specialized physical activities like dance (i.e., in social and theatrical settings), people construct perceptions and representations of who they and those around them are. In Mexico, these processes of identity formation intimately connect to how legacies of colonization influenced racialized power dynamics in transnational relations and intercultural encounters, including among dancers.

To comprehend the role dance played in the development of Mexican history and identities, I will briefly historicize processes of racialization and social stratification stemming from New Spain (colonial Mexico: 1521–1821). I do so to contextualize how ideas about race (and racism), social status, and representation continue to operate in different forms during Mexico's post/colonial and postrevolutionary eras.[27] This discussion will serve as a background to trace residues of colonialist racial and social ideologies integrated, explicitly and implicitly, in dance practices and artistic discourses analyzed in subsequent chapters.[28] Examining the enduring coloniality embodied in modernist dance practices facilitates understandings of the many forms dance artists have contributed to creating narratives about the modern Mexico they and others wanted to construct.

Mechanisms of Racial and Social Distinction in New Spain's Caste System

In Mexico—and Latin America more widely—skin color has served as the basis for complex racial taxonomies that categorize people along a continuum where indigenous Mesoamerican and mestizo peoples represent the brown area between the poles of black and white.[29] During the colonization of Mexico, Spaniards implemented the *limpieza de sangre* (blood cleansing) system they used in Spain as an attempt to preserve their blood purity as a group of people distinct from Jews and Muslims.[30] In Mexico, and the rest of the Americas, Spanish colonizers retained the religious and genealogical aspects of this mechanism of (racial) distinction while adopting other factors to distinguish themselves as a (racial) group apart from indigenous Mesoamerican, Black, and mixed-race

---

[27] For some studies on diverse dance practices during the Mexican colonial period, which is not the focus of this book, see Maya Ramos Smith, *La danza en México durante la época colonial* (México: Alianza Editorial Mexicana, CONACULTA, 1990), and *La danza teatral en México durante el Virreinato (1521–1821)* (México, DF: Escenologia Ediciones, 2013); Susana Hernández Araico, "Espectacularidad musical indígena: Desde cronistas y ritos novohispanos a Sor Juana," *Romance Notes* 59, no. 1 (2019): 41–49; Scolieri, *Dancing the New World.*

[28] For a discussion of how residual elements of ideologies persist into the formation of emergent and dominant ideologies, see Raymond Williams, *Marxism and Literature* (Oxford: Oxford University Press, 1977).

[29] Throughout the book, I use variations of *indigenous Mesoamerican* in reference to native people of Mesoamerican descent. Most of the literature on colonial Mexico refers to these people as "Indians," a designation implemented by Spanish colonizers referring to various non-European colonized subjects.

[30] María Elena Martínez, *Genealogical Fictions:* Limpieza de Sangre, *Religion and Gender in Colonial Mexico* (Stanford, CA: Stanford University Press, 2008).

people. It was in the seventeenth century that some of these additional "stains" as "sources of contamination" were made visible in *casta* paintings.[31] These visual records depicted people who belonged to one of many categories depending on whether they were born from combinations of Spaniards, Spaniards and indigenous Mesoamerican, Spaniards and Blacks, indigenous Mesoamerican and Blacks, offspring of these pairings, subsequent mixtures, etc. (Figure I.2).[32]

For the first time, people could see representations of skin color as integral to the institution of the highly complex *sistema de castas* ("caste/race system")[33] that the Spanish used to racialize the population relative to hierarchies of political power, social standing, and the accumulation of wealth.[34] It was then that the concept of *limpieza de sangre* was gradually linked to "white skin color and thus mapped ... onto the body."[35] In general, whiter people occupied upper positions in social and economic hierarchies, while darker bodies took lower ranks in the human stratification system.

However, whiteness was not only characterized by light skin color but also by factors such as birth legitimacy and family lineage traceable for generations. Religion was an important determining element. By virtue of their Christianity, white Spaniards considered themselves *gente de razón* (people of reason). In 1537, Pope Paul III formally declared that American "Indians" indeed had souls and were also capable of reasoning.[36] Yet, this capacity could develop if indigenous Mesoamerican people "progressed from a pagan mind-set to a westernized lifestyle like the more civilized Europeans."[37] Assimilation to racialized notions of white European culture, including religion, offered culturally civilizing and spiritually redeeming alternatives to dark-skin-color and mixed-race colonial subjects who aspired to be considered *gente de razón*. They thus could increase their prospects for social mobility within a racially and socially stratified colonial system.

Analyzing these racial and social distinction mechanisms reveals that whiteness represented a complex high social status characterized by light skin color

---

[31] Ibid., 21.
[32] For additional studies on different aspects of *casta* paintings and the complex classification system they represented, see María Concepción García Sáiz, *Las castas mexicanas: Un género pictórico americano* (s.l.: Olivetti, 1989); Ilona Katzew, *Casta Painting: Images of Race in Eighteenth-Century Mexico* (New Haven, CT: Yale University Press, 2004); Magali M. Carrera, *Imagining Identity in New Spain: Race, Lineage and the Colonial Body in Portraiture and Casta Paintings* (Austin: University of Texas Press, 2003); Ben Vinson III, *Before Mestizaje: The Frontiers of Race and Caste in Colonial Mexico* (New York: Cambridge University Press, 2018).
[33] Martínez, *Genealogical Fictions*, 1.
[34] For a discussion of the intersection between colonial racialization processes and early forms of capitalism, see Aníbal Quijano, "Coloniality of Power, Eurocentrism, and Latin America," *Nepantla: Views from South* 1, no. 3 (2000): 533–80.
[35] Martínez, *Genealogical Fictions*, 21.
[36] Gloria E. Miranda, "Racial and Cultural Dimensions of 'Gente de Razón' Status in Spanish and Mexican California, *Southern California Quarterly* 70, no. 3 (Fall 1998): 267.
[37] Ibid.

14   DANCING MESTIZO MODERNISMS

Figure I.2 "Cuadro de Castas." Eighteenth-century, oil on canvas painting showing sixteen caste combinations. Unknown author. Public Domain, Courtesy of Instituto Nacional de Antropología e Historia.

and other factors.[38] As a dominant ideology, whiteness's constructed racial and cultural supremacy denoted superiority in various domains of life and human valuation (i.e., cultural practices, access to prestigious occupations, wealth, political and social status, etc.). In this racialized social system, dark-skinned people could aspire to and thus strive to approximate themselves closer to whiteness as an enabling social status. Although on rare occasions and limited exclusively to elite people of mixed race who could prove exemplary loyal service to the king and the state, a petitioner could gain selected privileges of whiteness as a favor (*gracias al sacar*) by royal authorities or as a purchase for a price.[39] Both strategies, seeking the favor of the king and royal authorities through the *gracias al sacar* and purchasing mechanisms to circumvent some *limpieza de sangre* restrictions, helped mixed-raced people to achieve whiteness (as a social status). It also helped them attempt to eliminate their racial "defect,"[40] thus hoping to minimize further discrimination after being granted (partial) white status.[41]

In this colonial context, where dark skin color and other factors were considered "defects" (as sources of contamination to blood cleanliness and associated with decreased reasoning ability), prejudices and stereotypes developed across colonial Spanish America. By the 1560s, Peruvian authorities worried about the increased number of Blacks, mulattos, mestizos, and people of various mixtures in specific provinces. They asserted that many of these dark-skinned people "do not know their parents and they grow up in great vice and liberty without working, they have no occupation and eat and drink without order and mingle with the Indian men and women and join in their drunkenness and witchcraft and do not hear mass."[42] Mexican officials expressed similar concerns

---

[38] This meant that people who phenotypically might pass as white (i.e., light skin) could experience different forms of prejudice and discrimination if publicly discovered to have people of color in their family lineage, or were illegitimate children, and directly or indirectly associated with non-Christian religions.

[39] See the following three works by Ann Twinam: for an introduction to the topic, see "Racial Passing: Informal and Official 'Whiteness' in Colonial Spanish America," in *New World Orders: Violence, Sanction, and Authority in the Colonial Americas*, ed. John Smolenski and Thomas J. Humphrey (Philadelphia: University of Pennsylvania Press, 2007), 249–72. For an in-depth discussion of the nuanced workings of whitening mechanisms as applied to a mixed-status family of people of color whose eldest son was the only one granted status as white and the honorific title of "Don," see "Pedro de Ayarza: The Purchase of Whiteness," in *The Human Tradition in Colonial Latin America*, ed. Kenneth J. Andrien, 2nd ed. (Lanham, MD: Rowman & Littlefield, 2013), 221–36. For these two discussions in a broader context, see *Purchasing Whiteness: Pardos, Mulattos, and the Quest for Social Mobility in the Spanish Indies* (Stanford, CA: Stanford University Press, 2015).

[40] Twinam, "Racial Passing," 1.

[41] One should note that for mixed-race people, especially of dark skin color, white status did not guarantee full rights granted to whites, thus the desire to eliminate the implications of a person's racial "defect" as much as possible. Other "defects" were religion (i.e., Jewish lineage), and illegitimacy (i.e., a child born out of wedlock, or a mixed-race child not recognized by a white father). See Twinam's works cited above.

[42] Konetzke, quoted in Twinam "Racial Passing," 252.

about the "great quantities of mulattoes . . . that have bad inclinations," and at the turn of the seventeenth century, Mexican authorities continued to refer to mulattos derogatorily as "hucksters" and claimed that "their" women "dressed with great disorder."[43] Racist ideas like these had served to produce and justify the institution of slavery to which colonialists subjected Blacks.[44] Similar racist ideas functioned to institute diverse forms of violence in other systems of servitude and marginalization against Black, indigenous Mesoamerican, Asians, and mixed-race people of dark skin.

As this brief discussion illustrates, Spanish America's caste system was complex. It afforded the highest privileges to whiteness (as an unofficial racial category and as an official status), it permitted some social mobility to exceptionally loyal people of mixed race (primarily men) through whitening mechanisms, and it naturalized racial prejudices affecting people's lives and whose bodies were *marked* by racial and other "defects." Although all people of mixed race generally lived under the same repressive colonial system, those perceived as Black—free and enslaved—were often subjected to the harshest treatments. However, Blacks and other dark-skinned people were not passive colonial subjects. They found many ways to exercise their agency within a highly regulated colonial matrix of power that often failed to keep them (totally) subordinated.[45]

In the case of Mexico, as in other territories throughout the Spanish Empire, racialized power dynamics changed after the country's independence in 1821. Mexico's first president, Vicente Ramón Guerrero Saldaña, signed a decree

[43] Ibid.
[44] For a discussion on how racist ideas—formed and circulated by white and Black people—related to the dehumanization of Black bodies and the development of slavery, see Ibram X. Kendi, *Stamped from the Beginning: The Definitive History of Racist Ideas in America* (New York: Nation Books, 2016), especially the prologue and chapters 1–3. Although Kendi's historicizing of racist ideas focuses on how they took shape in the United States, his analysis shows the ways such ideas developed in Europe and Africa before traveling to the Americas.
[45] For an analysis of caste system limitations as a totalizing repressive structure, see R. Douglas Cope, *The Limits of Racial Domination: Plebeian Society in Colonial Mexico City, 1660–1720* (Madison: University of Wisconsin Press, 1994). For some examples of overt and subtle forms of rebellion and resistance by Black communities in colonial Mexico, see Octaviano Corro Ramos, *Los cimarrones en Veracruz y la fundación de Amapa* (Veracruz: Comercial, 1951); Patrick J. Carroll, "Mandinga: The Evolution of a Mexican Runaway Slave Community, 1735–1827," *Comparative Studies in Society and History* 19, no. 4 (October 1977): 488–505; Colin A. Palmer, *Slaves of the White God: Blacks in Mexico, 1570–1650* (Cambridge, MA: Harvard University Press, 1976); Adriana Naveda Chávez-Hita, "De San Lorenzo de los negros a los morenos de Amapa: Cimarrones veracruzanos, 1609–1735," in *Rutas de la esclavitud en África y América Latina*, ed. Rina Cáceres Gómez (San José: De la Universidad de Costa Rica, 2001), 157–74; Joan C. Bristol, *Christians, Blasphemers, and Witches: Afro-Mexican Ritual Practice in the Seventeenth Century* (Albuquerque: University of New Mexico Press, 2007); Frank Proctor III, "Slave Rebellion and Liberty in Colonial Mexico," in *Black Mexico: Race and Society from Colonial to Modern Times*, ed. Ben Vinson III and Matthew Restall (Albuquerque: University of New Mexico Press, 2009), 21–50. For an analysis of the development of Maroon communities across the Americas, including Mexico, see Alvin O. Thompson, *Flight to Freedom: African Runaways and Maroons in the Americas* (Jamaica: University of the West Indies Press, 2006).

abolishing slavery throughout Mexican territories in 1829.[46] Guerrero was the first Afro-Mestizo president in the Americas. He had joined forces with José María Teclo Morelos Pérez y Pavón, a local Catholic priest of African ancestry and a leading figure in the Mexican War of Independence.

However, reflecting now in the present, I ask myself, how it is that I, and the person working by my side as I write these sentences and who also grew up in Mexico, remember that Benito Juárez was the first Mexican president of indigenous Mesoamerican descent (1858–1872)? Neither of us remembers learning that Guerrero and Morelos were of African ancestry. This apparent forgetfulness might be prompted by a faulty or selective memory. It might also have been prompted by the disciplinary force of an elementary educational system, in which we were both educated, that has fostered selective erasures. Mine and other people's "faulty" memories, shaped by a "forgetful" educational system and a broader cultural environment, have contributed to the forgetting and erasure of Africanist, and Asian, influences in ideas about Mexican culture and Mexico as a nation.[47]

Excavating Racial and Social Genealogies

Again, the case of Pavlova can be illustrative here as an example of a de-essentialized Mexican *mestizaje*, a specific corporeality that embodies multiple cultural influences and neo/colonial histories. Her performance of a balleticized folkloric dance exemplifies how racial integration, invisibilization, and absorption processes functioned in constructing the Mexican subjectivity, body, and nation. As a white *china poblana* dancing the *Jarabe Tapatío*, "refined" by employing a Russian-European dance technique, she embodied other racial and cultural traces, African and Asian, already invisibilized and absorbed into the dance and the image of the iconic Mexican female figure. *Jarabe* historians have traced multiple genealogies in the formation of this dance and musical genre, including associations to people identified by colonial authorities as "mulatos y gente de color 'quebrado'" ("mulattos and people of 'broken' color").[48] Influenced by the Catholic Holy Inquisition, political and ecclesiastical officials

---

[46] White slave owners in Texas, then Mexican territory, resisted the decision and, after cessation from Mexico in 1836, legalized slavery.

[47] Although more and more people recognize the Africanist influence as the "third root" of Mexican culture (Mesoamerican and Spanish being the other two) in the last decades, prejudice and discrimination against Afro-Mexicans and Blacks from other countries continue to be prevalent. In this introduction, I use *Africanist* and *Black* as non-essentialist inclusive terms for diverse people and cultural practices of African descent, whether they are from Africa, Mexico, the United States, or other places.

[48] Josefina Lavalle, *El Jarabe... El Jarabe ranchero o Jarabe de Jalisco* (México, DF: Cenidi Danza/INBA, 1988), 33.

warned that performances of *jarabe* dancers replicated Black dancers' excessive lasciviousness, sexual degeneracy, and sinfulness. Hence, authorities prohibited dances like the *Jarabe Gatuno* for their perceived similarity to African dances.[49] Responding to the criminalization of these dances, *jarabe* dancers "cleaned" their performances making them more morally acceptable while retaining Africanist influences.

The *china* character, which would become the *china poblana* that Pavlova embodied in the twentieth century, is equally complex in her genealogical formation as an endearing figure in the Mexican popular imagination since the early nineteenth century. As a *mestiza* embodiment, the *china poblana*'s corporeality of multiplicity integrates indigenous and Spanish elements in her dress (i.e., cotton garments designed and colorfully embroidered in indigenous fashion as well as details evocative of women from Andalucía and Madrid).[50] Mexican dance historian Josefina Lavalle traces the *china*'s zapateado dancing (stomping of the feet) to various Spanish dance styles.[51] Although Spanish zapateado embodied influences by the Moors and people of other Arab descent, the dominant narrative of *mestizaje*, central to Mexican national identity, privileged the combination of indigenous Mesoamerican and (white) European influences. This *china poblana*'s mestizo corporeality further accentuated its Mexicanness through the Mexican flag's green, white, and red colors as distinctive features of her dress, shawl, and ribbons interlaced through her swaying braids.

There are other genealogical strands related to the many meanings the word *china* has carried and absorbed into the *china poblana* figure Pavlova embodied. *China* and *chino* can refer to a female and male person from China.[52] In colonial Mexico, *chino* became an arbitrary catch-all term that included people from East, South, and Southeast Asia. The use of this term as a general category for people of different Asian ancestry emerged from the belief that they all shared the same "Oriental" origin.[53] Also, all "*chinos*" crossed the Pacific Ocean before arriving in Mexico as free and enslaved people on board the Manila galleon, among them, Mirra, a young girl from India.[54] After being transported by the Portuguese as part of the slave trade to the Philippines then sold in a market

---

[49] "1802. Edicto inquisitorial prohibiendo el *Chuchumbé*, el *Jarabe Gatuno* y otros biales" (content originally published in *Gazeta de México*, December 6, 1802), in Maya Ramos and Patricia Cardona, comps., *La danza en México. Visiones de cinco siglos. Tomo II: Antología, cinco siglos de crónicas, crítica y documentos (1521–2002)* (México, DF: Cenidi Danza/INBA/CONACULTA/Escenología, 2002).

[50] Vázquez Mantecón, "La china mexicana."

[51] *El Jarabe*.

[52] In Spanish, the letters "a" and "o" at the end of a word (*china/o*) denote its female and male form, respectively.

[53] Tatiana Seijas, *Asian Slaves in Colonial Mexico: From Chinos to Indians* (New York: Cambridge University Press, 2014), 10.

[54] The Philippines played a crucial role in the Portuguese Asian slave trade, including transporting free and enslaved Asians to Mexico. Official Asian slavery ended in 1672; see ibid.

there, Mirra arrived in the Mexican port of Acapulco in 1619.[55] Once in the state of Puebla, she was renamed Catarina de San Juan and became a domestic servant for the Portuguese couple that had bought her. She had a short-lived, arranged marriage to a *chino* slave owned by her employer. By the time she died in 1688, she had developed fame as a pious woman and became a popular saint loved by people in Puebla.[56] Although there are contradicting narratives, de San Juan, and her *china* background, has been associated with the creation of the *china poblana* dress that became a beloved national symbol represented by a traditional, virtuous Mexican woman during Porfirio Díaz's dictatorship (1876–1911).

Some writers have referenced the *china poblana*'s Africanist elements related to the word *china/o* (here meaning curly hair) often based on prevalent stereotypes. In 1846, George Ruxton, a British explorer and travel writer, visited Mexico. He wrote about associations people made between the *china* and "pelo chino" (curly hair), which ostensibly added the Africanist presence to the mix of indigenous Mesoamerican and European in the *china*'s mestizo *nature*.[57] Other sources have traced the use of *china* and *chino* as referencing young girls of indigenous Mesoamerican and mestizo ancestry employed as servants by Spaniards and to children born to Black and indigenous Mesoamerican couples in Puebla.[58] Studies of *casta* paintings from the eighteenth century reveal that a *chino* could descend from a male wolf and a Black female or an indigenous Mesoamerican woman; a mulatto and an indigenous Mesoamerican woman; a coyote and a mulatta, etc. (Figure I.2).[59] These classifications reflected the low status of *chinos* among mixed-race people. It also demonstrated, even if symbolically, the dehumanizing nature of the colonial casta system that set the basis for racial relations and the formation of identities across the Americas for centuries to come, including stereotypical Mexican national symbols like the *china poblana*.

As is apparent in this brief genealogical sketch of the *Jarabe Tapatío*'s iconic female figure, much of the information sounds ambiguous, uncertain, and contradictory—the result of myths, legends, stereotypes, fantasies, and historical narratives. This body of knowledge, produced by colonial authorities, proud nationalists, European travelers, and historians, strives to create an "objective" historical account. My intention here is not to find and settle the *china poblana*'s true, authentic origin story but to highlight the constructedness of Mexican culture and Mexico as a nation. I want to emphasize the selective visibilization and invisibilization of racial and social histories—"true," tentative, and fictional—as

---

[55] Ibid.
[56] Ibid.
[57] Vázquez Mantecón, "La china mexicana," 129.
[58] Ibid.
[59] García Sáiz, *Las castas mexicanas*; Katzew, *Casta Painting*; Carrera, *Imagining Identity*; Vinson, *Before Mestizaje*.

part of the construction of Mexican individual and collective identities.[60] It is these multiple genealogical strands that constitute Pavlova's embodied mestizo modernism as her white body represents a *china poblana*, dancing a "traditional" Mexican dance "modernized" by a Russian-European dance technique. While doing so, Pavlova, like other international and national *Jarabe Tapatío* dancers, embodied not only the typical narrative of the *china poblana*'s European-indigenous Mesoamerican *mestizaje* but also its invisibilized Africanist and Asian histories.

This book includes brief discussions of the explicit Africanist and Asian presence in the production of Mexican culture and dance (i.e., the cakewalk craze in the late 1880s, the Caribbean musician Alberto Flachebba's collaboration with Norka Rouskaya in 1919, Michio Ito's tour in Mexico City in 1934).[61] However, although the book visibilizes this latent presence in some instances, it does not focus on excavating explicit Africanist and Asian influences in Mexican culture and nation-building processes.[62] As the genealogical traces of Pavlova's *china poblana* sketched above show, these influences, although systematically invisibilized, continue to have a potent impact in the development of mainstream

---

[60] In her seminal work, *Digging the Africanist Presence in American Performance: Dance and Other Contexts* (Westport, CT: Greenwood Press, 1996), dance scholar Brenda Dixon Gottschild theorizes the concepts of visibility and invisibility in the context of the United States. She uses these terms to make visible Africanist influences that have been made invisible in master narratives about "American culture" and "artistic geniuses" like choreographer George Balanchine. Her work inspires some of the ideas discussed above and below.

[61] Scholarship focusing exclusively on Black and Asian dancers' influence in the development of dance practices in Mexico is scarce. For some examples, see Anita González, *Afro-Mexico, Jarocho's Soul: Cultural Identity and Afro-Mexican Dance* (Lanham, MD: University Press of America, 2004); Miguel Lisbona Guillén, "Danzas como tradición y como disputa: La ilusión comunitaria china en el soconusco chiapaneco," *Península* 10, no. 1 (January–June 2015): 9–28.

[62] For some historical and contemporary studies on the contributions people of African and Asian descent have made in the development of different aspects of Mexico's life, including slavery, resistance movements, and cultural, intellectual, and economic advancements, see Ben Vinson III, *Bearing Arms for His Majesty: The Free-Colored Militia in Colonial Mexico* (Stanford, CA: Stanford University Press, 2001); Ben Vinson III and Matthew Restall, eds., *Black Mexico: Race and Society from Colonial Modern Times* (Albuquerque: University of New Mexico Press, 2009); Citlali Quecha Reyna, "La movilización etnopolítica afrodescendiente en México y el patrimonio cultural inmaterial, *Anales de antropología* 49-II (2015): 149–73; América Nicte-Ha López Chávez, "La movilización etnopolítica afromexicana de la Costa Chica de Guerrero y Oaxaca: Logros, limitaciones y desafíos," *Perfiles latinoamericanos* 26, no. 52 (2018): 1–33; Theodore W. Cohen, *Finding Afro-Mexico: Race and Nation after the Revolution* (Cambridge: Cambridge University Press, 2020). For a brief account of Mexican president Andrés Manuel López Obrador's recent apology for the massacre of 300 Chinese people in the city of Torreón in 1911 as part of the armed phase of the Mexican Revolution, see an AP report published on May 17, 2021, https://apnews.com/article/health-coronavirus-pandemic-d6202bf78 7c39865f743490221de2d7a. For this and other aspects of various people of Asian descent's role in the construction of Mexican culture and notions of nation, see Robert Chao Romero, *The Chinese in Mexico, 1882–1940* (Tucson: University of Arizona Press, 2010); Monica Georgina Cinco Basurto, "La expulsión de chinos de los años treinta y la repatriación de chino mexicanos de 1960" (master's thesis, Centro de Estudios de Asia y África, Colegio de México, 2009); Seijas, *Asian Slaves in Colonial Mexico*; Rubén Carrillo, "Asia llega a América: Migración e influencia cultural asiática en Nueva España (1565–1815)," *Asiadémica*, no. 3 (January 2014): 81–98.

"Mexican culture" and dominant narratives about Mexico as a mestizo nation. Thus, the book assumes these influences are integral to Mexican mestizo expressive cultural practices even when they are not brought fully to the surface.

Visibilizing and Racializing Whiteness

As I have begun to suggest, *mestizaje* as a corporeality of multiplicity can function as a hegemonic cultural ideology that marginalizes and often invisibilizes indigenous Mesoamerican, Black, and Asian peoples' lives and influences. However, *mestizaje* can also represent an alternative to colonial logic that upholds the ostensible supremacy of whiteness. Before elaborating on *mestizaje*'s anticolonial resistive potential, it is important to remember that whiteness often functions as a racially and culturally unmarked form of embodiment and an ideological mechanism in the hierarchical organization of human relations and cultural productions. It is then necessary to racialize the ideology of whiteness, mark it, make it visible, and expose its specific cultural associations. In so doing, one can uncover how whiteness operates when it attempts to be invisible, racially and culturally "neutral," to reproduce its supremacy and the privileges it receives. This need to visibilize and racialize whiteness resonates with critical dance scholar Anthea Kraut's efforts to "treat whiteness not as the absence of race but, rather, as a powerful and historically contingent racial formation."[63]

Similar investigations in various domains of life include dance. However, these studies do not address the role of Mexican dance in identity-formation processes during the historical times this book covers. Thus, this study examines how whiteness, *mestizaje*, and Mesoamerican indigeneity coexist in frictive negotiation in the development of dance practices, aesthetic discourses, and individual and collective (national) identities that have systematically excluded Africanist and Asian influences.

Racial Ideologies in the Production of Marked and Unmarked Bodies

The preceding discussion showed that the manufacturing of whiteness as a powerful racial formation developed in tensile interactions with blackness, Asianness, *mestizaje*, and the indigenous Mesoamerican. It demonstrated how whiteness's (ostensible) supremacy characterized Mexican colonial processes

---

[63] Anthea Kraut, *Choreographing Copyright: Race, Gender, and Intellectual Property Rights in American Dance* (New York: Oxford University Press, 2016), 30.

of racialization and social formation. It is important to emphasize here that for dark-skin-color people, an enduring desire to be white emerged out of the need to eliminate one's racial "defect" to obtain a higher social status associated with whiteness.[64] Accordingly, in Mexico, like in other colonized countries, racialization processes established whiteness as a referent of (Western) civilization and modernity. Historically, whiteness as an ideology of power has professed the universality of Western culture and the white body as the highest standard for the development of human civilization, notions of beauty, and modes of representation.[65] Legacies of this colonial perspective have often led people of diverse backgrounds around the world to embrace variations of the ideology of whiteness as they formed notions of who they were or wanted to be. The book assumes that this desire to be white, and other manifestations of whiteness's ideological force, take different forms in varied cultural contexts (i.e., urban, rural localities) and practices like dance.[66]

A prevalent manifestation of whiteness as an ideology of power holds that white bodies and Western ways of knowing are racially and culturally neutral— not possessing any markers that could anchor it as part of a racial and cultural form of ideology and embodiment. This ostensible neutrality has rendered whiteness as a universal representative of human experience.[67] In contrast, the nonwhite body often is figured as restricted to the trappings of its racial and cultural specificity, its "defects."[68] Such colonialist assumptions ignore visual markers of whiteness while marking nonwhite bodies as racially and culturally

[64] For instance, Twinam argues that during the last two decades of Spanish America's colonial period (1780s–1790s), pardos, mulattos, and other mixed-race people began to demand complete whiteness in their *gracias al sacar* petitions ("Racial Passing"; "Pedro de Ayarza"; *Purchasing Whiteness*).

[65] One can think here about the contemporary global industry of skin-whitening products. See a brief discussion on the use of these products in Mexico toward the end of the nineteenth century (chapter 1) and mid-1930s (chapter 4).

[66] For analyses of whiteness as an ideology relative to concepts such as homogenization, racialization, modernity, and capitalism in Latin America, including Mexico, see Bolívar Echeverría, *Modernidad y blanquitud* (Mexico, DF: Era, 2010); Bolívar Echeverría, ed., *La americanización de la modernidad* (México, DF: Era, Universidad Nacional Autónoma de México, 2008); Carlos Guevara Meza, *Conciencia periférica y modernidades alternativas en América Latina* (Ciudad de México: CONACULTA/INBA, Cenidiap, 2011); Quijano, "Coloniality of Power."

[67] European literature scholar Warren Montag has traced a genealogy of the Western philosophical tradition to explain how whiteness became "itself the human universal that no (other) race realizes" in "The Universalization of Whiteness: Racism and Enlightenment," in *Whiteness: A Critical Reader*, ed. Mike Hill (New York: New York University Press, 1997), 292.

[68] For example, in the case of the rhetoric of modernity and the ideology of universalism within the US artistic context, dance scholar Thomas F. DeFrantz notes that "the black body itself never achieves ["universal"] transcendence in any discourse of the West. Marked even before it can be seen, before it can exist, the black body carries its tangled web of work and sexual potentials, athletic and creative resources, and stratified social locations onto the stage of the modern." In other words, the Black dancing body is always already marked by corporeal, cultural, and social elements associated with its racialization. *Dancing Revelations: Alvin Ailey's Embodiment of African American Culture* (Oxford: Oxford University Press; 2004), 19.

other based on the visibility of their skin color and the categorization of their practices as "cultural" (e.g., fashion; ways of cooking, eating, dancing).[69]

These hierarchical colonialist ideas about culturally and racially marked and unmarked bodies constitute the colonial racial unconscious that informs the production of modernist dance practices.[70] In other words, analyses in this book attend to how national and international dancers often unintentionally reproduced colonial legacies of racial and social stratification because such legacies were normalized as part of the rhetoric of modernity. As subsequent chapters in this book demonstrate, this colonial racial unconscious often manifested in the ambivalence with which representations of *mestizaje* and indigeneity were conceptualized and integrated as part of dances, civic events, and notions of the nation (chapter 2). While tracing these unconscious colonial forces and ambivalence, the book analyzes debates about whether racial and cultural markers—as presumed sources of "contamination"—could constitute dance as a legitimate form of modern art without compromising its ostensible universal potential.

By drawing attention to the intricate relationship between modernist aesthetic practices and Mexico's colonial history, this study resonates with semiotician and decolonial scholar Walter Mignolo's assertion that "there is no modernity,

---

[69] Dance scholar Susan Manning discusses the concepts of *marked* and *unmarked* concerning racial and cultural particularity, whiteness, and universalism. She does so to theorize theatrical conventions such as *metaphorical minstrelsy* and *mythical abstraction* employed by modern dancers in the United States beginning in the first half of the twentieth century. *Modern Dance, Negro Dance: Race in Motion* (Minneapolis: University of Minnesota Press, 2004). Others critique the dichotomization of marked and unmarked bodies as a limited analytical paradigm that posits race as a mere *inscription* on the surface of the body rather than examining the complex nuances of the *performativity* of race—treating race as a performed social construct; Eva Cherniavsky, *Incorporations: Race, Nation, and the Body Politics of Capital* (Minneapolis: University of Minnesota Press, 2006). As Cherniavsky cautions, "To situate race as a bodily inscription is to posit that race makes a difference to the figuration of the body, exclusively, not to the fundamental condition of embodiment itself" (quoted in Kraut, *Choreographing Copyright*, 31). However, the material effects of whiteness as an ideology of power have literally marked the surface of black (and brown) bodies—their ankles, wrists, backs, and necks—across the Americas throughout history. Considering the contemporary time at this writing, we can realize how the visual markers of certain bodies—the inscription on the surface of their bodies—continue to subject them to potentially biased perceptions and treatment with even lethal consequences. Conversely, the inscriptive markers on white bodies can sometimes translate into diverse forms of privilege (i.e., safety, more accessible resources/spaces, generational wealth, etc.). Thus, how *inscription* marks bodies constitute forms of *performativity* that produce discriminatory perceptions and treatment of people as theoretical subjects and as bodies with specific flesh and skin. Rather than dichotomizing *inscription* and *performativity* as mutually exclusive processes, *Dancing Mestizo Modernisms* views these processes as mutually constitutive because visible markers translate into treatment that directly and profoundly affects the constitution of people's embodiment and subjectivity.

[70] In this context, colonial racial unconscious refers to the latent, yet unspoken, influence that colonial legacies of racialization and socialization have on different aspects of daily life for individuals and collectives, including social and power relations. For a formulation of the "racial unconscious" relative to racialized performances, see Eric Lott, "Love and Theft: The Racial Unconscious of Blackface Minstrelsy," *Representations*, no. 39 (Summer 1992): 23–50.

without coloniality."[71] Thus, this book contends that colonial legacies are not a sole determining factor but a very influential one in formulating the rhetoric of artistic modernity. This analysis is not an attempt to merely vilify modernist aesthetic practices, or to reduce them to their colonialist aspects. Instead, it is an effort to understand better how unconscious and conscious colonial legacies continue to operate through dance practices in forming hierarchical individual and collective identities and power relations within Mexico's modernization processes.

The Value of Embodied Mestizo Modernisms' Racial and Cultural Markings

This book challenges traces of the *limpieza de sangre* colonial logic that constructed racial and cultural others as "defective," as possessing "contaminants" that needed removal to attain privileges of white social (and artistic) high status. In this respect, the colonialist desire to be white, to become *gente de razón*—in the many shapes and forms it takes in dance practices and aesthetic ideologies— remains a focal point for analyses of case studies in this book. The study attends to (unconscious) colonial legacies shaping dance discourses that champion transcendence and the cleansing of markers of difference in the utopian pursuit of a racially and culturally neutral space, practice, and subjectivity. In its ideological foundation, this purported superior approach to dance-making, training regimes, movement practices, and modes of representation reproduces a desire for the cleanliness, invisibility, and neutrality with which whiteness has historically asserted its ostensible supremacy.

Dancing Mestizo Modernisms theorizes Mexican mestizo productions as *other* forms of modernity that expressed unique ways of being, thinking, feeling, moving, doing, making, and relating. Instead of merely replicating presumed universal, unmarked ballet and modern dance practices, national and international dance artists such as Pautret, Pavlova, Valencia, Rouskaya, the Campobello sisters, Sokolow, and Waldeen adapted these practices to create dances that conversed with the specificities of local histories. These dancers created mestizo dance practices that employed ballet and modern dance training regimes and

---

[71] Mignolo contends that "Coloniality names the underlying logic of the foundation and unfolding of Western civilization from the Renaissance to today of which historical colonialisms have been a constitutive, although downplayed, dimension." He also writes that "the idea of modernity and its constitutive darker side, coloniality, . . . emerged with the history of European invasions of Abya Yala, Tawantinsuyu, and Anahuac; the formation of the Americas and the Caribbean; and the massive trade of enslaved Africans." Accounting for these processes, Mignolo concludes that "there is no modernity without coloniality"; *The Darker Side of Western Modernity: Global Futures, Decolonial Options* (Durham, NC: Duke University Press, 2011), 2–3.

choreographic conventions associated primarily with Europe and the United States. They did so to "modernize" Mexican "traditional" dances, valued as cultural expressions but considered rudimentary regarding artistic rigor and technical proficiency. In so doing, they combined a neocolonial rhetoric of modernization with visible markers of Mexico's cultural and political histories, viewed as legitimate sources for choreographing dances that could speak to varied audiences. Rather than entirely rejecting foreign aesthetic elements and techniques as modernizing technologies—with all their implicit associations to the ideology of whiteness—these diverse dance artists combined the local and the transnational as a practice of modernist de-essentialized *mestizaje*. At the same time, these mestizo artistic embodiments represented an alternative to nativist practices of asserting "authentic," "traditional" dances intended as resistance to forms of "cultural imperialism."[72]

These processes of cultural modernization through dance continued to embrace the ideal of universalism. The book examines debates over efforts to develop a form of dance that was distinctively Mexican and universal in its reach, a form of Mexican universalism. The resulting danced *mestizajes* eschewed transcendentalist desires to cleanse visibly recognizable (Mexican) racial and cultural elements because of the view that they did not hinder production of art with universal appeal. While a modernist approach to creating mestizo dances assumed the need for "refined" technical proficiency, it did not regard overt Mexican cultural elements as if they were "defects" to be (totally) cleansed, invisibilized, neutralized, or erased. Although this tensile quest for a uniquely Mexican dance form included the idea of *uni*versality, the book suggests that the multiplicity of overt cultural elements integrated into modernist mestizo dances proposed *pluri*versality: "a world in which many worlds [can] coexist"[73] and be equally valued as sources of representation of the diversity of human experience.[74] These visibly marked mestizo dance practices avoid reproducing the rhetoric of invisibility and neutrality with which whiteness had historically established its

---

[72] Jane C. Desmond, "Dancing Out the Difference: Cultural Imperialism and Ruth St. Denis's 'Radha' of 1906," *Signs* 17, no. 1 (Autumn 1991): 28–49.

[73] Mignolo, *The Darker Side*, 54. In the context of environmental studies, Mexican economist Enrique Leff specifies further this idea as "not only 'a world in which many worlds [can] coexist' but a world shaped by a diversity of worlds" in *Saber ambiental: Sustentabilidad, racionalidad, complejidad, poder* (México: Siglo XXI Editores, 1998), 28. Both authors' ideas reflect the phrase "un mundo donde quepan muchos mundos" ("a world in which many worlds can fit/coexist"), a phrase attributed to Subcomandante Marcos, a leader of the Zapatista revolutionary movement in Chiapas, Mexico.

[74] For how the "pluriversal" has been theorized as an alternative to the "universal" as a concept more inclusive of diverse ways of being, thinking, feeling, moving, doing, making, and relating, see, e.g., Arturo Escobar, *Designs for the Pluriverse: Radical Interdependence, Autonomy, and the Making of Worlds* (Durham, NC: Duke University Press, 2018); María Regina Firmino-Castillo, "Dancing the Pluriverse: Indigenous Performance as Ontological Praxis," *Dance Research Journal* 48, no. 1 (April 2016): 55–73; Mignolo, *The Darker Side*; Bernd Reiter, ed., *Constructing the Pluriverse: The Geopolitics of Knowledge* (Durham, NC: Duke University Press, 2018).

supremacy, including its relation to notions of Western modernity. Embodied mestizo modernisms thus offer ways to think about *other modernities* based on Mexico's cultural and political histories.

Mestizaje's Contradicting Multiplicity and Decolonial Potential

Embodied legacies of colonial racialization in Mexico and across the Americas are central to the context where *mestizaje* and its multiplicity as a form of corporeality, ideology, and mode of representation was constantly reconfigured. This book joins a Latin Americanist intellectual tradition that has debated *mestizaje*'s different relationships to dominant notions of Western modernity as *the* foundational model for the development of human civilization. However, rather than pursuing what I see as the nearly impossible task of total "delinking" from what Mignolo calls the colonial matrix of power,[75] where notions of modernity and nation emerge, the book resonates with efforts to create "strategies for entering and leaving modernity"[76] and the nation-state's grip. These temporary moments of delinking (strategic entering and leaving) represent one among other "decolonial options"[77]—the exercise of individual and collective agency. In this respect, the book assumes colonial legacies and decolonial strategies as part of negotiating the rhetoric of (Western) modernity, nationalist ideologies, and the exercise of agency within a colonial matrix of power.[78]

Mexican Latin American historian Carlos Guevara Meza asserts that "En América Latina no hubo, ni hay, una modernidad, sino muchas" (In Latin America, there was not then, and there is not now one modernity, but many).[79] Other scholars of the region have long debated whether political movements and expressive cultures have reproduced or challenged European and US

[75] Mignolo, *The Darker Side*.
[76] Néstor García Canclini, *Hybrid Cultures: Strategies for Entering and Leaving Modernity*, trans. Christopher L. Chiappari and Silvia L. López (Minneapolis: University of Minnesota Press, 1995).
[77] Mignolo, *The Darker Side*.
[78] For scholarship that critically examines Western modernity and proposes diverse decolonial options relative to neocolonialism, visual culture, race, capitalism, legacies of slavery, and epistemology, see, e.g., Santiago Castro-Gómez and Ramón Grosfoguel, eds., *El giro decolonial: Reflexiones para una diversidad epistemica más alla del capitalismo global* (Bogotá: Siglo del Hombre Editores, 2007); Echeverría, *Modernidad y Blanquitud*; Echeverría, ed., *La americanización de la modernidad*; García Canclini, *Hybrid Cultures*; Guevara Meza, *Conciencia periférica*; Mignolo, *The Darker Side*; Quijano, "Coloniality of Power"; Silvia Rivera Cusicanqui, *Sociología de la imagen: Miradas Ch'ixi desde la historia andina* (Buenos Aires: Tinta Limon 2015; repr. 2018); George Ciccariello-Maher, *Decolonizing Dialectics* (Durham, NC: Duke University Press, 2017); Boaventura de Sousa Santos, *The End of the Cognitive Empire: The Coming of Age of Epistemologies of the South* (Durham, NC: Duke University Press, 2018).
[79] Guevara Meza, *Conciencia periférica y modernidades alternativas*, 16.

imperialism.[80] While analyzing *other modernities* that combined local cultural traditions with aesthetic elements and discourses from Europe and the United States, the book demonstrates that embodied mestizo modernisms often reproduced and challenged logics of imperialism and colonialism simultaneously. By combining the national and the transnational, danced mestizo modernisms embodied the tension between the colonial and decolonial, a tension that characterized intercultural encounters, modernization projects, and identity formation processes in colonized countries like Mexico. Thus, the work situates the exercise of agency—its efficacy and limitations—within a matrix of power where decolonial strategies exist as an ongoing process of constant negotiations with colonialism's legacies of racialization.

This ontological ambivalence, the exercise of decolonial agency within a colonial matrix of power, has characterized the multiplicity of Mexican *mestizaje*—its potential, contradictions, and violence. Thus, the book does not theorize embodied mestizo modernisms as a concept and practice that offers total delinking from neo/colonial racialization processes. As illustrated earlier, the racial and cultural markedness of modernist *mestizajes* can represent alternatives to the hegemony of whiteness as an ostensibly superior corporeality and foundation for artistic practices. However, *mestizaje* as a form of ideology, corporeality, and mode of representation—discursively composed by European and indigenous Mesoamerican elements—has also functioned to invisibilize Africanist and Asian influences in the production of Mexican culture, identity, and notions of nation.

Ironically, *mestizaje*'s exclusionary violence has also marginalized *Indios vivos* (live Indians) while strategically romanticizing the memory of *Indios muertos* (dead Indians) and their great Mesoamerican civilizations.[81] In Mexico, and other countries in the Americas, the perceived cultural backwardness of *Indios vivos* prompted benevolent civilizing efforts based on progressive tropes of *mestizaje*. Proponents hoped that Eurocentric cultural elements and notions of whiteness could help *improve* other cultures and races, including *Indios vivos*, explicitly and implicitly seen as inferior, as "defective,"[82] as in need of rescue (chapter 2). Representations of *Indios muertos*, their long-gone glorious civilizations, served as sources to strategically visibilize "uniquely Mexican" racial and cultural elements while invisibilizing less desirable "Indian," Africanist,

---

[80] Camilla Fojas, *Cosmopolitanism in the Americas* (West Lafayette, IN: Purdue University Press, 2005).

[81] For an example of the use of *Indios vivos* and *Indios muertos* as categories referencing indigenous Mesoamerican communities, see Verónica Zárate Toscano, "Los pobres en el Centenario," *Proceso*, Bi-Centenario: La Fiesta Interrumpida, Fascículos Coleccionables no. 6 (September 2009): 4–19.

[82] See, e.g., José Vasconcelos, *La raza cosmica: Misión de la raza iberoamericana* (México: Agencia Mundial de Librería, 1925); Juliet Hooker, *Theorizing Race in the Americas: Douglass, Sarmiento, Du Bois, and Vaconcelos* (New York: Oxford University Press, 2017); Vinson, *Before Mestizaje*.

and Asian influences in the creation of national imaginaries. However, as the following chapters show, these efforts to fashion representations of cultural uniqueness often implied processes of auto/exoticization[83] that relied on recycling previous and producing new stereotypical identities.

In sum, the book reckons with these tensions and contradictions not to offer embodied mestizo modernisms as a superior form of corporeality and mode of representation. This work is not an attempt to *replace* practices explicitly and implicitly based on the ostensible supremacy of whiteness as an ideology. Rather, the study illustrates how de-essentialized modernist *mestizajes* embodied a multiplicity of complex histories shaped by transnational influences crucial in constructing identities and the nation. In doing so, the book embraces the simultaneity of contradicting operations *mestizaje* embodies in its multiplicity: neo/colonial legacies, colonizing forces, and decolonial potentials.

Dancing Mestizo Modernisms' orientation joins ongoing efforts to decolonize dance histories and revalorize the diversity of bodies and experiences that shape them. While contributing to reconstructing the epistemological formation of the world, the book revalorizes embodied mestizo modernisms while challenging the hegemony of whiteness and its othering practices. It also acknowledges forms of anti-Blackness and other types of anti-dark-skin prejudice rooted in legacies of Mexico's colonial racial and social legacies, including the development of *mestizaje* as a dominant national discourse and identity. Thus, the study eschews the desire to offer idealized alternatives that provide a sense of resolution. Instead, it embraces human relations within a global social space as a wide-open field in constant change, friction, discomfort, and negotiation integral to constructing a pluriversal world. It examines the complex multiplicity of embodied neo/colonial histories and decolonial strategies that constitute Mexican corporeality and subjectivity—conceived, experienced, and expressed in multiple ways of being, thinking, feeling, moving, doing, making, and relating.

Further Notes on Methodologies and Chapter Content

To tell the story of how national and international dancers contributed to the construction of Mexican cultural and political histories during the periods covered, I relied on extensive archival research of primary sources written in Spanish conducted at various archives in Mexico City. Secondary sources from multiple disciplines produced in Spanish and English complement these analyses. This diversity of materials—books, newspaper articles, government documents,

---

[83] Savigliano, *Tango and the Political*.

INTRODUCTION 29

photographs, and video recordings—facilitate choreographic and discourse analyses throughout the book.

As suggested earlier, this study centers dance as a subject and method of critical inquiry to study dance and other forms of embodiment and representation in relation to forming identities and ideas about Mexico as a nation. Thus, the book adapts choreography as an analytical methodology to examine social relations beyond the dance floor. In so doing, choreographic analyses in this book consist of looking carefully at the choices made, the elements that constitute, and the logic that organizes how dances and other cultural practices and events produce conceptual meaning, affective associations, and kinesthetic sensations with sociopolitical implications. Choreography then represents a way to analyze the logics that determine rules, functions, and modes of operation employed by structuring mechanisms that attempt to prescribe, surveil, and regulate how bodies inhabit diverse social spaces.

The following chapters attend to the structuring logic and expectations about how bodies exist, think, feel, move, do, make, and relate in spaces such as the prestigious theater, the venue of low repute, the street, restaurant, city, and country—as dancers and audiences, as citizens and denizens. The study also accounts for how people circumvented predetermined expectations set by the state as a choreographic agent,[84] dancers' contrasting approaches to dance-making and aesthetic discourse, and colonial legacies of racial and social hierarchies that served as choreographic scores in daily life relations. In sum, choreographic analysis enables an appreciation of the forces that bodies negotiated as they constructed and performed a sense of who they and others were as racial, social, gendered, national, and transnational subjects in a variety of spaces.[85]

Discourse analyses attend to how dances and other cultural practices signify and what claims dancers, critics, audiences, and government officials make about those dances and cultural practices. Thus, this study assumes that people's claims about dance do not always reflect fully what a dance actually does in the world. In so doing, the book analyzes people's discursive claims and actual dances within the historically mediated sociopolitical and cultural contexts in which they were both produced. That is, the analysis of dance as a form of embodied discourse results in conversation with other forms of cultural and political discourses influential in the development of individual and collective identities (i.e., artistic, national). Two of the four following chapters (1 and 2) include choreographic

---

[84] For a discussion of "the state as a choreographic agent" that prescribes and regulates bodily practices and social relations, see Anurima Banerji, *Dancing Odissi: Paratopic Performances of Gender and State* (London: Seagull Books, 2019), 3.

[85] Like *mestizaje*, the concept of choreography has complex genealogies with conflicting implications. See, e.g., Foster, *Choreographing Empathy: Kinesthesia in Performance* (London: Routledge, 2011); and Kraut, *Choreographing Copyright*.

and discourse analyses beyond the realm of dance. They examine how *mestizaje*, whiteness, and the indigenous Mesoamerican related to ways of experiencing and representing diverse forms of Mexican modernity in exclusive streets and restaurants, in low-class venues, elite theaters, and private homes, in print media, and in civic events. That is, these two chapters weave dance studies and performance studies "to examine not just dance as culture but culture as dance."[86] Together, choreographic and discourse analyses reveal how oral, written, and kinesthetic forms of expression have political and social implications in shaping a sense of identity and power relations among people, including dancers, with diverse racial, social, and national backgrounds.

Although the order of the chapters is chronological, they do not intend to draw a linear development that traces stages of evolution from the ostensibly barbaric, rudimentary, or traditional to ideals of the civilized, sophisticated, or modern. Instead, by selecting specific moments in history, each chapter emphasizes how embodied mestizo modernisms—dance practices and other quotidian forms of embodiment—have contributed vitally to processes of subjectification. The chronology facilitates an analysis of how individuals and collectives have constituted themselves as distinctive subjects within specific ideological and corporeal dispositions that mediate (if not produce) their sense of agency. Thus, the book traces intersections of nationalist ideology and a rhetoric of modernization that emerged from neo/colonial legacies of racialization and transnational flows of bodies. It places the resulting modernist processes of *mestizaje*, including dance practices and aesthetic ideologies, as central to how people experienced themselves and their relation to others within Mexican national imaginaries. As the book traces how embodied mestizo modernisms changed over time, it emphasizes how they operated at different historical moments. These diverse forms of embodied mestizo modernisms have been crucial in forming Mexico's transnational nationalisms.

Chapter Descriptions

Dancing Mestizo Modernisms consists of four chapters and a coda. Chapter 1, "Mexico City's Ambivalent Spatial *Mestizaje*: Bodies in Motion from Independence to Dictatorship," is organized by two main concepts: spatial *mestizaje* and ambivalence toward *mestizaje* and indigeneity. The chapter examines major trends in dance, theater, and quotidian movement practices

---

[86] Performance studies scholar Rebecca Schneider, quoted by dance studies historian Susan Manning in "Inside/Beside Dance Studies: A Conversation, Mellon Dance Studies in/and the Humanities," *Dance Research Journal* 45, no. 3 (December 2013): 9.

by emphasizing the relation between space and bodies from the Mexican independence (1821) to the Porfiriato (1876–1911). In doing so, it shows how local and foreign bodies of different social classes, gender expressions, and racial backgrounds embraced and contested neo/colonial influences in diverse social spaces (prestigious theaters, venues of low repute, exclusive streets, and private homes). The chapter asserts that this multitude of diverse bodies dancing, acting, and walking within exclusive and shared public spaces represented a social kinesphere that constituted Mexico City as a racially and socially stratified mestizo space. While analyzing Porfirian ambivalence toward *mestizaje* and indigeneity, the chapter accounts for performative manifestations of the colonial desire to be white that Díaz himself, Mexican and foreign elites, as well as dancers and critics expressed in distinctive ways. The concepts of spatial *mestizaje* and ambivalence toward *mestizaje* and indigeneity illuminate how different social and racial groups negotiated colonial histories and transnational influences as they participated in constructing post/colonial Mexico as a modern nation and Mexico City as its cosmopolitan capital.

Chapter 2, "Choreographing the Indigenous Body in the Independence Centennial: From Dictatorship to Revolution," focuses on Porfirian ambivalence toward *mestizaje* and indigeneity during the 1910 Centennial celebrations of the Mexican independence. The chapter argues that while designing and structuring these festivities, Díaz's government instrumentalized *mestizaje* and indigeneity to create state performances of racial difference, tradition, and modernity. That is, after decades of forging a cultural context using Europe as a model, Díaz attempted to show the world his accomplishments in modernizing the country, including its mestizo and indigenous populations. Analyses of scientific and philanthropic efforts demonstrate how a re-emerging interest in the indigenous Mesoamerican reimagined Mexico's live and dead "Indians'" as figures of national representation and as objects of rescue and modernization. The chapter uses choreography as an analytical methodology to examine representations of the indigenous and modernity in dance and theater, art contests in print media and visual arts, massive parades, and other public events. While doing so, it provides a context to understand how this resurgent, ambivalent interest in *mestizaje* and indigenism subsequently integrated into the revolutionary governments' efforts to institute mestizo and indigenous cultures and histories as foundational to new nation-building projects.

Chapter 3, "Embracing the Indigenous while Establishing a Mestizo Nation: *Forjando* a Revolutionary *Patria*," focuses on three dance artists consecrated in Europe—Anna Pavlova, Norka Rouskaya, and Carmen Tórtola Valencia. While tracing the transition from the Porfirian dictatorship to a revolutionary state, it analyzes how these artists functioned as legitimizing agents who contributed to establishing *mestizaje* as the official cultural and racial ideology in postrevolutionary Mexico between 1919 and the mid-1920s. Rouskaya and Valencia exemplify the concurrent indigenism central to revolutionary ideology in the arts and politics. Rouskaya's work reimagined the Aztec as a figure of representation in a time when this "ancient" Mesoamerican civilization enjoyed a resurgent interest in Mexico and abroad. Mexican reception of Valencia's indigenized dance inspired by the Incas of Peru, performed in Mexico City in 1926, reflected Mexico's position within a Latin American pan-indigeneity integral to imagining post/colonial national and hemispheric identities. Although indigeneity was a central component of revolutionary rhetoric, Pavlova's performance of the folkloric *Jarabe Tapatío* en pointe consolidated the dance's prominent role in the nationalist dance repertoire and the state's project of establishing *mestizaje* as a dominant national, cultural, and racial identity. These artists' mestizo modernisms reveal aspects of the colonial racial unconscious underlying the coloniality of modernist dance practices and artistic subjectivities.

Chapter 4, "The Making of a Postrevolutionary Modern Dance Form: Debating National and International Politics and Aesthetics (1930s–1940)," argues that the effects of the Great Depression during the early 1930s and the rise of fascism in Europe later in the decade influenced how debates over the relationship between aesthetics and ideology in dance contributed to Mexico's institutionalization of the revolution and a mestizo state. The discussion starts with Russian dancer Hipólito Zybin's efforts to institutionalize professional dance training, exemplifying how dancers, government officials, and critics embraced different approaches to the relationship between (rigorous) dance technique and political ideology. The chapter discusses the Campobello sisters' mass dances in the early 1930s as choreographies that responded to national and international calls for socialist revolution in a time of disenchantment with capitalism prompted by the effects of the Great Depression. Critiques about the artistic merits of their dances extend to 1940 when Sokolow and Waldeen, two choreographers from the United States, prompted debates about to what extent visibly recognizable cultural elements, as opposed to abstraction, could be part of dance representations without compromising its ostensible universal potential. A choreographic analysis of Waldeen's 1940 dance *La Coronela*, offered as an example of a racially and culturally marked embodied mestizo modernism, challenges the ideology of universalism associated with Western forms of modernism that assumed or strived for racial and cultural neutrality. Ideas about auto/exoticism are part of this analysis. The chapter situates Waldeen's and Sokolow's divergent approaches to making dances within the context of President Lázaro Cárdenas's revolutionary "radicalism" and the rise of fascism in Europe during the late 1930s and early 1940s.

Finally, the "Coda: Contemporary Mestizo Modernisms and Transnational Nationalisms in the United States" provides a context to understand my personal involvement and motivation for writing this book and its emphasis on dance's relationship to colonial legacies of racialization and social formations. It also summarizes some of the main ideas analyzed in the book, and it briefly discusses developments prompted by Sokolow, Waldeen, and their respective associates during the 1940s and early 1950s when José Limón arrived from the United States. He, too, presented his mestizo modern dances and joined the contentious aesthetic and political debates then motivated by Cold War geopolitics. Taking Limón's experience as a Mexican who immigrated to the United States as a child with his family in 1915 because of the Mexican Revolution, the coda contextualizes Mexico-US migration patterns and their role in developing notions of US modernity. A discussion about Primera Generación, an up-and-coming contemporary dance collective formed by first-generation Mexican American dancers, highlights their work's explicit ethnoracial and class elements as a challenge to color-blind ideologies within the contemporary (experimental) dance tradition. It contextualizes their work within larger Latina/o/x/e communities shaping the United States as a nation while navigating racialization and social stratification processes.

1
Mexico City's Ambivalent Spatial *Mestizaje*
Bodies in Motion from Independence to Dictatorship

> There is always in infant countries the incarnation of a spirit of foreignness.... Spanish America has that faculty in the highest degree. Argentina is Italian; Chile is English; Brazil, Portuguese; Guatemala, German; and Mexico runs with full force toward becoming French, even though an impetuous current of American [US] immigration seems to run over everyone.[1]

These words were part of an article published by the *Diario del Hogar* in 1899, a newspaper originally geared toward middle-class families who embraced French culture championed during Porfirio Díaz's regime (1876–1911). However, the year before the note's circulation, the newspaper had already declared itself against Díaz's re-election, arguing that it was unconstitutional, a position that subjected the daily's founder, Filomeno Mata, along with other press members and political dissidents, to censorship and incarceration. The article, issued in this politically tensile environment, succinctly illustrated how for roughly eighty years since "Spanish American" colonies gained their independence, nation formation processes continued to be influenced by European countries. As its title suggested, the piece associated the Díaz-promoted "incarnation of France in Mexico" with neo/colonial processes of racialization and nation-building projects. Furthermore, only one year after the United States had taken over territory and control in the Philippines, Guam, Puerto Rico, and Hawaii, the article also alluded to the influx of US influences into the country through "immigration." In other words, neo/colonial and imperial forces continued exerting their power in the development of post/colonial "American" countries, including Mexico.[2]

---

[1] "Encarnación de Francia en México," *Diario del Hogar: Periódico de las familias*, domingo 20, 1899, 1. Unless noted, all translations are mine.

[2] Toward the end of the Porfiriato in 1911, the United States had invested over $1 billion, "controlled three-quarters of the Mexican mining and metallurgical industries," and its investment

This opening quote provides a brief but powerfully illustrative context to understand this chapter's primary goal: to demonstrate how diverse national and transnational forces contributed to shaping post/colonial and dictatorial Mexico as a nation and Mexico City as a racially and socially stratified mestizo space. The quote contextualizes neo/colonial influences that continuously impacted how people imagined, constructed, experienced, and expressed their identities as individuals and members of distinct collectives. As this chapter posits, dance, theater, and quotidian embodied practices played a crucial role in these processes of subjectification. Thus, it examines significant trends in these three forms of expressive embodiment to show how local and foreign people of different social classes and racial backgrounds embraced and contested colonialist influences. The chapter asserts that multitudes of bodies dancing, acting, and walking within specific social spaces constituted Mexico's body politic, its national corporeality of multiplicity.

The City's Kinesthetics and Spatial *Mestizaje*

By emphasizing the relationship between bodies and space, the chapter concentrates on Mexico City to theorize a form of *spatial mestizaje*.[3] In so doing, it adapts Michel Foucault's concept of heterotopia, which refers to a space inhabited by heterogeneous groups of people whose collaborative and tensile coexistence tends to produce progressive change toward utopian forms of social and political organization.[4] This idea contextualizes how local and foreign bodies with different racial, social, gender, and sexual backgrounds collaborated and competed with each other while constructing post/colonial Mexico City as a heterotopic mestizo space. Expanding Foucault's heterotopia concept, this chapter emphasizes how bodies in motion constituted the Mexican capital's spatial *mestizaje*. That is, this mestizo spatiality was not formed exclusively by the city's architectural elements but also by bodies' kinesthetic capacities, the sociocultural implications of their diverse ways of moving.[5] This proposition contributes to conversations about how dance

---

value was "twice that of Mexicans." Mark Wasserman, *Pesos and Politics: Business, Elites, Foreigners, and Government in Mexico, 1854–1940* (Stanford, CA: Stanford University Press, 2015), 7.

[3] For a discussion of the concept of spatiality (the "spatial turn") relative to literary analyses of time and history, as well as urban space and the city, see Robert T. Tally Jr., *Spatiality* (London: Routledge/Taylor & Francis Group, 2013).
[4] Michel Foucault and Jay Miskowiec, "Of Other Spaces," *Diacritics* 16, no. 1 (Spring 1986): 22–27.
[5] Kinesthetic relates to the term "kinesthesia," which refers to the use of sensory organs in the joints and muscles to sense the movement and position of body parts. For an analysis of aesthetic and political implications of kinesthesia relative to the concepts of empathy and choreography since the eighteenth century, see Susan L. Foster, *Choreographing Empathy: Kinesthesia in Performance* (London: Routledge, 2011).

scholars have theorized cities as kinesthetic spaces,[6] the borderlands between the United States and Mexico as a kinetopia,[7] and how within an "entire social kinesthetic" (i.e., in a city), mobilization is fundamental to see how dance can help us "rethink conventional views of politics."[8] In other words, the chapter proposes to think of Mexico City's spatiality as a mestizo social kinesphere. We can then see how a diversity of bodies moving within the city's urban spaces produced *mestizajes* that activated different forms of social and cultural meanings with specific political implications.

The discussion considers how these disparate social actors—dancing, observing, and walking bodies—performed choreographies of their individual and collective identities as dancers, audiences, and pedestrians who generated divergent discourses on modernity. It examines these performances in prestigious theaters, venues of low repute, exclusive streets, and private homes. As will be evident, analyzing various forms of embodiment in a diversity of spaces enables an appreciation of three forms of *mestizaje*: different pedestrian movement conventions and dance techniques cultivated within the same body; European, US, and Mexican dance forms performed as part of the same show on the same stage; and European, US, and Mexican dance artists commingling with diverse pedestrian bodies in the same urban metropolis, Mexico City. Examining how these forms of *mestizaje* formed and coexisted will facilitate understanding of the roles embodied mestizo modernisms played in Mexico City's formation as a post/colonial social and geopolitical space.

Post/Colonial Ambivalence toward Mestizaje and Indigeneity

Ambivalent attitudes toward *mestizaje* and indigeneity resulted from social and racial formations prevalent in colonial Mexico. As this book's introduction illustrates, colonial socialization and racialization processes set precedents for the country's development as an independent nation. Thus, this chapter demonstrates that Mexico's colonial legacies—establishing the supremacy of Europe as a cultural source and whiteness as a dominant ideology—shaped notions of post/colonial modernity and ambivalent attitudes toward *mestizaje*

---

[6] SanSan Kwan, *Kinesthetic City: Dance and Movement in Chinese Urban Spaces* (Oxford: Oxford University Press, 2013).
[7] Sidney Hutchinson, "Breaking Borders/Quebrando Fronteras: Dancing in the Borderscape," in *Transnational Encounters: Music and Performance at the U.S.-Mexico Border*, ed. Alejandro L. Madrid (Oxford: Oxford University Press, 2011), 41–66.
[8] Randy Martin, *Critical Moves: Dance Studies in Theory and Politics* (Durham, NC: Duke University Press, 1998), 24 (Martin theorizes mobilization in the introduction).

and indigeneity. How does a civilized, modern nation integrate people whose race (and other factors) deemed them "defective" and in need of assimilation to become *gente de razón* (people of reason) during the colonial era? Post/colonial ambivalence toward *mestizaje* and indigeneity manifested itself in quotidian social relations, modes of representation, and official public policies that fluctuated between the embrace of and contempt for *mestizaje* and indigeneity as forms of identity, corporeality, and sources of cultural practices. This chapter begins to illustrate how this ambivalence would take different shapes in dance practices and aesthetic discourses, including debates about the extent visible racial and cultural markers could constitute dance as a legitimate universal art form. In so doing, the analysis facilitates learning about how this racial and cultural ambivalence expressed itself during the independence Centennial celebrations and twentieth-century postrevolutionary Mexico in subsequent chapters.

Against Mexico's colonial historical background, the concepts of spatial *mestizaje* and post/colonial ambivalence toward *mestizaje* and indigeneity contextualize this chapter's story. The chapter reveals that although Díaz's regime championed French influences as the primary source for fashioning Mexico's elite culture and identity, the United States, Spain, and other European countries remained influential forces. It emphasizes how different social groups negotiated these transnational influences as they participated in the development of Mexico as a modern nation and Mexico City as its cosmopolitan capital.

This story begins only four years after Mexico's independence, made official in 1821, and traces developments into the Porfiriato in the second half of the nineteenth and early twentieth centuries. The first four examples illustrate different forms of embodied *mestizajes* as well as ambivalence toward them and indigeneity. Together, the cases of French choreographer Andrés Susano Pautret Chapalber, Mexican dancer María de Jesús Moctezuma, Plateros Boulevard, and critic Ignacio Manuel Altamirano demonstrate how a diversity of bodies' performances mobilized political dynamics shaping Mexico City's social kinesphere. The chapter then accounts for the emergence of theater and dance forms from Europe and the United States, and a new type of artist-entertainer. It discusses how these performances and different bodies contributed to creating notions about race, class, gender, and sexuality while critics and audiences debated what constituted legitimate, dramatic art. An emphasis on the case of modern dancer Loïe Fuller and performances of Spanish dances, and the *Jarabe Mexicano* by national and foreign dancers, leads to a final analysis of how the ambivalence toward *mestizaje* and indigeneity in dance practices and among Mexican elites resembled the colonial desire to be white.

Choreographing Post/Colonial Ambivalent and Integrative *Mestizajes*: Pautret and Moctezuma

After three centuries of colonialism in New Spain, a series of insurrections against Spanish rule in the late eighteenth century galvanized the independence movement, a struggle that resonated with liberal Enlightenment-era revolutions in Europe. Criollos (Mexican-born of European descent), mestizos (mixed-race people of European, Black, Asian, and Mesoamerican ancestry), and indigenous groups joined forces. They fought to overthrow *Peninsulares* (European-born Spaniards) and their local allies, who served as agents of royal power in what later became Mexico. More concerted revolts across the land took place from 1810 until 1821, when the establishment of an independent monarchy constituted the First Mexican Empire and declared independence from Spain. Three years later, in 1824, a new constitution established the Republic of the United Mexican States, named Catholicism as its sole religion, and granted equal citizenship to members of all races.

Although the new constitution granted rights to people of Black, Asian, indigenous Mesoamerican, and mixed-race descent as new citizens, and Mexico's first president, Vicente Ramón Guerrero Saldaña, was of Africanist ancestry, colonial prejudices against people of color continued. Post/colonial nation-building processes were fraught with tensions and contradictions. Colonial mechanisms to attain white status through a purchase deal or as a favor (*gracias al sacar*) from Royal authorities took new forms as mixed-race and indigenous Mesoamerican peoples *were* integrated into official notions of an emerging modern nation. Often, people of Black and Asian ancestry were strategically excluded. Explicitly and implicitly, Europe as a cultural source and whiteness as a dominant ideology remained influential in the development of post/colonial Mexico.

The case of Andrés Susano Pautret Chapalber and other international and national dancers illustrates how dance artists and people, in general, participated in complex processes of inclusions and exclusions in these nation-building projects. Looking at these diverse bodies' work demonstrates how they created post/colonial-embodied mestizo modernisms as dance strived to survive amid constant political conflicts, military interventions, and economic hardships.

Dancing a European-Inspired Mexican Independence: Pautret's *Allusion to the Cry of Dolores*

On September 16, 1825, some of the "most distinguished people from Méjico and abroad" gathered at the Teatro Provisional to see a group of national and international actors and dancers perform in Pautret's ballet *Alusión al grito de*

Dolores (Allusion to the Cry of Dolores).[9] According to the newspaper *El águila mexicana*, which published the ballet's libretto, the congregation of performers representing allegorical characters onstage "express with a colorful dance the joyful happiness that reigns within their hearts" as they demonstrate their support for the "liberty they wish for their nation."[10] After a series of belligerent struggles incited by Despotism, Love leads Liberty into "the temple of glory" and together they break the "chains that had bonded América" (a reference to Mexico).[11] Their victory prompted the heroes and all others involved in the liberatory movement to rejoice while performing more colorful dances. All equally jubilant, "deities, geniuses, and other people gather to demonstrate their joy with a military-like dance, ending with a group from which Love elevates itself above the ground in order to crown the Mexican Eagle."[12]

The dance was part of the official festivities celebrating the country's new status as a post/colonial nation. As such, it commemorated the Mexican war for independence, from 1810—when in the city of Dolores, Guanajuato, Miguel Hidalgo y Costilla emitted *el grito*, his famous call for insurrection against the Spanish viceroyalty—to 1821, when the insurgents prevailed.[13] Pautret was a French dancer and choreographer who had arrived in Mexico in 1824 after living in Spain and Cuba. His ballet relied on an aesthetic lexicon and repertoire of characters prevalent in a new form of nationalist theater emerging as Mexico affirmed its sovereignty. His performers personified heroes and archetypal figures such as América, Mexican Eagle, Liberty, Love, Glory, Patriotism, Despotism, Discord, Envy, Mars, and Apollo. Dressed in symbolic costumes, these actors and dancers enacted a drama of clashing forces, subordination, repression, and freedom.

As Pautret integrated himself into his newly adopted nationalist context, he dedicated the work to the "Illustrious Defenders of America Septentrional's Independence and Liberty."[14] It is likely that his interest in choreographing dances with nationalist content, and the implicit ideological functions they play, might have been influenced by his familiarity with European ballets about the

---

[9] *El águila mexicana*, September 20, 1825, in Silvia Ramírez Domínguez, *Alusión al grito de Dolores: El ballet se suma a las fiestas que celebran la independencia de México* (Ciudad de México: CENIDID, forthcoming), 26. (I have a copy of the unpublished work facilitated by the author.)
[10] Ibid., 26.
[11] Ibid., 26–27.
[12] Ibid., 27.
[13] "Grito" can be translated as "shout" and "scream." However, Hidalgo's call to arms in Dolores in 1810, "el grito" has been translated into English most commonly as "the cry of Dolores." I use this translation in the rest of the book.
[14] "América Septentrional" translates to "North America," which in this context refers to Mexico as the northern part of the Americas, now known as Latin America. The quote is from Pautret's libretto for his ballet. Ramírez Domínguez, *Alusión al grito*.

French Revolution.[15] Pautret's ballet was one among many other cultural activities such as allegorical floats, parades, and theater performances designed to entertain the masses, celebrate the formation of an autonomous nation, and instill a nationalist spirit in the citizenry.[16]

Allusion to the Cry of Dolores physicalized the energies, visions, and hopes that many Mexicans and their international allies had as they transitioned from colonial New Spain to a post/colonial nation-state, first as a monarchical Mexican Empire and then as a federal republic. In so doing, Pautret's theater-dance work created different forms of *mestizaje*. Although descriptions of the production suggest that pantomime characterized actors' movements, one wonders, given the limits of such descriptions, what the dances referenced in the libretto looked like. As the Mexican dance historian Silvia Ramírez Domínguez suggests, dancers in the piece most likely combined two styles of ballet vocabulary.[17] Training consisted of an academic ballet technique instituted in Mexico City from 1779 by the Italian dancers Giuseppe Sabella Morali, Peregrino Turchi, and his Spanish wife, María Rodríguez Turchi. Pautret probably relied on what his Mexican dancers already knew as he introduced his training on a more contemporary French ballet technique that integrated French "nobleness and elegance," Italian "virtuosity," and pantomime's "emotiveness."[18] Pautret's Mexican and European-allied performers embodied multiple corporeal histories integrated with ballet techniques as they celebrated Mexico's independence, dancing.

Allusion to the Cry of Dolores manifested *mestizaje* in other ways. There is no specific reference to how different actors and dancers dressed. However, the proliferation of theater and dance productions, including themes about the independence, featured América dressed as an indigenous woman, usually chained before her liberation.[19] Pautret's wife, María Rubio (Rodríguez) de Pautret, represented América. One can appreciate how the fact that she was a dancer of Spanish origin, dressed as an indigenous woman representing Mexico's independence, created a form of *mestizaje* powerfully symbolic at that historical moment. This embodied mestizo modernism implicitly symbolized a post/colonial reconciliation between Mexico's *former* Spanish colonizers and the integration of the country's colonized indigenous Mesoamerican communities in the same female, European, white body.

The nature of the allegorical characters in the work also assumed Europe as the driving force of América's independence. While figures such as Love and

---

[15] Ibid.
[16] For more context on Pautret's work, including several other productions, and the Independence festivities, see ibid.
[17] Ibid.
[18] Ibid., 32.
[19] Javier Ocampo in ibid., 29.

Liberty could have appeared as abstract, *universal* ideals at the time, they were reconceptualized within the European, revolutionary imagination that Pautret had embodied. As such, these ideals resonated with characters like Mars and Apollo, extracted from the pantheon of Greco-Roman mythological gods (Mars, the Roman god of war; Apollo, the Greco-Roman god of archery, music and dance, truth and prophecy). The inclusion of these laudable, enabling ideals and characters was indeed integral to the formation of the emerging Mexican identity and culture. However, a post/colonial ambivalence toward *mestizaje* and indigeneity revealed European elements' dominant role in this theatrical representation. In other words, this and other similar works at the time staged European ideals and characters as driving catalysts in portrayals of América's liberation from *former* European colonizing forces. As part of post/colonial revalorizations of indigenous Mesoamerican communities, the "Indian" body remained in a subordinated position in need of modernization utilizing European bodies, cultural sources, and artistic conventions.

These complex forms of *mestizaje*, produced by a French choreographer's ballet created in collaboration with Mexican, Spanish, and other actors, implicitly heralded the impact foreign forces would have in shaping the new nation geographically, politically, and culturally. While these inclusive combinations of diverse cultural elements and bodies were vital to forming a new country, they often established, if implicitly, the supremacy of Europe and later the United States as cultural sources and whiteness as a dominant ideology in constructing identities and notions of nation. National and international dancers developed these racialized theatrical conventions as they strived to keep concert dance alive amid continuous post/colonial political turmoil in mid-nineteenth-century Mexico.[20]

"Modernizing" the "Traditional": Moctezuma's Integrative *Mestizaje*

Pautret and his wife, María, stayed in Mexico for the rest of their lives, becoming influential figures in the development of dance practices and educational efforts amid more international cultural influences and geopolitical interventions. María de Jesús Moctezuma was one of the most prominent dancers to come out of the state-sponsored dance conservatory the Pautret couple founded in 1826.[21]

---

[20] For an account of the development of ballet in Mexico from independence to the Second Mexican Empire (1863–1867), see Maya Ramos Smith, *El ballet en México en el siglo XIX: De la independencia al Segundo Imperio (1825–1867)* (Ciudad de México: Alianza, CONACULTA, 1991).

[21] Maya Ramos Smith, *María de Jesús Moctezuma*, cuadernos del CID Danza, no. 18 (México, DF: CID Danza/INBA, 1987).

As she trained and danced in romantic ballets with the Pautrets, Moctezuma built her status as Mexico City's prima ballerina. Her acclaim gave her access to reputed visiting dance artists. She trained and danced with the highly regarded French ballet masters Adèle and Hippolyte Monplaisir, who arrived in the city in 1850. The same year, Moctezuma also trained in classical ballet techniques and danced with European visiting artists Celestina Thierry and Oscar Bernardelli. In turn, Moctezuma taught the artistic couple the *Jarabe Mexicano* (later known as the *Jarabe Tapatío*). According to the press, the performance of the national dance by these two foreign dancers represented a stamp of success, as was made evident by the enthusiastic applause of their Mexican audiences.[22] Moctezuma, Thierry, and Bernardelli successfully used ballet to stylize traditional Mexican dances like the *Jarabe Mexicano*.

These intercultural collaborations took place in a national and international tensile political environment. In 1850, the same year Moctezuma danced with visiting European dancers, the newspaper *El monitor republicano* noted the "ups and downs" of Mexican nationalism, perhaps reflecting the recent events' demoralizing effects. Only a few years earlier, the invasion of the newly sovereign nation by its neighbor to the north occurred after the US annexation of Texas and its failed first attempt to purchase Mexican land as part of Western expansion. The ensuing war between the two countries culminated with the incorporation of roughly half of Mexico's territory into the United States in 1848. While some segments of the population embraced US and European influences as modernizing forces, others resented what they saw as US imperialist incursions and European neo/colonialism, thus fostering a resurgence of nationalist sentiments. It is against this context that performances of ballet and stylized Mexican dances by Moctezuma and her European collaborators must be understood.

Moctezuma and other national and international dance artists' embodied mestizo modernisms corporealized debates about the extent to which one should embrace or reject external cultural and political influences. Writing about Moctezuma in 1850, *El monitor republicano* lauded her as a "national entity, . . . a presage of Mexican fine arts."[23] However, the previous year, the same publication responded to some of Moctezuma's critics by claiming that her "misfortune was . . . being Mexican, in this spiteful epoch in which youth raves for the spirit of foreign fashions."[24] As much as some people embraced her as a national treasure, Moctezuma's expressed Mexicanness apparently rendered

[22] *El daguerreotipo*, no. 32, December 14, 1850, in Maya Ramos and Patricia Cardona, comps., *La danza en México. Visiones de cinco siglos. Tomo II: Antología, cinco siglos de crónicas, crítica y documentos (1521–2002)* (México, DF: Cenidi Danza/INBA/CONACULTA/Escenología, 2002), 237.

[23] In Ramos Smith, *María de Jesús Moctezuma*, 17.

[24] *El monitor republicano*, 1849, in ibid., 16.

her culturally stagnant in the face of prevalent predilection for European and US (modernizing) influences. Moctezuma's ballet and stylized folkloric dance practices represented a point of contention amid ongoing debates over whether to embrace or resist foreign influences.

In this context of friendly intercultural collaborations, tensile international relations, and contentious cultural debates, Moctezuma and other local and foreign artists choreographed *mestizajes* that embodied simultaneous processes of resisting *and* embracing the foreign *and* the local. In doing so, their dance practices and dancing bodies were central to developing notions of what it meant to be an individual, a member of a national collective, and a cosmopolitan subject in mid-nineteenth-century Mexico City. Together, these dance artists helped establish a post/colonial tradition of stylizing local dances like the *Jarabe Mexicano*. While creating a form of de-essentialized *mestizaje*, Mexican and European dancers used ballet technique as an embodied modernizing technology in hopes of elevating Mexican dances to a legitimate art form. While Pautret's *Allusion to the Cry of Dolores* created a *mestizaje* produced by different cultural elements represented by diverse bodies on stage, Moctezuma, Thierry, and Bernardelli's *mestizajes* embodied European ballet and Mexican dance techniques within the same dancing body. Both approaches to choreographing mestizo modernisms would cause controversies among different population segments for decades to come.

Choreographing a Modern Country and Its Capital: From Post/Colonial Wars to Dictatorship

This brief overview of post/colonial Mexican wars provides a context for understanding the development of both dance practices and the conditions for Porfirio Díaz's rise to power. As part of political and cultural debates prompted by the aftermath of the Mexico-US war and the resurgence of long-standing European influences, dance continued to strive for its survival and relevance as a cultural activity in the second half of the nineteenth century. It did so while the struggle for power between neo/colonizers continued. A civil war between Mexican liberal and conservative factions occurred in 1857–1860. Liberals fought to implement radical reforms that would undermine the power of the Catholic Church and the military, while conservatives tried to resist such reforms and even advocated reinstituting a monarchy. Benito Juárez, a liberal, took the presidency in 1861, the first Mexican president of indigenous Mesoamerican descent. Seeking to extend France's dominion in the Americas, and in response to Juárez's suspension of interest payments to foreign creditors due to wartime expenditures, Emperor Napoleon III sought support from the United Kingdom and Spain to invade

Mexico in December 1861.[25] At Napoleon III's urging, Maximilian of Habsburg joined forces with conservative Mexican monarchists and the Catholic Church to overthrow Juárez, taking control of the country. This period, known as the Second Mexican Empire, lasted from 1864 to 1867, when the United States, coming out of its civil war, aided Juárez's forces in defeating Maximilian's French monarchy in Mexico.

During Maximilian of Habsburg's reign, he unsuccessfully attempted to institute a ballet company.[26] Moreover, the volatile social and political situation caused by the military resistance to his monarchy coincided with a worldwide decline in support for classical ballet.[27] Thus, after the French-imposed emperor's execution and the reinstitution of Juárez's Republican government in 1867, dance survived primarily as part of theater productions and variety entertainment shows, but international dance companies continued to visit the country from time to time.

The turbulence of constant wars in post/colonial Mexico continued briefly after Juárez's death in 1872, when Sebastián Lerdo de Tejada assumed the presidency. Díaz, a military general who had supported Juárez and helped defeat Maximilian's forces in the famous Battle of Puebla on May 5, 1867,[28] left for New Orleans and Texas, where he plotted a takeover of Mexico's presidency. Indeed, in 1876, Díaz overthrew Lerdo de Tejada, who went into exile in New York City. Although Díaz and his allies, primarily military officers, had justified his coup d'état with the *Plan de Tuxtepec*, a document that stipulated the principle of no re-election to the presidency, he modified the Constitution. He remained in power as Mexico's ruler for nearly three decades.[29] This transition from post/colonial wars to relative peace, from independence to autocratic governance, from stagnation to modernization fueled by foreign investors, enabled Díaz's favoritism for European culture, particularly French. He continued Maximilian of Habsburg's French-inspired transformation of Mexico City's architecture and urban design. As one of many Porfirian paradoxes, Díaz had fought to remove the French invaders from power, but he fully embraced their culture as the primary source to promote social identities as well as notions of cultural and industrial modernity. Porfirian elites fashioned and performed Europeanized modern

---

[25] Britain and Spain landed troops in the port of Veracruz in January 1862, but three months later, these countries withdrew from Napoleon's alliance.

[26] Ramos Smith, *Teatro musical y danza en el México de la Belle Époque: 1867-1910* (México, DF: Universidad Autónoma Metropolitana, Grupo Editorial Gaceta, 1995).

[27] For an account of the increasing decline of ballet in Europe at the time, see José Sasportes, "Grand Opera and the Decline of Ballet in the Latter Nineteenth Century: A Discursive Essay," *Dance Research: The Journal of the Society for Dance Research* 33, no. 2 (Winter 2015): 258-68.

[28] This battle is celebrated annually by Mexicans in Mexico, primarily Puebla and in the United States. In both countries, the celebration is Cinco de Mayo.

[29] Díaz governed first in 1876-1880 and then 1884-1911.

identities expressed through movements and (aesthetic) discourse in private and public spaces.

Performing Choreographies of Europeanized Modernity on Urban and Theatrical Stages: Plateros Boulevard and Altamirano's Cancan

Díaz's French-inspired social and cultural modernity coincided with the modernization of the country's infrastructure as well as its economic and educational institutions.[30] It is in this context that a multitude of bodies with diverse racial, social, gender, and sexual backgrounds created different forms of *mestizaje* as they moved within and through Mexico City's spaces. With US, British, and French investment, the railroad system expanded significantly and thus allowed commerce to grow exponentially by opening new markets between rural and urban centers. In 1891, the system added luxurious train cars in which wealthy people could comfortably travel to New York City in only five days. The comfortable spatial mobility that the train enabled within the country and between countries allowed those with means—Mexican and foreign—to travel to the Mexican capital.[31] These national and transnational economically mobile subjects reconstituted the metropolis as an increasingly important cultural stage of international reputation. The same year, with French investment and modeled after Parisian fashion department stores, the upscale emporium Palacio de Hierro opened its doors. Highlighting the correlation between the ascendancy of Porfirian upper classes, and the creation of consumer culture, Latin American historian Steven B. Bunker assures that "nothing made modernity more tangible for urban Mexicans than the department store."[32] Luxurious stores such as Palacio de Hierro provided opportunities for those who could financially afford it to re/fashion their modern identities.

---

[30] For analyses of Porfirian modernization and its consequences, see Michael C. Meyer, "The Making of the Porfiriato," "The Process of Modernization," and "The Cost of Modernization" in *The Course of Mexican History*, 7th ed. (New York: Oxford University Press, 2003); Claudia Agostoni, *Monuments of Progress: Modernization in Mexico City, 1876–1910* (Calgary: University of Calgary, 2003); Gilbert M. Joseph and Jürgen Buchenau, "Porfirian Modernization and Its Costs," in *Mexico's Once and Future Revolution: Social Upheaval and the Challenge of Rule since the Nineteenth Century* (Durham, NC: Duke University Press, 2013), 15–36.

[31] For cultural and ideological analyses of the railroad system as a hallmark of Porfirian modernization, see Michael Matthews, *The Civilizing Machine: A Cultural History of Mexican Railroads, 1876–1910* (Lincoln: University of Nebraska Press, 2014).

[32] *Creating Mexican Consumer Culture in the Age of Porfirio Díaz* (Albuquerque: University of New Mexico Press, 2012), 99. Palacio de Hierro [Iron Palace] was one of the first buildings in Latin America whose structure was primarily iron. The upscale store sold luxury products from Europe.

Plateros Boulevard, El Boulevard

An increased sense of mobility and purchasing power enabled Porfirian elites to experience exclusive social spaces as urban stages where they performed choreographies of Europeanized modernity. As the main artery of the fashionable shopping district, the Bulevar Plateros (Plateros Boulevard) was one such stage. As geographer Michael Johns suggests, for the "city's aristocracy," Bulevar Plateros "was the center of it all."[33] It "represented urbane, civilized, and modern Mexico: in a word, Europe."[34] More specifically, José Juan Tablada (1871–1945), a renowned poet and art critic influential in the transition from modernism to vanguardism in Mexico, hinted at what defined the bustling space he frequented. He said, "The love of everything French ... encouraged us to call Plateros, ... *el boulevard.*"[35]

People who could afford it bought their Parisian overcoats and other fancy clothing in one of the boulevard's fashionable boutiques or neighboring stores like Palacio de Hierro. They could purchase expensive European jewelry at the four-story La Esmeralda, the largest and most elegant of the many jewelry stores on *el boulevard*. They could buy life insurance just cross the street at the "flashiest building," La Mexicana. As people leisurely strolled on the street, buildings constructed with European architectural motifs surrounded them. La Mexicana included in its upper portion "a huge clock framed by a semicircular hood with dentils on its underside and a Greek goddess above it."[36] In its exterior, the exclusive Casino Español featured a highly detailed neoclassical façade, and its interior included glaring chandeliers that illuminated the most luxurious balls of the period. The Jockey Club, "the most illustrious association, ... was covered in bright tiles and crowned by finials. Here were the sharp frock coats and shiny top hats of the city's wealthiest men and the tight-waisted skirts, puffy blouses, and frilly hats of the women, who were all quite 'Parisian in the free use of rouge for lips and cheeks.'"[37] Members of this cosmopolitan class of people could enjoy themselves at the Casa de Plaisant, "a café where men in tailored suits sipped soft drinks and cordials" or at La Concordia, "whose large glass windows let 'the *snobs* eat their truffles and drink their champagne in plain view of less fortunate passersby.'"[38]

It was in these apparently straightforward leisure spaces characterized by European-inspired architectural motifs that local and foreign elites constituted

---

[33] *The City of Mexico in the Age of Díaz* (Austin: University of Texas Press, 1997), 17.
[34] Ibid., 11.
[35] Quoted in ibid., 17.
[36] Ibid., 16.
[37] Ibid., 17.
[38] Ibid.

themselves as social and cultural subjects through bodily performances. Their bodies displayed the latest fashions and other visual expressions of their purchasing power as consumers of high-end European products and cultural sensibilities. This display of European elements contextualized how their bodies in motion signified within the metropolis. They performed the implicit logic and scripted expectations associated with how they must move their bodies in space and relation to one another. They carefully performed highly rehearsed social choreographies expressed through the physically proper use of their arms and hands when sitting at dinner or tea tables, the measured softness of their gait's pace while shopping or strolling at *el boulevard*, the calibrated manners of subtly moving their necks to the side and slightly bending knees to bow while greeting each other, the restrained levels of excitement their whole body vocabulary should express while laughing among themselves, and the calculated distance between each other while talking about their fortunes and social lives. These specific ways of moving enabled US and European visitors and Europeanized Mexicans to assert themselves as members of an internationalized social class of modern individuals. Through these embodied performances of modernity at exclusive urban stages—luxurious cafés, restaurants, boutiques, clubs, and streets—elite people produced European-inspired social and cultural values that vied for dominance in shaping Porfirian Mexico City's life.

As the day waned on Bulevar Plateros, many of these cosmopolitan people went home, "some went to see a show" in one of three prominent theaters within the vicinity: the Principal, the Nacional, and the Arbeu.[39] Indeed, dance and theater productions also helped produce, readapt, and resist the Europeanized influences with which members of the Mexican bourgeoisie and other classes *learned* and *rehearsed* to become post/colonial Mexican subjects during the Porfiriato. Before examining various dance practices associated with diverse sectors of the population, it is necessary to understand the encoding of colonial legacies of racialization in artistic practices that implicitly and explicitly upheld hierarchies of superiority and inferiority. A look at Ignacio Manuel Altamirano (1834–1893), a prominent Mexican literary figure and cultural critic, can serve as an exemplar of such sociocultural dynamics.

Altamirano's Civilizing View of the Cancan

The case of the cancan's initial reception in Mexico further illuminates the tacit racial component embodied in people's choreographies of modernity while moving through *el boulevard* and other socially exclusive spaces. Forty-five years

[39] Ibid., 18.

after Pautret's ballet, the cancan debut in Mexico City stands as an example of how some Mexicans, including cultural critics, continued to embrace Europe as superior to mestizo and indigenous people and cultures, yet who also held a latent ambivalent proximity to *mestizaje* and indigeneity. In other words, this instance begins to illustrate how the colonial desire to be white, as a social status, and thus to distance from or try to erase one's ostensibly inherent racial "defect," manifested in aesthetic discourse as well as in music, theater, and dance practices.

Ignacio Manuel Altamirano was considered one of the foundational "fathers" of modern Mexican literature and became known, among other things, as *el maestro* (the teacher) who mentored new generations of writers.[40] His actual physical body and his body of literary work as a novelist and cultural critic who wrote about art, theater, and urban life can be seen as the very embodiment of ambivalence toward *mestizaje* and indigeneity. A strong Díaz ally, Altamirano advocated for French literature and culture's transformative role in Porfirian nation-building projects. Indeed, the editor for the *Echo du Mexique*, a French newspaper, once called Altamirano "the most French and Parisian of all Mexican writers he had personally known."[41] As a commentator remembered him in 1903, people who had never seen Altamirano physically but read his "speeches, verses or novels, imagined him as high, white and beautiful, a true son of Apollo."[42]

Notably, the influential *maestro* was an "Indian" of humble origins. A combination of his brown phenotypical characteristics made him publicly known as the "ugly Indian." His high standing as a literary figure did not make him immune to racist attacks, even by the press, which once referred to him as "Pygmy man" whose "ugliness" made him resemble "a clay idol."[43] Manuel Gutiérrez Najera (1859–1895), a renowned poet also influential in developing Mexican literary modernism, was one of *el maestro*'s "most adoring followers" and "saw in him a spiritual mentor whose capital was Paris, not Mexico City."[44] Yet Gutiérrez Najera referred to Altamirano's "Indian features" as "Satanic."[45] Alluding to his own "Indian" appearance, Altamirano himself admitted, "I am ugly, and I do not need big reasons to demonstrate it."[46] Although he did not usually identify as "Indian," but as a "Liberal, modern man who had risen from poverty through the regenerative power of education,"[47] he occasionally acknowledged his

---

[40] Christopher Conway, "Ignacio Altamirano and the Contradictions of Autobiographical Indianism," *Latin American Literary Review* 34, no. 67 (January–June 2006): 36–37.
[41] Quoted in ibid., 38.
[42] Gregorio Torres Quintero, "En honor de Altamirano," quoted in ibid., 34.
[43] In Conway, "Ignacio Altamirano," 38.
[44] Ibid., 39.
[45] Ibid.
[46] Quoted in ibid., 34.
[47] Ibid., 36.

indigenous Mesoamerican ancestry, as when he proudly told a Cuban reporter that he possessed, the "'splendid ugliness' of the Aztec race."[48]

Altamirano's ambivalence toward his indigeneity and his resolute adoption of European culture as the remedy to Mexico's ostensible racial and cultural stagnation informed how he viewed French performing arts and their role in the reconstitution of the Mexican individual self and collective nation. On July 3, 1869, the *Crónica de la semana* published an article reflecting the writer's assessment of a recent performance by the internationally renowned French cancan composer Jacques Offenbach and dancer Amelia Marguerite Badel, known by her stage name, Rigolboche, at the Teatro Nacional. A firm believer in the civilizing power of French culture, Altamirano viewed this artistic event as mocking those who lacked real cultural edification, especially elite Mexicans who already enjoyed high social status as marked by their efforts to embody a Parisian self. He addressed them directly by saying, "What a shame! You were behind Europe by a century, and while it is true that you fixed your clothing and hairdos like French figurines, you did not do the same with your heart and taste. You were merely boorish Americans[49] dressed like Parisians and nothing else."[50] In other words, these ostensible cultural inferiors' efforts to embrace a genuinely French way of being human led to mere superficial appearance, pretentious make-believe; there was no fundamental inner transformation, like the one he had experienced.

Nevertheless, there was hope. He added:

But light at last arrived to shine at your dark spirit. You are redeemed from ill taste and ignorance. Worry no more.

Let us salute, with hats in our hands, the arrival of the two missionaries of progress and happiness that have just entered furtively the National Theater's stage. *Offenbach* and *Rigolboche* are now among us. Let us strip away our gardens from their flowers and toss them on the artists' feet; let us get bronchitis by yelling repeatedly at them, *Hosanna*![51]

The critic concluded with a final exaltation of the French artists: "they had taken so long before visiting us; it was about time they came to reanimate our dejected spirit and to restore the fire in our American blood that was curdling in our veins."[52]

---

[48] Ibid., 38. See the same source for a discussion of what I call ambivalence toward *mestizaje* and indigeneity in Altamirano's novels.

[49] "Americans" refers to inhabitants of the American continent, including Mexico.

[50] *Crónica de la semana*, July 3, 1869, reprinted as "1869. Ignacio Manuel Altamirano. Debates sobre el cancán. La 'cancanomanía,' los 'jacalones' y el inicio de las 'tandas,'" in Ramos and Cardona, *La danza en México*, 269.

[51] Ibid.

[52] Ibid.

Altamirano's critique of his partially unconverted contemporaries and his praise for the recently arrived French music and dance artists evoked familiar colonial tropes, contributing to the presumed supremacy of Europe as a cultural source and whiteness as a dominant ideology. These Western colonial notions of progress and modernity assume a "traditional" Other, stagnating in the past, lagging behind, or even moving backward, while a modern self, reconstituted firmly in the present, always *progresses* moving toward higher states of being. If embraced in one's heart, this cultural progression would facilitate the formation of a Europeanized self. In gratitude to European redeemers, cultural subordinates must strip away their gardens in tribute—much as natural resources in Mesoamerican lands were stripped away in offerings to civilizing missionaries and colonizers. According to this Europeanized, brown "ugly Indian" critic, French cancan music and dance produced social and cultural values that reaffirmed the self and nation Porfirian elites would strive to construct in the following decades.

These examples demonstrate how within a cultural context that championed European culture's supremacy, pedestrian and dance choreographies performed on quotidian urban stages and in artistic spaces embodied racialized colonial histories. Together, Pautret's and Moctezuma's work, alongside Altamirano's relationship to French culture and cancan's music and dance, prepare the grounds for understanding how different forms of ambivalent and integrative *mestizajes* contributed to constructing Mexico City as a model for Díaz's national reformation. The following discussion focuses on a diversity of movement practices that national and international bodies of diverse racial, social, gender, and sexual backgrounds employed to perform choreographies of modernity in prestigious theaters, venues of ill repute, private homes, and exclusive streets. These analyses illustrate how dance contributed to Porfirian processes of post/colonial racialization and social stratification.

Dancing Race and Social Class: Ballet and the Emergence of New Artists, Theater, and Dance Genres

The dire economic crisis resulting from decades of political and military struggles affected the development of dance and theatrical forms in Mexico, including the capital, as Díaz took power in 1876. Ballet became a filler act in productions of various types. Visiting ballet companies whose productions satisfied the aesthetic tastes of the elites hired some dance artists but were often commercially unsustainable. Financial disparities exacerbated under Díaz's regime contributed to creating and maintaining economic and social hierarchies that determined who could afford to pay for access to see theater and dance companies in distinctive spaces. Consequently, impresarios had to strategize by adjusting to audiences' different budgets and expectations for shows by ballet companies and artists who offered more entertainment value at lower prices.

The economic dynamics involved in the production and consumption of dance and other forms of entertainment led to a growing popularity of US and European commercial dance and theater genres, especially toward the end of the nineteenth century. National and foreign ballet dancers who decided to stay in the country at length survived by appearing in short dance numbers in intermissions of musical theater shows such as Spanish *zarzuelas* and French operettas. While doing so, ballet dancers competed with the emergence of new types of dance performers and other entertainers.[53]

Enacting Neo/Colonialism: Ballets, *Féeries*, Cakewalk Dances, and *Zarzuelas*

Despite economic challenges and shifts in taste, ballet from the French and Italian traditions continued to draw audiences of balletomanes on the rare occasions when prestigious foreign dance and theater companies visited Mexico City. Some of these European dance artists adopted the country as their home. Such was the case for some members of the Spanish dramatic-choreographic company Bernis-Burón, which debuted at the Teatro Nacional on April 24, 1880. The three names behind this company's reputation raised hopes for those who longed for the reinstitution of ballet in Mexico as a serious art form: impresario Alberto Bernis, director and first/principal actor Leopoldo Burón, and director and choreographer Giovanni Lepri. This last was a disciple of the iconic Italian ballet teacher and theoretician Carlo Blasis. Lepri had also taught the influential Enrico Cecchetti, who developed his signature ballet style and teaching methodology known as the Cecchetti Method. Lepri and his daughter, Amalia Lepri, stayed in Mexico for the rest of their lives, influencing the development of various theatrical and dance genres in the capital.

As these and other visiting artists contributed to keeping ballet alive in Mexico, some of their works helped to naturalize neo/colonial international racial relations tacitly. The esteemed ballet company La Scala of Milan presented pieces such as *Coppélia*, *Excelsior*, *Brahman*, and *En el Japón* (In Japan) for the 1904–1905 season. Critics mentioned neither colonial histories between India and Holland nor imperial relations between Japan and England when

---

[53] See Ramos Smith, *Teatro musical y danza*, for a survey of local and foreign dancers and companies that visited the country and the theatrical trends that developed in Mexico City between 1867 and 1910, a period she calls Mexico's *belle époque*. I am deeply indebted to Ramos Smith's extensive research on this historical period.

52 DANCING MESTIZO MODERNISMS

commenting on *Brahman* and *En el Japón* respectively. Instead, they focused on these productions' formal and lavish visual aspects. They praised *En el Japón*'s "richness of the costumes, the correct execution of the dances, the harmonious ensemble of the company, [and] the magnificent decorations."[54] Further, they characterized *Brahman* as "a recreation for the eyes, a luminous and colorful kaleidoscopic game, a constant fluttering of figures and nuanced colors that for a moment fascinate and dazzle."[55] The two dance pieces featured heterosexual romantic and social relations between characters of different races, ethnicities, genders, and social classes. These choreographed interactions on stage enacted—and naturalized—human relations based on colonial histories influenced by Orientalism and the Western rhetoric of modernity.[56] Mexico's Europeanized audiences consumed such staged Orientalism as they cultivated their distinct modern cosmopolitan subjectivities.

Looking at European and US dance and theater practices shaping Mexico City's commercial dance and theatrical milieu reveals how social class was implicitly associated with racialization processes. The *Féerie* (fairy play) theatrical genre emerged in the early nineteenth century in France. It included elaborate sceneries and spectacular visual effects that combined theater, dance, music, acrobatics, and mime. The introduction of new technologies and apparatuses enabled astonishing magical tricks (e.g., the sudden disappearance of supernatural and human characters) and stage effects (e.g., flight or midair suspension of actors and dancers).[57] In Mexico, the *Féerie* bolstered the popularity of musical theater along with magic and musical comedy during the 1870s and 1880s. These shows enabled impresarios to make some profits while also providing the context for the ballet to thrive as a divertissement and for dancers to supplement their livelihood. However, by the mid-1880s, the complex theatrical infrastructure for magic comedies increasingly made their production financially prohibitive. In the early 1890s, the popularity of the *Féerie* waned as the Spanish *zarzuela* continued its dominance, and other dance forms from the United States made their way into Mexico City dance halls and theater stages.

In the early 1900s, African American dance forms gained traction in the city, including the cakewalk. The dance had emerged among enslaved people on plantations across the US South. White performers later appropriated it, many

---

[54] *El imparcial*, September 13, 1904, quoted in Ramos Smith, *Teatro musical y danza*, 441.
[55] *El imparcial*, August 18, 1904, quoted in ibid., 436.
[56] For analyses of how Orientalism and other forms of exoticism were constitutive of the rhetoric of Western modernity and colonialism, see, e.g., Edward Said, *Orientalism* (New York: Pantheon, 1978); Marta Savigliano, *Tango and the Political* (Boulder, CO: Westview Press, 1995); Walter Mignolo, *The Darker Side of Western Modernity* (Durham, NC: Duke University Press, 2011).
[57] To situate the *Féerie* within the broader history of ballet's development as an autonomous art form in mid-eighteenth-century France, see Foster, *Choreography and Narrative: Ballet's Staging of Story and Desire* (Bloomington: Indiana University Press, 1996).

donning blackface as part of minstrelsy shows that contributed to stereotyping Black people. In Mexico, some commentators characterized the cakewalk as "a return to the primitive,"[58] a description that resonated with the production of racialized stereotypes of non-European "primitive" peoples and which some Europeans used to justify colonization processes.[59] If *Féeries* tacitly enacted whiteness in their melodramatic plots, the cakewalk offered the allure of embodied Black culture as an exotic other. Perhaps this colonialist resonance led the cakewalk to cause quite a stir in a city that championed European, particularly French, culture. Professional dancers and bodies with less formal dance training began to dance the cakewalk in prestigious venues and *jacalones*, lower-class spaces considered to be of low repute for artistic performances.[60] Even if performers did not use blackface, they produced a form of metaphorical minstrelsy that enabled nonblack bodies to (mis)appropriate and (mis)represent embodiments of Black people's expressive culture.[61] Like its European ex/colonizers, Mexico City adopted dances inspired or danced by racialized bodies perceived as primitive, exotic others. As if having internalized a colonial whitened racial unconscious, the city itself would participate in producing and consuming metaphorical minstrelsy shows well into the twentieth century.[62]

While theatrical and dance forms like the *Féerie* and the cakewalk began to fall in and out of favor among general audiences, *zarzuelas* retained their dominance. Like *Féeries*, this Spanish genre combined theater, music, dance, singing, and spoken word, but *zarzuelas* did not, as a rule, require an elaborate production infrastructure.[63] Two years after the 1867 fall of the Second Mexican Empire, Spanish *zarzuela* and French operetta were the preferred musical theater forms in the city. During the 1870s, these two genres shared and competed for stages with *Féeries* and musical comedies. However, *zarzuelas* seemed to thrive more readily in precarious economic times when impresarios had to lower their prices. By the early 1880s, the Teatro Arbeu became one of the most popular venues and

[58] Ramos Smith, *Teatro musical y danza*, 418.
[59] For a discussion of how primitivism as a movement developed and functioned, see Marianna Torgovnick, *Gone Primitive: Savage Intellect, Modern Lives* (Chicago: University of Chicago Press, 1990).
[60] Venues known as *jacalones*, plural for *jacalón*, were named for a type of living quarters mostly inhabited by rural poor people, built with straw and coated with a thin layer of mud. Critics used this classist metaphor to denigrate specific low-class theatrical venues.
[61] For a discussion of the racial implications of metaphorical minstrelsy as a theatrical convention in the United States during the early decades of the twentieth century, see Susan Manning, *Modern Dance, Negro Dance: Race in Motion* (Minneapolis: University of Minnesota Press, 2004).
[62] See, e.g., Melissa Blanco Borelli, "¿Y ahora qué vas a hacer, Mulata?": Hip Choreographies in the Mexican *Cabaretera* Film *Mulata* (1954)," *Women & Performance: A Journal of Feminist Theory* 18, no. 3 (2008): 215–33. For a discussion of the concept of the racial unconscious in performance, see Eric Lott, "The Racial Unconscious of Blackface Minstrelsy," *Representations*, no. 39 (Summer 1992): 23–50.
[63] Some *zarzuelas* did include more complex production machinery and were known as *zarzuelas de gran aparato* (*zarzuelas* of grand apparatus).

devoted its programming almost exclusively to *zarzuelas*. Despite their popularity, *zarzuelas*—which continued to provide a cultural link to Spain, Mexico's ex/colonizer—had a worthy competitor, the cancan.

To appreciate the significance the cancan had in the city, one needs to understand how the proliferation of new theater and dance genres coincided with the emergence of a new type of artist. By the 1890s, professionally trained dancers, who specialized in ballet and Spanish dances, had to compete with *tiples*, versatile female dancer-singer-actors akin to vaudeville performers. These new artistic subjects sparked frictions over what constituted dance as a form of legitimate, serious art. They did so in part by redefining how actors, dancers, and audiences performed choreographies of gender and sexuality.

Although audiences from distinct social classes expected differences in technical proficiency between professionally trained female dancers and *tiples*, the two figures faced similar expectations of physical attractiveness. The *tiple* had to perform as a singer, actor, and dancer, roles she executed with different levels of proficiency. As Mexican dance historian Maya Ramos Smith notes, "the *tiple* was asked to perform a little bit of everything and was forgiven for not doing it all so well, but on this she could not fail, she had to be beautiful, funny, spontaneous, and above all have a voluptuous form, the most exuberant the better, generously exposed."[64] The influx of *tiples*, mainly from Spain, created a new market, more avid audiences, and a class of appreciative writers who praised the versatile performers' raw talents and bodies.

As *zarzuelas* consolidated their dominance among audiences, the multitalented *tiples* further displaced professionally trained dancers. In these shows, *tiples* performed their multiple talents and often exposed more of their body. As the next section shows, the cancan and other dance forms gave theater and dancing bodies, including *tiples*, opportunities to perform varied gender expressions and eroticized encounters in public and private spaces, even as authorities criminalized their dancing bodies.

Scandalizing the City: Un/Lawful Bodies Performing Choreographies of Gender and Sexuality in Public and Private Spaces

The Cancanization of the City

As the previous discussion began to demonstrate, performances in various theater and dance genres enacted racial and social class dynamics. These bodily

---

[64] Ramos Smith, *Teatro musical y danza*, 372.

performances also produced notions about the experience of gender and sexuality during the Porfiriato. In a context of highly policed morality where naturalized heterosexuality was the norm, a diversity of gendered and sexual dancing bodies with different racial and social backgrounds scandalized the city through their performances on and off theatrical stages. In 1869, the newspaper *El renacimiento* declared that "the *zarzuela* had dethroned the dramatic arts, and that the cancan had dethroned the *zarzuela*."[65] While this latter statement is an exaggeration, the cancan certainly influenced the *zarzuela* and many other genres.

Emerging in the early decades of ninetieth-century France, the cancan (much like the cakewalk that would come after it) was initially danced in music halls and eventually became a craze worldwide. It initially carried an aura of rebelliousness that young men and women adopted as a form of protest and expression of nonconformity to social norms. The eventual commercialization of the form produced female dancers who showed their legs and crotches in fishnet or black stockings as they kicked their legs as high as possible, bent over to show their bottoms to the audience, hopped around the stage, and ably landed on split legs. Conservative elites regarded these commercial versions of the cancan as a form of social and moral degeneration and took the dance's improvisational nature for a lack of choreographic rigor and thus far from being a legitimate art form.

As eroticized female cancan performers gained popularity, the form was fully embraced in many countries by audiences from the lower classes. People in Mexico City adopted the dance form so fervently that it had a "cancanization" effect in the city's dance and theatrical scene.[66] Artists such as *tiples* and other performers took up the form, and the craze for the cancan took hold in Mexico City's *jacalones* and all other venues. The dance style heightened expectations for seeing both professional and commercial female dancers' eroticism.

Il/licit Eroticized Encounters: High- and Low-Class Heterosexual Dancers and Audiences

Growing numbers of scandalous sexualized encounters at high- and low-class venues led to theatrical and social pandemonium. Although *tiples* and formally trained female dancers had different bodily training trajectories, heterosexual men held similar expectations for the physical attractiveness of these gendered artist-entertainers. As in other cities the world over, heterosexual men of all classes would roam about, accessing backstage areas, hallways, lobbies, and

---

[65] July 8, 1869, in Ramos Smith, *Teatro musical y danza*, 449–50.
[66] Ramos Smith, *Teatro musical y danza*, 59.

entrance doors according to their level of privilege, hoping to gain the attention of a female singer, dancer, or actress.[67] For one of the rare showcases of ballet as a serious dramatic art in the city, *El monitor republicano* created a heightened sense of expectancy among audiences by emphasizing that a renowned European opera and dance company was bringing twenty-six beautiful female dancers. As if to incite heterosexual men's erotic desire, the note assured its readers that "there is no greater novelty in [the company] than the dancers' . . . legs—and mind you, it is all going to be about plenty of beautiful legs for three months," and thus the announcement predicted that "Twenty-six female dancers are more than sufficient as a magnet to draw a full house."[68]

With a similar audience in mind, other companies were more proactive in their marketing strategies.[69] The Lilly Clay's Colossal Gaiety Company brought a group of twenty female dancers whose fishnet-stockinged legs in marketing posters enticed prospective audiences of love-seekers. This heterosexual male fascination for romantically pursuing actresses, chorus girls, singers, and dancers became so intense that some dance companies hired bodyguards to keep their female artists safe.[70] Also, some theaters prohibited the practice of courting during intermissions because it delayed the start of the show's following act.[71]

At the low-class *jacalones*, passionate expressions of admiration from heterosexual men for female performers scandalized state authorities and critics who upheld conservative moral values coded in aesthetic terms. In venues such as El Principal and El Triunfo de América—the latter described by Enrique Chávarri Juvenal as "a type of a parrot's cage, a barracks . . . the cancan's Babylon"[72]— heterosexual men "frantically applauded and joyfully howled when female dancers lifted up their clothing to reveal that which women have most hidden."[73] With similarly animalistic metaphors, Javier Santa María captured the scene at one of these performances at El Teatro de América in 1873. He wrote:

> That was definitively something to shield one's eyes from. Just imagine half a dozen robust female dancers executing the hops and contortions of the cancan,

---

[67] For an example of how sexual exchanges between dancers and patrons were part of the ballet scene in eighteenth-century France, see Lorraine Coons, "Artiste or Coquette? *Les Petits Rats* of the Paris Opera Ballet," *French Cultural Studies* 25, no. 2 (2014): 140–64.

[68] *El monitor republicano*, September 21, 1873, in Ramos Smith, *Teatro musical y danza*, 121–22.

[69] The primary target audience for these ads might have been heterosexual men, but female audiences who felt attracted to other women could connect equally to these marketing materials. For the concept of "cross viewing" relative to how audience members might relate to a dance work from their own specific social, gendered, and racial perspectives, see Manning, *Modern Dance, Negro Dance*.

[70] The Lilly Clay's Colossal Gaiety Company implemented this practice; *El monitor republicano*, October 26, 1890, in Ramos Smith, *Teatro musical y danza*, 351–53.

[71] Ibid., 351–53, 358.

[72] *El monitor republicano*, February 9, 1873, quoted in ibid., 115.

[73] *El monitor republicano*, September 24, 1871, quoted in ibid., 101.

with all the unrestrained possible and imaginable. Just imagine one hundred *pollos* [male audience members][74] standing tightly together on the benches, forming a great compacted human mass, while others, hanging like lizards, grabbed onto the theater box columns, wishing their whole beings were eyes to see and mouths to scream.... Terpsichore's [the Greek Muse of dance] disciples hopped, their dresses [moving] up and down letting the women's enticing forms be seen, and the *pollos*, then, frenetically, deliriously, desperately did not scream; they howled, they emitted frightening yowls. That was like a cage full of mentally insane men.[75]

Despite some critics' condemnation of these "Babylonian" venues for the "mentally insane"—uninhibited female performers and lascivious male audiences—the popularity of *jacalones* and their shows continued well into the early 1900s. Such was the passionate effervescence between female performers and male audiences that their overflowing eroticized enthusiasm spilled beyond the theater walls. In many cases, not only critics but also neighbors and the police had to intervene.

Law enforcement officers, government officials, and morally concerned citizens policed scandalous sexualities.[76] In addition to dance and theater companies' measures to protect their female performers from unsolicited romantic and sexual requests by male audiences, more aggressive city ordinances attempted to control these morally transgressive heterosexual interactions by further regulating female dancer's bodies. By decree, the city government demanded that "female dancers present themselves with the fantastic costume they had traditionally used, or if the dance requires a long and informal dress, make sure not to lift it, thus, as it ought to be done, respect social mores."[77] Further stipulations fined women for disobeying city ordinances designed to regulate their performing bodies. However, in defiant complicity with men in their performance of erotically scandalous encounters, women defied the state policing of morality. Women continued displaying their voluptuous forms while their fervent audiences collected money to pay the fines and bailed the transgressive dancers out of jail.[78]

---

[74] "Pollo" can mean male chicken or chick in Spanish.
[75] Santa María, *El siglo XIX*, February 2, 1873, quoted in Ramos Smith, *Teatro musical y danza*, 113.
[76] For an analysis of Porfirian precedents in the systematic criminalization of the urban poor in Mexico City before and after the revolution, see Pablo Piccato, *City of Suspects: Crime in Mexico City, 1900–1931* (Durham, NC: Duke University Press, 2001).
[77] Olavarría y Ferrari, II: 856, quoted in Ramos Smith, *Teatro musical y danza*, 118.
[78] Ibid.

Staging Acceptable Fluid Gender Expressions and Sexual Identities: Fregoli and the *Potosí submarino*

Female dancers, with their devoted heterosexual male audiences, were certainly not the only social agents shaping notions of race, class, gender, and sexuality in Mexico City. Some shows featured male performers dressed as women, while others presented effeminate male characters. Undoubtedly, audiences for these shows included members of the homosexual community who kept their sexual identity a secret known only by people they trusted. In the mid-1890s, for instance, the celebrated Italian entertainer Leopoldo Fregoli "amazed some and scandalized others" with his character transformations, especially his imitations of known female figures.[79] Comparing the cross-dressing entertainer with female performers of the serious dramatic arts and their assumed inherent feminine *nature*, the highly respected poet and critic José Juan Tablada categorized Fregoli's "effeminate movements" as reflective of a "grotesque femininity."[80] That is, the entertainer's grotesque masculine *nature* could not express a graceful femininity.

Other shows, like the *Potosí submarino*, featured effeminate male characters. Only four years after its debut in Europe, this *zarzuela cómico-fantástica de gran espectáculo* [comical-fantastic zarzuela of grand spectacle][81] arrived in Mexico City for the 1874–1875 season. Much of the work's drama takes place in a fantastic underwater world whose anthropomorphic characters coexist with human protagonists, often dealing with romantic stories. The *Potosí submarino*'s success in Mexico was such that it led some impresarios to restage the show intermittently from the mid-1870s through the early 1900s.

With all its appealing spectacle, the comical-fantastic *zarzuela*'s three acts represented a denunciation of corrupt investors in Spain and a call for their punishment. However, the presence of an amphibian effeminate male character named Escamon appeared to provide a subtext with which Mexico City's gay men could identify. According to the original libretto, Escamon was to act with an "effeminate air and manners."[82] He took pride in spending a great deal of time at the vanity desk taking care of himself by applying "tohalla de Venus and pachouly,"[83] an activity and products considered proper for female skincare and appearance embellishment at the time, in Spain and Mexico.

---

[79] Ibid., 377.
[80] *El universal*, January 17, 1897, in Ramos Smith, *Teatro musical y danza*, 379–80.
[81] This is how the original libretto characterizes the work. Rafael García y Santisteban, *El potosí submarino: Zarzuela cómico-fantástica de gran espectáculo en tres actos y en verso*, music by Emilio Arrieta (Madrid: Imprenta de José Rodríguez, 1870).
[82] Ibid., 40.
[83] Ibid., 58.

Perhaps in response to Escamon's effeminate gestures, melodic inflection, and careful grooming, Cardona, a male human, asked him whether he was a "prince or princess."[84] In an apparent paradox, Escamon tacitly declared his fluid gender expression by identifying as a prince at one point[85] and a member of the "sexo débil" ("the weak sex," an allusion to the female gender)[86] at another. Indeed, Escamon's girlfriend, the female-identified Perlina, complained that her boyfriend was "always making up excuses" in reference to Escamon's sexual unavailability.[87] For this and other expressions of Escamon's effeminacy, Cardona calls him "Mr. Mariquito" (a variation of the word *maricón*).[88] Finally, the effeminate, heterosexually elusive male amphibian escapes to the surface of the earth with Misisipí—a male human, corrupt impresario who confesses that he never really loved Celia, the woman he had intended to marry before submerging himself into the underwater world. Before being caught by amphibians they defrauded, Escamon and Misisipí cohabitate in luxury thanks to the money they stole from the underwater creatures.

No apparently documented direct link between the underwater world of the *Potosí submarino* and the "underwater," closeted gay community in Mexico City exists. However, both the explicit and the tacitly coded fluid male gender and sexuality portrayed in *Potosí submarino*, together with cross-dressing shows by performers like Fregoli, surely resonated with gay and bisexual men who helped create notions about gender and sexuality in Porfirian Mexico City. Many men who pursued women romantically in respectable and low-class performance venues were known as *lagartijos* [dandies], men concerned with fashion and style as a marker of social status and Europeanness.[89] Many *lagartijos* and other men were married to women and had children. As discussed below, like Fregoli, Escamon, and Misisipí, many of these men also cross-dressed or were bisexual or gay. They either pretended to have girlfriends or hid in marriages and formed families, the fundamental unit of the Porfirian heteronormative imagined community.

---

[84] Ibid., 43.
[85] Ibid., 41.
[86] Ibid., 43.
[87] Ibid., 51.
[88] Ibid., 41. The term *maricón*—much like the former slurs *faggot* and *queer*—has been resignified by scholars and many self-identified gay people as a term of self-affirmation and identification. The term is still used derogatorily by some people.
[89] Víctor Macías González, "The *Lagartijo* at the *High Life*: Masculine Consumption, Race, Nation, and Homosexuality in Porfirian Mexico," in *The Famous 41: Sexuality and Social Control in Mexico, 1901*, ed. Robert McKee Irwin, Edward J. McCaughan, and Michelle Rocío Nasser (New York: Palgrave Macmillan, 2003), 227–49.

Dancing Clandestine Fluid Gender Expressions and Sexual Identities: The Forty-One Upper-Class "Maricones"

Socially sanctioned dance-theater shows that included gender fluid and sexually ambiguous male characters, coded as "funny" or "entertaining," like those by Fregoli and the *Potosí submarino*, provided male audiences with a model of non-normative gender and sexual practices in a safe space, the theater.[90] There, these men could affirm their humanity while sheltered from the repressive, homophobic cultural context that surrounded them. One can imagine these shows functioning in tandem with clandestine social spaces and activities—"taverns, god-forsaken sites, procurers, 'rentable' young men, and 'specialized' brothels"—to enable Mexico City's closeted sexualities to exist and eventually emerge to the light.[91] According to the renowned Mexican intellectual Carlos Monsiváis, in reference to homosexuality during the Porfiriato, "for the sexually segregated, the greatest stimulus is the existence of others like themselves."[92] Thus, legal and illegal social spaces and activities produced for the sexually marginal an empowering sense of not being alone as they navigated Porfirian homophobia and European-based notions of manliness.[93]

It was precisely through situations like clandestine dance balls in private homes that gay men's self-affirmation and Porfirian state homophobia collided to constitute the "invention of homosexuality in Mexico."[94] In mid-November 1901, the police raided a house and arrested forty-two men, half of them dressed as women, purportedly (according to one newspaper) for "ataques a la moral" [attacks to morality].[95] The number would eventually be known as forty-one, as one well-connected man would largely disappear from the official record. The event caused quite a stir among political and cultural circles and became the talk of the town among all social classes.[96] There were *corridos* [traditional Mexican ballads] that spoke of the forty-one "*maricones*." Famous artist José Guadalupe Posada circulated a series of lithographs that portrayed pairs of men dancing, the

---

[90] Here, one can think of Manning's concept of cross-viewing referenced earlier.

[91] Carlos Monsiváis, "The 41 and the *Gran Redada*," trans. Aaron Walker, in Irwin et al., *The Famous 41*, 146.

[92] Ibid.

[93] Héctor Navarro, "Creating Masculinity and Homophobia: Oppression and Backlash under Mexico's Porfiriato," *Historical Perspectives: Santa Clara University Undergraduate Journal of History*, Series II, 22, Article 8 (2017): 30–48.

[94] Monsiváis, "The 41," 164.

[95] *El popular*, November 20, 1901, reprinted in *The Famous 41*, 36. These charges alluded to regulations stipulated in article 785 of the 1871 penal code against "Ultrajes a la moral pública, o a las buenas costumbres" [affronts to public morality and good (virtuous) customs]. Monsiváis suggests that the Porfirian regime used the article's ambiguity to police non-normative sexualities and thus protect the heterosexual family (Monsiváis, "The 41," 155–56).

[96] *La patria*, "Los cuarenta y un bailarines," November 22, 1901, reprinted in Irwin et al., *The Famous 41*, 38.

effeminate partners wearing "really elegant lady dresses, wigs, prosthetic breasts, earrings, embroidered slippers, and makeup on their eyes and cheeks."[97] As a newspaper noted about the arrested dancers, "the costumes were so well done that it was difficult to know at first glance whether those individuals were men."[98] Perhaps satirically, some of Posada's and other artists' renditions of men dressed as women gave them fashionable mustaches, like those worn by upper-class men of the day (Figure 1.1).[99]

Members of the press took the opportunity to vent their homophobic prejudices coded in political and patriotic terms by taking some creative license in their reporting. Their moralism inflected their language with violence. Some described the event as "repugnante" [repugnant],[100] and others refrained from providing more details, for they found them "sumo asquerosos" [extremely disgusting].[101] According to a newspaper note, a "seasoned" police officer became nauseous at the scene of male cross-dressed social dancers; he also struggled to calm his "rightly justified rage," thus preventing himself from physically punishing the moral aggressors "with fist and sticks."[102] The ultraconservatives took the scene as symptomatic of the sickness caused by the liberalism they accused Díaz of embracing. In reference to the dance ball attended by the forty-one men, the conservative Catholic newspaper *El país* exhorted "society" to see this event as "a symptom of the depravation to which we are descending."[103]

However, the clash between religious and political ideologies was not as vital a concern as was the social class of the arrested men. What many commentators and the public took as the most shameful and irritating sign of the extreme degradation of society was the fact that the men were members of well-known wealthy families.[104] They were the same men seen leisurely strolling in Plateros Boulevard, the epicenter of choreographies of Porfirian Europeanized modernity. Some of these men, then, might have been seen routinely holding hands with their girlfriends, wives, and children while strolling on the exclusive boulevard or attending a theater to see popular performances like Fregoli's female impersonations or the *Potosí submarino*.

---

[97] *El popular*, "Un baile clandestino sorprendido: 42 hombres aprehendidos, unos vestidos de mujeres," November 20, 1901, reprinted in Irwin et al., *The Famous 41*, 36.

[98] *El popular*, "El baile de los 41: Los enviados a Yucatán," November 24, 1901, reprinted in Irwin et al., *The Famous 41*, 42.

[99] The pronoun "men" is arbitrary here as it is unknown whether some of the arrested persons might have identified differently.

[100] *El diario del Hogar*, "Baile de señores solos," November 19, 1901, reprinted in Irwin et al., *The Famous 41*, 35.

[101] *El popular*, "Un baile clandestino," 1901, reprinted in Irwin et al., *The Famous 41*, 36.

[102] *El universal*, "Baile de afeminados," November 19, 1901, reprinted in Irwin et al., *The Famous 41*, 35.

[103] *El país*, "El baile nefando," November 22, 1901, reprinted in Irwin et al., *The Famous 41*, 36–37.

[104] Monsiváis, "The 41," 148.

Figure 1.1 José Guadalupe Posada's drawing of the "41 *Maricones*" event, published in a newspaper in 1901. Public Domain, Courtesy of the Harry Ransom Center, The University of Texas Austin.

Some of the arrested men's wives, mothers, and brothers attempted to intercede on behalf of their arrested relatives.[105] Among these wealthy women was

---

[105] "El baile de sólo hombres: Cuatro individuos piden amparo," reprinted in Irwin et al., *The Famous 41*, 40–41.

none other than Porfirio Díaz's daughter. As Monsiváis notes, "the gays of the [Porfirian] elite, 'made invisible' by their status, only suffer the snares of rumor, and the exception that breaks the rule is the halo of Nacho de la Torre . . . the 'First Son-in-Law' of the nation."[106] Porfirio Díaz's son-in-law was the forty-second man, allegedly arrested but cleared, not included later among the group of forty-one *jotitos*.[107] Unfortunately, despite the intercessions of influential relatives, the rest of the men were not as lucky. Most of them, particularly those caught dressed as women, were sent to a maximum-security prison in Yucatán, in southern Mexico.

As the men were transferring to Yucatán, the general public, the press, and soldiers mocked the men's "aberrant" effeminacy in various ways. A popular rhyme, told from the dancers' perspective, named dancing as both the source and the consequence of the men's plight:

> Look at me as I march
> with my shako to Yucatán
> where I'll find myself in a convoy
> dancing *jota* and cancan.[108]

Jota is a popular form of Spanish dance whose associated origins are with the region of Aragon, Spain. Coincidentally, *jota* resonates with the word *joto* referencing a gay man. The inclusion of the cancan in this mockery was not only because of its popularity but perhaps also for its feminine eroticism, in this case performed by effeminate men.

Like female cancan dancers pursued by heterosexual admirers in low-class venues, these effeminate men dancing among themselves in a private home tested the limits of law codes that functioned as forms of social control.[109] In so doing, their eroticized movements defied Porfirian notions of proper morality and decency. Female dancers and male audiences performing overflowing heterosexual desire in low-class venues formed alliances to circumvent state regulations against female bodies' eroticized performances. The visibility of

---

[106] Monsiváis, "The 41," 148.

[107] Used with endearing intent, *jotito* is the diminutive form of *joto*, a word that since the late nineteenth century in Mexico references a gay man. It can also be used as an expression with homophobic intent.

[108] Eduardo Castrejón, "Los cuarenta y uno: Novela crítico-social (selecciones)" (originally published 1906), reprinted in Irwin et al., *The Famous 41*, 93–137.

[109] For a discussion of how emerging discourses on sexuality constituted a form of control in Mexico at the turn of the twentieth century, see Robert McKee Irwin, Edward J. McCaughan, and Michelle Rocío Nasser, "Sexuality and Social Control in Mexico, 1901," in Irwin et al., *The Famous 41*, 1–18.

effeminate characters such as Fregoli and those in the *Potosí submarino* provided identification models among men of diverse gender expressions and sexualities. The criminalization of upper-class effeminate men's dancing bodies in a private space resulted from interpretations of the law that penalized them for wearing the wrong clothes, expressing the wrong gender, embodying the wrong sexuality, and dancing with the wrong partner. During the Porfiriato, a diversity of bodies performing distinctive choreographies of class, race, gender, and sexuality helped develop and challenge social values that different people considered foundational in the formation of a modern person, city, and nation.

Marked and Unmarked Bodies Choreographing Mestizo and Other Modernisms: Fuller, Spanish Dance, and the *Jarabe Mexicano*

The following discussion extends the analysis of how performances of race, class, gender, and sexuality by low- and high-class bodies in public and private spaces also played a crucial role in determining what criteria constituted dance as a legitimate art form. Examining Loïe Fuller's visit to Mexico City in 1897 alongside Spanish dances and performances of the *Jarabe Mexicano* by local and visiting artists sheds light on the ideological aspects of artistic discourses and their relation to notions of modernity. In so doing, these analyses illuminate the intersection of transnational dance histories and Mexico's nation formation processes.

Constructing the Deracialized, Chaste Body as a Modernist Artistic Subject: Fuller's Serpentine Dance

Loïe Fuller's case demonstrates how ideas about aesthetic originality and experimentation as components of modern theater-dance performances were also implicitly related to race and sexuality. In the Mexican context, her experimental approach to modernizing theater and dance in the late nineteenth century reinforced the idea of European and Euro-American cultural superiority as central to the rhetoric of (white) Western modernity. Her case illuminates how whiteness, thought of as a racially neutral ideology, and the body's desexualization functioned as aesthetic values in the formulation of dance as a high art form. Fuller had already established herself in her native United States and her adopted Europe, particularly France, as a modern dance artist. She became famous for the innovative use of lighting technologies to project a multitude of lights on her as she manipulated dresses that extended far beyond her body, aided by sticks held through her sleeves. She seemed to be almost a human kaleidoscope, as lights emanated from her moving body, enlarged by surplus fabric that constantly produced sinuous, undulating motions.

Previous to Fuller's debut in Mexico City on January 14, 1897, at the Teatro Nacional, some imitators of her so-called serpentine dance caused debates in the city.[110] One such imitator was the crossdresser performer Fregoli, whose "effeminate movements" and "grotesque femininity," according to critic José Juan Tablada, would disappear from the public's memory after seeing the *original* serpentine, Loïe Fuller, in "agile elegance" and splendid action.[111] Two other internationally known artists performed variations of Fuller's serpentine dance. Stella Follet debuted in 1894, followed soon after by Jossie Lindsay. While still awaiting Fuller, the press speculated, "Who among the three, Loïe Fuller, Stella Follet, or Jossie Lindsay, will win the prize for the [serpentine] dance? We already know Stella and are about to see Jossie; we will only need to see Loïe Fuller to decide who among the three can be considered the true Serpentine."[112]

As Fuller arrived in the city, members of the press and impresarios competing for audiences debated the visiting artist's merits. Some individuals defended the *original* serpentine, while others claimed that she had nothing new to offer Mexico's dance-theatrical scene.[113] A few critics sought to lessen Fuller's impact during her visit to the city by defending imitators hired by impresarios with whom these detractors sympathized. However, others praised the authenticity of Fuller's serpentine dance after they experienced her astonishing lighting effects, as if "a rain of erratic stars has settled on that [human statue], a great flower of beauty akin to a flock of celestial butterflies."[114] Fuller's astonishing visual effects resulting from her artistic and technological inventiveness resonated with Mexico City's cosmopolitan, modern identity forged during the Porfiriato.

Race and sexuality were not always an explicit component in dance content or claims dancers, critics, and audiences made about dances and dance practices. However, modernist dance-theater performances like Fuller's tacitly enacted notions of race, gender, and sexuality. For instance, critical dance studies scholar Anthea Kraut asserts that "white women" like Fuller—and other early dance modernists such as Isadora Duncan, Ruth St. Denis, and Martha Graham—differentiated themselves "from racialized, sexualized dancing bodies ... to gain

---

[110] Fuller had some legal battles with people who performed variations of her dance style. For an analysis of Fuller's claims to ownership of her work as intellectual property concerning gender, race, and property rights, see Anthea Kraut, "White Womanhood, Property Rights, and the Campaign for Choreographic Copyright: Loie Fuller's *Serpentine Dance*," *Dance Research Journal* 43, no. 1 (Summer 2011): 3–26.

[111] *El universal*, January 17, 1897, reprinted in Ramos and Cardona, *La danza en México*, 304–5.

[112] *El renacimiento*, January 1894, "Revista de la semana," quoted in Ramos Smith, *Teatro musical y danza*, 368.

[113] *El diario del Hogar*, January 15–17, 1897, quoted in Ramos Smith, *Teatro musical y danza*, 379.

[114] Tablada, *El universal*, January 17, 1897, reprinted in Ramos and Cardona, *La danza en México*, 304–5.

legitimacy for themselves as artists (not objects) on the theatrical stage."[115] More specifically, dance theorist Susan L. Foster has argued that modern dancers like Duncan, a Fuller contemporary, embraced ideas about spirituality to create a "chaste" dancing body distinct from commercial female dancers who eroticized themselves on stages, and thus to legitimize her innovative modern dance practice as a high art form.[116] While doing so, Foster suggests, it was against the "African dancer, [ostensibly] possessed by a sexual frenzy, [who] demonstrated a primitive and unrefined variety of bodily responsiveness" that "Duncan asserted her own naturalistic cultivation of the body."[117] One can conclude, then, that by contrasting her aesthetically experimental body with the presumably primitive, sexually overflowing Black African dancer, Duncan constructed her modern, chaste white body as an ostensibly superior artistic corporeality.

There were some parallels in the Mexican context. Just as Duncan's whiteness and sexuality sublimated into a chaste modernist artistic discourse, Fuller's white, lesbian body disappeared literally and figuratively under her massive costumes and technological experimentation.[118] Covered by surplus fabric and colorful lights, her momentarily deracialized and desexualized body fueled an aesthetic ideology associated with notions of what constituted serious dramatic modern art in Mexico. In reference to the serpentine dance as a genre, "de moda" [in vogue] performed by Fuller and her imitators, the newspaper *El nacional* noted that "this dance sets itself entirely apart from all theatrical events currently taking place [in the city . . .]. While in all other theatrical dances female dancers perform almost nude, in the Serpentine they are covered in a very wide tunic. *Es un baile casto* [It is a chaste dance]."[119]

The note alluded implicitly to commercial dancers' eroticism, performed by *tiples*, cancan dancers, and similar movement-based entertainers. In so doing, it reiterated the discursive convention that legitimate, *serious* modern art inherently reflected higher levels of civilization, restraint, decency, morality, and spirituality. For its capacity to tame the instincts of the flesh while providing

---

[115] "White Womanhood," 7.

[116] Susan L. Foster, "Closets Full of Dances: Modern Dance's Performance of Masculinity and Sexuality," in *Dancing Desires: Choreographing Sexualities on and off the Stage*, ed. Jane C. Desmond (Madison: University of Wisconsin Press, 2001), 147–207 [see 150–52]). In this chapter, Foster analyzes the desexualization of heterosexual and homosexual dancing bodies as foundational discourse on the formation of Western modern and experimental dance practices as "chaste"; thus, legitimate art forms, by Ruth St. Denis, Ted Shawn, Merce Cunningham, Mangrove, and Matthew Bourne.

[117] Ibid., 153.

[118] Like some of the forty-one men arrested for dancing with one another, Fuller had also lived in a heterosexual marriage for three years (1889–1892). Soon after this marriage ended, she traveled to Paris, where she consolidated her artistic acclaim. She met her French lifelong companion and collaborator Gabrielle Bloch, who became an art promoter, filmmaker, set designer, and choreographer known professionally as Gab Sorère.

[119] *El renacimiento*, January 21, 1894, quoted in Ramos Smith, *Teatro musical y danza*, 369.

a visually astonishing model of what a truly high art form could be, the newspaper *El universal* declared Fuller, the originator of the serpentine dance, to be "really a modern wonder."[120] Tablada concurred by characterizing the "famous Serpentine" as the "heroine of modern choreography."[121]

As a heroine of Western aesthetic modernity, Fuller's dancing body mobilized tropes central to modernist art, for which critics like Tablada seemed to claim affinity. In other words, at the very moment of dancing, and consuming a dancing body as a spectator, Fuller was no longer a gendered, racial, sexual body but a purported universal body, a conveyor of higher ways of being human. In so doing, her veiled body illuminated by shifting patterns of light anticipated mid-twentieth century universalist discourses on the role abstraction played in developing "modernist formulas" in Europe and the United States. In dance, these formulas "meant framing bodies as forms in motion, not necessarily as people [who] share movements from specific historical, cultural, or geographical contexts."[122] Modernist dancers like Fuller and Duncan represented early embodiments of this aesthetic ideology. Their efforts to forge abstract, desexualized dance practices as forms of universal modern art rendered the body a "hallowed place" that "promised a glimpse of the human soul, its changingness, its transcendent veracity."[123] Being a part of this discursive lineage of Western modernist dance, Fuller's abstract, universal body served as a conduit for conveying higher, universal truths and ways of being modern. Embracing these ideas enabled Mexican critics and audiences to experience and claim affinity with like-minded people in other "civilized," modern countries.

This ideological, aesthetic discourse resonated with Díaz's notions of modernity based on European culture and its implicit whiteness as Mexico transitioned into the twentieth century. Fuller's body offered a model for modernist formulas that valued the utopic desire to create an ostensible racially and culturally superior body—usually an assumed white body—that could represent the condition of modern humanity. Meanwhile, non-white bodies' representational capacity, dancing Spanish and Mexican dances, continued to be evaluated through the lens of their racial and cultural specificity. Under the veil of extra luminous fabric, Fuller's deracialized and desexualized body in motion fueled the desire for universal connections and modern aspirations among Mexican critics and audiences. Under and outside the modernist veil, Fuller—a white, lesbian from the United States and an artist consecrated in Europe—resonated with Porfirian notions of Western cultural modernity on and off dance and theater stages.

---

[120] *El universal*, January 16, 1897, quoted in Ramos Smith, *Teatro musical y danza*, 379.
[121] *El universal*, January 17, 1897, reprinted in Ramos and Cardona, *La danza en México*, 304–5.
[122] Clare Croft, *Dancers as Diplomats: American Choreography in Cultural Exchange* (Oxford: Oxford University Press, 2015), 66.
[123] Foster, "Closets Full of Dances," 152.

Mestizajes on the Same Stage and within the Same Body: Dancing Spanish and Mexican Mestizo Modernisms

There were reports that for her performances in Mexico City, Fuller made $5000 pesos, of which she spent "$4000 at various jewelries in [the] capital."[124] She commingled with a diversity of cosmopolitan bodies as she shopped at Plateros Boulevard's jewelers and other urban, social stages. Fuller also shared theatrical stages with bodies choreographing other mestizo modernisms that integrated legacies of the country's colonial histories. She performed alongside a *zarzuela* company owned by the brothers Luis and Pedro Alcaraz y Chopitea.[125] This seemingly unusual combination of disparate artistic bodies, dance genres, aesthetic discourses, and embodied histories was not at all atypical. The coexistence of different types of performers on the same stage and the cultivation of diverse dance techniques within the same body enabled dance and dancers to survive mid-nineteenth-century precarious times financially. While these practices augmented job opportunities and a more expanded sense of artistry, they became expected theatrical conventions by the end of the century. However, as the following examples show, these forms of *mestizaje*—sharing stages and embodying diverse techniques—often cause heated debates about what constitutes dance as a legitimate art form and a dancer as a legitimate artist.

It should not be surprising that Fuller shared the stage with a *zarzuela* company in 1897. During the Porfiriato, Spanish theater and dance forms enjoyed the sustained favor of audiences from various social strata in their respective venues.[126] A constant influx of *tiples* from Spain continued to populate Mexico City's stages, where they popularized *boleros, jotas, oles,* and other Spanish dance forms as part of Spanish *zarzuelas* and French operettas. Among many other dancers, Francisca (Paca) Martínez caused quite a stir as she specialized in what many considered the "immoral" *jota*, the same dance performed by the male crossdressers on their way to prison in Yucatan. Early in the 1890s and into the next century, artist-*tiples* such as the sisters Ursula and Laura López, Conchita Martínez, Conchita Narvaez, and the innovative Trinidad Huertas ("La Cuenca") helped consolidate flamenco as a favorite among audiences.[127]

---

[124] Quoted in Alberto Dallal, "Loie Fuller en México," *Anales del Instituto de Investigaciones Estéticas* XIII, no. 50, Tomo 2 (México: UNAM, 1982), 305.

[125] Ibid.

[126] There was a constant crossover between audiences and venues. However, members from the upper classes, particularly men, who wanted to enjoy more eroticized shows without being seen by respectable members of their class (or their wives or girlfriends) would attend shows in venues of "ill repute." Audiences from lower classes were more frequently unable to attend shows in "prestigious" venues because of prohibitive ticket prices, a mechanism of social distinction, and social stratification.

[127] Ramos Smith, *Teatro musical y danza*.

Writing for *El monitor republicano*, Enrique Chávarri Juvenal said of La Cuenca's impactful dancing in "Corrida de toros" [Bullfight], "[when she] dances over the platform, it causes vertigo to see her feet move with inconceivable speedy lightness [as she] executes all the tricks of the bullring—maneuvers the cape, sticks *banderillas* onto the bull's shoulder, stabs and kills [the bull]— without stopping for a single moment the movement of her feet to the rhythm of the music."[128] While exhibiting such an extraordinary sense of musicality and masterful footwork, La Cuenca's female dancing body performed gender fluidity while appropriating a male-dominated practice. It was the simultaneity of the expert bullfighter motions of her upper body and the speed of her dancing feet that led audiences' enthusiasm to reach "delirio" [delirium][129] as they experienced in a dance show the bullfight, one of Spain's (and its ex/colonies') beloved traditions. Like other Spanish dancers, La Cuenca offered to Mexican and foreign audiences performances of cultural traditions from the *madre patria* [motherland], a label used by some Mexicans as a symbolic gesture of appreciation for the colonial mother, Spain, that had *birthed* them into Western modernity.

Taming the *Jarabe Mexicano*: From Diabolical Eroticism to a Chaste Modernized Dance

As flamenco and other Spanish dance forms gained momentum toward the end of the nineteenth century in Mexico City, they shared an intimate coexistence with Mexican dances, often on the same stages. The *Jarabe Mexicano* evolved from its contentious colonial precedents into its iconic post/colonial status in Mexico's dance repertoire. During colonial Mexico, when the viceroy shared governing power with the Catholic Church, various *jarabes* were considered morally transgressive and thus policed by both royal and religious officials. Authorities prohibited dances such as *El Jarabe Gatuno* [The Feline Jarabe] due to its alleged lasciviousness and the dancers' "diabólica intension" [diabolical intention] to "lose Souls, already redeemed by Jesus Christ."[130] In 1782, Don José Gregorio Alonso de Ortigosa, bishop of Oaxaca (a state in southern Mexico), assured the populace that "the devil himself—father of deception—has confessed that he was the author of the dances," and therefore Christians must not dance or see them.[131] Those who disobeyed the royal and religious authorities' prohibition

---

[128] *El monitor republicano*, February 10, 1887, quoted in ibid., 336.
[129] Ibid.
[130] Don Bernardo Ruiz de Molina, 1802, reprinted as "Edicto inquisitorial prohibiendo el *Cuchumbé*, el *Jarabe Gatuno* y otros bailes" in Ramos and Cardona, *La danza en México*, 120.
[131] Reprinted as "Edicto del Obispo de Oaxaca contra varios bailes" in ibid., 118.

of the dances would face total excommunication from the church.[132] Additional punishments included fines,[133] "vergüenza pública" [public shaming], and two-year prison terms for men and women who participated in dancing, singing, watching, or listening to the *Jarabe Gatuno*.[134]

In post/colonial Mexico (after the declaration of independence in 1821), people among the masses continued performing *jarabes*, including the *Jarabe Mexicano*, thus defying religious edicts and an upper-class sense of propriety. However, in a context in which the country endeavored to assert itself as a new sovereign nation, sexually chaste versions of the *Jarabe Mexicano* would also arise, providing an emblematic embodiment of respectable Mexicanidad [Mexicanness]. Often, efforts to sanitize the dance by taming its potentially excessive heterosexual eroticism coincided with strategies to stylize the "traditional" *Jarabe Mexicano* by employing dance techniques considered more prestigious and modern. In its chaste yet coquettish, stylized choreographic iterations, the adoption of the dance into many local and foreign artists' repertoires represented an embodied exotic Mexican distinctiveness within a still Europeanized neocolonial cultural context. Danced by national and international artists, the stylized *Jarabe* became a gesture of cultural appreciation, collaboration, and exchange. It was also part of a marketing strategy to attract audiences with nationalistic sentiments and those with a desire for racial and social exotic others. In its multiple forms, the performance of the *Jarabe Mexicano* became a tradition that served different purposes alongside other dance forms in diverse social and cultural contexts.

As the nineteenth century unfolded, ballet artists continued to share stages with dancers of other dance forms while pleasing Mexican audiences with stylized renditions of the *Jarabe Mexicano*. In the mid-1880s, Augusta La Bella, who had recently danced with Giovanni Lepri, his daughter Amalia, and Paca Martínez (the Spanish dancer of the "immoral" *jota*), performed a variation of the *Jarabe*'s sanitized "lascivious caprices." La Bella presented a show that included various dance genres and closed with the *Jarabe Mexicano*, as audiences celebrated her gesture of appreciation to her host nation.[135] In 1882, dancer Magdalena Puig debuted in Mexico City by performing with Paca Martínez a "*Jota* Aragonesa."[136] Puig was highly regarded for her virtuosic footwork *en pointe*, a technique she used as many other dancers did to stylize the *Jarabe Mexicano*. *El monitor republicano* reported that Puig's *Jarabe* was "enloquecedor" [maddening] as audiences saw how "the china [poblana] gets over the tip of her feet and dances

---

[132] "*excomunión maior trina canonica monitione en dro*," Alonso de Ortigosa, 1782, reprinted as "Edicto del Obispo..." in ibid., 118.
[133] Ruiz de Molina, 1802, reprinted as "Edicto inquisitorial...," in ibid., 120.
[134] Felix Berenguer de Marquina, 1802, reprinted as "Bando del Virrey..." in ibid., 121.
[135] Ramos Smith, *Teatro musical y danza*, 317.
[136] Ibid., 298.

the national hopping steps in a thousand diverse ways."[137] Audiences' enthusiasm suggests that visiting European dancers who performed the *Jarabe Mexicano* successfully created a de-essentialized mode of *mestizaje*, one constituted by combining varied cultural elements. That is, their (white) European dancing bodies, dressed in Mexican attire, could tap into a purported Mexican essence as they tiptoed on the point of their ballet shoes the "modernized" *Jarabe Mexicano* steps they learned from their Mexican collaborators.

Mexican dancers also participated in the "modernization" of *their* emblematic dance. Moctezuma emerged from the Pautret's conservatory in 1830 as a favorite among ballet audiences and taught the *Jarabe Mexicano* to European dancers Thierry and Bernardelli in 1850. Similarly, Felipa López emerged from Amalia Lepri's youth ballet group as a promising Mexican star in the early 1880s. Midway through the decade, López danced Spanish and Mexican dances accompanied by her father, Melesio, during intermissions. By the end of the 1880s, López's talents and Mexicanness had rendered her "the smartest choreographic artist of the country."[138] In addition to her ballet training, she specialized in Spanish dance and performances of the *Jarabe Mexicano*; she even took the place of Paca Martínez and started dancing her Spanish duets with Amalia Lepri. In 1887, she danced as part of a show by the magician Bosco.[139] In a detailed account that is worth quoting at length, *El monitor republicano* asserted that when the *Jarabe* began,

> that *china* [*poblana*] beats the floor with her feet moving like an eel, raising her handkerchief while on the tip of her feet; she seems to embroider the national dance on the surface of the floor. Those feet that exude sparks, sequins hit by the light, move with vertiginous speed, interlacing one another, confusing one another, getting lost amid the moving lace [of the skirt]. The public applauds with maddening enthusiasm; the dancer, with her serpentine movements, nears her dancing partner; she puts on *his* Mexican hat and while stretching her neck spinning around the *charro*, as one who asks for a kiss, she increases the speed of her footwork, she hops more, and the people in the space touched by the tiny feet's work, respond to the echo of that harmony that produces tickles and makes the heart of all Mexicans beat. How beautiful *chinas* are in my land! We had never seen a *jarabe* danced like this.... "Bravo! Bravo!," we repeated with the public.[140]

---

[137] *El monitor republicano*, November 19, 1882, quoted in ibid., 30.
[138] Olavarría y Ferrari, II: 1197 [Enrique de Olavarría y Ferrari, *Reseña histórica del teatro en México*, 5 vols (México, 1961)], quoted in ibid., 332.
[139] Reports of the show did not specify the name of the dancer. However, Ramos Smith, who has studied the historical period extensively, concludes that the dancer was very likely Felipa López (ibid., 332–34).
[140] *El monitor republicano*, May 15, 1887, quoted in ibid., 334.

López's speedy dancing feet symbolically embroidered the "national dance" on the floor. In other words, as the nation's body, her Mexican female dancing body weaved itself into the floor as the land, the nation as territory. In response to this balleticized choreographic patriotism, the audience embroidered themselves affectively into a broader choreography of transnational nationalism. During the early 1890s, Felipa López, and others, continued enchanting audiences with the *Jarabe Mexicano* in ways that brought "shivers to the patriotic public."[141]

As these accounts suggest, post/colonial choreographic versions of the *Jarabe Mexicano* served different purposes simultaneously. Staged for and sanitized to please the taste of prudish audiences, and often infused with ballet technique, the dance emphasized the spectacular footwork, the exotic costumes, and the resulting Mexicanness that national and international bodies produced as they danced. For some, the dance satisfied the desire for exotic others. For others, it cultivated their nationalist sentiments as they witnessed a presumed Mexican essence in motion. As the second half of the nineteenth century unfolded, the performance of the popular dance, along with ballet and Spanish dances, enabled dance, dancers, and impresarios to survive and thrive. Dancers became more technically versatile, competing for roles as performers of different dance genres. As they embodied and performed different techniques, these artists' individual and collaborative efforts often sparked heated discussions on aesthetic and nationalist grounds.

Conceptualizing Dance as Art and Dancers as Artists: Debating the Aesthetics of Social and Racial Formations

As national and international dancers made their way as versatile artists and bodies-for-hire[142] before and during the Porfiriato, critics and audiences actively participated in determining which dance forms circulated and which venues were appropriate for these cultural practices. Their opinions favored the artistic productions of some dance artists while also devaluing the work of other dancers and entertainers. These discursive aesthetic evaluations carried colonialist undertones, which contributed to the naturalizing values and interests of social hierarchies and nationalist sentiments.

---

[141] *El monitor republicano*, October 9, 1892, in ibid., 359.
[142] Here, one may think of a version of "the hired body" that Susan L. Foster theorizes in "Dancing Bodies," in *Meaning in Motion: New Cultural Studies of Dance*, ed. Jane C. Desmond (Durham: Duke University Press, 1997), 235–57. However, in the Mexican context, these bodies-for-hire performed within specific cultural and historical contingencies.

Local and visiting dancers' choreographies of Mexicanness on post/colonial Mexican stages were often a point of contention. While many audiences and critics embraced Europeanizing cultural tendencies, reflected in quotidian life, theater, and dance productions, others resisted these acculturation processes. In response to a show by a performer of popular dances in 1869, *El renacimiento* lamented the Europeanization of one of the most revered figures of Mexicanness: the *china poblana* of the *Jarabe Mexicano*. The note asserted that "the *china* of this time, adulterated as if closely emulating French fashion of [certain] dresses; the *china* . . . falsified . . . entirely botched . . . it's a shame that also this character, so representatively Mexican, gradually dies out due to the irruption of French fashions, the baleful result of a dominating intervention in our customs, even from across the Ocean!"[143] While the account implies the disfiguration of an imagined "authentic" Mexican *china poblana*, it also seems to resent colonial dynamics, in which the foreign power—once the Spanish King, now French fashion—exerts its influence even from across the Atlantic.

As critics and audiences debated what constituted legitimate, serious dramatic art—and thus its embodied social values—they also disputed the artistic merits of European dance forms and those who danced them. As Paca Martínez rose to fame dancing the Spanish *jota*, leading critics pitted this dance form against ballet. With a dramatic metaphor, Gutiérrez Nájera averred that Martínez "has killed Elisa Mancini," a ballet dancer popular in Mexico City at the time. He added: "Italian dances and Parisian pantomimes run away ashamed in the presence of the graciously spicy *jota*."[144] However, French and Italian newspapers in the city responded in defense of ballet by arguing that Martínez's *jota* offended the moral sensibility of many audiences and thus was no worthy rival to the "decent and gracious dances by Misses Lepri and Mancini."[145] Even when performed by European bodies, dance forms continued to be evaluated hierarchically by people with different affective and aesthetic ideological investments, often informed by a racial unconscious of whiteness associated with classical ballet.

The case of Moctezuma and her former rival Ambrosio Martínez, a Spanish dancer, also illustrates the aesthetic-ideological quarrels of critics and audiences in response to the pair's collaboration in 1850. This artistic duet was not a light accomplishment; fervent admirers of these dancers got into fistfights defending their favorite artist.[146] Most likely due to economic reasons, Moctezuma and Martínez danced a series of *pas de deux* together. Ambrosio Martínez received criticism for his deficiencies in performing dance forms outside Spanish dances, namely ballet. *El daguerreotipo* recommended that he remain devoted

[143] June 28, 1869, in Ramos Smith, *Teatro musical y danza*, 84.
[144] Gutiérrez Nájera, *El cronista de México*, September 18, 1880. *Obras* III: 283, quoted in ibid., 262.
[145] *La scintilla italiana*, October 12, 1880, quoted in ibid., 263.
[146] Ramos Smith, *María de Jesús Moctezuma*.

"exclusively to the specialty he had adopted in the choreographic art [Spanish dance]."[147] Furthermore, the note characterized the couple's performance as a "bland parody of the admirable groups led by the Monplaisir couple,"[148] a reference to reputed French dance artists Hippolyte and Adèle Monplaisir. Being the most prestigious company visiting Mexico in 1850, the French artists set the measurement standards for Moctezuma and Martínez's performances.

As these examples illustrate, elite critics endeavored to cultivate a Europeanized cosmopolitan Mexican subjectivity while they had to contend with artists' collaborative practices. Artistic collaborations between dancers such as Moctezuma and Ambrosio Martínez in 1850 seemed to have defied some critics and audiences through their very pairings (Amalia Lepri and Paca Martínez experienced a similar situation in 1880). Likely due to economic considerations, the production of low-budget shows also fostered a drive for more diverse audiences for the daring, if not risky, cultural collaborations between "incompatible" dance artists and dancers who did not perform with equal proficiency in various dance forms. Regardless of whether some critics considered these danced *mestizajes* to be aesthetic failures—based on ballet's technical standards—and whether audiences, as well as national and foreign dancers, regarded their performances across various dance forms to be *correct*, they all set in motion notions about aesthetics, nationality, gender, race, and class. The tensile coexistence of disparate agents, aesthetic discourses, and embodied practices produced different forms of artistic *mestizajes*. Together, these cultural forces transformed theatrical and urban stages into specific social spaces where diverse dancing and pedestrian bodies helped shape how different people experienced Mexico City culturally, socially, and racially.

Embodying Ambivalence toward *Mestizaje* and Indigeneity: Performing the Desire to Be White

This chapter has illustrated some of the ideas Mexican and foreign critics, audiences, and dancers used to conceptualize dance as a pivotal cultural activity to the formation of post/colonial Mexico as a modern nation and its capital as a cosmopolitan center. Relying on a Eurocentric framework, Pautret's *Allusion to the Cry of Dolores* ballet exemplified early post/colonial manifestations of ambivalence toward *mestizaje* and indigeneity in its choreographic representation of Mexico's independence. Altamirano's case began to illustrate how some mestizo and indigenous Mexicans experienced ambivalence toward *mestizaje*

---

[147] December 14, 1850, quoted in ibid., 23.
[148] *El daguerreotipo*, December 14, 1850, quoted in ibid.

and indigeneity while fashioning Europeanized identities and performing choreographies of Western modernity. In this vein, national and international dancers used ballet to "modernize" the *Jarabe Mexicano*, producing more "refined" mestizo modernisms throughout the nineteenth century. These and other dancers commingled in Mexico City streets, private homes, and theater stages. As they performed distinctive embodied histories through different dance practices, they produced unique forms of cultural *mestizajes*. Their dancing often defied normative moral codes and aesthetic ideologies thus causing debates among audiences and critics.

As guardians of good taste and ostensible experts on legitimate forms of theater and dance, critics evaluated dancers' performances in terms of the civilizing impact they could have on audiences' modern identity formation. In response to audiences' enthusiastic reception of ballet dancer Amalia Lepri in 1880, Gutiérrez Nájera celebrated that "the crapulent, libertine mass is gradually becoming civilized."[149] Similarly, *El imparcial* declared that the influx of European ballets such as *Coppélia*, *Brahman*, and *En el Japón* in the early 1900s represented a solid "first step" in the development of "modern theatrical arts" in Mexico.[150] Newspaper assessments celebrating the professed transformative power of artistic productions, performed primarily by white artists from Europe and the United States, included comments by critics like Alatamirano (Gutiérrez Nájera's mentor)—who lauded Offenbach and Rigolboche's cancan music and dance as civilizing, and Tablada—who characterized Fuller as a "heroine of modern choreography."

These civilizing processes of modernization manifested, in subtle and overt ways, different forms of post/colonial ambivalence toward *mestizaje* and indigeneity. Dance practices, audience responses, and critics' assessments participated in forging a Europeanized identity that defied essentialist notions of Mexican identity based on purported biological traits. Simultaneously, dances, dancers, audiences, and critics contributed to forming social values and the cultural context in which Porfirian Mexican elites performed the colonial desire to be white. In so doing, these elites garnered the cultural capital and other privileges associated with whiteness as a social status, a process with roots in colonial Mexico. In some cases, they also sought a transformation in their physical appearance. A brief final view into these dynamics illustrates further the context in which dance practices played a crucial role in the formation and contestation of Mexico City's social and racial hierarchies.

As the Platero Boulevard discussion revealed, highly distinguished wealthy men and women who consumed modern dance forms in theater spaces also

---

[149] *El cronista de México*, December 12, 1880, quoted in Ramos Smith, *Teatro musical y danza*, 276.
[150] *El imparcial*, August 18, 1904, quoted in ibid., 437.

performed choreographies of cultural and economic modernity on urban stages. They constituted their embodied subjectivities by wearing the latest European fashions as their bodies executed well-rehearsed movements and actions while they strolled, sat, and ate in upscale stores, restaurants, cafés, and clubs on *el boulevard*. These public social spaces constituted the urban stages where some of the forty-one men arrested for dancing among themselves (some of them dressed as women) were routinely showing off their fashionable suits and expensive jewelry.

Latin American and gender and sexuality historian Víctor Macías González suggests that Porfirian men were "extremely obsessed with their appearance," as advertisements, magazines, and literary works of the era make evident.[151] One can imagine how some of these men could identify with effeminate characters like Escamon in the widely popular *Potosí submarino*, who admitted to spending a great deal of time at the vanity desk taking care of himself by applying "tohalla de Venus and pachouly." The preoccupation of these men with taste and physical appearance was such that many considered it a part of the "sinister feminization of the [male] elite."[152]

Not only fashion and gender fluidity but also phenotype—perceived appearance and race—was a component of Mexican Europeanized modernity, as is apparent in references to dancers from Europe and the United States and men and women among socialites. According to Macías González, the Porfirian government favored "European-phenotyped" people as clerks and presidential guards.[153] Nacho de la Torre (the "son-in-law of the nation" arrested at the dance ball raid) "surrounded himself with young, handsome, blond European male servants," a widespread practice among Mexican elites.[154] Men and women of "mixed race" who might be perceived by others, or view themselves, as too "Indian-looking" used a wide variety of products to whiten and soften their skin, a practice that would continue into twentieth-century postrevolutionary Mexico (Figure 1.2).[155] Macías González asserts that the avid display and consumption of European "finery and sumptuary objects" had the additional benefit of allowing the Porfirian elite to "distance itself from its [biological-phenotypical] *mestizo* roots."[156] That is, if a brown mestizo complexion was frowned on, Blackness remained at the extreme margins of desirability. Dark skin seems to have rendered indigenous Mesoamerican, mestizo, and Black bodies, literally, as the *darker* side of Western modernity.[157]

[151] Macías González, "The *Lagartijo* at *the High Life*," 233.
[152] Ibid., 227.
[153] Ibid., 241.
[154] Ibid., 240.
[155] Ibid., 236
[156] Ibid., 230.
[157] Mignolo, *The Darker Side of Western Modernity*, 2011.

Figure 1.2 Advertisement for a whitening product that could help men and women treat "black color and other unpleasant conditions." *Revista de revistas*, June 29, 1930, 8. Public Domain, Courtesy of the Biblioteca Miguel Lerdo de Tejada de la Secretaría de Hacienda y Crédito Público.

In linking consumption habits with notions of race and modernity at the turn of the twentieth century, Macías González asks, "Did the purchase and display of a European appearance—constructed through clothing, but also contrived through cosmetics like skin whiteners—indicate that the average Porfirian, elite male [and female] consumer perceived himself [or herself] as racially inferior, as biologically unmodern? I will certainly say so."[158] Macías González's provocative question points to at least two other assumptions implicit in the desire to be white as central to identity formation processes: the desire not to be oneself and the desire to improve a perceived inferior self.[159] This chapter attempts to illustrate how dance practices contributed to these processes of self-fashioning depending on where in the social and racial hierarchies individuals positioned themselves and were positioned by others.

In this respect, dance practices also served as mechanisms for dancers, audiences, and critics to cultivate (to purchase and display) a European appearance—and the experience of corresponding feelings—as a marker of an acceptable, if not superior, social and racial identity and corporeality. In other words, in agreement with Macías González—that to some extent Porfirian elites might have implicitly felt "racially inferior [and] biologically unmodern"— dance along with other performances of cultural and economic modernity helped them consolidate the supremacy of whiteness as an idealized form of embodiment and ideology. As Fuller's case illustrates, markers of difference such as race, gender, and sexuality became literally veiled by the material and visual effects of abundant fabric and experimental use of technology. Her momentarily degendered, sexually chaste, and racially neutral dancing body, associated with her serpentine dance, transformed her into an ostensible conduit of universal connections, sensations, and truths. As an exemplar of how this aesthetic discourse operated, Fuller's serpentine dance demonstrated how a white body, in the moment of performance, was constructed to be consumed as a racially, socially, and culturally unmarked body. This ostensibly neutral body represented an idealized aesthetic value associated with universal art. The ideas of cultural neutrality and artistic universalism played an implicit role in Fuller's experimentalism, as well as in ballet's classicism. Both Fuller's experimental modern dance and classical ballet represented distinctive models of embodied Western modernity and its attendant aesthetic, social, and racial values.

---

[158] Macías González, "The *Lagartijo* at *the High Life*," 242.
[159] Even today, this desire is often expressed in Mexico with phrases such as "para mejorar la raza" [to improve the race], for example, when speaking about potential partners to procreate, even to the point of favoring the influx of immigrants and asylum seekers perceived as white over other racial groups. The global industry of whitening products also continues to thrive.

The fact that Fuller, and ballet companies, shared stages with *zarzuela* dancers and actors illustrates the different forms of *mestizaje* people experienced in Porfirian Mexico City. Mexican, Spanish, Italian, French, and dancers from other nationalities performed dance forms that explicitly revealed the specificity of their associated racial and cultural difference (i.e., Spanish dances, the *Jarabe Mexicano*). Dancers often used ballet as a (universal) form of embodied technology to "modernize" dancing bodies and dance. Racially and culturally marked bodies produced embodied mestizo modernisms, performed in urban and theatrical stages, that were central to how people experienced themselves, the city, and the nation. As white, brown, and Black dancers performed racially, culturally, and often sexually marked dances, they challenged the mythology of neutrality while valorizing different ways of being in the world through dancing.

In sum, all these bodies in motion, with their diverse backgrounds—light and dark skin; local and foreign; upper and lower class; heterosexual and homosexual; men, women, and gender-fluid—performed ideas and assumptions about who they and others were. As they formed Mexico City's social kinesphere, they grappled implicitly and explicitly with the legacies of colonial processes of socialization and racialization. Different embodiments of the ambivalence toward *mestizaje* and indigeneity, as well as performances of the desire to be white, took different forms on urban and theatrical stages from independence to the dictatorship.

Díaz himself, one of the most ardent champions of French culture as a model for the post/colonial reconstruction of the Mexican individual self, the nation, and its capital, had in his "veins . . . the blood of the primitive Mixtec with that of the invading Spaniards."[160] An ambivalence toward (his personal) *mestizaje* and indigeneity led him to favor the advancement of the upper classes and the marginalization of indigenous communities as part of his national modernization project. Indeed, his modernizing accomplishments under his autocratic rule would be celebrated on a grand scale during the 100-year celebration of the Mexican Independence in 1910. As the next chapter demonstrates, the Centennial Celebrations included the strategic integration of mestizo and indigenous histories and bodies as objects of study and (national) representation. In so doing, Díaz's Centenario choreographies represented an ambivalent performance of nationalist mestizo modernity.

---

[160] James Creelman, "President Díaz: Hero of the Americas," *Pearson's Magazine* XIX, no. 3 (March 1908): 231. Mixtec [Mixteco] refers to indigenous Mesoamerican people living in La Mixteca, a region that expands across the states of Oaxaca, Puebla, and Guerrero. Díaz was born in 1830 in Oaxaca to a mestizo woman of Mixtec ancestry and a criollo man of Spanish descent.

2
Choreographing the Indigenous Body in the Independence Centennial

From Dictatorship to Revolution

As discussed in chapter 1, a variety of choreographic performances in prestigious proscenium theaters, popular *jacalones*, public balls, private homes, and the streets represented contested spaces where (dancing) bodies corporealized social and cultural values before and during Porfirio Díaz's dictatorship (1876–1911) (Figure 2.1). On these artistic and urban stages, diverse bodies in motion constituted themselves as racial, social, gendered, and sexual subjects contributing to Mexico City's mestizo spatiality. That is, as a social kinesphere, Mexico City was a space where different forms of *mestizaje* coexisted in an ambivalent relationship to European culture as a model for transforming the city and the nation under Díaz's regime.

This chapter extends this discussion by focusing on post/colonial ambivalence toward *mestizaje* and indigeneity formed during the 1910 Centennial celebrations of the Mexican independence. The analysis will highlight the beginning of a shift from representations favoring European elements to ones that gave more prominence to indigenous Mesoamerican bodies, histories, and cultures toward the end of the Porfiriato. This shift contributed to the formation of emerging identities and new forms of embodied mestizo modernisms as the country transitioned from autocratic rule to a revolutionary state.

During September 1910, the historic "month of the Centenario,"[1] authorities organized dance, theater, and other artistic, civic, and scientific events with the aim of creating a sense of European-inspired modernity. Selecting specific aspects of Mesoamerican indigeneity, officials also attempted to honor and reimagine the country's indigenous past and present. The Mexican social sciences emerged with international assistance on such a momentous occasion. A group of *científios* [scientists], as they were known, included social scientists, politicians, bureaucrats, and philanthropists who embraced positivism as they embarked on the mission to modernize the country and civilize descendents of

---

[1] *El imparcial*, "Del palco escénico: Ester Zanini," Suplemento Dominical 3ra. Parte, September 4, 1910: 22.

CHOREOGRAPHING THE INDIGENOUS BODY   81

Figure 2.1 "Afrancesadas" [Frenchified] Bourgeois ladies dancing for Porfirio Díaz and his male dictatorial entourage. "Porfirio Díaz y su Gabinete." Detail from David Alfaro Siqueiros's mural *From the Dictatorship of Porfirio Díaz to Revolution— The People in Arms* (1957). Public Domain, Courtesy of Instituto Nacional de Antropología e Historia.

Mesoamerican people. Artistic contests invited artists to represent the peace and prosperity Díaz's governance brought to the country after the tumultuous post/colonial period. A series of parades and the culminating Cry of Dolores ceremony drew people from throughout the nation and the world.

This chapter argues that while designing and structuring these celebrations, Díaz's government instrumentalized *mestizaje* and indigeneity to create state performances of racial difference, tradition, and modernity. In other words, after decades of forging a cultural context characterized by Europe as a model, Díaz had the opportunity to showcase to the world his accomplishments in modernizing the country, including its mestizo and indigenous populations. To do so, his government strategically integrated (ambivalent) representations of *mestizaje* and indigeneity in the celebration of the 100 years since Catholic priest Miguel Hidalgo y Costilla led a rebellion in 1810 seeking Mexico's independence from Spain.

The chapter develops this argument using choreography as an analytical methodology to examine how compositional elements in different forms of representation relate to one another to create meaning. It analyzes these meaning-making processes among diverse bodies in motion on dance and theater stages, in parades, and in other public ceremonies. It focuses on the conceptualization of indigenous Mesoamerican bodies portrayed in civic performances, scientific discourse, philanthropy, and print media. These analyses illustrate how this ambivalent integration of indigeneity into the Centennial celebrations began to construe indigenous Mesoamerican people as part of the national (historical) imaginary while also probing their capacity to be rescued, civilized, and modernized.

Examining the participation of indigenous people in these celebratory activities—as sources of inspiration, actors, and objects of study and philanthropic benevolence—reveals how their performing bodies contributed to creating notions of national modernity that reflected social and racial hierarchies prevalent during the Porfiriato. Thus, the discussion provides an insight into how social and racial ideologies shaped the contexts in which dance functioned in tandem with other forms of cultural practices in Porfirian nation-building projects. In so doing, the chapter prepares the ground for understanding how Porfirian ambivalence toward *mestizaje* and indigeneity extended into and changed during and after the armed revolution that removed Díaz from power. Thus, examining this resurgent interest in indigeneity during the Centenario provides the bases for analyzing the social and racial ideologies that national and international dancers negotiated in their choreographic mestizo works in postrevolutionary Mexico (chapter 3).

To contextualize these developments, the discussion starts with a brief account of how foreign capitalist allies from the so-called civilized world supported Díaz's dictatorial rule and project of modernization. Subsequent sections analyze different figurations of the indigenous Mesoamerican body as both objects of study and figures of (national) representations in dance and theater, science and philanthropy, art contests in print media and visual arts, massive parades, and other public events. The chapter concludes with a choreographic analysis of Díaz's Cry of Dolores civic performance enacting the onset of the independence struggle 100 years earlier.

"President Porfirio Díaz, the Creator and Hero of Modern Mexico"

To comprehend how Díaz's ambivalence toward his personal *mestizaje* and indigeneity led to ambivalent integration of the indigenous Mesoamerican body in/as the nation during the Centenario, one needs to understand the construction of Díaz's persona as a modernizer.[2] The title of this section appeared in the caption for a Díaz picture published alongside an extensive interview by US journalist James Creelman with the dictator in *Pearson's Magazine* in 1908.[3] Like Creelman, Díaz's US allies used hyperbolic expressions of admiration to describe the Mexican ruler as the creator and hero of modern Mexico. During a visit to Mexico City in 1907, US secretary of state Elihu Root told Díaz in a public event, "Mr. President, the people of the United States feel that the world owes this great change [from a country torn by civil war, sunk in poverty, in distress, in almost helplessness] chiefly to you. They are grateful to you for it, for they rejoice in the prosperity and happiness of Mexico."[4] For his accomplishments, Root looked at Díaz "as one of the greatest men to be held up for the hero worship of mankind."[5] David A. Thompson, ex-ambassador to Mexico, agreed that "[a]ll this change can be accredited to the guiding mastermind of this one man; and the work of this master in war and in civil life [reflect] over sixty years of self-sacrificing life devoted to one effort, the welfare of his country."[6] With a tone of religious reverence, the industrialist and philanthropist Andrew Carnegie asserted that Díaz was the "Moses and the Joshua of his people."[7] Indeed, an article published in the *New York Times* in March 1910 asserted that "Porfirio Díaz, President of the Mexican Republic, should be a very happy man, for he not only enjoys the ardent admiration of the civilized world but knows he has fairly earned it."[8]

Díaz knew that he enjoyed such admiration and believed he earned it, even if by autocratic rule. Only a few days before September 15, the official day of the Centenario, Díaz held a toast in front of "the highest dignitaries in the Universe," who had gathered in Mexico City for the celebrations.[9] He asserted that

> Mexico ... has moved from anarchy to peace, from misery to wealth, from discredit to credibility [in terms of financial credit], from international isolation to ... the widest and cordial friendship with all civilized humanity.
>
> We have chosen to celebrate our Centenario with works of peace and progress. We want that humanity, congregated here through your presence, to judge

---

[2] Díaz was of Mixtec and Spanish ancestry.
[3] "President Díaz: Hero of the Americas," *Pearson's Magazine* 19, no. 3 (March 1908): 231.
[4] Quoted in "Porfirio Díaz of Mexico," *New York Times*, March 19, 1910: unpaged.
[5] Ibid.
[6] Ibid.
[7] Ibid.
[8] Ibid.
[9] *El imparcial*, "El banquete de anoche en palacio fue todo un suceso," September 12, 1910, 1.

what a *pueblo* [nation] and its government can accomplish when a common purpose motivates them: love of country [and] national progress.

... For many years we have worked to make our motherland richer, more noble, more worthy of the respect and appreciation by all *pueblos cultos* [cultured nations].

... Your presence here demonstrates that our Republic has gained such appreciation and respect ... only because we have worked peacefully, we have become deserving of our autonomy and liberty.[10]

With a Spanish inflection that "cultured" Mexicans used at the time, President Díaz concluded: "I toast for civilized humanity who with upmost dignity you embody in this solemn occasion, and for the health of the illustrious, sovereign Heads of State that so lustrously you represent."[11] Díaz's speech exalted the two ideals that he hoped would define his legacy: the *peace* resulting from his regime's governance after decades of tumultuous post/colonial history, and the *work* that had made Mexico a prosperous, modern country worthy of a place among sovereign civilized nations.

As chapter 1 illustrated, Díaz's words were not entirely empty. During his long tenure in power, his policies enabled an upper middle class to prosper. A relatively small group of privileged domestic and foreign families had accumulated much of the wealth produced through advances in the country's infrastructure. However, the Centenario provided grounds for choreographing depictions of *national* prosperity and modernity as if this progress was enjoyed universally across the country. A presidential mandate mobilized government officials in all Mexican states to invest in public works, infrastructure, buildings, and monuments. Designs for many of these new constructions took their inspiration from similar structures and symbols in Europe (i.e., the Mexico City monument called the Angel of Independence resembled the Victory Column in Berlin and the July Column in Paris). If the monument of the Aztec emperor Moctezuma, designed with Greco-Roman compositional motifs (completed in 1887), was to symbolize Mexico's indigenous past and *mestizo* present, monuments like the Angel of Independence (completed in 1910) were to highlight Mexico's historical lineage also as European.

The task for the Centenario's official organizing apparatus was to create a symbology reflecting the country's material and cultural modernity. Symbolic representations were to include different sectors of the population as members of an imagined national collective. They organized dance balls to entertain

---

[10] *El imparcial*, "Brindis del Sr. Gral. Díaz en el banquete del domingo," September 13, 1910, 1.

[11] Ibid. "Señores: Brindo por la humanidad civilizada que tan dignamente encarnáis en este solemne momento, y por la salud de los ilustres Soberanos y dignos Jefes de 'Estado que con tanto brillo representáis.'"

diplomats who poured in from around the world, and people from Europe and the United States who had established themselves in the country. Different venues presented theater and dance shows as part of the celebrations. Like all these social and artistic events, the streets also became stages for a wide array of choreographic performances of what it meant to be a modern post/colonial Mexican.

The composition of Mexico City as a mestizo heterotopic space (chapter 1) consisted of many factions colliding in micro clashes of civilizations. Those in power desiring to socially engineer a modern society experienced varying levels of ambivalence toward *mestizaje* and Mesoamerican indigenous people, culture, and identity. Colonial racism, including the desire to be white, mediated Porfirian elites' cultural and economic relationships with indigenous communities. As noted in chapter 1, some brown-skinned elites used whitening products on their skin to distance themselves from racial associations to "Indians" and *mestizos*, even if these identities were part of their personal background.[12] They also adopted European costumes and corporeal mannerisms to constitute themselves as modern (white/ned) subjects, and thus achieve higher social status. However, the desire for culturally exotic others among transnational elites in Mexico and abroad shaped relations to and representations of the indigenous as part of Mexico's post/colonial formation as a modern nation.

For all these material and cultural accomplishments, influential politicians, journalists, and philanthropists from the United States lauded Díaz as a modernizer whose mastermind constructed a nation worthy of joining the rest of the civilized world. However, in apparent contradiction, some of these Porfirian eulogists noted, as Creelman did, that "[i]f he [Díaz] has shed blood freely, if he has governed with an iron hand, if he has seemed to deny the democratic principles for which he fought on the field, if he has retained office when he yearned for retirement, it was principally for the sake of the down-trodden peon."[13] Díaz's civilized supporters rationalized his nearly three-decade repressive and violent dictatorial rule as an inevitable necessity to help Mexico's "aboriginals," seen "everywhere loafing in the sunlight against their little adobe huts—inert, content, procrastinating, lazy," and thus usher "the ultimate rise of these wonderful tribes to the highest plane of civilization."[14] It seemed a "miracle," Creelman declared, "that one man could have changed the most corrupt, confused and helpless country on earth into modern Mexico,"[15] "a strong, steady, peaceful, debt-paying

---

[12] Macías González, "The *Lagartijo* at *the High Life*."
[13] Creelman, "President Díaz," 255.
[14] Ibid.
[15] Ibid.

and progressive nation."[16] Such rationalizations also helped justified the fact that Mexico proved to be a great economic partner. By the end of the Porfiriato in 1911, the United States had invested over $1 billion, its investment value was "twice that of Mexicans," and it "controlled three-quarters of the Mexican mining and metallurgical industries."[17] Certainly, the confluence of a "necessary" iron hand and foreign economic interests reveals that democracy and capitalism were flexible ideals in Porfirian Mexico-US relations and influenced Díaz's nation-building project by repressive, autocratic rule.

Creelman expanded his interview with Díaz into a book-length study of the Porfiriato. Published in 1911, his *Díaz Master of Mexico* included a chapter titled "The Real Mexican Problem." In sum, the "aboriginals" were the problem on two accounts. First, indigenous groups such as Yaquis in the northern state of Sonora and Mayas in the southern states of Yucatan and Quintana Roo continuously resisted Díaz's appropriation of local natural resources. Second, Mexico's "real" problem was "due to the natural laziness and political indifference of the Indians and part Indians [mestizos] who constitute more than three quarters of the citizenship of the country."[18] Díaz suggested that indeed "Indians" inherited this political apathy and inability "of thinking for themselves" from Spaniards.[19] However, Creelman noted that no one had understood better than Díaz "the futility of attempting to deal with his people as though they were Anglo-Saxons developed by ancestry, tradition, racial instinct, education, and habit to sustain the individual burdens and responsibilities of citizenship contemplated by the Anglo-Saxon Constitution."[20] As he elaborates, Creelman concludes that not all peoples in the world are, like Anglo-Saxons, capable of democracy and dutiful citizenship. It seems that Díaz's embracement of racist ideologies from Mexico's colonial past (and present) intersected with Creelman's racialized eugenic notions of democracy and citizenship.

In Díaz's (mestizo) and Creelman's (white) articulations of the "Indian problem," the task was not just to contain "Indian" rebels like the Yaquis and Mayas but also to rescue "Indians" from their "natural" laziness and political apathy associated not only to legacies of Spanish colonization but also to their inherent racial "defects" (introduction). During the Centenario, indigenous Mesoamerican bodies were embraced as figures of representation in public events while being regarded as a problem in political discourse. The following survey of theater and dance productions demonstrates how racial ideologies in theatrical presentations resonated with Porfirian notions of "Anglo-Saxon" superiority and

[16] Ibid., 232.
[17] Wasserman, *Pesos and Politics*, 7.
[18] Creelman, *Díaz Master of Mexico* (New York: D. Appleton & Co., 1911), 397.
[19] Creelman, "President Díaz," 241.
[20] Creelman, *Díaz Master*, 397.

the reimagining of the assumed inferior "Indian" as an increasingly idealized symbol of national pride. This discussion contextualizes subsequent analyses of efforts to rescue and civilize the indigenous as part of choreographies of mestizo modernity during the Centenario and after the revolution.

Dance and Theater during the Month of the Centenario

As was characteristic throughout Mexican post/colonial history, dance and theater performances continued to set the stage for the corporealization of racialized class values in the Mexican capital during 1910. During the month of the Centenario, prestigious venues presented theatrical works featuring national and international artists. The cosmopolitan metropolis drew crowds of thousands from throughout Mexico and abroad who enjoyed theatrical productions before, during, and after the grand centennial performance and reenactment of the Cry of Dolores on September 15. Some of these shows featured ensembles generally known as *cuerpos coreográficos* [choreographic bodies], which contributed to the "visual pleasure and elevation of the spirit" in spectacles like those offered in early September at the distinguished Teatro Arbeu by the opera company Rabinoff, its principal dancer Ester Zanini, and its extraordinary group of dancers.[21] A newspaper alluded to performances by soprano Marie La Salle Rabinoff in the opera *Rigoletto*, which revived a long-declined enthusiasm for opera among the public in the capital.[22] Her versatile voice also captivated audiences in Gaetano Donizetti's opera *Lucía [de Lammermoor]*.[23] Furthermore, Giacomo Puccini's operas *Tosca* and *Madame Butterfly* were likewise big successes, with the former wowing the public at the Coliseo de San Felipe Neri,[24] and the latter lauded by one critic for the way it opened up the audience's "souls" to "jubilee and beauty."[25]

In addition to attending these opera performances, audiences attended exclusive theatrical galas explicitly branded as part of the Centenario in the same prestigious venues. Such was the one attended by President Díaz at the Teatro Arbeu, an event characterized by ostentatious luxury, "with jewelry, lights, and beauty" displayed by the socialite attendees.[26] Local and visiting bourgeoisies

---

[21] *Cuerpos coreográficos* might be read as equivalent to a corps de ballet, a collective of dancing bodies supporting main actors or dancers. It also referred to groups of dancers included in theater pieces. See, "Del palco escénico," *El imparcial*, Suplemento Dominical, 3ra parte, September 4, 1910, 22.

[22] *El imparcial*, "Crónicas teatrales: Ruidoso éxito de Rigoletto," September 18, 1910, 4.

[23] There are no more references in the sources consulted to dancers that accompanied Rabinoff's performances. *El imparcial*, "Crónicas Teatrales: 'Lucía,'" September 29, 1910, 5.

[24] *El imparcial*, "Crónicas teatrales: 'Tosca,'" September 21, 1910, 9.

[25] *El imparcial*, "Crónicas Teatrales: 'Madame Butterfly,'" September 26, 1910, 4.

[26] *El imparcial*, "La función de gala en el Teatro Arbeu: Fue un derroche de joyas, de luz y de belleza," September 12, 1910, 1, 11.

affirmed their Europeanized cosmopolitan subjectivities at these theater and dance events. Prestigious artists performed theatrical and dance choreographies on stage, while audiences of high social standing performed choreographies of refined corporeal gestures and mannerisms as they consumed art on the stage and socialized in the theater house.

Theater and dance productions that were not as glamorous represented opportunities for forming other subjectivities. Venues of lower social status presented *tandas* [variety shows] that attracted large audiences. Some theaters reserved Sundays to present shows respectful of moral boundaries so that families could attend.[27] Spanish *zarzuelas* dominated these *tandas* in theaters such as Teatro Briseño, Rosa Fuertes, Principal, Colón, and Lírico.[28] Other productions alluded to the national victory of independence celebrated that month. Through a racialized romantic relationship between a brown, blind man and a white, blue-eyed woman, *Idilios en la sombra* [Idylls in the shadow] theatrically enacted the triumph of love over death and light over darkness, themes resonant with Porfirian triumphalist rhetoric.[29] Some of these shows featured *tiples* [a type of vaudeville performer] who had been on hiatus from Mexico City stages. Characterized as part of the Centenario, *La nueva vida* [A new life] (a title perhaps referring to the new life toward which Díaz led the nation) included Mexican and Spanish dances performed by the returning popular *tiple* María Conesa and her partner Bezares.[30] Other popular *tiples* such as Virginia Fábregas and Esperanza Iris appeared in *tandas* before and during the Centenario.[31]

Other Spanish dance artists remained dominant on theatrical stages. The Trio Lara, known as the "colossuses of dance" for their ability to perform a wide array of international dance forms, presented Russian dances in the same *La nueva vida* production.[32] The two male dancers garnered more praise than their female companion, as one paper noted "their agility, precision, and rhythmic movements, which makes one think of impossible [body] dislocations."[33] Other critics, however, thought them incomparable as a group, finding it difficult to imagine anyone else surpassing the trio's dance ability.[34]

---

[27] *El imparcial*, "Correo de espectáculos," September 2, 1910, 9.
[28] *El imparcial*, "Correo de espectáculos," September 29, 1910, 9. See chapter 1 for analyses of performances and performers considered lowbrow or of ill repute (i.e., *tandas, zarzuelas, jacalones* [lower-class venues], and *tiples*).
[29] *El imparcial*, "Pequeño teatro Lírico: Idilios en la sombra," September 18, 1910, 20.
[30] *El imparcial*, "Crónicas teatrales: La tanda del Centenario," September 8, 1910, 7.
[31] See respectively *El mundo ilustrado*, "La próxima temporada de Virginia Fábregas," Sec. Teatrales, Año XVII, tomo II., núm 20, September 11, 1910, unpaged; and *Revista de revistas*, "Tres estrellas de la tanda," Sec. Vida Artística, July 31, 1910, unpaged.
[32] *El imparcial*, "Crónicas teatrales: La tanda del Centenario," September 8, 1910, 7.
[33] *El imparcial*, "Trio Lara ...," Sec. Del Palco Escénico, September 25, 1910, unpaged.
[34] *Revista de revistas*, "El trío Lara en el Principal," Sec. Vida Artística, September 25, 1910, 5.

Some shows presented during the "month of the Centenario" explicitly included mestizo and indigenous representations. In their pursuit of a somewhat exoticized "authenticity," these portrayals were not so different from those later choreographed during the parades in the streets of Mexico City as part of the celebrations. *El pájaro azul* [*The Blue Bird*] at the Teatro Principal included one of the most "poetic" Mexican types, the Tehuana from the southern state of Oaxaca. A newspaper note described the Tehuana as "beautiful women of *tez morena* [brown complexion], sculptural curves, and fantastic dresses from a fairy tale."[35] It explained the different uses of the *huipil*, an iconic square-shaped garment worn by Maya women in southern Mexico and Central America, and carried by Tehuanas when they danced.[36] These representations and appropriations of indigenous and popular performance practices helped create the sense of an inclusive nation as Mexico celebrated its first hundred years of independence. Examining the relationship of indigeneity to *mestizaje* and whiteness, not only in theater and dance events but also in scientific and philanthropic activities, shines a light on the historical, transnational forces that shaped Porfirian mestizo modernity during the Centenario.

Beneficence and Scientific Discourse: Rescuing the Indigenous

A positivist Darwinian scientism informed the concurrent development of expressive cultures and the social sciences during the Porfiriato.[37] Scientific discourse and humanist philanthropy combined to selectively valorize indigeneity as both a figure of representation and an object of rescue.[38] To showcase Porfirian

---

[35] *El imparcial*, "Las Tehuanas," Sec. Del Palco Escénico, July 3, 1910, 5.

[36] Ibid. For a discussion of the Tehuana in various forms of representation in the postrevolutionary period, see chapter 2 in Manuel R. Cuellar, *Choreographing Mexico: Festive Performances and Dancing Histories of a Nation* (Austin: University of Texas Press, 2022).

[37] To different extents and for different reasons, many people did not fully agree with the application of Darwinian evolutionary principles to the hierarchization of social and racial groups. For some arguments made at the turn of the twentieth century regarding indigenous communities as better equipped for survival than white people, see Moisés González Navarro, "Las ideas raciales de los científicos," *Historia mexicana*, El Colegio de México, 37, no. 4 (April–June 1988): 565–83. For a discussion on how Mexican social scientists and politicians aligned with, or claimed to resist, positivism, and Darwinian scientism, specifically in terms of the "Indian problem" of national integration, see Carlos Guevara Meza, *Conciencia periférica y modernidades alternativas en América Latina* (Ciudad de México: CONACULTA/INBA, Cenidiap, 2011). I posit that to whatever extent different people embraced positivism and social Darwinism, these ways of knowing represented a dominant influence on how the non-European, nonwhite population was imagined and treated by modern science, including the social sciences, in Porfirian Mexico.

[38] I adapt here the concept of "object of rescue" formulated by Inderpal Grewal, a founder of the field of transnational feminism. Grewal employs this conceptualization to discuss a repressed subject within the discourse of human rights as someone in need of rescue from an ostensibly objective observer who often neglects to account for its or others' contributions (i.e., militarism) to the violation of human rights; "On the New Global Feminism and the Family of Nations: Dilemmas of

efforts to modernize the nation and its people, the Centenario celebrations featured two scientific events focusing on Mesoamerican people's history and well-being.

Early in September, the famous anthropologist Franz Boas arrived in Mexico City from the United States for the Congreso Internacional Americanista [International Americanist Congress].[39] About 100 social scientists gathered to share and discuss knowledge about indigenous communities in Mexico and across the Americas. One could trace the congress's origins to the 1875 Americanist International Congress, which took place in France and reflected that country's desire for "cultural globalization" and its "frustrated imperial impulse."[40] To some extent, the press reflected vestiges of that French colonial mentality in connection with the Mexican congress's goal of systematically knowing the indigenous. A newspaper article applauded the Mexican government's efforts to preserve "our archeological treasures" and "scientific jewels" in museums, suggesting they could be rediscovered there by those studying indigenous cultures.[41] Other articles reminded readers that Mexico City, constructed on a "prehistorical culture" preceding the Aztecs, offered the scientific community opportunities to find traces of "primitive" life under the very soil on which they were standing.[42] An editorial for *El imparcial* concluded that in its abundance of materials for archeological investigation, Mexico was equal to Egypt or India, in terms of the proportion of riches that each of them held on its respective continent.[43]

Transnational Feminist Practice," in *Talking Visions: Multicultural Feminism in a Transnational Age*, ed. Ella Shohat (Cambridge, MA: MIT Press, 1998), 501–30. However, I came to this concept through Heather Rastovac-Akbarzadeth's work who uses the notion of "object of rescue" to theorize the concept of "savior spectatorship" in the context of dance in "Do Iranian Dancers Need Saving?: Savior Spectatorship and the Production of Iranian Dancing Bodies as 'Objects of Rescue,'" in *Futures of Dance Studies*, ed. Susan Manning, Janice Ross, and Rebecca Schneider (Madison: University of Wisconsin Press, 2020): 453–70.

[39] *El imparcial*, "Un delegado al Congreso Americanista," September 7, 1910, 4–5. Boas trained Latin American anthropologists (including Manuel Gamio, who was instrumental in developing the indigenista movement that set the basis for Mexico's postrevolutionary indigenous and mestizo racial discourse as part of state-sponsored nation formation projects). Boas was also influential in the foundation of the Escuela Internacional de Arqueología y Etnografía Americanas [International School of American Archeology and Ethnography] during the Centenario (Guevara Meza, *Conciencia periférica*, 2011). For a discussion of Boa's influence in Mexico and other Latin American countries, see Afef Benessaieh, "Boas Goes to Americas: The Emergence of Transamerican Perspectives on 'Culture,'" in *Mobile and Entangled Americas*, ed. Maryemma Graham and Wilfried Raussert (London: Routledge, 2016), 301–20.

[40] "Congreso Internacional de Americanistas desde 1875," *Filosofía en Español*, accessed August 5, 2017, https://www.filosofia.org/ave/001/a051.htm.

[41] *El imparcial*, "La primera sesión del Congreso Americanista," September 9, 1910, 1.

[42] *El imparcial*, "El Congreso de Americanistas," Sección Editorial, September 8, 1910, 3.

[43] Ibid.

This enthusiasm for offering Mexico as a ready-to-be-exploited mine of "prehistorical" life and great civilizations long gone was seemingly motivated by support from international research institutions. Universities, including "Columbia, Harvard, Pennsylvania, Berlin, and Paris," provided funding to establish the School of American Archeology in Mexico.[44] However, these enthusiastic announcements, offering the so-called ruins of Mesoamerican peoples and cultures, seem to enact a marginalization if not an erasure of indigenous people living in the present. It was as if the descendants of great Mesoamerican civilizations had vanished, and only their *remnants* remained to be discovered and conquered again. The "distinguished" Spanish delegate to the congress, Mr. Sánchez Moguel, "evoked the great queen Isabel la Católica, whom he called mother of the Indians," as evidence of Spain's (Mexico's former colonizer) appreciation for the indigenous.[45] At the same time, his statement revived the violent memory of conquest and colonization that his apparent benevolent affirmation masked. These scientists' valorization of Mesoamerican historical culture selectively situated it as a valuable relic in the national imaginary, opening it up to more colonial scenarios of re/discovery.[46]

According to the *Crónica Oficial* [Official Chronicle] for the Centenario, a new organization, the Primer Congreso Indigenista [First Indigenist Congress], would concern itself with the study of the "diverse problems related to our indigenous races and especially to their betterment . . . [for] they are deserving of living a life that progress has to offer."[47] This civilizing project coupled positivist scientific discourse and humanist philanthropic sentiments as part of Mexico's mission to rescue and modernize. This initiative resulted in the formation of the Sociedad Indianista [Indianist Society].[48] According to newspapers, the new "altruistic institution" began attracting experts from states throughout Mexico.[49] Some reported that "Indians" from Yucatan and Oaxaca sent official

[44] Ibid.
[45] *El imparcial*, "La primera sesión."
[46] For a discussion on the recurrence of "scenarios of discovery" in post/colonial Mexico and Latin America more broadly, see Diana Taylor, *The Archive and the Repertoire: Performing Cultural Memory in the Americas* (Durham, NC: Duke University, 2003).
[47] *Crónica Oficial de las Fiestas del Primer Centenario de la Independencia de México*, publication director Genaro García (Ciudad de México: Secretaría de Gobernación, Talleres del Museo Nacional, 1911), 236.
[48] The Sociedad Indianista lasted for only four years and took other forms in subsequent decades. It would serve an instrumental role in the production of indigenous intellectual knowledge. For a detailed analysis of how this organization embraced ideas from evolutionist theory and philanthropy in the development of ethnological social sciences in Mexico, see Beatriz Urías Horcasitas, "Etnología y filantropía: Las propuestas de 'Regeneración' para los Indios de la Sociedad Indianista Mexicana, 1910–1914," Serie de *Historia Moderna y Contemporánea—Instituto de Investigaciones Históricas, UNAM*, no. 37, ed. Claudia Agostini and Elisa Speckman (México, DF: Universidad Autónoma de México, 2001), 223–39.
[49] *El imparcial*, "La sociedad indianista," August 12, 1910, 10.

letters "celebrating and thanking the efforts the Society had made to civilize them thus elevating them on par with any other cultured man."[50] The reportage noted that the Indians declared their desire to be under the *amparo* [protection] of the philanthropic organization. The reporter interpreted this voluntarism as "the perfect sign that our *aborigenes* [aborigines] have the desire and willingness to learn, to cultivate their intelligence with a methodical and efficient education."[51] The reference to willing *aborigenes* from Yucatan and Oaxaca is specially significant because indigenous communities from these places had been part of Díaz's "Indian problem." The association's mission seemed to be on its way to transforming living members of *traditional* indigenous bodies into enlightened, peaceful, *modern* subjects.

From the scientific and altruistic standpoint, the International Americanist Congress and the Indianist Society reflected and influenced official efforts to choreograph dead and living indigenous Mesoamerican people in the national imaginary. Dead Indians figured as valorized embodiments of ruins and relics of great civilizations, propelled scientific advances, and inspired exoticized pride and commercial allure. Live Indians were strategically represented as mnemonic proxies for great but "dead" civilizations. The view that live Indians were objects of rescue, needing, and willingly embracing, a state-sponsored civilizing process offered the idea that they could become people on par with any other "cultured man," capable of enjoying the life of progress that modernity promised.[52] As a discursive othering mechanism, this neocolonial relational paradigm constructed the "traditional" indigenous as "premodern." This maneuvering functioned to naturalize the rhetoric of capitalist modernity, whose network of authoritative experts and investors could redeem the indigenous from their purported cultural (existential) stagnation. As a golden opportunity to showcase Mexico as a peer among civilized nations of the world, the independence festivities selectively represented dead and live Mesoamerican indigenous bodies and cultures in integrative choreographies of mestizo modernity, including in print media and visual arts.

---

[50] Ibid.
[51] Ibid.
[52] As discussed in chapter 3, people like Manuel Gamio, an influential Mexican anthropologist, reproduced this patronizing rhetoric in postrevolutionary Mexico. Obviously, not all so-called Indians voluntarily accepted the Porfirian civilizing project of white/ned Western modernity. Many had been rebelling against it all along during the Porfiriato.

Drawing and Painting the Indigenous Modern into National Imaginaries

As part of the Centenario, a series of contests took place in the sciences and the arts. Analyses of a drawing contest and a painting included in an art exhibition illustrate the ambivalent ways artists and critics created visual and discursive narratives. These representations reflected imagined indigenous communities within Porfirian national modernity. A local newspaper organized a competition of *caratualas alegóricas* [allegorical posters]. It aimed at celebrating while forging a collective consciousness of the peace and prosperity that the Díaz regime had brought to the nation after years of constant post/colonial wars. An examination of the three winning entries, with texts by commentators, suggests that these images represented distinctive forms of modern *mestizaje* that resonated with colonialist racial politics at the time.

Ornamental Indigeneity in the Construction of a Peaceful Post/Colonial Nation

Carlos Alcalde won third place with his drawing *Alegoría de "La Paz"* [Allegory of Peace] (Figure 2.2).[53] Three white-looking women stand in the center, flanked by a few rather decorative Mesoamerican symbols placed on the image's upper margins. This choreographic visual representation of Mexico's indigenous peoples and cultures makes them appear as nothing more than marginal ornamentation in the nation. Evoking the Mexican flag's coat of arms, a drawing of an eagle devouring a snake spreads its wings wide behind the woman in the center, whose arms extend as if they are part of the eagle's wings.[54] This woman gazes upward. Her clothes are green, white, and red, the colors of the Mexican flag; she is the embodiment of the victorious independent nation. The woman on the left writes what is perhaps a new constitution; she is the embodiment of a new system of justice. The woman on the right wears an olive wreath. She holds a branch of the same plant as a symbol of peace and seems about to drop it on the peasants working the land below her gaze; she is the embodiment of harmony that advents prosperity. The three women stand on a pile of ruins—a royal crown, an old law book, and other symbols—all remnants of an old colonial empire. The image constructs a *mestizaje* where the abstract existence of the indigenous within the

---

[53] *El imparcial*, "Alegoría de 'La Paz,'" Suplemento Dominical: 3er Sec., September 11, 1910, 19.

[54] The symbolic image of the eagle resting on a cactus while devouring a serpent has been at the center of the Mexican flag since its conception after Mexican independence from Spain in 1821.

Figure 2.2 *Alegoría de "La Paz"* by Carlos Alcalde. *El imparcial*, Suplemento Dominical, 3a. Parte, September 11, 1910, 19. Public Domain, Courtesy of Biblioteca Miguel Lerdo de Tejada de la Secretaría de Hacienda y Crédito Público.

frame remains as the cultural specter of great civilizations long gone. The ornamental citations of indigenous cultures on the upper margins of the drawing frame the three female figures standing as the liberal embodiments of a post/colonial national modernity forged under Díaz's rule.

CHOREOGRAPHING THE INDIGENOUS BODY 95

Figure 2.3 *Gloria* by the Tarazona brothers. *El imparcial*, Suplemento, 3a. Parte, September 16, 1910, 19. Public Domain, Courtesy of Biblioteca Miguel Lerdo de Tejada de la Secretaría de Hacienda y Crédito Público.

Assimilating the (Invisible) Indigenous into Díaz's Prosperous National Organism

The Tarazona brothers won second place with *Gloria* [Glory] (Figure 2.3).[55] This drawing represents an unapologetic *glorification* of Díaz. The image seems to have assumed indigenous existence as an assimilated component of the mestizo

[55] *El imparcial*, "Gloria," Suplemento, 3ra. Parte, September 16, 1910, 19.

nation that the Mexican flag stood for. A flying eagle soaring across the arch of "peace" carries the Mexican emblem in its beak while looking over a peaceful and prosperous nation. A dense forest serves as the background for the flattened green landscape, where a newly constructed pedestal stands and a few sculptors continue at work. One of the artists is giving form to a Napoleonic-looking male figure—Porfirio Díaz, the "Hero of Peace"—atop a horse as if at leisure. One imagines the placement of Díaz's statue atop the pedestal on its completion. Contemplating the scenery, the mythological patron of History, the Greek muse Clio, sits at the forefront of the drawing's imagery. She looks over her shoulder as if witnessing how this fertile land enabled the construction of a great leader and nation. The iconography of this poster, including the architectural composition of the sculpture's base, resembles that of monuments such as the Angel of Independence and the one honoring Cuauhtémoc, both placed along the French-inspired Paseo de la Reforma avenue in Mexico City.[56] The Tarazonas' image symbolically places Díaz's effigy as part of the ruler's nationalizing sculptural program mandated across the country during the Centennial celebrations.[57]

The drawing seems to exclude overt representations of indigenous peoples and cultures. Perhaps their implicit existence as part of the national project of modernization could be inferred because Díaz's maternal grandmother was of indigenous descent. Perhaps one could infer the existence of the Mesoamerican as assimilated into a racial unification ostensibly necessary to form the national body politic that the flag, a precious national emblem, seems to embody.

In response to the Tarazonas' drawing, an unidentified writer characterized the preceding thirty years of peace, alluding to Díaz's prolonged "benevolent" governance and Mexico's arrival at a "distinguished place among civilized nations."[58] The author noted that "wealth and well-being are undeniable within the Republic, . . . work abounds not just for us but also for foreigners who bring their virtues to us . . . an atmosphere of happiness, tranquility and safety fills our organism with oxygen and hope."[59] Claiming to be from among the generation of "sons" young enough not to remember the past, the grateful commentator evoked this bygone time. He expressed appreciation for the hard-won sovereignty, peace, and prosperity that characterized the modern nation under Díaz. He recreated a memory of a past "filled with revolutions, hatred and bloodshed, . . . devastated towns, farms, and ranches looted and burned to the ground,

---

[56] See Barbara A. Tenenbaum, "Streetwise History: The Paseo de la Reforma and the Porfirian State, 1876–1910," in *Rituals of Rule, Rituals of Resistance: Public Celebrations and Popular Culture in Mexico*, ed. William H. Beezley, Cheryl English Martin, and William E. French (Wilmington, DE: Scholarly Resources Press, 1994), 127–50.
[57] I am grateful to Dr. Mary K. Coffey for drawing my attention to this connection.
[58] *El imparcial*, "Gloria," 19.
[59] Ibid.

families always in bereavement, hearts in constant oppression expecting fatal news."[60]

Ironically, these descriptions of Mexico's post/colonial armed struggles mirrored the current armed insurgencies scattered across the country, whose collective efforts would very soon give rise to a revolution. Whether the indigenous were overtly excluded from or tacitly assimilated into the drawing and the writer's comments, indigenous peoples would soon affirm their vibrant existence, along with other factions of the population, as revolutionary fighters to overthrow Díaz's regime. The widespread peace and prosperity discourse proved to be a myth that would be destroyed just a few months after the Centenario. Not everyone was part of the Mexican "organism," and not everyone's organism was filled with the same "oxygen and hope," no matter what this optimistic commentator asserted.

Reimagining the "Ferocious" Indigenous Barbarian into a Peaceful Mexican Subject

Contrasting the classically styled imagery of the third- and second-place entries, Jorge Enciso's drawing, "El águila y el olivo" [The eagle and the olive tree], won first place. Unlike the other two drawings' ornamented symbolism evocative of European (and Greco-Roman) culture, Enciso's work was seemingly the least elaborate yet the most decidedly indigenous in style and content. It employed a modernist minimalist approach to represent Mesoamerican symbolism as "traditional," a mestizo aestheticism in itself. The piece's title conjures a mental picture of an eagle as the symbol of the nation and an olive branch as the referent for peace.[61] However, it fails to reference the centerpiece of the image, a muscular, brown body of an indigenous Mesoamerican man (Figure 2.4). Yet, his presence is so significant that he is the center of attention. While the eagle devouring a serpent represents the marker, as legend had it, where Tenochtitlan, the core of the Aztec Empire, later Mexico City, would be founded, the indigenous man performs a peaceful gesture by holding an olive tree. In a context in which indigenous rebel communities constituted part of Díaz's "Indian problem," Enciso's image and José Juan Tablada's accompanying commentary represented the integration of the peaceful indigenous body into the national project of Porfirian modernization.

The indigenous man stands on a small mound of land facing an almost empty background. He is nude except for a white-and-blue belt wrapped around his

---

[60] Ibid.
[61] *El imparcial*, "El águila y el olivo," Suplemento: 2a. Parte, September 16, 1910, 13.

98 DANCING MESTIZO MODERNISMS

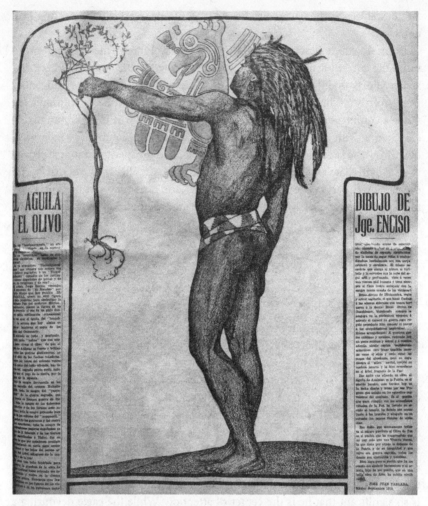

Figure 2.4 *El águila y el olivo* by Jorge Enciso. *El imparcial*, Suplemento, 2a. Parte, September 16, 1910, 13. Public Domain, Courtesy of Biblioteca Miguel Lerdo de Tejada de la Secretaría de Hacienda y Crédito Público.

waist. Blue and green feathers hang from his headdress midway down his back. A green, ornamented earring decorates his left ear. One sees most of his entire body's back side, including his buttocks and, only slightly, his left profile—face, chest, and abdominal area. His left knee bends as his spine and head slightly curve backward in response to the motion of his left arm, reaching forward. He offers a small olive tree to a stylized red eagle devouring a snake and floating in a somewhat "neutral" space in the background. One can see the choice of having the indigenous man's gaze and body orientation away from the viewers, toward the bird of prey, as a mere compositional decision. However, this choice is also a mediating choreographic strategy for the visual and spatial relationship between this representational body and its viewer. It portrays the indigenous man as a less confrontational subject while rendering him a more vulnerable body as we watch him. We do not have to face him (or have him face us) but only witness his noble act of peaceful offering from behind. If we all stand behind him, including those who saw the drawing in 1910, we can feel like part of the collective body that he, the indigenous man, leads into a new national reality.

A comment published in two columns flanking the full-page drawing reframes one's perception of the indigenous man's nonconfrontational vulnerability in terms resonant with the author's contemporary racial politics. The writer was none other than José Juan Tablada, considered by some the "most complete Mexican artist" and others as one of the "most complex modernists."[62] Tablada praised Enciso for having achieved a simple design that represented "with wise ornamental stylization" the figure of the "virile" nude "indian" in front of the "same eagle that today flutters in our flags to the winds of the Centenario."[63] It was a rather austere design but, as Tablada interpreted it, one filled with complex transtemporal political implications. Yes, it was an eagle, but as he noted, it was a glyph, a Mesoamerican-like representation of the winged creature devouring a serpent, although in this case, floating in space instead of being set on a cactus. This emblematic Aztec imagery, which also appears on the Mexican flag, in official civic activities, and in expressions of popular culture, became a beloved symbol of Mexico in the early nineteenth century. The indigenous imagery of the eagle and the brown male body was to be read not exclusively as the revalorization of Mesoamerican culture and people. In the context of the Centenario, it also represented indigenous people's peaceful assimilation into a white and mestizo project of modernization led by Díaz.

Tacit colonial notes in the rhetoric of modernity resonated with the Porfirian narrative of national peace and prosperity that Tablada celebrated. Obviously familiar with Aztec history and mythology, he summarized aspects of what for contemporaneous Western ears might sound like the *barbarous* cosmology that organized the lives of Mexicas.[64] He remembered "all the blood spilled in the old *teocalis* [temples] of Huitzilopochtli," the god of war and patron of the city of Tenochtitlan (later Mexico City).[65] Tablada evoked the "holy war," the so-called

---

[62] José María González de Mendoza, quoted in Sophie Bidault de la Calle, *La escenificación del cuerpo en la crónicas modernistas de José Juan Tablada* (México, DF: Amate Editorial, CENIDID-Danza, INBA, CONACULTA, 2010), 11.

[63] José Juan Tablada, "El águila y el olivo," *El imparcial*, September 16, 1910, 19.

[64] Mexicas were people who founded and inhabited important cities, such as Tenochtitlan and Tlatelolco, part of the Aztec Empire.

[65] Tablada, "El águila y el olivo," 19.

wars of the flowers.[66] He visualized "all the blood from the painful penances and auto sacrifices; all the blood inexhaustibly dripping from the zompantli [*tzompantli*, wooden racks for the display of human skulls], from the chests of warriors, from the faces of the priests; all the blood from voluptuous women, decapitated on the altar of Xiutecutli [Xiuhtecuhtli: god of fire, patron of kings and warriors], and from all the tender children sacrificed to Tlaloc [Tláloc, god of rain and lightning]."[67]

The modernist writer's evocation of this bloody carnage provided a context for the viewer and the reader to appreciate the transformation of the "ferocious" indigenous body into an appeased indigenous member of the modern nation, represented in Enciso's drawing. Tablada suggests that all the bloodshed "transformed into the sap that nourished the olive branches and leaves" the Mesoamerican man holds in his hand. That is, the bloodshed nourished the ground on which subsequent post/colonial Porfirian peace and concord emerged. Seemingly assuming that indigenous populations no longer suffered different forms of colonial violence, Tablada muses that clods of dirt—from the *patrio suelo* [sacred patriotic soil]—hanging from the olive tree are "saturated by the juices of the earth, blood from the legend."[68] However, in striking contrast to his nationalist rhetoric, the tree roots in the image are bare, no fertile soil crumbling from them. Tablada seems to suggest that the blood that had saturated the *patrio suelo* nourished seeds of peace that grew into this olive tree. Accordingly, he characterizes Enciso's placement of the olive tree in the right hand of the "ferocious Aztec" as a "beautiful hyperbole," a choreographic strategy that enables the artist "to consecrate the greatness [of] the oeuvre of national peace."[69] Tablada suggests the success of the colonialist impetus of modernity's civilizing mission within the context of selectively curated Porfirian nationalist *mestizaje*.

Evoking archeological codices and monoliths, Tablada attempted to illustrate the transformation of the violent indigenous barbarian into a peaceful member of the nation. He reminds his readers of the Aztec people's "terrible arms [upper limbs] . . . brandishing weapons of extermination, hoisting war trophies, wearing frightening symbols, *encallecidos* [hardened] by the task of exterminating lives."[70] As if wishing for indigenous populations to read his comments about the drawing and learn a lesson about how to be peaceful, he notes that the Mesoamerican man's "sublime and contemporary gesture"—extending his arm offering the

---

[66] Ibid. The people whom the Aztec Empire comprised fought the wars of the flowers. For an analysis of these wars in the context of empire building, see, e.g., Ross Hassig, *Aztec Warfare: Imperial Expansion and Political Control* (Norman: University of Oklahoma Press, 1988).
[67] Tablada, "El águila y el olivo," *El imparcial*, 19.
[68] Ibid.
[69] Ibid.
[70] Ibid.

olive tree—responds to the Aztecs' violent history by utilizing "another arm, also brown" extending it with offerings of peace.[71] Then, as if addressing a general readership, Tablada asserts that the "indian who offers an olive [tree] to the eagle of Anáhuac, is the *Patria* [Nation], [he] is the heroic *pueblo* [populace], more heroic now in the daily and tenacious fight for that Progress."[72] According to the writer, this "peaceful Indian" stands for "the *pueblo* that in order to complete the harmonious rituals of Peace has taken their shield to the temple, surrendered their arms alongside the laurels and mitigated in their hearts the raucous fury of times past."[73]

By representing the indigenous man's body as the embodiment of the nation itself, Tablada suggests that contemporary indigenous people have experienced transformative assimilation from their uncivilized barbarous instincts to the functions of the faculty of reason. His rhetorical hyperbole figures the indigenous as part of the national (mythological) project toward peace and progress. Their terribly ferocious brown upper limbs have surrendered the murderous instruments of their historical "rage" and now (must) labor in constructing the peaceful, prosperous modern nation.

Tablada concludes his analysis of Enciso's drawing with a similarly inclusive sentiment yet a subtle warning tone. He says, "that indian who serenely offers the Olive [branch] of Peace to the warrior eagle is the *pueblo* that has comprehended that there is only one Holy War, the one whose only objective is the defense of the *Patria* [Nation] and its integrity, and that aside from that holy war, all others are despicable and *malditas* [accursed]."[74] While Tablada fails to account for the colonial barbarism of the [Spanish] Empire in his analysis, he highlights the barbarism of the [Mesoamerican] "barbarians."[75] In other words, at the same time he neglects to mention any of the barbaric violence perpetrated against indigenous communities since the arrival of Europeans to what became Mexico, Tablada contrasts the Aztec's *barbaric* holy war—its war of the flowers—with Mexico's *noble* post/colonial holy wars, which helped construct a modern nation-state.

Furthermore, Tablada's hint of warning might reference the increasingly recurrent indigenous uprisings across the country among people living materially and ideologically at the margins of prosperity and progress, in the underbelly of Porfirian modernity. If the commentator for the second-place drawing was more discreet in referencing the reality of increasing dissatisfaction with Díaz's

---

[71] Ibid.
[72] Ibid.
[73] Ibid.
[74] Ibid.
[75] I am evoking here Raquel Serur, "La barbarie del imperio y la 'barbarie' de los Bárbaros" [The Barbarism of the Empire and the Barbarism of the Barbarians], in *La americanización de la modernidad*, ed. Bolívar Echeverría (México, DF: Universidad Nacional Autónoma de México. 2008), 269–87.

regime, Tablada seems to actively want to intervene by issuing an indictment to would-be subversives. Like many of his contemporaries, including members of the Sociedad Indianista [Indianist Society], Tablada placed faith in civilizing projects intended to appease "ferocious Indians" and their allies. White and *mestizo* social engineers and architects of modernity assumed (and desired) that indigenous peoples, imagined as docile bodies, would always produce unconditionally peaceful subjects.

As part of his hyperbolic rhetoric, Tablada participated in the difficult challenge of integrating the country's Mesoamerican history and living bodies into official modern national imaginaries. In an observation that Enciso had "evoked the virile figure of the *old* [primitive] Anahuac to symbolize the triumphant Peace of the *modern* Mexico [emphasis added],"[76] Tablada tacitly produced a mestizo modernity. He implied the necessity of constructing the barbaric Mesoamerican as uncivilized and premodern to constitute the Western as civilized and modern.

Centering the Indigenous Body as Figure of National Representation: Enciso's "Anahuac" at the Exposición de Artistas Mexicanos

Notably, Enciso's work related to this racial and cultural project of modernization in complex ways. The same month of the Centenario, when he won the contest of allegorical posters with his work "El águila y el olivo," he presented another painting, "Anahuac," in an art exhibition. The show organized by the Asociación de Pintores y Escultores [Association of Painters and Sculptors] and led by artist Gerardo Murillo (known as Dr. Atl after the Mexican Revolution in 1911), opened on September 19 at the Escuela Nacional de Bellas Artes [National School of Fine Arts].[77] Established artists and students participating in the exhibition attempted to carve their own space as Mexican artists felt excluded from the official Centenario art exhibition featuring art primarily from Spain and Japan. For many, it was ironic that during Porfirian celebrations of independence from Spain, Spanish art enjoyed official support and patronage. The Mexican artists' alternative art showcase, titled Exposición de Artistas Mexicanos [Mexican Artists Exhibition], signaled ongoing efforts to develop a nationalist art form. This impetus would carry on after Díaz's ousting from power.

The choreographic compositions of Enciso's two works, "El águila y el olivo" and "Anahuac"—especially the orientation of the featured bodies in space

---

[76] *Anahuac* is a Nahuatl word that means "close to water." Many interpreted it as the "valley of Mexico," the geographical core of the Aztec Empire.

[77] *1910, el arte en un año decisivo: La exposición de artistas mexicanos* (Mexico City: Museo Nacional de Arte, 1991). Thanks to Dr. Mary K. Coffey for suggesting this connection.

and the embodied actions they conjure—reveal the ambivalence with which artists like him embraced indigenism. They did so as a strategy to simultaneously satisfy Porfirian notions of Europeanized modernity and growing resistance to it. On the one hand, the indigenous Mesoamerican man in "El águila y el olivo" presents a less threatening body-facing-backward while extending an olive branch as a symbol of peace. In this action, he embodies the trope of the barbarian-turned-peaceful "Indian" that modernist critics like Tablada helped construct in his commentary about the work. Perhaps, Enciso's image won the first place in a contest intended to celebrate Porfirian rhetoric of peace and progress because his poster suggested that the barbarian had already assimilated into a peaceful subject and thus could integrate into the modern national imaginary.

On the other hand, "Anahuac" featured a similar indigenous Mesoamerican man, but unlike the "Indian" in Enciso's poster, this man faces forward, slightly in a diagonal, not completely facing or confronting the viewer; he seems absorbed in the action he is executing. His arms and hands extend out diagonally about shoulder height to the sides of his body, as if he is measuring the wide extent of the horizon in front of him. His spine tenuously arches back, thus very minimally propelling his sternum and left hip forward, leaning his body weight subtly to the left. This subtle bodily motion suggests he has just taken a deep breath in preparation to make a verbal proclamation. His gaze seems directed toward the wide-open horizon as he stands assertively in front of a cactus, a lake, and a hill. One can interpret these concerted motions as the moment of enunciation when the Nahua man declared the foundation of Tenochtitlan, the center of the Aztec Empire, and centuries later, Mexico City. In the context of an art exhibition intended to present an alternative to Porfirian predilection for European art, Enciso's "Anahuac" represented an assertion of a new nationalist artistic landscape. Accordingly, a critic responded to Enciso's piece by commending the artist for "painting what belongs to our country, what is ours."[78] In this emerging nationalist art form, indigenous bodies and cultures would have a central place on the horizon opened by the armed revolution that overthrew Díaz's regime just several months after the festivities.[79]

As this discussion suggests, in a context of renewed interests in indigenous populations and cultures through dance, social sciences, and philanthropy, works like Enciso's began to signal a shift in the formation of embodied mestizo modernisms from those that favored European elements to new forms that revalorized the indigenous. This emerging indigenism would become

[78] *El imparcial*, "La exposición de los artistas mexicanos: Ha sido un verdadero éxito," September 20, 1910, 1–9.
[79] For another example of artistic representations of Mesoamerican indigeneity as representative of the nation, specifically the Aztec Palace included in Mexico's pavilion at the 1889 Universal Exposition in Paris, see Cuellar, *Choreographing Mexico*, chapter 1.

central to postrevolutionary racial and cultural ideologies of *mestizaje*, including ones produced by dancers (chapters 3 and 4). At the same time, as artists like Enciso and writers like Tablada, among others, negotiated the frictions within Porfirian cultural and racialized relations, they formulated narratives of the modern/ized indigenous and an indigenized modernity. Their visual and discursive representations of indigenous corporealities informed choreographies of *mestizaje* also performed in parades and other civic events during the Centenario celebrations.

Parades of Indigeneity in the National Public Sphere: Mass Choreographies of the Mestizo Nation

Although representations of indigenous bodies on printed pages in the newspaper contest and the art exhibition evoked bodily motions endowed with meaning, they were two-dimensional static images. Nevertheless, the Centenario also included a few carefully orchestrated displays of living, moving indigenous bodies in public spaces. Reflecting racial assumptions about indigenous populations prevalent at the time, these "Procesiones Publicas" [Public Processions] included "Indios vivos" [live Indians] to represent "Indios muertos" [dead Indians]. That is, indigenous bodies, socially marginalized at the time, acted as mnemonic proxies for indigenous bodies of great civilizations in the distant past. Alongside bodies representative of Mexico's international investors, these Mesoamerican actors also participated in enactments of their colonization, past and present. While indigenous populations and their allies in various parts of the country organized and conducted rebellions against Díaz's regime, Mexico City served as the central stage for Porfirian choreographies of embodied mestizo modernities. Analyzing three parades illustrates how these performances embodied and displayed the transnational nature of Díaz's national modernization project.

The Public Procession on September 4 featured an array of allegorical floats representative of Mexico City's most prosperous commercial corporations (Figure 2.5). Framed by a discourse of peace and progress, the first four floats implicitly evoked the confluence of forces that had shaped Mexico's post/colonial history, including its current capitalist modernity. El Centro Mercantil [the Mercantile Center] led the parade with a float decorated with Mexican and French flags. It staged the genealogy of patriotic heroes. These proceeded from Miguel Hidalgo y Costilla, often referred to as the "father of independence"; Benito Juárez, the first Mexican president of indigenous descent, who led the 1867 defeat of the Second Mexican Empire under French Emperor Maximilian

Figure 2.5 This article shows allegorical floats representing the banking, mining, and commerce industries. "Por principales avenidas desfilaron ayer los suntuosos carros alegóricos," *El imparcial*, September 5, 1910, 1, 6. Public Domain, Courtesy of Biblioteca Miguel Lerdo de Tejada de la Secretaría de Hacienda y Crédito Público.

of Habsburg; and Porfirio Díaz, the current president, who had brought peace and progress, enabling an oligarchic class to emerge.

A female figure placed a crown on the head of each of these representative male nation builders. "Motherland (Patria)," "Justice," and "Peace" crowned Hidalgo, Juárez, and Díaz respectively.[80] It was as if the three static female figures in the drawing *Allegory of Peace* in the poster contest had become living bodies. Their actions anointed the patriarchal lineage of the *men* who led the *mother*land's formation, a metaphorical reversal in the gendered rhetoric of national formation. Four men dressed as Louis XIV led the horses that dragged this allegorical float. These four Louis were simultaneously pulling the float and leading Mexican

[80] *Crónica Oficial*, 1911, 128.

history through a well-structured public display of France's crucial role in the formation of Mexican post/colonial history and modern capitalism.

The second allegorical float represented the upscale department store Palacio de Hierro [Iron Palace], which opened its doors in 1891 with French investment. According to the *Crónica Oficial*, the float "powerfully called people's attention" through its display of luxurious decorations and garments representing patriotic symbols.[81] Following the float were three motor cars owned by the store, a true sign of wealth and modernity at the time.[82] The third float represented agriculture. It carried a replica of a mountain, "rustic deities, and scenes of rural life performed by people wearing clothing from Tehuantepec, Jalisco, and Yucatan."[83] While the cars that accompanied the Palacio de Hierro's allegorical float represented the (iron) embodiment of material modernity, the yoke of oxen guided by cattlemen that pulled the agriculture float embodied premodernity. In this choreography of Porfirian racialized social formation, representations of the modern and premodern constituted one another as dialogic elements of a national de/industrialized *mestizaje*. These choreographic representations kept different social actors in their *respective* places within hierarchical modes of production, circulation, and consumption of goods and services. The symbolic power of this stratifying dynamic resonated, too, with the fourth allegorical car in the parade, sponsored by the Gautier Cognac company. This float "simulated a tavern occupied by several French female peasants and some musketeers."[84] "Innumerable" indigenous people dedicated to the production of flowers in Xochimilco followed the distillery's float.[85] They carried floral offerings intended for the cathedral where urns held the remains of the independence heroes.

On September 14, another parade, El Desfile Cívico [Civic Parade] attempted to include representations of all sectors of Mexican society. *Revista de revistas* reported that participants came "from the highest ranked employees in our government to the last indigenous from our country ... all the classes that form our society gathered to pay homage to the memory of our heroes."[86] Thousands of people passed through the doors of the cathedral to place flowers by the heroes' urns. If indigenous bodies took an important, yet strategic, role in choreographic representations of the modern mestizo nation in this and previous parades, they took center stage in the Desfile Histórico (History Parade) on September 15, the day of the official celebration of 100 years of Mexican independence. This

---

[81] *Crónica Oficial*, 1911, 129.
[82] The first car arrived in Mexico City, from France, in 1895. According to Manuel Salinas Álvarez, by 1908 around 800 cars were on roads across the country. *Los caminos de México, History of the Roads of México* (México: Banco Nacional de Obras y Servicios Públicos, 1994).
[83] *Crónica Oficial*, 1911, 130.
[84] Ibid.
[85] Ibid.
[86] *Revista de revistas*, September 18, 1910, no. 35, 2.

celebration, arranged like a grand choreography of a mass dance, also consisted of various performances throughout the day. It started early in the morning with the parade and ended with the traditional Grito de Independencia, also known as the Grito de Dolores [Cry of Dolores], by Porfirio Díaz.

The Performers

Early in the morning, an estimated 2,800 people began to take their places to perform their assigned roles in the History Parade.[87] There were "Indians," mestizos, and Spaniards. Organizers made painstaking efforts to ensure the authenticity required to represent the different historical actors in this re-enactment of post/colonial Mexican history.

The Audience

El imparcial reported that an estimated 70,000 people attended the event, attempting to see the performances amid the "restless [human] ocean."[88] One can imagine the multitude of bodies performing the mass dance trying to find a better vantage point, pressing against each other, trying to carve space, pushing and tugging, sometimes out of one's volition and other times as the result of others' physical efforts to move, finally staying still until the mob would push again, seeking the renegotiation of the space as they inhabited the Zócalo plaza.[89] While the masses populated the plaza and streets that led to it, President Díaz, his cabinet, foreign dignitaries, and the "most distinguished" families in Mexico City witnessed this performance of historical memory from the balconies of the Palacio Nacional [National Palace].[90]

---

[87] Ibid.

[88] *El imparcial*, "Vimos pasar ayer una época de hist. nacional," September 16, 1910, 1.

[89] These descriptions are also informed by my personal muscle and visceral memories of sensations experienced at the same Zócalo plaza precisely 100 years later during the Bicentenario celebration in 2010. I experienced the parade (albeit in a different choreographic composition) and the Cry of Dolores, enacted by President Felipe Calderón. The plaza was indeed packed. Seven years later, in September 2017, I had a similar experience while attending the Cry of Dolores festivities at the Zócalo, led by President Enrique Peña Nieto. As in 1910, attendance at the Grito ceremony in 2010 and 2017 was massive. In my experience, the vast accumulation of bodies pressing against one another was such that one's slow advancement through space was not always the result of one's own volition but of bodies negotiating the space while squeezing one another. Attendance at these two Grito celebrations offered a glimpse into what it might have been to be a body navigating the space on September 15, 1910, while producing collective (patriotic) affect amid a "human ocean."

[90] *Crónica Oficial*, 1911, 140.

The Stage

It seems that there could not be a more appropriate stage for a re-enactment of a scenario of discovery and conquest than the Zócalo, also known as the Plaza de Armas.[91] The Zócalo—built atop the ceremonial core of Tenochtitlan, the most important of Aztec cities—and its surrounding buildings represent the centers of power that ruled post/colonial Mexico. The ruins of Templo Mayor [Major Temple], a place considered by the Aztec people to be the center of the universe, are located less than a block away from the plaza. Adjacent to this sacred site stands the Catholic cathedral constructed by Spanish colonizers starting in 1573 as a symbol of the church's political alliance during the conquest and colonization of Mexico. Near the main doors to the cathedral, thick glass plates on the floor allow visitors to see the remnants of Aztec structures buried under the colonial religious building. For the Centenario, the cathedral housed national heroes' remains to be venerated by the thousands of attendees to the celebrations. From the balconies of the contiguous National Palace, President Díaz and his distinguished entourage enjoyed choreographic representations of the birth of the mestizo nation and its post/colonial history on a stage that included actual physical remnants that embodied cultural memories of that history.[92]

The Performance

At approximately eleven o'clock in the morning, the first of three acts started as the contingent representative of the Aztec emperor Moctezuma stopped in front of the presidential balcony. Over 100 warriors—*caballeros tigres* [tiger knights] and *caballeros águila* [eagle knights]—priests, and noblemen and noblewomen accompanied their Mexica leader.[93] The *Crónica Oficial* insisted that the selection of the noblewomen was from the "purest types among their race."[94] As Moctezuma arrived, carried by his servants on a palanquin made of gold and decorated with brilliant colors, Hernán Cortés, the Spanish conquistador, arrived at the site riding a horse.[95] While Moctezuma's warriors held arrows and spears as weapons, Cortés's soldiers carried rifles. The conqueror's entourage consisted of other conquistadors accompanied by friars, and his mistress, Doña Marina, la

---

[91] For the concept of "scenarios of discovery," see Taylor, *The Archive and the Repertoire*.
[92] For a historical account of the Zócalo's significance as a contested site for different forms of performance, including political protests, see Ana Martínez, *Performance in the Zócalo: Constructing History, Race, and Identity in Mexico's Central Square from the Colonial Era to the Present* (Ann Arbor: University of Michigan Press, 2020).
[93] *Revista de revistas*, September 18, 1910: 2.
[94] *Crónica Oficial*, 1911, 140.
[95] *El imparcial*, "Vimos pasar ayer."

Malintzin, a Nahua woman. She was also known as La Malinche and served as his interpreter.[96] The choreography of La Malinche in the scenario of conquest for the Centenario seems to portray her as one among many local allies who joined Cortés's war against Moctezuma's forces. Following the conquistador's army was the Tlaxcaltecas, a diverse ethnic group from neighboring Tlaxcala whose ancestors had proved a critical Spanish ally in the defeat of the Aztec Empire. These two contingents wore colorful costumes and carried banners decorated with brilliant colors and feathers, all of which magnified the visual spectacle as they marched toward and converged at the Zócalo (Figure 2.6).[97]

This celebratory choreography did not include representations of the actual bloody encounter 400 years earlier. The most enigmatic sign of the violence of the Spanish conquest was a banner carried by one of Cortés's soldiers. The black ensign featured a red cross at the center, framed by the inscription, "Con la cruz y esta enseña venceremos" [With the cross and this emblem, we will win].[98] As a performative gesture, carrying this banner symbolized the military, religious, and political powers that fueled the European's barbaric civilizing mission. *El imparcial*'s choreographic analysis characterized the encounter between Moctezuma and Cortés in front of the presidential balcony as "friendly."[99] The conquistador, prevented from his attempt to greet the Aztec emperor with a hug, marked the differences between the two cultures meeting (clashing). Nevertheless, Cortés placed a necklace of glass beads on Moctezuma's neck, a gesture that "the Indian" received as "an extraordinary present."[100]

The second act in the 1910 History Parade at the Zócalo was the "Jura del Pendón" [Oath of Allegiance], a re-enactment of a Spanish tradition by which viceroys in cities across the Spanish Empire took a public oath on behalf of their colonial subjects, pledging unconditional loyalty to the king of Spain.[101] At the National Palace, the same *pendón* [banner] used more than 200 years earlier by viceroys waved to the rhythms of the wind.[102] A platform outside the

---

[96] Ibid. The scope of La Malinche's role as Cortés's interpreter and advisor has been debated, including accusations that she was a traitor to her people. In contemporary Mexican colloquial language, Malinchista refers to a traitor of any sort, but especially one who favors foreign people, goods, products, and customs over Mexican ones. For this and more nuanced alternative perspectives on La Malinche's historical significance and her place in the Mexican imaginary, see, e.g., Octavio Paz, *El laberinto de la soledad*, 5th ed. (Mexico: Fondo de Cultura Económica, 1967 © 1959); Sandra Messinger Cypress, *La Malinche in Mexican Literature from History to Myth* (Austin: University of Texas Press, 1991); M. Kasey Hellerman, "The Coatlicue-Malinche Conflict: A Mother and Son Identity Crisis in the Writings of Carlos Fuentes," *Hispania* 57, no. 4 (December 1974): 868–875.

[97] *El imparcial*, "Vimos pasar ayer," 6.

[98] *Crónica Oficial*, 1911, 140.

[99] *El imparcial*, "Vimos pasar ayer," 6.

[100] Ibid.

[101] "Jura del Pendón" translates literally as "Swearing of the Banner." Some scholars translate the phrase as "The Oath Ceremony." Here, I translate it as "Oath of Allegiance" to capture the intention of the symbolic ceremony.

[102] *El imparcial*, "Vimos pasar ayer," 6.

Figure 2.6 The History Parade on Independence Day, September 15, 1910. *Top row*: Cortés on his way to meet Moctezuma; *middle row, from left*: La Malinche, Agustin de Iturbide (an Independence hero), the emperor Moctezuma carried on a palanquin; *bottom row, from left*: Moctezuma and his entourage, Cortés with Moctezuma's brother, the royal pendón [banner] being brought for the re-enactment of allegiance to the king of Spain. "Vimos pasar ayer una época de hist. nacional," *El imparcial*, September 16, 1910, 6. Public Domain, Courtesy of Biblioteca Miguel Lerdo de Tejada de la Secretaría de Hacienda y Crédito Público.

government building served as the stage for the symbolic (post/colonial) ceremony that re/confirmed Spanish domination over its colony. Decorative drapery featuring embroidered images of lions representing Castilla, Spain, flanked four public functionaries who were "rigorously" attired to reflect the setting of the original ceremony. A performer acting as the *alférez real*, an administrator for a *cabildo indiano* [municipal chapter] of a city in the empire, arrived at the platform accompanied by a large entourage. Four viceregal representatives placed on the colonial administrator's hands the *pendón* with the royal emblem made of crimson damask, embroidered in gold, trimmed with a flounce of gold cords and silk tassels, and surrounded by the inscription, "[sic] Non in multitudine Exercitus Consistit sed in Voluntate Dei" [Victory does not Depend on the Size of the Army but on the Will of God].[103] As an embodied performative utterance that confirmed the official (legal) submission to the king's rule, the *alférez real* performed a short choreography. With slightly bent elbows, his arms extended forward, he ceremoniously motioned up and down three times while the palms of his hands held the symbolic *pendón*, the symbol of the colonial pact.[104] Among the performers needed to validate such a ceremony of imperial allegiance was a contingent of Spanish colonial administrators and military personnel, as well as "Indians, dressed according to the historical time."[105] Adhering to tradition, many among the indigenous group would have been barefoot, while others wore sandals as they carried "their typical square blankets, wide trousers, [and] a cape."[106]

The insistence on fidelity to historical representation, particularly of indigenous peoples recruited as performers for this History Parade's mass dance, revealed the Mesoamerican person's embodiment of multiple ontologies and temporalities. As part of the choreographic historical re-enactment of the conquest, the "live Indians," their dark skin and "traditional" garments, served as mnemonic proxies for a remembrance of a glorious civilization ("dead Indians") that existed in the distant past. However, "live Indians'" authenticity outside the context of the theatrical mass dance was viewed as undesirable in the present. To demonstrate Mexico's state of modernity to thousands of foreign visitors during the Centenario, the state fostered campaigns to *pantalonizar* indigenous peoples who would be visible to visitors—to dress them in modern pants, rather than their *calzones de manta* (wide cotton trousers wrapped around the waist and groin area).[107] With assistance from the United States, Díaz's administration distributed 5,000 pants free of charge among "Indians" throughout the city.[108] His government, along with philanthropic organizations, also gave away clothing to

---

[103] Marie Robinson Wright, *Mexico: A History of Its Progress and Development in One Hundred Years* (Philadelphia: George Barrie & Sons, 1911), 198. The phrase in this source seems to miss a reference at its beginning. The phrase's meaning likely has altered for different purposes throughout history. Late in the fourth century it was included in the Vulgate, a translation of the Bible. Thanks to Dr. Zoa Alonso Fernández for insight into the potential meaning variations of this phrase.

[104] *El imparcial*, "Vimos pasar ayer," 6.

[105] Ibid.

[106] Robinson Wright, *Mexico*, 198.

[107] Verónica Zárate Toscano, "Los pobres en el Centenario," in "Bi-Centenario: La fiesta interrumpida," *Revista proceso*, no. 6 (September 2009): 11.

[108] Ibid.

Figure 2.7 Clothing and toy giveaway to poor children. *El mundo ilustrado*, September 11, 1910: unpaged. Public Domain, Courtesy of Biblioteca Miguel Lerdo de Tejada de la Secretaría de Hacienda y Crédito Público.

people from poor communities to wear (Figure 2.7). As a note in *El imparcial* reported, they made these efforts so that those among the "*clase desheredada*" [disinherited class], including children, *puedan "presentarse decentemente"* [could attend] the Centenario [in a decent manner].[109] As another article noted, in the spirit of the festivities "*las damas de la alta sociedad*" [the ladies of high society], including President Díaz's wife, Carmen Romero Rubio de Díaz, were instrumental in this form of "*alto altruismo*" [great altruism]. Moreover, the largess manifested as an "*obra pía*" [pious deed], underscoring "*el cristiano precepto de 'vestir al desnudo'*" [the Christian precept to "clothe the naked"].[110] The systemic disinheriting of indigenous and other poor social groups continued, but at least during the celebrations they would appear to be less far behind *modern* white and mestizo Mexicans if they no longer wore their *primitive* and dirty, tattered clothing.

---

[109] "Reparto de ropa," September 6, 1910: 12.
[110] *El imparcial*, "El reparto de ropa a los niños pobres, por las damas de la alta sociedad," September 3, 1910, 4.

While "authentic live Indians" were desirable in these mass theatrical performances, they were embodiments of premodernity in the streets of Mexico City. The intricacies of colonizing encounters rendering native cultures and bodies as part of capitalist circulations of their representations reveal the complexities of experiencing multiple ontologies and temporalities. Critical dance studies scholar Jacqueline Shea Murphy argues that although Native Americans in the United States participated in shows portraying them in a seemingly passive and stereotypical manner, they were, in fact, not *re-enacting* but rather *enacting* their own indigenous subjectivities and cosmologies in the context of staged performances.[111] Similarly, indigenous Mesoamerican people participating in staged performances during the Centenario negotiated their acting roles in these historical *re-enactments* while also *enacting* their specific cosmological subjectivity and cultural memory. In addition, their seemingly passive role as representative instruments for the purposes of the Mexican state would soon transform into an active revolutionary enactment that would attempt to transform the national sociopolitical, economic, and cultural stage. While indigenous and other groups across the country were forming a revolutionary movement that would explode just two months later, the staged show celebrating Mexican independence and capitalist modernity on Mexico City's grand stage continued.

The third act in this mass choreography of the History Parade represented Mexico's transition to independence from Spanish domination, a period of history that, in 1911, Marie Robinson Wright characterized as Mexico's "modern times."[112] The parade's contingent of actors followed an allegorical float honoring Miguel Hidalgo y Costilla and one honoring José María Morelos y Pavón, two key figures in the war of independence. A group of actors representing (male) leaders in the independence movement—Agustín de Iturbide, Vicente Guerrero, Manuel Mier y Terán, Guadalupe Victoria, and Anastasio Bustamante—preceded the victorious entrance of the army of the Three Guarantees to Mexico City.[113] The allegorical floats previously featured on the September 4 parade followed this procession as the day waned and the grand finale of this great mass dance choreography approached (Figure 2.8).

---

[111] Jacqueline Shea-Murphy, *The People Have Never Stopped Dancing: Native American Modern Dance Histories* (Minneapolis: University of Minnesota Press, 2007).

[112] Robinson Wright, *Mexico*, 199.

[113] The Army of the Three Guarantees was a consolidation of a new military body established in the Plan de Iguala. Its goal was to guarantee that the new sovereign nation enjoyed independence, unity, and religion (thus including the influence of the Catholic Church in the construction of post/colonial Mexico).

114 DANCING MESTIZO MODERNISMS

Figure 2.8 The History Parade on Independence Day, September 15, 1910. *Top row, from left*: floats to Hidalgo, mercantile/commerce center, and industry; *bottom row, from left*: floats to peace, Guerrero, independence, and agriculture. "Vimos pasar ayer una época de historia nacional," *El imparcial*, September 16, 1910, 1. Public Domain, Courtesy of Biblioteca Miguel Lerdo de Tejada de la Secretaría de Hacienda y Crédito Público.

The Cry of Dolores Ceremony: The Grand Finale

As the sun set on the Zócalo and surrounding streets, electrical lights, a recent modern accomplishment in Mexico, provided an impressive theatrical setting for Díaz's re-enactment of the Grito de Dolores [Cry of Dolores]. Thousands of bright bulbs accentuated the architectural details of the buildings they decorated. According to *El imparcial*, the lights looked like a luminous serpent squirming along the buildings' columns, crawling around window frames, following the contours of the architectural edges and cornices: a gigantic serpent of light that had "coiled around all the buildings in the city."[114] The dome of the cathedral, which for this occasion housed the remains of the heroes of independence for veneration, was covered with thousands of blue lights of soft, tenuous tones that visually rendered the round shape a "gigantic turquoise stone."[115] On its tower to the left, bright lights formed the word "Libertad" [Liberty] with the date 1810 above it and Miguel Hidalgo y Costilla's image below. The tower to the

[114] *El imparcial*, "El grito: Fue anoche el canto glorioso de libertad," September 16, 1910, 6.
[115] Ibid.

right displayed lights spelling the word "Progreso" [Progress], flanked on top by the date 1910 and below by an image of Porfirio Díaz. Between the two towers, the word "Paz" [Peace] shone brightly. The luminous decoration at the National Palace, located just to the right-hand side of the cathedral, framed the presidential balcony with the words "Libertad" and "Progreso."[116]

The restless human ocean—the audience for this patriotic spectacle—eagerly awaited the re-enactment of the Grito, which in 1810 had marked the official start of the Mexican war for independence. That year, Miguel Hidalgo y Costilla, a Catholic priest, rang his church's bell in Dolores, Guanajuato, summoning people to rise against the colonial viceroyalty. In 1910, the thousands of enthusiastic bodies tightly filling the surface of the Zócalo waited for Díaz to perform the Cry of Dolores. A designated area in front of the National Palace accommodated the most distinguished among the attendees, including entire elegantly dressed families. They wore silk dresses and suits, fashionable top hats for men, and extravagant feathered hats for women.[117] The bodies of police and military forces cordoned off this area from the thousands of other attendees.[118] According to *El imparcial*, as 11 P.M. neared, the crowds of people with enchanting images of the History Parade still fresh in their memory shivered with emotion as the music of various choirs and bands magnified their "patriotic love" still further.[119]

Finally, an entourage of cabinet members and foreign ambassadors accompanied the leading actor, who served as an embodied proxy for Father Hidalgo. President Díaz held the Mexican flag on a pole as he walked solemnly forward to appear on the main balcony. The national anthem played right on cue, as if it was "sacred music," elevating the patriotic emotions and ovations to a deafening magnitude.[120] While people performed as a gigantic mass choir chanting the Mexican anthem, Díaz waved the flag repeatedly to each side of his body as if in a sign of victory, as if at the same time blessing his fellow citizens with the sacred national symbol that for his regime stood for peace and progress. Then, he enunciated the much-expected words that interpolated the modern nation-state as sovereign and intimate with the Catholic Church. He exclaimed, "Long live our most holy Mother of Guadalupe: Long live America, and death to bad government."[121] Then, joined by the multitude of "vibrating hearts," he led them into a collective exclamation, "Long live Freedom, Long live the Independence, long live the Heroes, long live the Mexican people . . . long live Mexico!!"[122] According

---

[116] Ibid.
[117] Ibid.
[118] Ibid.
[119] Ibid.
[120] Ibid. I had a similar experience at the Cry of Dolores festivities in Mexico City I mentioned earlier, both in 2010 (the Bicentennial of independence celebration) and in 2017.
[121] Robinson Wright, *Mexico*, 199.
[122] *El imparcial*, "El Grito."

to *El imparcial*, the collective *Grito* [Cry] was, "a sincere, profound, and desperate cry by a son who clamors to his mother: 'MY MOTHER!' "[123]

With such an effervescent and nationalist grand finale, this one-day mass choreography of mestizo modernity enacted the consolidation of Díaz's regime of law and order, positioning Díaz as the preserver of Mexico's sovereignty and constructor of a peaceful and prosperous modern nation-state. In 1911, Robinson Wright summarized Díaz's post/colonial accomplishments succinctly as Mexico gained "a place in the world of great republics."[124] Resonating with other foreign journalists, politicians, and philanthropists, particularly from the United States, who characterized Díaz, the dictator, as the "master-mind," the "creator and hero of modern Mexico," she said:

> In the early days, after the reign of the viceroys was over, the Mexicans had to fight for their rights, which were overrun by highwaymen and guerrilla bands, and until a man could be found who would have the strength to cope with the situation there was no safety for life or property. With the advent of General Díaz all this changed. Mexico proudly stands before the world as one of the best regulated governments.[125]

Ironically, at the same time as the publication of Robinson Wright's chronicle of Porfirian Mexico, several months after the Centenario, groups of "highwaymen and guerrilla bands," including indigenous communities, were again proliferating across the country. Díaz's dictatorship established an oligarchic class that benefited more than the rest of the population from his regime's efforts to institute Western (European-US) cultural and material modernity.

In many respects, his post/colonial form of governmentality developed into bourgeois liberalism. It was modeled more on a positivist social Darwinism than on a socially revolutionary democracy seemingly promised by the independence movement and embraced by other "civilized" nations. The many accomplishments of Díaz's regime clashed with the needs of those left out on the *darker side* of his version of Western modernity, one founded on liberalist and positivist neocolonial governance.[126] The history of Porfirian cultural modernity was also the history of the development of oligarchic Mexican modern

---

[123] Ibid.
[124] Robinson Wright, *Mexico*, 180.
[125] Ibid. Although Robinson Wright's book provides detailed accounts of different moments in Mexico's post/colonial history, including events related to the Centenario, it is written from a celebratory perspective. She dedicated the book "To his Excellency, General Porfirio Díaz, President of the Republic of Mexico, a great man among the eminent men of the world, who on his eightieth birthday is still active in body and soul; a powerful administrator of the spiritual and material good of his country." (Ibid., Beginning of her book, unpaged.)
[126] Mignolo, *The Darker Side of Western Modernity*.

capitalism, which brought "peace and progress" to the few, and which divided the population along the lines of gender, sexuality, ethnicity, race, and class (chapter 1). In 1910, as Díaz strategized for his sixth election after nearly thirty years of rule, the rebel "highwaymen and guerrilla bands" composed of brown working-class and indigenous bodies together with mestizo and white allied liberal intellectuals mobilized throughout the country, and the United States, to overthrow his dictatorial regime.[127] These insurgent coalitions would prevail in a fierce battle that would attempt to transform the country from a bourgeois dictatorship into a revolutionary nation-state.

Efforts to celebrate Mexico's sovereignty—the dance and dances for socialites and working classes in balls and theaters, the new monuments and public buildings, the scientific and philanthropic endeavors to "modernize" indigenous Mesoamericans, the public contests in science and art, and the series of exuberant parades—constituted parts of the Porfirian state's ideological apparatus. Together, these activities helped forge the Centenario as a majestic choreography of mestizo modernity. In so doing, they spurred growing interests in indigenous Mesoamerican bodies, histories, and cultures, thus signaling a shift from European-inspired to indigenous-centered forms of embodied mestizo modernisms in various modes of representation. At the same time, this renewed emphasis on the indigenous and *mestizaje* further erased Africanist and Asian influences in constructing the modern nation.

These racial and cultural ideologies that served as the foundation for representations of indigeneity, *mestizaje*, and whiteness during the Centenario would remain active after the Mexican Revolution. However, as the armed insurrection led to a revalorization of the indigenous in forming a culturally, socially, and politically progressive nation-state, postrevolutionary governments would eventually institute *mestizaje* as an official racial and cultural ideology. In this new context, as had been the case since the colonization of Mexico, the influence of transnational forces, including dance artists, continued shaping the country's versions of what nationalism, modernity, and *mestizaje* could mean. As the next chapter analyzes, the constant flows of national and international aesthetic ideologies and dancing bodies reproduced and challenged Porfirian modes of representation. In so doing, dancers created new forms of embodied mestizo modernisms that played a central role in constructing postrevolutionary Mexico.

---

[127] For the influential role the Flores Magón brothers played in organizing the revolutionary upheaval during their exile in the United States, see Kelly Lytle Hernández, *Bad Mexicans: Race, Empire, and Revolution* (New York: W. W. Norton, 2022).

3
Embracing the Indigenous while Establishing a Mestizo Nation
Forjando a Revolutionary *Patria*

On September 11, 1910, four days before the official day of the Centenario celebrating 100 years of Mexican independence, the newspaper *El imparcial* published a half-finished drawing of a dancing couple (Figure 3.1). This illustration, in which the outline of a *charro* danced the iconic *Jarabe Tapatío* with a *china poblana*,[1] was part of various scientific and artistic contests honoring the centennial (chapter 2). The newspaper invited children to complete the image and send it in as a contest entry. The completed figure of the dancing female *china poblana* seemed to be waiting for youngsters, the future of the nation, to participate in the process of bringing the *jarabe* into full visibility as their hands traced the contours of the male *charro*'s silhouette.

This innocuous image, denoting a gradual process of completion by children, serves as a powerful metaphor for how dance participated in gradual processes of nation formation as the country transitioned from Porfirian autocratic rule to a revolutionary state. Indeed, the *Jarabe Tapatío*—and, more broadly, the *mestizaje* it corporealized—would become foundational to producing new forms of postrevolutionary modernity and nationalism. However, as chapter 2 illustrated, a resurgent interest in Mesoamerican indigenous peoples, histories, and cultures during the centennial celebrations also became an essential component of revolutionary ideology. If the Exposición de Artistas Mexicanos [Mexican Artists Exhibition] led by Gerardo Murillo revitalized the pursuit of a nationalist art form toward the end of the Porfiriato, works by artists like Jorge Enciso unapologetically featured the image of the indigenous Mesoamerican body as a central figure of nationalist representation (see 102–103). In other words, this resurgent indigenism prompted by mestizo artists during the Centenario participated in subsequent revolutionary governments' efforts to embrace mestizo and indigenous cultures and histories as part of new nation-building projects. During the 1920s, writers, musicians, and muralists created new narratives, sounds, and

---

[1] For analysis of the *Jarabe Tapatío*'s multiple genealogies and functions in different contexts, see the introduction and chapter 1 in this book.

ESTABLISHING A MESTIZO NATION 119

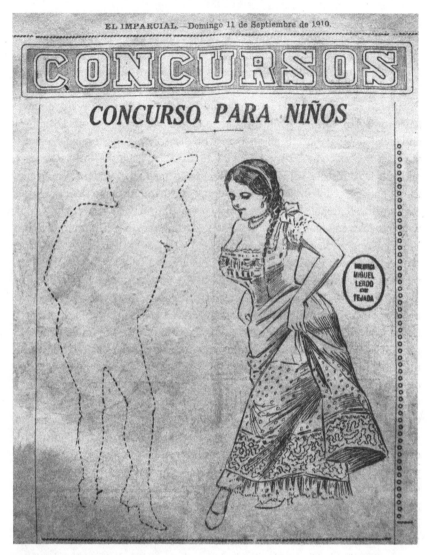

Figure 3.1 A newspaper illustration from 1910 featuring an outline of a *charro* dancing the *Jarabe Tapatío* with a *china poblana*. *El imparcial*, "Concurso para niños," September 11, 1910, 17. Public Domain, Courtesy of Biblioteca Miguel Lerdo de Tejada de la Secretaría de Hacienda y Crédito Público.

images reflective of the country's cultural and racial diversity as a vital element in the nation's political development.

This chapter focuses on the role dancers played in these postrevolutionary processes of nation formation. Although indigeneity and *mestizaje* took a prominent role in creating new national imaginaries, a patronizing state held the view that indigenous communities needed rescue as part of national modernization. That is, legacies of colonial racial and social formations, which favored European culture during the Porfiriato as a model for individual and collective identities, continued to operate even while the indigenous Mesoamerican body became a figure of national representation. This chapter illuminates this ambivalence toward indigeneity while the state solidified *mestizaje* as an official cultural and racial ideology. Specifically, it focuses on the work of three foreign dance artists visiting Mexico in 1919 and the mid-1920s: Anna Pavlova, Norka Rouskaya, and Carmen Tórtola Valencia. This discussion facilitates understanding how these dancers contributed to developing aesthetic mestizo practices that corporealize nationalist ideologies. In so doing, the analysis sheds light on how whiteness as a colonialist ideology continued to operate in collaborations among Mexicans and between Mexicans and foreign artists.

By focusing on visiting dancers who collaborated with local artists, government officials, critics, and audiences, the chapter posits that dancing bodies from abroad served as vital legitimizing agents in creating new embodied mestizo modernisms. The combination of their fame and associations with European art forms as modernizing technologies enabled visiting dancers to influence the reformulation of local aesthetic, cultural, and political discourses. In other words, the white foreign body was central to the production of de-essentialized forms of *mestizaje* that included the "modernization" of local cultural traditions.[2] If Octavio Paz, one of the most revered Mexican poets and cultural critics of the twentieth century, asserted that *La Revolución Mexicana fue el descubrimiento de México por los Mexicanos* [the Mexican Revolution was the discovery of Mexico by Mexicans],[3] this chapter illustrates how foreign dancers also participated in these "discovery" processes. It emphasizes how these international artists and their cosmopolitan Mexican collaborators contributed to transforming the nation while re-enacting "scenarios of discovery" echoing colonial tropes of the "discovery of America" by Europeans.[4] As I elaborate below, Pavlova's, Rouskaya's, and Valencia's cases share commonalities and offer unique perspectives that help us understand relations between aesthetics and coloniality. Together, these dancers' work demonstrates the crucial role transnational artists

---

[2] See the introduction to this book for a discussion of the concept of *de-essentialized mestizaje* as the result of cultural mixings rather than biological factors in the creation of cultural practices (i.e., embodied mestizo modernisms) and (national) identities produced by artists from different national, racial, social, and cultural backgrounds.

[3] Paz, *México en la Obra de Octavio Paz* (México, DF: Fondo de Cultura Económica, 1987), 229.

[4] For a discussion on the recurrence of scenarios of discovery, see Diana Taylor, *The Archive and the Repertoire: Performing Cultural Memory in the Americas* (Durham, NC: Duke University Press), 2003.

played in constructing a mestizo state at a crucial historical moment in Mexico and the world.

Touring the Americas: Forging New Nations

The three artists had established their reputation in Europe, Pavlova as one of the most famous female ballet dancers at the time, Rouskaya as a violinist-dancer, and Valencia as a modernist performer of "oriental" dances. Events related to World War I (1914–1918), including the geopolitical reordering of the world, prompted Europe-based artists like them to tour across North and South America in the late 1910s.[5] As this chapter shows, the three dancers visited Lima, Peru, before coinciding in Mexico City in 1919 and two of them, Pavlova and Valencia, returned to the city in the mid-1920s.[6] These artists' touring trajectories illuminate the transnational circuits that influenced their practices as well as how their artistry impacted different aspects of national reconstruction processes in Peru and Mexico.[7] By following these women's transnational circuits, the chapter illustrates the influence their political and cultural work had in forming new individual and collective identities as they crossed geographical and ideological borders. Moreover, looking at specific aspects of these dancers' artistic trajectories through Europe and South America demonstrates how transnational aesthetic and political discourses intertwined with the development of Mexican history.

Pavlova's, Rouskaya's, and Valencia's cases also contribute unique perspectives of the legitimizing role foreign dancers played, as cultural co-discoverers, in the restructuring of Mexico as a postrevolutionary nation. Analysis of Pavlova's performance of the *Jarabe Tapatío* en pointe suggests how this dance became institutionalized as part of the state's governing apparatus (i.e., included in primary school curricula). It also emphasizes how the ideological investment in the dance was central to establishing *mestizaje* as a dominant national, cultural, and racial

---

[5] For a survey of the development of modernist dance practices relating to race and class in some countries in Latin America during the twentieth century, see Jose L. Reynoso, "Racialized Dance Modernisms in Lusophone and Spanish-Speaking Latin America," in *The Modernist World*, ed. Stephen Ross and Allana C. Lindgren (London: Routledge, 2015), 392–400. For a discussion of dancers such as Tórtola Valencia and Vaslav Nijinsky as they toured across Europe and the Americas in the early twentieth century, see Michelle Clayton, "Modernism's Moving Bodies," *Modernist Cultures* 9, no. 1 (May 2014): 27–45.

[6] Pavlova returned to Mexico City in 1925 for a shorter season than the one in 1919 discussed in this chapter. For an analysis of her 1925 visit, see Reynoso, "Choreographing Politics, Dancing Modernity: Ballet and Modern Dance in the Construction of Modern Mexico (1919–1940)" (PhD diss., University of California Los Angeles, 2012).

[7] For subaltern voices and bodies participating in these contested nation-building processes in both countries, see Florencia R. Mallon, *Peasant and Nation: The Making of Postcolonial Mexico and Peru* (Berkeley: University of California Press, 1995).

identity. Rouskaya and Valencia exemplify the concurrent indigenism central to revolutionary ideology in the arts and politics. Rouskaya's work highlights the reimagining of the Aztec as a figure of representation in a time in which this "ancient" Mesoamerican civilization enjoyed a resurgent interest not only in Mexico but also abroad. Her case reveals how Mexican critics and audiences experienced her work as proof that *their* Mexican cultures and histories were as valuable as European ones. Valencia offers an example of a different embodied mestizo modernism inspired by the Incas of Peru. The favorable reception of her Inca-inspired dance in Mexico, performed in the mid-1920s, suggested a pan-indigenism that simultaneously pointed to shared values among indigenous peoples across the Americas while homogenizing their diversity. The three cases—Pavlova, Rouskaya, and Valencia—enable understanding of different transnational circuits, transtemporal dimensions, and aesthetic ideologies. They shed light on the formation and reception of postrevolutionary mestizo dance practices (co)created by white female dancers consecrated as artists in Europe.

The Coloniality of Modernist (Mestizo) Artistic Practices

Responses to Pavlova's, Rouskaya's, and Valencia's work enacted legacies of colonial Mexico's racial and social formations. Their individual cases illustrate how specific traces of colonial legacies informed the production of their works and collaborations with Mexicans of different classes and ethnicities. Pavlova's case begins to exemplify the role these artists took as "discoverers" of Mexico's popular cultures, thereby leading to processes I call "racialized interclass colonization." Analysis of Rouskaya's work emphasizes how the colonialist trope that romanticized "dead Indians" over "live Indians" enabled the modernist dance artist and her collaborators to "resurrect the Aztec race" through her European white body and symbols. Valencia's case exemplifies the concept of "colonial affectivity," which refers to the coexistence of the dance artist's genuine sympathy for indigenous Mesoamerican cultures, colonial racial assumptions, and extractivist practices.

Far from characterizing these and other artists as mere colonialists, the following analyses attempt to illuminate processes through which traces of a colonial racial unconscious influenced national and international dance artists' modernist imagination. Thus, their cases illustrate that modernist aesthetics and latent, yet unspoken, colonial legacies of racialization and socialization continue to coexist in the creation of mestizo modernisms. In other words, analyzing the processes of producing these dancers' works demonstrates that "there is no modernity [modernist dance practices] without coloniality."[8] As such, these forms

---

[8] Mignolo, *The Darker Side*, 2–3. The phrase "modernist dance practices" within his quotation is my addition.

of embodied *mestizaje* represent a corporeality of multiplicity that contributed to forming new modern identities in postrevolutionary Mexico. The following discussion begins with a brief account of the transition from Díaz's autocratic rule to revolutionary governance. This account contextualizes the significance of Pavola's, Rouskaya's, and Valencia's work in the reconstruction of Mexico after the revolution. The chapter continues with the cases of Pavlova, Rouskaya, and Valencia respectively before ending by offering some conclusions on the distinctive roles these artists played in establishing a mestizo state.

Revalorizing the Indigenous, toward a Mestizo Nation: From the Porfiriato to Revolution

Despite Díaz's declared readiness for democracy after ruling Mexico since 1876,[9] he once again sought to retain power through a highly dubious victory in the 1910 elections. Accumulated collective frustration added to the political turmoil created by the contested electoral process. Contrasting Díaz's rhetoric of "law and order" and "peace and progress," widespread dissatisfaction with his highly "regulated governance"[10] grew across the country during previous years (see Chapter 2). At the turn of the twentieth century, various insurgents and disparate factions engaged in local struggles had already begun to create a collective consciousness of rebellion.

The ideological impetus fueling these scattered revolts coalesced in the body of a wealthy landowner from Northern Mexico, Francisco Ignacio Madero González. In a 1908 book that was part prediction and part warning to Díaz, *La sucesion presidencial in 1910* [The presidential succession in 1910], he acknowledged the dictator's accomplishments related to his regime's rhetorical slogans. However, Madero emphasized the increasing social and political repression that Díaz's centralized power had inflicted on the lives of marginalized and exploited populations, especially among certain groups from Northern Mexico—the Yaqui people and protesting workers in mines and factories in Cananea.

Known as the apostle of democracy among people seeking to overthrow Díaz, Madero became the face of a movement that pushed for free elections. He led the Democratic Party's organization under a motto reflecting the desire to respect the popular vote, "Sufragio efectivo, No reelección" [Effective suffrage, No reelection]. After Madero's nomination as his party's presidential candidate, Díaz ordered his arrest, but Madero eventually escaped to Texas, where he published

---

[9] "President Díaz," 242.
[10] Robinson Wright, *Mexico*, 180.

the *Plan of San Luis Potosí* on October 5, 1910.[11] This document's publication marked the (official) beginning of the revolutionary transition of power. Indeed, nearly 90 percent of voters elected Madero on October 15, 1911, as Mexico's first democratic president in decades. He took the oath of office on November 6, but the country would continue to experience several years of bloody battles for power among revolutionary factions whose nation-building projects responded to national and international sociopolitical, economic, and cultural forces.[12]

As the previous chapter demonstrated, the Centenario celebrations included a renewed interest in indigenous peoples, cultures, and histories. Government officials and social scientists under Díaz's governance employed positivist evolutionary rhetoric to *rescue* indigenous communities from their ostensible barbarism and cultural backwardness in the advancement of their modernization. Artistic representations such as Enciso's featured the once "ferocious" indigenous body as an assimilated, peaceful subject. Parades included indigenous communities as embodied mnemonic proxies for glorious civilizations of the past. The display of their seemingly docile bodies in these civic performances contrasted with their marginalized reality of the day. If Díaz's highly regulated government imagined, represented, and treated the indigenous as passive objects of rescue and strategic representation, new liberal revolutionary initiatives attempted to integrate the indigenous Mesoamerican and working-class mestizos as active agents in the formation of a new type of modern nation. However, this integration would continue to embrace paternalistic evolutionary approaches to the "modernization" of the indigenous and the popular masses while appropriating their expressive practices. With the revolution, some things changed while others remained, albeit in different manifestations.

The arts became an important instrument in the state's project of national formation. Combinations of elements from Europe and the United States, intermixed with Mexico's indigenous Mesoamerican and popular cultures (with populations of Asian and African descent largely excluded), constituted the manufactured mestizo racial identity dominant in cultural discourse and policy during most of the twentieth century.[13] In the realm of dance, the rhetorical polarity between modernity and tradition, including their various combinations, found expression in postrevolutionary choreographies of mestizo modernisms. In response to shifting national and international sociopolitical contingencies,

---

[11] The brothers Ricardo, Enrique, and Jesús Flores Magón were also instrumental in instigating the Mexican Revolution while in exile in the United States. See Kelly Lytle Hernández, *Bad Mexicans: Race, Empire, and Revolution* (New York: W. W. Norton, 2022).

[12] For instance, General Victoriano Huerta conspired in President Madero's and his vice-president's assassinations on February 22, 1913, thereby succeeding Madero. Three years later, Huerta died in a Texan prison after US president Woodrow Wilson intervened to remove him from the Mexican presidency.

[13] For a discussion of these erasure processes, see the introduction to this book.

the fusion of disparate dance forms, performed by artists from different national, racial, and social backgrounds, represented powerful embodiments that the state attempted to employ in forging a mestizo national identity. While finding themselves within a vortex of competing interests prompted by revolutionary struggles and World War I, national and transnational dance artists participated willingly and reluctantly, implicitly and explicitly, in forming Mexico's notions of nationalism.

Racialized Interclass Colonization and the Discourse of Cultural Re/Discovery: Pavlova's *Fantasía Mexicana*

Anna Pavlova rose to prominence while dancing as a principal dancer, first with the Imperial Russian Ballet and later with the Ballets Russes—a ballet company that revolutionized dance early in the twentieth century.[14] By the time she formed her dance group in 1911, Pavlova had consolidated her reputation as one of the most famous contemporary ballerinas. She was also one of the first to tour worldwide with her own ballet company. Like Rouskaya and Valencia, Pavlova toured a similar transnational circuit in the Americas. She presented shows in Lima while Rouskaya performed there "with enviable success,"[15] and not long after, Valencia visited the Peruvian capital. In January 1919, the same month that Valencia offered her last shows in Mexico City and Rouskaya's collaborations with Mexican artists and intellectuals were underway, the three dance artists' names appeared in newspapers promoting their respective performances through ads, previews, and reviews.

Although delayed until the second half of January, Pavlova's arrival in the Mexican capital, chronicled in advance by the newspapers, created a sense of high expectancy for her visit. A note reported that as Pavlova boarded *Esperanza* [Hope], the ship that would transport her from Havana, Cuba, to Mexico, the artist expressed her enthusiasm, sending her regards to the Mexican people and President Venustiano Carranza.[16] When she arrived in the port of Veracruz, the press reported that the Mexican president had sent federal troops to guard the train that transported the star of the ballet to the capital. Unlike Rouskaya and Valencia, Pavlova traveled with a group of dancers from her company. These dancers were reportedly "appalled to see the corpses of bandits hanging from poles beside the railway track," a holdover from the more violent period of the Mexican Revolution.[17] While in 1919, scattered groups of rebels continued to

---

[14] For an analysis of the Ballets Russes' influence on various forms of cultural production, see Lynn Garafola, *Diaghilev's Ballets Russes* (New York: Oxford University Press, 1989).
[15] Clitandro, "Las 'Danzas Aztecas' de Norka Rouskaya," *El universal*, January 18, 1919, 7.
[16] *El universal*, "Anna Pavlowa envía un saludo al señor presidente," January 16, 1919, 7.
[17] Keith Money, *Anna Pavlova: Her Life and Art* (New York: Knopf; 1982), 272.

fight across the country, Pavlova and her fellow artists enjoyed the Mexican capital's relative safety. There, she forged alliances with members of different social classes as she danced for a variety of audiences who experienced Mexico's emerging mestizo modernity differently.

Enchanting the Elites: Heterosexual and Queer Pavlovians

Pavlova debuted her two-month season at the prestigious Teatro Arbeu on January 25, 1919, to an audience of "old and young *cultured* aficionados and all the most relevant and distinguished among Mexican society" (emphasis added).[18] Pavlova's Europeanized ballet repertoire initially enchanted these cultured elites, both national-born and emigrant alike, many of whom continued cherishing Porfirian cultural values. Dances like "La muñeca encantada" [The enchanted doll] enacted the purchasing power of these audiences' affluence and social status choreographically. Other dances conflated social class with representations of male and female nonwhite racial others whose misplaced amorous desires rendered them violent or irrational (e.g., "Amarilla" and "Raymunda"). The "Bacchanale" relied on the same heteronormative choreographic framework that all the other dances employed. However, it attempted to emphasize a more "daring" sexuality, one prudishly refined to remain "far away from the spirit of corruption to which it might very readily degenerate."[19]

As an embodied technology of knowledge production, Pavlova's classical and modern ballets produced for Mexico City's most distinguished audiences a sense of being members of an international class of modern cosmopolitan subjects who shared similar social values.[20] In turn, these audiences enacted their own orchestrated choreographies of appropriate comportment at the theater. Through these performances, this racially diverse class of social similars realized corporeally their ostensibly superior moral character. While they corporealized their social status, they also enacted their actual or desired whiteness as they consumed choreographies danced by Pavlova and her dancers on a prestigious Mexican concert stage.[21]

[18] González Peña, "La presentación de Ana Pavlowa," *El universal*. Sección: *Crónicas de arte de El universal*, January 26, 1919: 4.

[19] *The Graphic*, quoted in Money, *Anna Pavlova*, 104.

[20] After World War II, dependency theorists conceptualized this class of elite people's interactions and shared values as "transnational elite alliances" and studied their role in sustaining international relations based on wealth inequality between developed and developing countries. See, e.g., Ana Margheritis and Anthony W. Pereira "The Neoliberal Turn in Latin America: The Cycle of Ideas and the Search for an Alternative," *Latin American Perspectives* 34, no. 3 (May 2007): 25–48. I am grateful to Mexican and Mexican American studies scholar Dr. Adrián Félix for pointing me toward making this connection.

[21] For a detailed discussion of these dances and their impact on Mexican audiences, see Reynoso, "Choreographing Politics."

Pavlova's Europeanized ballets also inspired a segment of this class of Mexican elites who had non-normative identities and had to express them clandestinely behind closed doors in private homes. The tradition of having (illegal) private parties among queer male elites seemed to have continued after the revolution. As if evoking the 1901 arrest of forty-one men dancing with one another in a private home, half of them dressed as women—for dressing in the wrong clothes, dancing with the wrong partner, and embodying the wrong gender (chapter 1, 606–63), Pavlova, inadvertently, prompted a similar event in 1919. The newspaper *El pueblo* reported that neighbors from the "aristocratic" Colonia Roma summoned the police to stop a disrupting, loud party taking place late at night.[22] As the authorities arrived, people inside the residence in question turned off the lights and began jumping through the windows attempting to escape. The police arrested twenty "effeminate" males and told them to dress like men before being taken into custody.[23] The effeminate aristocrats were all wearing dresses and costumes "exactly as those dressed by Pavlova's female dancers."[24] The owner of the home was identified by his "perverted cronies" as the "beautiful Volinine," referencing one of Pavlova's principal male dancers.[25] He too was wearing stockings in point of mesh and a skirt with "hardened, undulated fabric" [a tutu] "exactly as the one dressed by Pavlova in the 'Dying Swan.'"[26]

The police pressed moral misconduct charges against the men and booked them with their names and feminized aliases; Eduardo Aroche, for example, was "Jericho's little Rosie," and Heriberto Castillo Villasana was "Liz's Flower."[27] Because some of the effeminate moral transgressors had associations with socialite families, as it was the case in the 1901 incident, they attempted to clear their names. In a subsequent note entitled "Did Not Dress as Pavlowa [*sic*]" published by the newspaper *El universal*, Heriberto Castillo Villasana begged to clarify that he was not the man identified a few days earlier in the report by *El pueblo* as "Heriberto Castillo, 'Liz's Flower.'"[28] He assured readers that he was not among the men arrested while dressing "in Pavlowa's style" at the Colonia Roma party.[29] Whether men like Heriberto Castillo Villasana cleared their names or not, Mexico City's government officials sentenced the men arrested in the incident to the Islas Marias, a federal high-security prison on the outskirts of the state of Nayarit.

---

[22] *El pueblo*, "Fueron anoche sorprendidos veinte afeminados," March 13, 1919, 5.
[23] Ibid.
[24] Ibid.
[25] Ibid.
[26] Ibid.
[27] Ibid.
[28] "No se viste de Pavlowa," *El universal*, March 16, 1919: 8.
[29] Ibid.

Pavlova's classical and modern ballets impacted Mexico City's elites in ways that they could affirm their sense of individual racial, social, gender, and sexual identities. While sharing membership in an internationalized class of cosmopolitan subjects, some created their own spaces to circumvent the state's policing gaze or else pay the consequences for choreographing their fluid gender identities. Although it may seem a world apart, some of these elite's values and assumptions about individual and collective identities informed the ambivalence with which they and the revolutionary government embraced indigenism as part of the project of establishing the "primacy of a mestizo state."[30] Pavlova's balleticized Mexican dances participated in this resurgent enthusiasm for institutionalizing *mestizaje* as official racial and cultural ideology.

Cultural Architects and Social Engineers as Choreographing Agents: Toward Reconstructing a Modern Nation

As a foundational discourse for an emerging revolutionary nation with modern/izing aspirations, *Mestizaje* found its fullest expression in the early 1920s under José Vasconcelos. He served first as rector of the National University (1920–1921) and then as minister of education (1921–1924). Although Vasconcelos held these posts for only a few years, his influence shaped public life for many decades. Cultural production, and its role in the formation of national identity, became integral to Mexico's system of formal education. As part of his nationalist pedagogical agenda, Vasconcelos's Cultural Missions program sent experts on agriculture, literacy, hygiene, and physical education across the country to rural and indigenous communities with the mandate to improve daily conditions among Mexico's diverse ethnic groups. Simultaneously, cultural missionaries researched indigenous and popular expressive practices to create cultural repertoires used in producing mestizo national manifestations, a project embraced by many writers, musicians, and muralists during the 1920s. These cultural missions satisfied the revolutionary impetus for inclusivity and revalorization of "traditional" indigenous people. They also served as instruments in the rhetorical project of national modernization. In 1919, Pavlova's "modernized" Mexican dances actively participated in this evolving nationalist *mestizaje*.

As part of this effervescent nationalism, cosmopolitan Mexicans who had left the country due to the revolutionary struggle returned from exile to participate in constructing a new mestizo nation. The state employed many of these artists and intellectuals through Vasconcelos and others before and after he took

---

[30] Tace Hedrick, *Mestizo Modernism: Race, Nation, and Identity in Latin American Culture, 1900–1940* (New Brunswick, NJ: Rutgers University Press, 2003), 5.

office. They assumed dual roles as cultural architects and social engineers whose efforts shaped postrevolutionary Mexican society. Some collaborated with visiting artists like Pavlova, pursuing a renewed interest in formulating a *genuinely* Mexican art form. In 1919, Pavlova and her local artistic allies produced *Fantasía Mexicana*, a series of folkloric Mexican dances she performed en pointe after presentations of her company's classical and modern ballet repertoire. Many conceptualized this cultural *mestizaje*—the fusion of the "traditional" Mexican and the "classical-modern" European—as the advent of the much sought-for modernized Mexican art form.[31]

Many government officials, artists, and intellectuals—primarily white and mestizo—involved in the national reconstruction tacitly embraced evolutionist positivism that shaped their interests in indigenous and working-class cultural practices. Their modernizing artistic intentions implied both interracial and interclass power dynamics. Pavlova's case begins to show how racial formations in artistic discourses and practices upheld hierarchies that favored whiteness, *mestizaje*, Mesoamerican indigeneity, and blackness (if not totally erased), in that order. Echoing New Spain's colonial legacies, these postrevolutionary racialization processes often intersected with what I term interclass colonization. The concept refers to those in positions of institutional power and social privilege (e.g., by inheritance, social networks, or capital accumulation) who endeavor to establish a sense of reality based on their personal classist worldview. This reality functions as a contested site wherein members of different social classes resist, negotiate, and reconstitute their terms of social and political engagement, parameters of access to discursive and physical spaces, and the distribution of wealth and material resources.

In the case of dance, foreign artists like Pavlova, together with Mexicans (both those who had remained in the country and those who had returned from abroad), participated in transforming *traditional raw* cultural materials into *refined* works of *modern/ized* art. While doing so, Pavlova's Mexican collaborators experienced "the simultaneous feeling of a familial intimacy with indigenous people and a social (and temporal) distance from them."[32] They relied on their privileged social status to negotiate their racial anxieties and sublimate any seemingly negative associations their mestizo bodies might have had with indigenous populations.[33] They projected their embodied ambivalence toward indigeneity

---

[31] For a feminist perspective on the paradoxical processes of becoming modern by embracing tradition, see Adriana Zavala, *Becoming Modern, Becoming Tradition: Women, Gender, and Representation in Mexican Art* (University Park: Pennsylvania State University Press, 2010). See the introduction to this book for a more nuanced discussion of Pavlova's *Jarabe Tapatío* as a corporeality of multiplicity.

[32] Hedrick, *Mestizo Modernism*, 6.

[33] Ibid.

and *mestizaje* onto their appropriations of indigenous and working class expressive cultures.

Interracial and interclass appropriations of indigenous and popular cultural practices became part of Mexico's ideological state apparatus. Notably, this did not always translate into bettering the lives of "the humble classes," whose practices served as "raw" cultural materials for the production of Mexico's "nationalist modernity and aesthetic liberation."[34] As dance scholar Marta Savigliano notes, "the social practices of the poor—... food, fashion, music, and dance—[have been] 'borrowed' and 'refined' for the pleasure of those who could afford them,"[35] and also one may assert, by those with the legitimized power to transform them. Pavlova and her collaborators' process of "refining" cultural practices they "borrowed" had the colonizing effect of naturalizing a socially stratified worldview as inherent to the rhetoric of modernity.

Crossing Social and Ideological Boundaries: Choreographing *Fantasía Mexicana*

Interracial and interclass choreographies of mestizo modernisms also embodied forms of colonialist exoticism. Like Rouskaya and Valencia, Pavlova and her dancers found the exotic allure of Mesoamerican people and cultures fascinating. During a newspaper interview, one of Pavlova's dancers asked the interviewer, a writer identified as Buffalmacco, whether he was "completely Mexican," and he responded that he was.[36] After confirming the ethnoracial authenticity of her interlocutor (coded in terms of nationality), the dance artist declared that, in "Hispano-America," her interest above all else was in the Inca (from Peru) and the Aztecs (from Mexico).[37] Further, the artist confided that she felt a profound attraction for the "indian's primitive arts."[38] Pavlova, herself, drew exclamations of admiration for visiting the most "picturesque" places in the city, including the working-class neighborhood of Xochimilco[39] and the iconic Chapultepec Park.[40]

---

[34] Francisco Zamora, quoted in Rick A. López, "The Noche Mexicana and the Exhibition of Popular Arts: Two Ways of Exalting Indianness," in *The Eagle and the Virgin: Nation and Cultural Revolution in Mexico 1920–1940*, ed. Mary K. Vaughan and Stephen Lewis (Durham, NC: Duke University Press, 2006), 29.

[35] Savigliano, *Tango and the Political*, 92.

[36] Buffalmacco, "Volinine y Vlasta Maslowa, Intimos," *El pueblo*, febrero 4, 1919, 7.

[37] Ibid.

[38] Ibid.

[39] Carlos González Peña, "Los intérpretes rusos de la danza." *El universal*, March 2, 1919, 9. Buffalmacco, "Pavlowa, emperatriz de Rusia desea conocer Xochimilco y visitar el Teatro Lirico," *El pueblo*, January 21, 1919, 3.

[40] See photos of Pavlova at the park in *El universal*, "Anna Pavlowa en Chapultepec," February 7, 1919, 3; *El universal ilustrado*, "La reina de lava y la frondas del bosque," February 7, 1919, 14.

She further stepped over class boundaries by drinking a purely "authentic" Mexican drink, *pulque*, associated with the lower classes.[41] With a tone of classist disdain, the prestigious critic Carlos González Peña incredulously declared of Pavlova's daring act, "be amazed! She found it [*pulque*] delicious."[42]

However, as the critic seemed to suggest, Pavlova was not a mere tourist fascinated with Mexico's exotic culture but a serious artist "powerfully interested" in Mexico's archeology and history.[43] As the revered international artist that she was, Pavlova had exclusive access to archeological sites and museum galleries closed to the public. Accompanied by the Russian consul in Mexico City, Vladimir Wendhausen, she visited the National Museum, where she and her dancers marveled at archeological artifacts and codices that very few people in contemporary Mexico had ever seen.[44]

Discursively endowed with unique sensibilities, artists like Pavlova, legitimized as modern/izing agents by members of their class, sought to discover the hidden significance of ancient cultures, both Oriental and Mesoamerican. However, unlike those of Rouskaya and Valencia, Pavlova's dances engaged not the Mesoamerican indigenous directly but only its already assimilated presence in a mestizo corporeality of multiplicity (see introduction). Her *Fantasía Mexicana* was a series of Mexican folkloric dances in which the *Jarabe Tapatío* figured as the centerpiece.[45] Despite efforts by some of her prestigious Mexican informants to dissuade her,[46] Pavlova searched for local culture among the "humble classes." She attended performances at venues considered by some critics to be "stinky miasmas" of "old sewers,"[47] where "the most abominable clownish individuals

---

[41] Pulque is a beverage that Mesoamerican people have consumed for millennia. It has a thick, viscous consistency made from fermented maguey juice with a milky color. For a history of pulque before the colonization of Mexico and the development of the drink's negative connotations during the colonial era, see Joan Bristol, "Health Food and Diabolic Vice: Pulque Discourse in New Spain," in *Substance and Seduction: Ingested Commodities in Colonial Mesoamerica, The Atlantic World, and Beyond*, ed. Stacy Schwarzkopf and Kathryn Sampeck (Austin: University of Texas Press, 2017), 128–46. For a discussion of pulque as a national drink during the postrevolutionary period, see Amie Wright, "'La bebida nacional': Pulque and Mexicanidad, 1920–46," *Canadian Journal of History* 44, no. 1 (2009): 1–24.

[42] "Los intérpretes rusos de la danza.".

[43] Ibid.

[44] "Ana Pavlowa [*sic*] visitó el Museo Nacional" (1919). (Clipping at CENIDID; no bibliographic reference available. A digital copy of the newspaper article in the author's archives.)

[45] Primary and secondary sources mention *Fantasía Mexicana* as the umbrella term for the series of Mexican dances presented. All sources make specific reference to the *Jarabe Tapatío*. The focus on this dance was likely due to its popularity as representative of (*mestizo*) Mexicanness since the mid-nineteenth century (chapter 1).

[46] Buffalmacco, "Pavlowa, emperatriz de Rusia."

[47] González Peña, quoted in Josefina Lavalle, "Anna Pavlova y el Jarabe Tapatío," in *La danza en México: Visiones de cinco siglos*, ed. Maya Ramos Smith and Patricia Cardona Lang, Antología: Cinco Siglos de Crónicas, Crítica y Documentos (1521–2002). Vol. I, CENIDID, INBA, CONACULTA (México: Escenología, 2002), 641–42.

from our lowest social strata" performed.[48] She likely viewed renditions of Mexican folkloric dances, including the *Jarabe Tapatío*, during these trips.

However, she was more purposefully introduced to the dance in early March 1919 during a performance in her honor, arranged to showcase the country's nationalist music and dances in a more socially controlled environment. The *tiples* Eva Pérez Caro, Mimi Derba, Columba Quintana, and Marieta Fernández performed in the show.[49] Leopoldo Beristain, the organizer, offered Pavlova a pair of wax figurines representing a *charro* and a *china poblana*, the central figures of the *Jarabe Tapatío*.[50] The event seemed to have been so emotive that the *tiples* approached Pavlova in her box seat to drop rose petals on the ballet's acclaimed empress, while Beristain, overwhelmed with emotion, "wetted three handkerchiefs" with his tears.[51]

As Pavlova began to express interest in working on Mexican dances, González Peña reported that two young artists "took it upon themselves to bring her lovely idea to life [under the title] 'Fantasía Mexicana.'"[52] He claimed that J. Martínez del Rio, "dilettante of exquisite taste," and Adolfo Best Maugard conceived of "a popular scene" consisting of Mexican dances with music by Manuel Castro Padilla.[53] The latter had played at the show in Pavlova's honor. The critic Buffalmacco reflected that in addition to bringing their "good taste" and "good artistic sense," these "three *paisanos* [co-nationals]" exalted "*our* popular dances" through their sense of "spiritualism" (emphasis added).[54] This confluence of ideas about taste and spirituality complemented a discourse of artistic refinement among dance connoisseurs and enthusiasts. This specialized knowledge enabled foreign artists like Pavlova, Rouskaya, and Valencia, as well as their local collaborators, to create forms of aestheticized spirituality out of the raw "social practices of the poor,"[55] from "the spontaneity and primitiveness of the humble classes."[56]

Like her international peers, Pavlova enjoyed the collaboration of Mexican artists and intellectuals with whom the renowned dancer *rediscovered* indigenous and popular cultures and developed approaches to *refine* them. At age twenty-two, Best Maugard, one of Pavlova's collaborators, had returned from

---

[48] Luis A. Rodríguez, "La Fantasía Mexicana," *El universal ilustrado*, Sección: Teatros y Música, March 28, 1919, 10.
[49] *El universal*, "El homenaje," Sección: Por los Escenarios: Grandes y Pequeños Sucesos, March 4, 1919, 7.
[50] Ibid.
[51] Ibid.
[52] "Ana Pavlowa y el baile popular mexicano," *El universal*, Sección: Crónicas de arte de El universal, March 19, 1919, 3.
[53] Ibid.
[54] "La Fantasía Mexicana: Ballet de merito," *El pueblo*, Sección, Los Espectáculos, March 19, 1919, 7.
[55] Savigliano, *The Political Economy*, 92.
[56] Zamora (1921), quoted in López, "The Noche Mexicana," 29.

Europe, where he had lived and studied since he was nine years old. Upon his arrival, Maugard began teaching at the semirural *Escuelas de Pintura al Aire Libre* [outdoor/open art schools]. He also worked with US anthropologist Franz Boas, for whom he created illustrations of thousands of Mesoamerican decorative objects collected from archeological sites.[57] This intense work helped him develop his theory and practice of drawing based on seven principles that he argued established the basis of Mesoamerican and other "primitive" arts. His 1923 book *Manuales y tratados: Método de dibujo: Tradición, resurgimiento y evolución del arte mexicano* [Manuals and treatises: Drawing method: Tradition, resurgence, and evolution of Mexican art] became the foundational textbook for the institutionalization of his method in public schools. It also directly affected the development of influential artists such as Rufino Tamayo, Leopoldo Méndez, Agustin Lazao, Manuel Rodríguez Lozano, Carlos Mérida, and Miguel Covarrubias.[58]

With a passionate nationalism, Best Maugard pleaded, "*we* must love [popular art] for it is part of *ourselves*, of *our* idiosyncrasy. Rather than falling into servile imitation of imported arts . . . expressed in artistic languages not *our* own and therefore lacking *our* own characteristics, imported arts would need to slowly be assimilated, *mexicanized* before they could be used as part of *our* own expressions [and as we give] form to *our* emotional world" (emphasis added).[59] The cosmopolitan artist envisioned a genuinely Mexican art form as rooted in nationalism: "it is undeniable that to foster the evolution of *our* national art— and with this *we* want to say, popular art—is to strengthen a sense of nationality, it is to build nation" (emphasis added).[60] Best Maugard's words seemed to echo the project that the influential Manuel Gamio, one of his mentors, had laid out in his book *Forging Nation: Pro-Nationalism* only a few years earlier (more on this later in Rouskaya's discussion). Best Maugard's efforts, directed at artists, intellectuals, and government officials, intended to enable artistic agents to reconfigure popular arts into expressions of the country's cultural modernization. As a form of rhetorical address, the use of plural pronouns in the influential artist's prose emphasized an imagined collective of cultural architects and social engineers that cohered in forging a new nation.

As modernizing agents, Pavlova, Best Maugard, and other collaborators around them engaged in racialized interclass processes of extraction and

---

[57] CENART, BMP 59. For a characterization of these art schools as Eurocentric with the intention to produce a Mexican art form, see David Craven, *Art and Revolution in Latin America, 1910–1990* (New Haven, CT: Yale University Press, 2002), 34. For more on Boas's relationship with Mexico before the revolution, see chapter 2.

[58] CENART, BMP 59.

[59] *Manuales y tratados: Método de dibujo: Tradición, resurgimiento y evolución del arte mexicano* (México: Ediciones la Rana; Departamento de la Secretaria de Educación Pública, 1923; Secretaria de Educación Pública, 1964), 52–54.

[60] Ibid.

appropriation that rendered them discoverers and refiners of cultural products. González Peña lauded the "colorful decorative designs" that Best Maugard used for the staging of *Fantasía Mexicana*.[61] While valorizing the "popular" and "vernacular" arts, he noted as well that Best Maugard had "renewed" the *charro* attire "in part by turning to its *primitive* purity."[62] The critic mused that the beautiful simplicity of the stage "captivates *our* eyes, it makes *us* think about the many enchanting things contained in the vernacular arts of *our* country, things that pass before *everybody's* eyes every day, and which can only be grasped, discovered, by artists who, like Adolfo Best, seek for interpretations of profound beauty in the artistic work."[63] As with Best Maugard's writings, the critic employed inclusive pronouns denoting an imagined collective readership that shares similar aesthetic taste and social status. These writing strategies evinced the writers' personal classist worldview, conflated with the dual rhetoric of modernity and nationalism.

An apparent affective sympathy enabled these artists and intellectuals to exalt the potential cultural value of popular arts while ignoring the real-world class divide that separated marginalized populations from themselves. González Peña reiterated a common colonial logic in his assessment of Best Maugard's work. According to the critic, the cosmopolitan artist had not only discovered but also refined the vernacular arts that he drew from, arts that (in their "primitiveness") went unnoticed by "everybody's eyes every day," until he, as a cultural architect, interpreted them for "those who could afford them."[64] Best Maugard made these expressive cultural practices visible to those who had not been able (perhaps due to their racialized classism) to grasp the value of *their own* country's popular arts.

González Peña neglected to acknowledge the performance of these artistic forms for years in events he had dismissed as "coarse . . . pseudo plays characterized by vulgarity and lack of common sense,"[65] by performers whom he had called "whores" and whom his colleague Luis A. Rodríguez identified as "the most abominable clownish individuals from our lowest social strata."[66] Through their respective labor, Best Maugard, González Peña, and Rodríguez—the artist and the critics—participated simultaneously in the production of artistic mestizo national modernity and their individual subjectivities as aesthetic arbiters and modern subjects. At the same time, they contributed to the naturalization of hierarchical class relations.

---

[61] "Ana Pavlowa y el baile," 3. Many primary sources used the letter "w" instead of a "v" in Pavlova's name.
[62] Ibid.
[63] Ibid.
[64] Savigliano, *Tango and the Political*, 92.
[65] González Peña, quoted in Lavalle, "Anna Pavlova y el Jarabe," 641–42.
[66] "La Fantasía Mexicana," 10.

Although Pavlova formed alliances with these Mexican *cosmopolitan* artists and intellectuals, she transgressed the sacrosanctity of class allegiances that demarcated specific spaces for particular dance productions, performers, and audiences. She visited venues considered to be of ill repute and engaged corporeally with performers from those places as she learned their dances. Eva Pérez Caro, one of the "humble" *tiples* who had participated in the tribute in Pavlova's honor at the Lírico, taught the steps of the *Jarabe Tapatío* to the empress of the ballet.[67] Pavlova's interclass appropriation informed her racialized intercultural collaborations in the selective rechoreographing of the popular dance. The combination of ballet as embodied modernizing technology and the *Jarabe Tapatío* as "traditional" *raw* material produced a refined version of the iconic dance. This modernized *mestizaje* satisfied bourgeois conceptions of good taste and the representative populism claimed as integral to revolutionary ideology and official nationalist rhetoric.

The assumption that an ostensibly civilizing force inherent in high art would help propel the country toward a mestizo modern state fueled the revolutionary impetus for "popularizing" high art forms, including Pavlova's shows. Thus, in making her (civilizing) dances accessible to the masses, Pavlova did not modify the pieces in her Europeanized repertoire. Their choreographic codes and conventions, coupled with their ballet physical vocabulary, which embodied social values shared among international upper classes, remained relatively unaltered. However, in their "modernization," "raw," "primitive," and "traditional" dances from her Mexican vernacular repertoire had to undergo an inevitable significant corporeal modification.

This modernization reconfigured the mestizo dancing body culturally, as in the case of Pavlova's white body and other dancers like her, reimagining its shape and form, recalibrating the amount of energy and effort employed in movements of body parts, in concert or isolation, while standing or moving across the space. The corporeality of this refined dancing body adhered to expectations of morality and comportment that determined what distance men and women should keep from one another and how they should embrace or not while dancing. This selective corporeal rechoreographing would have cultivated (in Pavlova, her dancers, and audiences) both the body's sense of *being* a specific self and its ability to *represent* a civilized, refined modern subject. A successful modernizing process of selective rechoreographing created (and naturalized) the broadest possible ideological and physical distance between the modern (re)*creators*, thus

---

[67] For an imaginative reconstruction of the kinesthetic interactions between Pavlova and Pérez Caro during the transmission of the *Jarabe Tapatío*, see Reynoso, "Choreographing Politics," and "Choreographing Modern Mexico."

owners of the newly refined dance, and the "traditional" bodies for whom they felt a genuine interclass sympathy and whose "raw" dances they appropriated. As Mexico was forging forms of postrevolutionary *mestizaje*, Pavlova became an influential Mexicanized *china poblana*, and the *Jarabe Tapatío* a modernized *mestizo* dance (Figure 3.2).

Figure 3.2 Anna Pavlova as *china poblana* en pointe. Luis A. Rodriguez, "La Fantasía Mexicana," *El universal ilustrado*, March 28, 1919, 10. Public Domain, Courtesy of Biblioteca Miguel Lerdo de Tejada de la Secretaría de Hacienda y Crédito Público.

Democratizing Access to the Arts: Modernizing the (Revolutionary) Body Politic

From their respective national imaginaries, bourgeois capitalist and institutional revolutionary agents sought to choreograph their specific culturally civilizing missions as they negotiated their economic and ideological interests. On February 8, 1919, *El universal* reported that Mexico City's government, to promote *Cultured* spectacles, had reduced by 50 percent the tax contributions paid by the company that hired Pavlova at the Teatro Arbeu.[68] As promised by Pavlova's promoters, they granted this concession in exchange for organizing several shows at reduced prices. While theater impresarios hoped to increase profits, government officials continued their project of including the masses in Mexico's national modernity and promoting the revolutionary democratization of the arts. The press lauded these efforts to "popularize selected art"[69] by noting that "all social classes will be able to enjoy [Pavlova's] shows given the significantly reduced prices."[70]

Others emphasized the cultural significance of extending access to Pavlova's shows, as made evident by the reportedly 16,000 people who attended one of her productions at the Plaza el Toreo. *El universal* concluded that the outpouring of people proved that Mexico could support spectacles of importance and that the enthusiastic acclaim that Pavlova and her company received represented "an encouraging sign for those of us who desire the *Cultural* development of our popular classes" (emphasis added).[71] In comparing her success in Mexico and other countries across the Americas, Pavlova claimed that in all other places, "the interest has been limited to the intellectual classes," whereas in Mexico, a country where "everybody likes music and dance," she had seen "the most numerous public in the entire world."[72] In the same interview for *El Pueblo*, she confided to Buffalmacco that neither in the United States nor in any other place had so many people attended at the same time a spectacle of the type she was offering. She declared that something "really rare" occurred to her in Mexico; she said, "I have worked in five different theaters, something that has never happened [to

---

[68] "Se reducen los impuestos a la empresa del Arbeu," *El universal*, February 8, 1919, 8.

[69] "Anna Pavlowa: Con su asombroso éxito 'Fantasía Mexicana,' únicamente hoy en el Teatro Granat," *El universal*, March 22, 1919, 3.

[70] "Anna Pavlowa podra ser admirada hoy, por todas las clases sociales en el Teatro 'Granat,'" *El universal*, March 20, 1919, 7. The "popularization" of Pavlova's shows also attempted to remedy the decreasing attendance to her performances in venues considered to be prestigious (see Reynoso, "Choreographing Politics, Dancing Modernity," chapter 2).

[71] "México manifiesta su cálida admiración al extraordinario arte de Anna Pavlowa," *El universal*, February 17, 1919, 1.

[72] Interview with Buffalmacco, "Lo que dijeron a la Señora Pavlowa en el extranjero, respecto a México, y lo que ella ha venido a encontrar: Palabras de sinceridad y entusiasmo," *El pueblo*, March 27, 1919, 3, 5.

me] before. Isn't this a record...? Isn't it?... The Arbeu, the Principal, the Iris—in Mrs. Mayendia's show—, the Plaza el Toreo and the Granat."[73]

Indeed, Pavlova danced in the "right" and "wrong" places. The variety of performance venues in which she danced reveals the diversity of audiences that attended her shows and the implications these performances had in developing postrevolutionary racial and social formations. As Pavlova prepared to dance in venues deemed by some to be of ill repute, critics' commentary about these shows included classist undertones. González Peña, one of the most reputable cultural arbiters at the time, reported this news with a tone of incredulousness:

> In Mexico's theater life we are about to witness a surprising phenomenon: Art has transferred from the Arbeu to El Principal... The Arbeu, ennobled by a long tradition of culture, dignified [by a series of international figures]... [Well, the Principal will] be purified by opening its doors to that wonder of winged grace, of light, of diverse genius that is Anna Pavlova's Art... who will convert into subtle perfumes—at least for two weeks—the stinky miasmas of that old sewer.[74]

Rationalizing what for him was an otherwise improbable occurrence, the critic contrasted the social and artistic pollution of the Principal with the apparently inherent purifying capacity of Pavlova's dancing. In so doing, he naturalized class demarcations while asserting the ostensibly civilizing power of high art.

Those ambivalent toward the populist democratization of "selected" arts would have been astonished when Pavlova and company also performed at the Plaza de Toros el Toreo, one of the venues she named for the newspaper as evidence of her far-reaching performances among socially and racially diverse audiences. The Plaza el Toreo was a bullfight ring used for a great variety of popular events. Just two weeks before Pavlova's debut there, a wild female lion fought a bull as part of a "magnificent" program offered by the Grand Rivero Circus.[75] Also, a group of comedians from Spain presented a buffo-bullfighting-burlesque show, which included an act in which "Charlot," one of the troupe's leading comedians, imitated in some of his acts "the genius Anna Pavlowa."[76] It was in this populist environment that Pavlova attracted a crowd of 16,000[77] people—well beyond the usual "intellectual crowd" that attended her shows in prestigious

---

[73] Ibid.
[74] González Peña, quoted in Lavalle, "Anna Pavlova y el Jarabe," 641–42.
[75] *El pueblo*, "La eximia bailarina Anna Pavlova celebra esta noche su beneficio," February 11, 1919, 7.
[76] *El universal*, "Plaza de Toros 'El Toreo': Gran Festival Bufo-Taurino-Burlesco," Anuncio en Sección: *Teatros y Cines*, March 9, 1919, 8.
[77] *El universal*, "México manifiesta su cálida admiración al extraordinario arte de Anna Pavlowa," February 17, 1919, 1.

Figure 3.3 Pavlova and her company performing dances from her Europeanized ballet repertoire at the Plaza el Toreo. Xavier de Bradomin, "Por los escenarios," *El universal ilustrado*, March 7, 1919, 10. Public Domain, Courtesy of Biblioteca Miguel Lerdo de Tejada de la Secretaría de Hacienda y Crédito Público.

venues and other countries.[78] Indeed, according to Marian Heinly Page, who was traveling with the troupe and was mother to one of Pavlova's dancers (Ruth Page), "there was the most picturesque audience imaginable, every grade of society and variety of costume. Whole families of Indians, peons and street people watching the performance with the same delight . . . the great bullring was filled, except the section where the stage was built" (Figure 3.3).[79] Through this democratizing gesture at the Plaza el Toreo, even Mexicans from the lower social classes had access to experiencing high art by seeing dances from Pavlova and her company's Europeanized ballet repertoire.

Certainly, many of these diverse social groups were even more delighted to see a "refined" version of their beloved *Jarabe Tapatío* performed by one of the greatest ballet stars as ads began to announce the departure of Pavlova's company from the country (Figure 3.4). One can imagine how these socially and ethnically diverse human masses cheerfully celebrated the ballet empress's dancing body minimally bouncing up and down, her *china poblana* braids and *rebozo* (shawl) swaying, the tip of her point ballet shoes tapping the *modernized* steps of the *Jarabe Tapatío*, while she flirtatiously danced around her partner's sombrero lying on the floor (Figure 3.5).

---

[78] Buffalmacco, "Lo que dijeron a la Señora Pavlowa."
[79] Quoted in Andrew Wentink, "Pavlova, Humphrey and Page," *Dance Magazine*: "A Dance Magazine Portfolio Produced by William Como and Richard Philp," January 1976, 54.

Figure 3.4 Ad announcing the inclusion of *Fantasía Mexicana* and the *Jarabe Tapatío* as part of Pavlova's farewell show at the Plaza el Toreo. *El universal*, March 23, 1919, 8. Public Domain, Courtesy of Biblioteca Miguel Lerdo de Tejada de la Secretaría de Hacienda y Crédito Público.

There must have been hundreds of sombreros flying as "many men hurled their own hats onto the stage, hoping that [Pavlova] would dance on them too."[80] The audience's euphoric expressions of approval might have reflected how Pavlova's dancing made the heart of the Mexican "race palpitate" and its blood precipitate in a "wild uncontrollable torrent," as Gabriel Fernández Ledesma wrote in response to Pavlova's balleticized *El Jarabe Tapatío*.[81] It would not have been unusual to hear a proud multitude yelling in such a moment of collective consciousness a deafening, "Viva Mexico! Viva Mexico, Viva Mexico!" The effusive mass of bodies corporeally enunciated their patriotism as they felt and saw the movements of a group of white dancing bodies of such prestigious artistic status *modernize* their dances and rechoreograph their own sense of transnational Mexicanness.

The *Jarabe Tapatío* culminated the Mexican dance set following pieces from Pavlova's Europeanized ballet repertoire. The performance of her modernized

---

[80] Money, *Anna Pavlova*, 273.
[81] Quoted in Luis Bruno Ruiz, "Homenaje a Anna Pavlova: Bajo los puntos suspensivos de tus pies, mi raza palpita," *Balletomania: El mundo de la danza* 1, no. 1 (September–October 1981): 23.

ESTABLISHING A MESTIZO NATION 141

Figure 3.5 Pavlova as *china poblana*, dancing on a *charro*'s hat in the *Jarabe Tapatío*. *El universal ilustrado*, March 28, 1919, 10. Public Domain, Courtesy of Biblioteca Miguel Lerdo de Tejada de la Secretaría de Hacienda y Crédito Público.

mestizaje for multitudes at the Plaza el Toreo served as a window into how the Mexican dance corporealized the dual rhetoric of modernity and nationalism. The bourgeois ideological impetus of civilizing the masses, an impulse that combined the capitalist drive for profit, existed within a revolutionary state apparatus with its ideology of inclusive populism. Participants in this stratified revolutionary democracy engaged in intercultural and interracial collaborations undergirding a process of interclass colonization intended to shape collective modern subjectivity, a new mestizo Mexicanness. This calibrated inclusivity kept different population segments within their *respective* social and economic spaces.

Modernized Mexican dances, like those included in Pavlova's *Fantasía Mexicana* and her European repertoire, performed in populist venues and prestigious theaters, contributed to the production of racial and social formations as part of re/building the nation. Only nine years after the onset of the armed Mexican Revolution, the cheerful jumping bodies of "indians, peons and street people," their celebratory movements and vocalizations coming from the bottom of their guts, confirmed their embodied belonging to a postdictatorial country. Their enthusiastic bodies seemed to be performing their collective hope for the betterment of their livelihoods within the revolutionary Mexico they were a part of, as Pavlova performed *Fantasía Mexicana* dances on her ballet pointe shoes. At this moment in Mexican history, government officials, impresarios, dance artists, and audiences actively debated through their embodied practices whether the sociopolitical, economic, and cultural democratic impetus of the revolution was a mere populist *Fantasía Mexicana* [Mexican fantasy].

While Pavlova contributed to rearticulating Porfirian appropriations of the *Jarabe Tapatío's mestizaje* into new revolutionary rhetoric, Rouskaya embodied the indigenous Mesoamerican that Jorge Enciso and other nationalist artists began to center as a figure of national representation toward the Porfiriato's end. Rouskaya, like Pavlova, created a unique modernist mestizo dance work that enacted legacies of the country's colonial history while participating in the construction of a postrevolutionary nation.

Dead over Live Indians: Rouskaya "Resurrecting" the Aztec Race

The dancer-violinist Delia Franciscus, known as Norka Rouskaya, was not Russian, as many thought she was, but rather Swiss-Italian. Before traveling to Mexico, she arrived in Lima, Peru, on October 17, 1917.[82] Looking briefly at Rouskaya's visit to Peru in a time of cultural reconstruction casts light on the Latin American avant-garde sensibilities that influenced her work in Mexico. Her passage through Lima also illuminates how Latin American countries' national renewal histories intertwined with one another. Within a few weeks of her arrival in Lima, she performed to great acclaim works by Schubert, Mozart, Chopin, Saint-Saëns, and Beethoven at the Teatro Municipal.[83] Like Mexico

---

[82] Like Pavalova and Valencia, Rouskaya performed in various South American countries.
[83] José-Carlos Mariátegui, "El baile de Norka Rouskaya," *El comercio*, Sec. El Dominical, November 5, 2017. This author is not to be confused with his father, who is referred to and quoted below, as one of the members of Colónida. Mariátegui (1894–1930), the father, was a highly respected

and other Latin American countries in the early twentieth century, Peru experienced cultural shifts that would lead the country from a República Aristocrática [Aristocratic Republic] to La Patria Nueva [the New Nation]. In the 1911 novel *La ciudad de los tísicos* [The tubercular city], a young intellectual, Abraham Valdelomar, described the tumultuous shifts experienced by urban middle and upper classes as "physical and spiritual tortures endured by a country of sick people trapped between life and death."[84]

Valdelomar, also known as Conde de Lemos, led a group of artists and intellectuals under the name Colónida an allusion to their modernist literary works representing a new cultural re/colonization. In the words of José Carlos Mariátegui, a member, Colónida was more than a group of young, novice writers with heterogeneous aesthetic visions and methodologies. It was an "attitude, a state of mind/*animo*" that served a "transformative function" and that resonated with "heretic, heterodox, and solitary" Peruvian writers opposed to "academic values, reputations, and temperaments."[85] Its members also repudiated the "monopoly of national fame associated with an antiquated, official and 'pompous' art."[86]

According to Peruvian historian Carmen McEvoy, these avant-garde thinkers centralized the written word as the catalyst for cultural change.[87] However, the body—Rouskaya's dancing body—would have a lasting impact on Peru's national cultural and social debates. Those aligned with the Colónida sensibility frequented the Palais Concert, where foreign artists socialized with their likeminded hosts. They shared the urban snobbism that often characterized national and international cosmopolitan artists' subjectivities. At one of these events, Colónida writers proposed to Rouskaya that she dance to Camille Saint-Saëns's "Danse Macabre" [Dance of death] at the Cemetery Presbítero Maestro. She accepted the invitation. Based on various accounts of the event, they believed that a performance of this specific dance and music in a cemetery would resonate with the life-and-death struggle that Valdelomar discussed in *La ciudad de los tísicos* and serve as a cultural leitmotif of Colónida's historical time.[88]

---

political thinker, journalist, and literary writer devoted to developing a socialist revolution shaped by the unique characteristics and needs of people in Latin America, including indigenous communities. See, e.g., his famous book, *Siete ensayos de interpretación de la realidad peruana* (Santiago de Chile: Editorial Universitaria, 1955; orig. ed., 1928). It is specified when the text below refers to Mariátegui, the father.

[84] Carmen McEvoy, "Entre la vida y la muerte: A cien años del baile de Norka Rouskaya en el Cementerio Presbítero Maestro," *El comercio*, Sec. Mirada de Fondo, November 4, 2017.
[85] Mariátegui (father), quoted in Alberto Tauro, "'Colónida' en el modernismo peruano," *Revista iberoamericana* 1, no. 1 (May 1939): 77–80.
[86] Ibid.
[87] McEvoy, "Entre la vida y la muerte."
[88] There was also the precedent that the internationally famous modern dancer, Isadora Duncan, had danced in cemeteries.

Moreover, perhaps as a gesture toward imagining a more mestizo *patria nueva* [new nation], the performance would take place by President Ramón Castilla's (1797–1867) mausoleum. The group intended to pay homage to the man who, on December 3, 1854, abolished the slavery of Afro-Peruvians and terminated tributary payments by indigenous people.

Although the dance event lasted scarcely one minute, it caused a national uproar. On short notice, Colónida writers convinced skeptical city authorities to grant permits for Rouskaya to visit the cemetery the night before her departure from the country on the pretext that she wanted to take a last "original" impression of such an iconic place.[89] Accompanied by a city official, a group of writers, artists, and intellectuals, including Rouskaya and her mother, they entered the Cemetery Presbítero Maestro at around one o'clock in the morning on November 5, 1917. To the extent that reportage of the event reflects the reality, it seems that the group had planned a choreographic score for the swift performance at the cemetery, perhaps because they knew that their transgressive artistic plans would take place under the policing eyes of the city official who escorted them. As soon as they arrived at President Castilla's mausoleum, Luis Cáceres, the first violinist with the Teatro Colón Orchestra, began playing the mournful notes of Saint-Saëns's "Danse Macabre," as members of the group lit candles in the dark. In the tenuous lights, Rouskaya—dressed only in a gray tunic—began moving sinuously around the mausoleum area. Coming out of this improvisatory motion, she then performed what might have been a dramatic choreographic choice: she collapsed suddenly on her knees, and her long hair fell, covering her face.[90] Within this performance context, both the dancer and her collaborator-witnesses might have experienced this fleeting choreographic gesture as a potent emotional moment.

Highly alarmed and taken by surprise, the city official intervened to stop the performance. Rouskaya, her mother, and some of the organizers (among them Mariátegui, Cesar Falcon, J. Varas, Cáceres, Sabastian Lorente, and Gillermo Angulo y Puente Arnao) ended up in jail, where they spent at least two days.[91] The brief moment of legal and moral transgression scandalized the city. The Senate debated the "issue at the Lima Cemetery"; the newspaper *El comercio* characterized the event as "the desecration of the cemetery," and the archiepiscopal newspaper *La unión* condemned the incident under the title "The current degeneration."[92] Rouskaya's dancing body left an indelible mark. Through this fleeting performative act, she and her modernist avant-garde collaborators in

---

[89] José-Carlos Mariátegui (son), "El baile de Norka Rouskaya."
[90] Ibid.
[91] *El comercio*, Redacción, "Norka Rouskaya, la bailarina que escandalizo Lima en 1917," November 6, 1917.
[92] José-Carlos Mariátegui (son), "El baile de Norka Rouskaya."

Lima influenced ongoing efforts to contest official cultural dogma, political ideology, and social mores while forming a new national imaginary.[93]

The Greco-Roman and the Aztec: Rouskaya as a Mestizo Body

In Mexico City, Rouskaya's avant-garde sensibilities aligned with distinctive embodied mestizo modernisms that Mexican artists and intellectuals, bourgeois capitalists, and revolutionary government officials endeavored to produce for different purposes. Rouskaya arrived in Mexico early in 1918 and lived there for over a year. As Pavlova would do a year later, she too enchanted elite audiences with her Europeanized and exotic dances. At the time, critics and audiences who championed and consumed "serious" art forms—classically inspired music, theater, and dance on proscenium stages—professed romantic notions that held *ancient* (white) Western culture, namely Roman and Greek, as the highest standard of human civilization.[94] Contradictorily, those *culturally specific* Eurocentric referents—established as the foundation for *universal* art—ostensibly could transcend temporal and cultural limitations.

To observers, Rouskaya seemed to embody these ideals, a measure of legitimation for her in the eyes of local critics and audiences. In response to her debut at the prestigious Teatro Arbeu, the same theater where Pavlova would debut later, Xavier Sorondo assured his reader that Rouskaya, "the dancer of Russian name and of Roman facial features," was one of the "most notable dancer[s] in the world" and had graciously performed "rhythmic movements as a Greek dancer."[95] A year later in 1919, when Pavlova and Valencia were also presenting their shows in the city, Alvaro de Alhamar asserted that Rouskaya's "butterfly-like aerial agility gave color and shape to the music with emotions so vivid" that no other dancer attempting to evoke Greek motifs on Mexico City stages had ever matched her.[96] Rouskaya's light yet potent expressive physicality "animated classical dances with intense artistic truth."[97] Unlike previous dancers, according to Alhamar, Rouskaya "revived on our stages the winged grace of the Hellenic nymphs; her soft figure evoked breezes from Greece."[98]

---

[93] For more historical context on this incident and the uproar it caused in Lima, see William W. Stein, *Dance in the Cemetery: José Carlos Mariátegui and the Lima Scandal of 1917* (Lanham, MD: University Press of America, 1997).

[94] This was true in Mexico and other countries. Early in her career at the turn of the twentieth century, Isadora Duncan relied on evocations of Greek imagery as foundational to legitimizing dance as a high art form in the United States and Europe.

[95] "Norka Rouskaya: Desde mi butaca," *El universal ilustrado*, April 1918, unpaged.

[96] "Norka Rouskaya se va," *El universal*, January 13, 1919, 3.

[97] Ibid.

[98] Ibid.

While Rouskaya satisfied critics' and audiences' desires for ("ancient") European references as a measure of high art, a mechanism of social distinction carried over from the Porfirian era, those with nationalist affinities sought an opportunity to elevate their particular ("ancient") culture. Just as she had done in Lima, Rouskaya collaborated with Mexican experts on Mesoamerican cultures involved in scientific inquiry produced by such institutions as the International Americanist Congress, the First Indigenist Congress, the Indianist Society, and the School of American Archeology, all instituted under Díaz's regime (chapter 2). Under the "learned guidance" of experts, Rouskaya "patiently studied the Aztec civilization" in preparation for choreographing her mestizo works.[99] The writer Clitandro and entourage visited the dancer at her hotel, where she showed them drawings of stage sets and decorations by Carlos E. González, an artist with a "solid vernacular culture" capable of combining "exquisite taste and profound aesthetic sentiment."[100] Acknowledging the impossibility of creating accurate historical representations, González admitted that even if faithfully reproduced, Aztec dresses displayed on codices and archeological reliefs would lack sensuality.[101] Thus, the sets and dresses for Rouskaya would not be reproductions of historical truth. Instead, the goal of these "polychromatic and suggestive" stylized decorative elements was to create an "attractive exoticism,"[102] to "theatricalize, give color and luster to the spectacle,"[103] to highlight Rouskaya's "irradiating beauty" and "eurythmic figure."[104]

González reproduced colonialist tropes that romanticized "dead Indians" as members of great civilizations while implying that "live Indians" no longer existed or did not have the same cultural value. It was the indigenous imagined in a glorious distant past, not in the present, representing a source of cultural raw materials readily available for rediscovery and reconstitution by the modernist artist's creative imagination. González suggested that instead of futilely trying to reproduce faithful representations of movements from the "extinguished races," Rouskaya "must *feel* the civilization of the "época precortesiana" [pre-Cortesian epoch] (emphasis added).[105] This avant-garde exoticizing spectacle was not intended to produce mimetic visual representations of Aztec civilization with any sort of "authenticity," as had been the goal in the 1910 Centenario History Parade (chapter 2). Instead, the synergy of theatrical elements and Rouskaya's

[99] Ibid.
[100] Clitandro, "'Danzas Aztecas' de Norka Rouskaya," *El universal*, January 18, 1919, 7.
[101] Quoted in ibid.
[102] Orion, "Norka Rouskaya resucitara el pasado artístico de la raza azteca," *El universal*, February 1, 1919, 3.
[103] González quoted in Clitandro, "'Danzas Aztecas' de Norka," 7.
[104] Orion, "Norka Rouskaya resucitara el pasado," 3.
[105] Quoted in Clitandro, "'Danzas Aztecas' de Norka," 7. "Pre-Cortesian" refers to the period before the conquest of Mexico by the Spanish.

presupposed ability to *feel* the ancient civilization would produce a metonymic evocation of "Aztecness."[106] Although knowing that historical accuracy was not possible because of the temporal distance between the past and present and that Aztec imagery lacked "sensual" appeal, these modernist artists believed it possible for a white, European dancing body to tap into a temporality enabling embodiments of the *spirit* of the Aztec, its ontology and subjectivity. In so doing, they could "resurrect the artistic past of the Aztec race," as a newspaper reported[107] (Figures 3.6 and 3.7).

This indigenized theatrical production—dance, scenery, and music—interacted with other expressive practices, helping institute *mestizaje* as national cultural discourse reflecting transnational influences. The Mexican Arnulfo Miramontes and the Antillean Alberto Flachebba composed the music for Rouskaya's piece. Flachebba moved to Mexico early in the 1900s and was known for combining "modern techniques" with colonial and indigenized themes in works such as the opera *El indiano* and a ballet with choruses titled *Quetzalcoatl*.[108] As if acknowledging the music's resonances with the country's colonial and *mestizo* history, Orion noted the de-essentialized nature of pieces like *El indiano* and its composer.[109] The writer praised this work as a "gem" to be added to the national "repertoire of lyrical jewels," even if Flachebba, noting his Caribbean otherness, was an "Antillean pearl."[110] A diversity of local and international artists contributed to "modernizing" the nationalist artistic repertoire. As they choreographed their exoticizing musings of Aztec "dead Indians," they simultaneously constructed their subjectivity as modern artists.

Forging Nation: Rouskaya's Greco-Roman-Aztec(ized) Modernity

National Museum director Manuel Gamio praised González's scenic designs for effectively evoking the Aztec epoch, even in the theater context. The influential Gamio had studied at the Mexican School of American Archeology, founded under Díaz's regime with the support of foreign universities and notable anthropologists, such as Franz Boas (chapter 2). In 1916, three years before

---

[106] For a theory of different modes of representation, see Susan L. Foster, *Reading Dancing: Bodies and Subjects in Contemporary American Dance* (Berkeley: University of California Press, 1986).
[107] Orion, "Norka Rouskaya Resucitara," 3.
[108] "Indiano" or "Indiana" refers to an "Indian" from various cultures. It also references someone from Spain who traveled to colonized lands in the Americas seeking fortunes before returning to their country. Quetzalcoatl is a Nahuatl word that means "feathered serpent" and refers to a central deity in Mesoamerican religions. In Aztec mythology, Quetzalcoatl is the god of wind and learning.
[109] "Norka Rouskaya resucitara el pasado," 3.
[110] Ibid.

Figure 3.6 Article announcing that Norka Rouskaya will resurrect the artistic past of the Aztec race. Orion, "Norka Rouskaya resucitará el pasado Artístico de la raza azteca," *El universal*, February 1, 1919, 3. Public Domain, Courtesy of Biblioteca Miguel Lerdo de Tejada de la Secretaría de Hacienda y Crédito Público.

Rouskaya's collaboration with Mexican artists and intellectuals versed in "vernacular cultures," Gamio published *Forjando patria: Pro-Nacionalismo* [Forging nation: Pro-nationalism].[111] This book set the stage for the future development of Mexican anthropology, archeology, and ethnological studies. Moreover, it was influential to official nationalist projects seeking to assimilate the indigenous into a dominant mestizo culture, a project pursued intently by Vasconcelos between 1921 and 1924 as secretary of education.

[111] Manuel Gamio, *Forjando patria* (México: Librería de Porrúa Hermanos, 1916).

ESTABLISHING A MESTIZO NATION 149

Figure 3.7 Article announcing Norka Rouskaya's Aztec Dances. Clitandro, "Las 'Danzas Aztecas' de Norka Rouskaya," *El universal*, January 18, 1919, 7. Public Domain, Courtesy of Biblioteca Miguel Lerdo de Tejada de la Secretaría de Hacienda y Crédito Público.

Arguing against evolutionism, Gamio advocated for the revalorization of indigenous cultures. He asserted that "the indian . . . has intellectual aptitudes comparable to any race."[112] However, vestiges of liberal positivism remained in some of his somewhat patronizing propositions. He admitted that "[the Indian] is timid, lacks energy, [and] aspirations and lives always afraid of the humiliation and derision by 'people of reason,' the white man."[113] Gamio called for

[112] Ibid., 32.
[113] Ibid.

efforts to convince the indigenous in "simple and objective" ways that *his* "innate fear" no longer had reasonable foundation because *he* had become a "brother who [would] never again be humiliated."[114] In other words, Gamio, Rouskaya, and collaborators—as well as Pavlova and Valencia—tried to narrow the gap between indigenous peoples in the distant past and the present as they reimagined them within the mestizo national body politic. By "resuscitating the artistic past of the Aztec race,"[115] Rouskaya's "vernacular dances" helped produce the postrevolutionary context in which intellectuals and artists appropriated Mesoamerican imagery and knowledge while forging a new *patria*, a renewed national subjectivity. As she did in Peru, her transnational dancing body participated in processes of nation-building in Mexico.

Rouskaya's white European body, albeit with much less time in Mexico than some of her national and international collaborators, tapped into various temporalities and cultural repertoires, producing a mestizo modernity that embodied two "ancient" cultures. Orion offered an interesting interpretation of Rouskaya in one of her "Aztec" dresses (Figure 3.8). The critic noted her "warrior's tunic, a radiant aureole on her forehead holding an iridescent plumed headdress, one hand firmly holding an oval shield [and the other] a truncheon that would replace the *puñal* [dagger] [with which], as if in Hellenic sword dances (*xiphism*), the dancer [Rouskaya] simulates an attack on her adversary."[116] As one can infer from the Hellenic evocations, the description mixes cultural codes. The confluence of referents intensifies as Orion interprets the performative implications of the dancer's kinetic actions contextualized by what she is wearing. "Dressed like this," Orion writes, "Norka [Rouskaya] makes one think of an Aztec reincarnation of *salios romanos* [Roman Salians], [dance] priests of Mars, who rather than officiate before the Latin god's altar, elevate their prayers to the abstract Teotl [god] of the Mexica."[117]

Rouskaya's modernist *mestizaje* embodies a multiplicity of corporeal expressions and temporal dimensions: she was frequently perceived as Russian but was Swiss-Italian, she collaborated with cosmopolitan international artists and Mexicans (who were born in Mexico and educated in other countries), and her work produced embodiments of the Aztecs while citing the Romans, evoking the Roman god Mars to praise the *Mexica* god Teotl. Rather than attempting to blur or erase sources, as often happens with "cultural borrowings," this appropriation of disparate elements by a diverse group of artists demands a perceptual apprehension of the coexistence of dissimilar sources. Although culturally

---

[114] Ibid., 33
[115] Orion, "Norka Rouskaya resucitara el pasado," 3.
[116] Ibid.
[117] Ibid. *Mexicas* were Nahua people who founded and inhabited important cities such as Tenochtitlán and Tlatelolco, part of the Aztec Empire.

Figure 3.8 Rouskaya dressed as an Aztec warrior. Alvaro de Alhamar, "Norka Rouskaya se va," *El universal*, January 13, 1919, 3. Public Domain, Courtesy of Biblioteca Miguel Lerdo de Tejada de la Secretaría de Hacienda y Crédito Público.

different, in the critic's mind, the European and the Mesoamerican coexist on an equal plane.

Contextualized by conventions of theatrical representation and a discursive revalorization of the indigenous, this culturally inclusive modernist production echoes Gamio's assertion that "the indian ... has intellectual aptitudes comparable to any race" and thus could coexist along with " 'people of reason,' the white man."[118] Rouskaya's European, white female body participated in this revalorization of the indigenous while her Mexican collaborators' "knowledge" of Mesoamerican cultures lent some legitimacy to her Aztec dance.

[118] Gamio, *Forjando patria*, 32.

Rouskaya's indigenized avant-garde work fused exoticized citations of the Aztec and Roman "ancient" civilizations as the armed phase of the revolution began subsiding, and Mexico reconstructed its cultural identity. Her dance appropriated imagery from the "glorious" indigenous past, attempting to revalorize its existence in the present by presenting Mesoamerican indigeneity alongside ancient Roman culture. This form of mestizo modernism simultaneously embodied Mexico's revolutionary de/colonizing efforts and the country's neo/colonial histories.

Rouskaya and the Transnational Life of the Aztec

As in Pavlova's case, many expected Rouskaya to serve as a legitimizing agent helping to spread Mexican culture internationally. El Abate de Mendoza hoped that as Rouskaya toured her Aztec dance outside Mexico, she could show "the world an aspect of Mexico's inexhaustible beauty."[119] However, the writer clarified that it was not a matter of exporting Mexican dances (read "traditional") but "theatrical dance, cosmopolitan art, [with] matiz Mexicano [Mexican character]."[120] In fact, "the Aztec" as a stereotype of Mexican mestizo modernity began to have currency internationally in 1889 during the Porfiriato when a group of Mexican cultural architects participated in the Paris World's Fair, the Universal Exposition. There, they built a neo-Aztec temple and created other related art and history productions and publications.[121] Toward the end of the Porfirian era, these and other nationalist artists, including Jorge Enciso, inspired the centrality of the Aztec and other Mesoamerican cultures that postrevolutionary governments adopted.

Several years after the Paris Universal Exposition, the United States consolidated its imperialistic dominance, which included an increased interest in intercultural knowledge and understanding inside and outside the United States.[122] Indeed, "spectacularized" Aztec representation by filmmakers such as Cecil B. DeMille and choreographers like Ted Shawn resonated with the Manifest

---

[119] "El arte creador de Norka Rouskaya," *El universal ilustrado*, April 1926, 36–37.

[120] Ibid.

[121] For an analysis of Mexico's participation in this World's Fair and others after the Mexican Revolution, see Mauricio Tenorio-Trillo, *Mexico at the World's Fair: Crafting a Modern Nation* (Berkeley: University of California Press, 1996). See also chapter 1 of Manuel R. Cuellar, *Choreographing Mexico: Festive Performances and Dancing Histories of a Nation* (Austin: University of Texas Press, 2022).

[122] After 1900, these efforts were institutionalized by privately funded organizations such as the Institute of International Education and the Carnegie Corporation. Helen Delpar, *The Enormous Vogue of Things Mexican: Cultural Relations between the United States and Mexico, 1920–1935* (Tuscaloosa: University of Alabama Press, 1992).

Destiny ideology with which the United States justified its "sacred duty to expand across the North American continent."[123] In the early 1920s, "the Aztec" as a theme became associated with the United States to the point that Russian-born dance artists like Mikhail Fokine, Vera Fokina, and Theodore Kosloff "redefine Aztec exoticism as evidence of the 'Americanness' of their works developed for new-world audiences."[124]

In 1929, Ted Shawn, a pioneer of modern dance in the United States, and 100 students from his Denishawn dance school participated in "Aztec Gold," a massive pageant with 1,000 performers at New York's Madison Square Garden, which "was transformed into the capital of ancient Mexico."[125] The benefit event's massive cast included socialites, artists, and philanthropists from Mexico and the United States, many of them exuberantly dressed as indigenous people. The main roster of characters featured Moctezuma, the Aztec emperor, alongside a Hopi Indian chief. Shawn and his dancers performed Native American dances.[126] With all its exoticism, "Aztec Gold" assumed an inclusive category of representation that referenced a pan-indigeneity between Mexico and the United States in a time in which the two nation-states continued to mend their strained relations caused by the Mexican Revolution.

Rouskaya then participated in the development of the Aztec as a stereotype of Mexican indigeneity early in the postrevolutionary period. She did so during Mexico's resurgent interest in Mesoamerican cultures as an integral part of national imaginaries that expanded to other countries like the United States. While she and her collaborators focused on resurrecting the Aztecs, Valencia gained inspiration from the Incas of Peru for a work that had resonances with Mexican audiences and critics. While the "Aztec Gold" pageant conveyed a generalized indigeneity, functioning as an (exoticized) indigenous link between the United States and Mexico (i.e., via native American and Aztec dances), I suggest that Valencia's Inca dance symbolized a Latin American pan-indigeneity when performed in Mexico in the mid-1920s.

---

[123] Weeks, quoted in K. Mitchell Snow, "Orientalized Aztecs: Observations on the Americanization of Theatrical Dance," *Dance Research Journal* 51, no. 2 (August 2019): 35.
[124] Snow, Ibid., 36.
[125] Delpar, "The Enormous Vogue," vii.
[126] Ibid. For an analysis of how Shawn's Native American dances challenged and reproduced aspects of the US federal Indian policies of the 1920s and 1930s, see Jacqueline Shea Murphy, *The People Have Never Stopped Dancing: Native American Modern Dance Histories* (Minneapolis: University of Minnesota Press, 2007).

Artistic Collaborations and Colonial Affectivity: Valencia's Inca-Inspired Latin American Pan-Indigeneity

On January 1, 1919, *El universal* featured an article reminiscing about Carmen Tórtola Valencia's arrival in Mexico City over a year earlier. The note remembered how Valencia transformed the theater stage into an "opulent and sumptuous palace of artistic emotions," where audiences' astonished eyes would appreciate the *"eximia"* [illustrious] artist's legendary choreographies.[127] The newspaper lauded Valencia's virtues as a dancer and her capacity to aesthetically probe historical dances, a characteristic of the "great intuitive temperaments."[128] While exalting Valencia's finely fused spirituality and body as the "most suggestive choreographic miracle of modern times,"[129] the article anticipated the artist's departure after her final show early in January—a month with a fleeting confluence of international touring dancers in the Mexican capital. The following discussion focuses on what happened before and after this brief window of time in which Pavlova, Rouskaya, and Valencia coincided in Mexico City early in 1919. Following Valencia's trajectory from Europe to Lima and again to Mexico City in 1926 illuminates the cultural and power dynamics that enabled the creation of her pan–Latin American choreography of indigeneity and the colonial logics it embodied.

Valencia built her fame by performing exotic representations of dances from various cultures for her European audiences. Her repeated and prolonged visits to Latin America contributed to the Spanish-born, London-raised dancer's reconceptualized and extended repertoire of exotic dances.[130] Valencia, who had no formal dance training, reformulated early twentieth-century audiences' expectations of dancers and their level of technical proficiency. Her rise to international fame may owe a debt to the fact that her primarily upper-class audiences were not always knowledgeable enough to evaluate the technical proficiency of the dance forms Valencia reinterpreted. Undoubtedly, the potent expressive physicality of her moving body—dressed and surrounded by costumes and sceneries evoking mysterious cultures—also appealed to her cosmopolitan admirers.[131]

---

[127] *El universal*, "Todavía Tórtola Valencia," January 1, 1919, 8.

[128] Ibid. Other Mexican writers participated in producing this narrative of Valencia as having a unique intuition with which she could "assimilate" historical knowledge into dance representations. For instance, on May 1, 1918, Apolodoro characterized Valencia as "the dancer of historical intuition," quoted in Iris Garland, "Early Modern Dance in Spain: Tórtola Valencia, Dancer of the Historical Intuition," *Dance Research Journal* 29, no. 2 (Autumn 1997): 11.

[129] El universal, "Todavía Tórtola Valencia," 8.

[130] Michelle Clayton, "Touring History: Tórtola Valencia between Europe and the Americas," *Dance Research Journal* 44, no. 1 (Summer 2012): 28–49.

[131] Most published comments about Valencia (not unlike those about Pavlova and Rouskaya) expressed hyperbolic admiration for her performances. In the spirit of modernist literary experiments in Latin America from the mid-nineteenth century through the early twentieth,

She indeed fueled Western consumers' fascination for nonwhite exotic others, particularly Oriental/ized cultural products and bodies. Circulating as part of a market in which exoticism produced various forms of capital (i.e., money, objects, affects, passion), Valencia contributed to neocolonial projects while also playing a role in the formation of Western cosmopolitan subjectivities.[132] In this context, *strangeness*, as an Orientalized aesthetic approach in Valencia's performances (and those of others, like Ruth St. Denis in the United States), resonated with expectations of modern/ist art and its innovative daringness as avant-garde.[133] In Mexico, Valencia's experiments with the strangeness of Orientalism and other forms of exoticism served as modernizing technology. With it, she produced a mestizo modernism that had a Latin American pan-indigenist appeal to some Mexican audiences.

Through embodying exotic cultures, Valencia—much like Pavlova and Rouskaya—activated the affective link with audiences already cultivated over the years as members of an international class of social similars with shared values. This imagined collective of cosmopolitan internationalists helped construct the iconic status of specific bodies enacting their class worldview and values through exchange between dancers on stage and consuming these dances in the theater. In Valencia's case, the circulation of her distinctive expressive physicality as she crossed geographical and ideological spaces demonstrated her class status's power in constructing her artistic persona. Understanding affective

writers, some of them established literary figures, customarily employed (hyperbolic) poetic prose to describe dancers' performances and personalities. Valencia, for her part, was active in strategizing how to get commentators to write positively about her (Garland, "Early Modern Dance in Spain, and Clayton, "Touring History"). Although these are subjective accounts by writers who saw these dancers perform, they remain some of the primary sources from which one can infer the power of these dance artists' expressive dancing bodies, among other aspects of their interactions with people and places across Latin America.

[132] For an analysis of exoticism as part of neocolonial maneuverings specifically concerning tango, as a case study, and its associated production, circulation, and consumption of passion (affect, emotion, desire) as intangible currency, see Savigliano, *Tango and the Political*.

[133] See André Lepecki for an argument about how the *strangeness* of (contemporary) "experimental performance" enables avant-garde artists to engage in "moments, or singularities when a choreopolitical operation into neoliberal conditioning undoes them [neoliberalism's conditioning forces]," from within." *Singularities: Dance in the Age of Performance* (Abingdon: Routledge, 2016), 22. Although in a different historical moment, this argument resonates with what follows in my discussion insofar as the conceptualization of strangeness, as a referent for the unfamiliar, is not the only option for creating avant-garde art. One may argue that innovation and experimentation in the production of embodied mestizo modernities (as alternatives to white Western modernity) include, rather than attempt to transcend, elements or referents recognizable as belonging to a specific culture, even if deemed stereotypical (e.g., a Mesoamerican headdress). In this dance-making approach, the familiar is made strange to different extents. From this perspective, innovative, experimental performances—those which attempt to transcend markers of difference and those that highlight them and make them "strange"—have the potential to activate artists' capacity to negotiate (perhaps not entirely "undo") the forces that shape their subjectivities within the specific contexts in which they exist (neoliberalism in the case of Lepecki's analysis and neocolonialism in postrevolutionary Mexico in this chapter).

and ideological aspects in these identity formation processes illustrate how a consolidated European artist like Valencia served as a legitimizing agent in Peru and Mexico. Discussing the development of Valencia's artistic subjectivity and the performance of her Inca-inspired dance in Mexico expands further on the idea that modernist art-making and colonial histories intertwine with identity formation processes (i.e., racial, social, national).

Artistic and Ideological Aspects in the Construction of the Modernist Artist

After her 1908 debut in London, where she had been reared and educated, Valencia became a sensation on the music hall circuit for performing the much-in-vogue Oriental dances. However, she would find different music hall audiences in Madrid. Upon arriving in the Spanish capital for her debut in December 1911 at the Teatro Romea, Valencia was ill-prepared for skeptical music hall regulars. Many of them used obscene language to express their discontent with her abstract, expressive dance style.[134] Cultural elites in Madrid did not attend venues of such ill repute. However, Valencia's fame in other European cities, and her background as an educated woman in French and English boarding schools, contributed to her recognition as a social similar. She quickly established a close relationship with the local press and the *modernista* elites. A determined contingent of authorities on matters of (modern) aesthetics joined forces to turn one of their own, who had triumphed in major European cities, into a representative embodiment of Spanish sophistication. They hoped that Valencia's fame could serve as a refutation of the barbarism with which other countries in the region often charged Spain,[135] as well as a rejection of the country's perceived status as an "exotic other" (a status that would last until Franco's death in 1975).[136] These cultural architects contributed their talents through various media by writing hyperbolic poems about the dancer, analyzing her repertoire, publishing interviews with her, circulating prurient images and descriptions of her body, and highlighting her success on European stages.[137]

In a strategic appropriation of Teatro Romea, these cultural authorities, Valencia's admirers, exerted their influence to raise prices and exclude the working-class audiences that generally frequented the venue.[138] By performing exclusively for the upper classes, Valencia consolidated her position among

---

[134] Garland, "Early Modern Dance in Spain."
[135] Clayton, "Touring History."
[136] Garland, "Early Modern Dance in Spain."
[137] Clayton, "Touring History."
[138] Ibid.

ESTABLISHING A MESTIZO NATION 157

Madrid's highest social strata. With sponsorship by the Association of Writers and Artists, the Circle of Fine Arts, the Academy of Fine Arts, and the *Ateneo* [Athenaeum] of Madrid, she enchanted her elite audiences. At her induction to the *Ateneo*, an "elite cultural institution of elected artists, writers, and intellectuals," she gave the institution's first-ever dance performance on January 24, 1913.[139] The collective efforts to discursively manufacture Valencia as a modern artist and (her) dance as high art had a legitimizing effect, as evidenced by one critic's assertion that her dances were "elegant, serious, religious, and not appropriate for the masses."[140] It was these qualities of elegance, seriousness, and religiousness (or spirituality) that authorized Valencia's performance of (Eastern, Oriental, exoticized) sensuality. While many appreciated these artistic characteristics as progressive avant-garde art, others considered them immoral transgression.[141]

These classist assumptions intersected with Valencia's gender in constructing her artistic persona and status. That Valencia was a woman also endeared her to the (primarily male) Spanish elites. Their musings about the Oriental within Hispanic literature and poetry placed "woman" as reflective of the archetypal attributes of mystery and irrationality personified by "priestesses, pagan temptresses, sorceresses, and assassins."[142] Valencia's dancing body corporealized Spanish (male) *modernistas*' Orientalizing desires, even if her personal sexual desire was not for men, as many thought. Moreover, when Valencia eventually added Spanish-themed dances to her Oriental repertoire, she did not include the customary flamenco castanets or *taconeo* (rhythmic heel stomping). Unlike famous Spanish dancers like La Argentina, Valencia did not perform "authentic" regional dances; instead, she performed "Spanish impressions" through her dances, effectively embodying the "Spanish spirit."[143] While Valencia cultivated her artistic subjectivity and status in Madrid, her exoticized gendered body rendered the *strangeness* of her *singular* dancing in aesthetic terms, as part of an internationally itinerant European modernist avant-garde.[144]

[139] Garland, "Early Modern Dance in Spain," 9.
[140] Ibid.
[141] Ibid. For discussions about how the confluence of aesthetics, sensuality, and spiritual discourses functioned in producing modern artistic subjectivity and the legitimization of dance as a form of high art for artists such as Ruth St. Denis and Isadora Duncan, see Jane Desmond, "Dancing Out the Difference: Cultural Imperialism and Ruth St. Denis's 'Radha' of 1906," *Signs* 17, no. 1 (Autumn 1991): 28–49; Ann Daly, *Done into Dance: Isadora Duncan in America* (Middletown, CT: Wesleyan University Press, 2002; orig. ed. Bloomington: Indiana University Press, 1995); Foster, "Closets Full of Dances: Modern Dance's Performance of Masculinity and Sexuality," in *Dancing Desires: Choreographing Sexualities on and off the Stage*, ed. Jane Desmond (Madison: University of Wisconsin Press, 2001), 147–207.
[142] Garland, "Early Modern Dance in Spain," 9.
[143] Ibid.
[144] For an account of Valencia's contributions to the development of early (dance) modernism in Western Europe, Spain, and Latin America, see ibid. For an argument about how the case of Valencia and other "early modern dancers" can serve as case studies to revise dance history and trace

The Modernist Artist and the Colonial Logic of Cultural and Material Extractivism

Valencia's contributions to modernist discourse and practices in Europe and Latin America paralleled the relational logics of (neo)colonial intercontinental histories. Her aesthetic approaches to modernist dance-making resembled colonial logics of extraction and appropriation of cultural and natural resources. Although the view of Rouskaya was that she could "feel" and embody an abstracted Aztec spirit by "patiently" studying this Mesoamerican civilization under her collaborators' "learned guidance,"[145] Valencia claimed the ability to get a "feeling" for "ancient" cultures by interacting directly with actual objects from the past. She avidly collected textiles and all sorts of objects from places she visited. One newspaper writer justified this practice by saying that she was not a "vulgar collector" but an "artist who seeks information and surrounds herself with objects to evoke in her the voices of the past."[146] In other words, the accumulation of objects served as an archive from which the *sophisticated artist*—unlike the *vulgar collector*—could source materials to make contemporary art capable of capturing and evoking *the essence* of the past.

As she looked at her favored objects and fabrics in the privacy of her home, Valencia saw in them a life, a volition of their own. In an interview, she claimed that antique fabrics suggested the most exotic dances to her and asserted that those fabrics had a soul and life.[147] She reasoned: how could they not, if "they are in constant contact with our bodies."[148] This rhetorical relationship between the body and the soul of a culture, woven in the threads of historical fabric, enabled the modernist artist to assume "legitimate" access to an "authentic" essence. She could then inscribe it on her body and within her soul to express it in contemporary embodiments.

Valencia's extensive collection of objects, which served as sources for representations of "ancient" people's cultural "soul," exceeded merely artistic purposes. After one of her tours in Latin America, she returned to Spain "from Méjico *satisfechísima* [greatly satisfied]," bringing within her heart the applause of her audiences while also carrying "twenty-five trunks full of beautiful

---

"cross-cultural modernists entanglements," see Clayton, "Touring History," 46. See also Clayton "Modernism's Moving Bodies."

[145] González, quoted in Clitandro (1919, January 13, 7); Alhama (1919, 3).
[146] *La prensa*, October 12, 1921, quoted in Isabel Bargalió Sánchez and Monserrat Bargalió Sánchez "¿Colección o inspiración? Los textiles americanos de Carmen Tórtola Valencia / Collection or Inspiration? Carmen Tórtola Valencia's Latin American Textiles," *Datatèxtil*, no. 22 (2010): 33.
[147] *El comercio*, February 6, 1922 (Lima, Peru), quoted in Bargalió Sánchez and Bargalió Sánchez, "¿Colección o Inspiración?," 33–36.
[148] Ibid., 33.

costumes and a multitude of objets d'art [as well as] a few thousands of dollars, which add to her already large fortune."[149] Indeed, Valencia's trunks increased in number from thirty to more than seventy, weighing 2,300 kilograms, while touring Latin America.[150] Valencia's modernist dance practices embodied avant-garde aesthetic innovations and cultural collaborations. They also embodied a logic of extraction and appropriation justified as the product of her capitalist artistic entrepreneurship. Indeed, the accumulation of her cultural and financial capital was also the result of her and her assistants's arduous physical labor as an artist and as laborers respectively.[151] Her work reflected the close interrelation between her modernist artistic practice and the forces of capitalism and neocolonialism.

These processes of extraction and appropriation, which often were part of developing modernist avant-garde aesthetic practices, also functioned as mechanisms of *access and capture*. In the realm of representation, ostensibly unique inner faculties enabled (dance) artists like Valencia (and Rouskaya) to transcend time, thereby accessing the past to capture its purported essence or "spirit." In contemporary embodied renditions, this type of artistic agent could communicate to equally receptive audiences endowed with similar perceptual faculties. As members of a racially diverse international class of socially similar people, dancers and their patrons could establish this aesthetically mediated communication enabled by shared ideological, social, and cultural values. These forms of danced cultural practices served as a mechanism for producing artistic subjectivity, material wealth, privileged status, and membership in an imagined community.

Reconstructing the Inca Indigenous Soul: Valencia and the Peruvian Avant-Garde

As was also true for other dancers consecrated in Europe, Valencia's tours through Latin America, including Mexico, illuminate these simultaneous functions of modernist art: the coexistence of aesthetics and coloniality. In 1916, Valencia toured Latin America for the first time. Upon her arrival in Lima, her associates—the Colónida writers—invited her to perform at a cemetery. She declined, claiming to have other pressing commitments (Rouskaya would take them up on this proposal the following year).[152] While Valencia could not join

---

[149] P. Sorel, *La lucha*, March 14, 1919, quoted in ibid., 33.
[150] Clayton, "Touring History."
[151] Clayton notes the exhausting demands of Valencia's touring schedules, including transportation and handling of large quantities of stage materials for her performances (ibid.).
[152] José-Carlos Mariátegui (son), "El baile de Norka Rouskaya."

her hosts for this performative action, she joined in their discursive revalorization of popular cultures and indigenous peoples (both past and present). They intended their transnational collaborative efforts to echo revolutionary gestures in twentieth-century Latin American construction of *patrias nuevas* [new nations].

Like Pavlova and Rouskaya, Valencia collaborated with artists, intellectuals, and government officials invested in populist initiatives, while also performing in public and private venues for the upper classes. As she imbued herself in the *mestizaje* of liberal populism and bourgeois elitism in Lima, she pledged to choreograph a dance with indigenous themes. Although it took her nine years to fulfill that promise, Valencia performed a short indigenous-theme dance in various places, including New York City. However, being an astute co-creator of her persona, she used those opportunities to produce and circulate her staged photos costumed as a prototypical representation of Latin American indigeneity.

In a similar process experienced by Rouskaya in Mexico City, Valencia's collaborations with local experts in Lima enabled her to arduously study indigenous cultures to access, capture, and corporealize their ostensible essence and *soul*. Valencia garnered the support and guidance of people such as composer José María del Valle Riestra, who was experimenting with Peruvian music. She also studied ceramics and costumes at the Museo Larco and the Museo Histórico Nacional [National Museum of History].[153] Lima reporters lauded Valencia's efforts. A writer for *El comercio* claimed that "the famous dancer has admirably documented the life and customs of the imperial Incas, to such an extent, that if she so desired she could write a book on the subject that would produce a sensation."[154] Perhaps as one of her many fabricated stories,[155] Valencia claimed that the Casa Municipal [Municipal House] gave her complete access to an authentic Inca war costume.[156] She claimed feeling the "spirit" of the person who had used the dress in ancient times when she wore it.[157] In this brand of mestizo avant-garde art, the valorization of authenticity continued as a legitimizing element. However, it was not based merely on faithful replication of the source. Instead, authenticity rested in an evocative physical enactment of what it meant *to be* part of the (imagined) source, an enactment of the abstract/ed *cultural essence* that composed the source, its purported soul, or spirit.

In 1925, nine years after expressing her initial intentions, Valencia premiered *La Danza Incaica Guerrera* [The Inca War Dance or Inca Warrior Dance] at the Teatro Forero in Lima during her second tour of South America (1921–1925). Apparently, Valencia consulted writings by Inca Garcilaso de la Vega

---

[153] Clayton, "Touring History."
[154] September 19, 1925, quoted in Garland, "Early Modern Dance in Spain," 13.
[155] Ibid.
[156] *Heraldo de Madrid*, March 27, 1926, in ibid.
[157] *El día gráfico*, March 31, 1926, Barcelona, Spain, in ibid.

(1539–1616), a mestizo of indigenous and Spanish descent who chronicled the demise of the Mesoamerican empire incited by the Spanish and the death of the last Inca ruler, Huayna Capac, in the early 1490s.[158] Through a series of "exotic sculptural poses," some static and some in movement sequences, Valencia embodied Capac's daughter.[159] This characterization was at times corporealized, with "fiery" physicality, motions of a spear, and her father's warlike spirit; she eventually turned into the "grateful daughter" embracing her returning "imagined father" with repeated kisses on his cheeks.[160] Valencia's female dancing body thus performed archetypal gendered *mestizaje* through choreographies of aggression and emotional solace associated with masculinity and femininity respectively.

While responding to these Latin American–embodied mestizo modernisms, choreographed by dance artists such as Valencia, writers used terms like *soul* and *spirit* to link the present with the past rhetorically. As if echoing themes in Mexican critics' evaluations of Pavlova's and Rouskaya's mestizo dances, Peruvian commentators praised Valencia's work for tapping into the Oriental and Latin American past. A writer for *El comercio* in Lima asked, "with someone who has so fully understood the artistic soul of the Orient, why should it be a surprise that her soul should also have opened itself to that of our glorious Inca race?"[161] The writer implies the possibility of a direct soul-to-soul connection between two "premodern" exotic others (Oriental and indigenous) from a distant past, through the soul of a modern artist in the present. Another commentator admitted that although Valencia's Inca War Dance did not reconstruct Inca history, "she expresses the concept that the artist has of the soul of our ancestors. And she expresses it [in] an impeccable manner. This dance is the psychological synthesis of an omnipotent people."[162]

The creative license that allowed the modern dance artist to create contemporary renditions of the soul, and the psychology of the Inca people, resulted from Valencia's "penetrating spirit" and her "own intelligent observations."[163] At the same time, her collaborations with local artists, intellectuals, and government officials, coupled with her social privilege and European lineage, enabled her creative efforts. While she toured Latin America, the confluence of these forces allowed her to expand her repertoire of approaches to making embodied mestizo art. By relying on Orientalizing and indigenizing dance practices, she bridged the "ancient" past and the "modern" present, a mestizo temporality in itself. As

---

[158] Ibid.
[159] Ibid., 13
[160] Ibid.
[161] September 19, 1925, quoted in Clayton, "Touring History: Tórtola Valencia," 46.
[162] *El comercio*, September 18, 1925, Lima, quoted in Garland, "Early Modern Dance in Spain," 13.
[163] *El comercio*, September 19, 1925, Lima, quoted in ibid., 15.

these aspects of Valencia's artistic trajectory show, she developed a corporeality of multiplicity that enabled her to resonate with notions of indigeneity as a vital representational element in Peru. Her indigenized work also resonated with Mexico's construction of postrevolutionary mestizo modernity.

Performing "the Soul of Indigenous America": Valencia's Inca Dance in Mexico

Valencia first arrived in Mexico City in late 1917 to stay for over a year. She, like Pavlova and Rouskaya, rapidly established relationships with and garnered the admiration of the press and cultural and economic elites. That same year, after the ratification of a new Constitution under President Venustiano Carranza, the armed phase of the Mexican Revolution (1910–1920) began to wane. Valencia's Mexican fellow artists responded to the revolutionary rhetoric of the era, sometimes in accord and at other times in opposition. Together, all these voices participated in the discursive revalorization of indigenous populations (both living and dead) as fundamental in forming a modern nation-state.

In this mestizo nationalist context, resonant with that of other Latin American countries like Peru, a Mexican newspaper tacitly reproduced the neocolonial logic that informed recurrent scenarios of discovery.[164] Thinking about European artists who toured across "Hispanic America," the writer noted Valencia's intentions to find in the "New World" the right music to communicate a "complete vision" for an indigenous dance.[165] Writing for *Novedades*, Luis de Larroder contended that it was in the Inca cultural repertoire that Valencia's "nomadic and selective spirit" found the "character, delicacy, and elevation" she sought for the creation of a dance that could embody and communicate "the soul of indigenous America."[166]

Almost ten years later, in 1926, a year after Valencia premiered the Inca War Dance in Lima, she danced it in Mexico City. Witnessing the work, Antonio de Hoyos y Vinent asserted that he could see a "strong condensed vision" of what the American version of Venice could be: Tenochtitlan, the capital of the Aztec Empire.[167] The writer *saw* in Valencia's choreographic evocation of the Inca the specter of the Aztec emperor Moctezuma and that of the supreme *Mexica* pontiff Tehuatecotl. The critic also claimed to *feel* the air of the Peruvian Andes, where

---

[164] Taylor, *The Archive and the Repertoire*.
[165] Luis de Larroder, *Novedades*, December 1917, quoted in Bargalió Sánchez and Bargalió Sánchez, "¿Colección o Inspiración?," 46.
[166] Ibid.
[167] Antonio de Hoyos y Vinent, "Las rutas ideales de la bailarina de los pies desnudos," *Revista de revistas*, 1926, quoted in Bargalió Sánchez and Bargalió Sánchez, "¿Colección o inspiración?," 47.

the condor flies and where the Son and the Virgins of the Sun coexisted with the Inca people's sacred humanity.[168] The essentializing discourse of a homogeneous Latin American indigenous soul thus continued to have currency in Mexico. Together with international artists like Valencia (and Pavlova and Rouskaya), national collaborators and writers cultivated an affective relationship with their sources of inspiration. While doing so, they constructed an imagined archetypal class of Latin American indigeneity.

It seems that the ability of the modern artist's soul to connect to the soul of two similar, but not identical, exotic others in a remote past could also communicate to the soul of receptive modern audiences and critics. Perhaps this colonialist affective connection between the dance performance and perceptive interlocutors like De Hoyos resulted from the shared core values among members of an international class of social similars. This idealization of a singular American indigenous race erased the rich diversity of Mesoamerican cultures. Artists, critics, and audiences manufactured an aesthetic discourse that helped them fashion their modern mestizo identities in a country (and continent) where legacies of colonial logics continued to inform their artistic imagination.

As much as Valencia studied Inca ceramics and history, visited archeological sites, and circulated photos of her visits with different ethnic groups to exalt their culture, she also harbored colonialist assumptions. Often, artists like Valencia, who assumed themselves to be modern subjects, tacitly and explicitly considered indigenous people (like the objects of her aestheticized studies) uncivilized barbarians. Valencia shared in an interview with Mexico City's *El universal* that in one of her visits to an indigenous group, she and her entourage were taken captive by "bloodthirsty natives" she could not appease until she danced for them.[169] Valencia may have fabricated this story (as she later claimed), but it reveals her colonialist views of indigenous people and the seemingly civilizing effect that her modern dancing body could have when facing potentially aggressive savages.

Valencia's fascination with Mesoamerican indigenous cultures, informed by her colonialist early twentieth-century European imagination, reflected *colonial affectivity*. Notably, international artists who toured the Americas and their cosmopolitan local collaborators shared this form of affect. Colonial affectivity refers to a genuine admiration for cultural diversity and an interest in learning, borrowing, collaborating, embodying, and in this case representing an Other's culture. However, as Valencia's anecdote above illustrates, a genuinely affective admiration and interest for an Other, based on culture and social class, often coexisted with implicit colonialist assumptions.

---

[168] Ibid.
[169] September 19, 1917, quoted in Clayton, "Touring History," 43.

As a practice of racialized interclass colonization, modernist artists asserted their privileged access to "raw" cultural materials to produce "refined" representations of "exotic" cultures and "humble classes." In so doing, dance artists like Valencia, Pavlova, and Rouskaya and their local collaborators implicitly positioned themselves as culturally superior agents of progress. Together, they advanced civilizing projects that imagined indigenous populations as objects of rescue (chapter 2). While genuinely interested in interacting with indigenous people, who represented contemporaneous embodiments of the "ancient" sources of her artistic imagination, Valencia's (made-up) encounter with the "bloodthirsty natives" enacted a familiar colonial trope.[170] That is, the civilized, cosmopolitan, "modern" artist interfaces with a savage, parochial, "traditional" Other who can only be domesticated and modernized by the transformative power of her modernist artistry. Valencia's complex colonialist affectivity (similar to Pavlova's and Rouskaya's) infused her choreography of pan–Latin American indigeneity as she participated in forging transnational nationalisms in Peru and Mexico.

Nationalizing *Mestizaje*: Establishing the National Dance Repertoire

Looking at international artists like Pavlova, Rouskaya, and Valencia as legitimizing agents illuminates how aspects of colonial legacies informed the development of mestizo artistic practices and individual and collective identities. As Mexican cultural authorities embraced the indigenous while instituting *mestizaje* as a dominant racial and cultural ideology, the three artists created different forms of modernist *mestizaje* that played specific roles in Mexico's postrevolutionary formation. Pavlova's and Rouskaya's mestizo performances of folklore and indigeneity in 1919 helped fuel Mexico's nationalist effervescence, just as Vasconcelos was instituting massive investment in the arts as instruments of the state's ideological apparatus. Rouskaya's Aztec-inspired dance was part of a transnational trend establishing the Aztec as a symbol of pan-indigeneity in Mexico and the United States as the cases of the "Aztec Gold" pageant and works by dancers like Fokine, Fokina, Kosloff, and Shawn suggest. The reception of Valencia's Inca War Dance, performed in Mexico in 1926, reflected the country's position within the Latin American imagination that upheld regional pan-indigeneity as integral to postcolonial national and hemispheric identities.

---

[170] For an example of how the trope of the "bloodthirsty savage" in the Americas has been reproduced and sometimes contested by European travel literature writers and Latin American novelists, respectively, see Lesley Wylie, *Colonial Tropes and Postcolonial Tricks: Rewriting the Tropics in the Novela de la Selva* (Liverpool: Liverpool University Press, 2009).

Mestizo works by Pavlova, Rouskaya, Valencia, and other international artists prompted government officials and critics to advocate for creating a national dance form that could be distinctively Mexican and universal in its appeal. Indeed, mestizos' appropriations of indigenous Mesoamerican symbols, images, and dances will continue to be in the national dance repertoire (e.g., *La Danza del Venado* [the deer dance] from the Yaqui people in Northern Mexico). However, in a country invested in embracing the indigenous while establishing a mestizo state, the *Jarabe Tapatío's mestizaje* best suited revolutionary efforts to modernize a representative "traditional" national culture.

In this context of rising mestizo consciousness, massive audiences gathered to see Pavlova and her company performing the endearing mestizo dance on pointe shoes at places like the Plaza el Toreo. Surely, such an enthusiastic response positioned her as a salient source of inspiration for creating a new dance form. A hopeful González Peña conceded that Pavlova's *Fantasía Mexicana* provided such a "wide perspective that it opens before our eyes, the vast horizons that it represents for the future development of a great and genuinely national art."[171]

Jiménez Rueda admitted that "with our eyes placed on the exterior world, we had not realized the aesthetic import of the jarabe [tapatío], a drama that realizes in its apparent simplicity a mischievous and passionate conflict, just like the soul of our country is."[172] The writer seems to suggest that Pavlova's dancing revealed the rediscovered national soul embodied in the dance that people like him had been unable to see. Similarly, Rodríguez asserted that Pavlova's "miraculous gift of spiritualizing dances . . . has deciphered the secret of our ancestral soul; She has comprehended our emotiveness."[173] Implying a universalist discourse, the writer claimed that "all the tradition of our country lives in the [bodies of the] Russian dancers."[174] He tacitly rationalized the artists' ostensibly de-essentialized mestizo soul as capable of being both Russian and Mexican. The idea of this type of dual mestizo embodiment through dancing—a "raw" Mexican traditional dance "refined" by legitimizing white Russian bodies—sparked interest in developing a dance form that could participate in forging a new mestizo patria.

The half-finished drawing of the *Jarabe Tapatío* at the opening of this chapter (Figure 3.1) represented the incompleteness of a nationalist project that children would finish under Díaz's dictatorial regime in 1910. However, it was under post-Porfiriato revolutionary governance that this project would be institutionalized. As Jóse Vasconcelos arrived at the Ministry of Public Education in 1921, under President Álvaro Obregón (1920–1924), his belief that art was "México's

---

[171] González Peña, "Ana Pavlowa y el baile," 3.
[172] Quoted in Lavalle, "Anna Pavlova y el Jarabe," 649–50.
[173] "La Fantasía Mexicana," 10.
[174] Ibid.

only salvation" characterized his efforts to re-educate the nation's children.[175] His cultural missions researched and disseminated regional dances throughout the country and became part of official educational curricula. The *Jarabe Tapatío*, with its contentious post/colonial history as a marker of varied classes (depending on who danced it and how), became representative of the nationalist dance repertoire. Mexican dance historian Josefina Lavalle noted the paradoxical turn the iconic dance took in early postrevolutionary Mexico:

> the version of el jarabe [tapatío] that had been despised while danced by "Mexican tiples" as part of tandas in theaters [of ill repute] became—via Anna Pavlova—the official *jarabe*, danced by the nation's children as a national emblem—as the Mexican national dance par excellence [and] accepted by the country's educational authorities as didactic material in schools. The jarabe tapatío or national . . . should have been named instead, [the] official jarabe . . . [as] we found it established and "respectable," mingling at festivities with the best of society.[176]

In 1919, the confluence of modernizing rhetoric embedded in aesthetic discourse, and the equally ideological project of mestizo nation-building, enabled Pavlova and her local collaborators to legitimize the *Jarabe Tapatío*. The dance became the cultural connective tissue of a stratified body politic. It brought together the children of the masses and their parents with high-society members into an idealized national imaginary still fragmented by the actual material conditions of different social realities.

As an embodied national emblem central to identity formation processes, the *Jarabe Tapatío* integrated children's and their parents' dancing bodies into efforts to complete the revolution's mestizo modernity project. Indeed, in 1921, only two years after Pavlova's performances of the *Jarabe Tapatío*, hundreds of *chinas poblanas* danced en pointe with their *charros*, the iconic dance as part of festivities commemorating the Mexican War of Independence's end centennial. In 1924, 500 couples performed the *Jarabe Tapatío* during Vasconcelos's inauguration of the National Stadium.[177]

As he established this venue for massive sports and cultural events, Vasconcelos began to think about a dance form that could synthesize high and popular art and bring the masses together as members of a revolutionary nation. He imagined the creation of a nationalist dance form that could be

---

[175] Vasconcelos, quoted in Margarita Tortajada Quiroz, *Danza y poder* (México, DF: Instituto Nacional de Bellas Artes; Centro Nacional de Investigación, Documentación e Información de la Danza José Limón, 1995), 41.
[176] Lavalle, "Anna Pavlova y el Jarabe," 650.
[177] Tortajada Quiroz, "*Danza y poder*," 45.

simultaneously modern and traditional, a dance form like the one created by "the Russian dancers, technically perfect [and] expressive of their own temperament."[178] Pavlova's balleticized *Jarabe Tapatío* and other folkloric dances in her *Fantasía Mexicana* seem to have pointed toward a Mexican high art form akin to Serge Diaghilev's Ballets Russes, one of the most famous ballet companies at the time to whom Vasconcelos alluded.

Despite Vasconcelos's enthusiasm and advocacy for developing a national dance form, the state did not institutionalize professional dance training until the 1930s. As the next chapter shows, state-sponsored dance schools trained the first generations of dancers who worked with national and international choreographers to create a modernized dance form that could embody the Mexican character, the country's "soul," while aspiring to universal appeal. As these dancers, along with government officials, critics, and audiences, debated what constituted dance as a legitimate art form during the 1930s and 1940s, their aesthetic quarrels reflected the national and transnational politics that continued to shape Mexico as a mestizo nation.

[178] Vasconcelos, quoted in ibid., 46.

4
The Making of a Postrevolutionary Modern Dance Form

Debating National and International Politics and Aesthetics (1930s–1940)

As chapter 3 illustrated, performances in Mexico City by international dancers such as Anna Pavlova, Norka Rouskaya, and Tórtola Valencia in 1919 and the mid-1920s revived a search for a modern dance form that could be genuinely Mexican in character and universal in its appeal. Although some of these efforts included the indigenous Mesoamerican as a figure of national representation, a new modern dance form would help consolidate *mestizaje* as an official cultural and racial ideology. As this chapter demonstrates, this emerging dance practice was to achieve its goals by relying on the country's post/colonial history, revolutionary impetus, and modernist aspirations—including its embodied colonial legacies of racialization[1]—as tacit sources of inspiration.

In early December 1940, drawings by Germán Horacio complemented Horacio Quiñones's commentary about *La Coronela* [female colonel], a dance work choreographed by US dancer Waldeen Falkenstein in collaboration with local artists (Figure 4.1).[2] Horacio's sketches provided readers with a visual referent of *La Coronela*'s creative process as the artist and the writer experienced it while attending rehearsals of Waldeen's work.[3] The images incited viewers' kinesthetic imagination to appreciate the dancing bodies' forceful muscle tension and release, their motions while traversing the space, collapsing on the ground in despair or defeat, raising their fist or rifle militantly—whether dancers wore plain clothing or evoked figures from José Guadalupe Posada's popular artwork. Although the drawings portrayed seemingly abstract (universal) bodies, the viewer could recognize cues that situated those dancing bodies within the Mexican context. For many people at the time and some scholars afterward, *La*

---

[1] See the introduction and chapter 3 in this book. For an analysis of the forms that racism took in Mexico's postrevolutionary nation-building projects, see Beatriz Urías Horcasitas, *Historias secretas del racismo en México (1920–1950)* (México, DF: Tusquests Editores, 2007).

[2] Quiñones's article is discussed later in the chapter.

[3] I will use "Waldeen," as she was known.

MAKING A POSTREVOLUTIONARY MODERN DANCE FORM   169

Figure 4.1 Drawings of *La Coronela* by Germán Horacio. Text by Horacio Quiñones, "El Ballet Mexicano," *Hoy*, December 7, 1940, 72–73. Public Domain, Courtesy of Biblioteca Miguel Lerdo de Tejada de la Secretaría de Hacienda y Crédito Público.

Coronela represented the first genuinely Mexican modern dance work with universal import, the inception of a nationalist modern dance form.

This chapter surveys the 1930s and ends in 1940 to trace key developments that led to the creation of works such as *La Coronela*. It traces the formation of a postrevolutionary dance practice that embodied the rhetoric of modernization and the ideologies of nationalism and universalism. In so doing, the chapter emphasizes how these efforts took different forms depending on who produced, discussed, and evaluated them. For example, as relative peace and prosperity unfolded in the early 1920s after the armed phase of the revolution (1910–1920) waned, some people embraced modernity's associations with capitalist industrialization. Others favored progressive movements toward revolutionary sociopolitical and cultural nationalism as hallmarks of a new form of being modern. However, during the early 1930s global economic depression, other social actors advocated for an abstract new socialist "man" to transcend national specificity. While some people embraced universality as solidarity with international working-class struggles for social justice and socialist economic reforms, others claimed universal affinity with internationalized bourgeois elites. Some dance artists embraced revolutionary and nationalist ideology as foundational to a modern cultural and political identity. Other dancers saw the particularity of those markers as compromising the universal potential of legitimate modern art.

This chapter illustrates how dancers joined other artists, government officials, critics, and audiences in these debates through their public statements, writings, and choreographies. Their collective discussions sought to define what characterized a new Mexican dance form to be considered a legitimate art form instead of mere ideological propaganda. Thus, the chapter contends that analyzing disputed relationships between politics and aesthetics is crucial to understanding what role dance and other arts played in the formation of a mestizo nation and its relationship to the world.[4] It does so by examining the state's systematic efforts to create a dance form that could replicate what muralists, musicians, and writers had achieved since the 1920s: the synthesis of revolutionary ideology and artistic, technical sophistication. As the chapter illuminates, disputes about the right combination of political ideology and artistic rigor took specific forms in Mexico. However, they were also part of international debates about how politics should relate (or not relate) to dance and other arts as forms of representation and shared solidarity. In sum, the chapter argues that the effects of the Great Depression during the early 1930s, and the rise of fascism in Europe later in the decade, influenced how debates over aesthetics and ideology in dance contributed to Mexico's institutionalization of the revolution and a mestizo state.

This chapter begins with a brief account of Russian dancer Hipólito Zybin's initial efforts to institutionalize professional dance training in the early 1930s. Zybin's endeavors offer insight into the quest for a Mexican dance form relative to the debates between arts and politics. This discussion examines how these schools' first generation of students and hundreds of other bodies participated in mass choreographies created by Mexican dance artists and half-sisters Nellie and Gloria Campobello. Analyzing their mass dances, primarily *Ballet Simbólico 30-30* [Symbolic Ballet 30-30], reveals how these massive events extended José

---

[4] For examples of these debates as artists aligned with and resisted official nationalist projects in visual arts, literature, and music, see Mary K. Coffey, *How a Revolutionary Art Became Official Culture: Murals, Museums, and the Mexican State* (Durham, NC: Duke University Press, 2012); Rubén Gallo, *Mexican Modernity: The Avant-Garde and the Technological Revolution* (Cambridge, MA: MIT Press, 2005); Leonora Saavedra, ed., *Carlos Chávez and His World* (Princeton, NJ: Princeton University Press, 2015).

Vasconcelos's educational agenda to choreograph the revolutionary national body politic inside and outside the National Stadium he inaugurated in 1924. Examining the reception of the Campobello sisters' mass dances also illustrates how these grand choreographies, rooted in Mexican history, helped shape debates about political ideology and rigorous aesthetics while establishing universalist solidarity with international movements for socialist revolution.

The story then accounts for the turn government officials took toward the United States to find a foundational modernist formula for creating a truly revolutionary dance form: Mexican in "essence" and, unlike most performers in the Campobello sisters' mass dances, rigorous in modern techniques. This second part of the chapter focuses on two choreographers from the United States, Waldeen and Anna Sokolow, and their distinctive approaches to dance-making and questions of representation. Sokolow's collaborations with Spanish artists exiled in the country caused some Mexican nationalists to evaluate her works as emphasizing Spanish references, even when the artist intended them to be abstract and universal. Others praised Waldeen's willingness to embrace themes that referenced the specificity of Mexican history more overtly. In a time when fascism in Europe, especially during Spain's Civil War (1936–1939), was in full force, analyses of these artists' works illuminate how their unique artistic approaches contributed to the search for a dance form that could be politically revolutionary, aesthetically rigorous, and universalist in its reach. The chapter ends with an analysis of Waldeen's *La Coronela*'s inherent contradictions as a form of embodied mestizo modernism and its potential to reimagine a more inclusive pluriversal world.

Collectively, these dancers' cases—Zybin, the Campobello sisters, Sokolow, and Waldeen—demonstrate dance artists' vital contributions to forming a postrevolutionary mestizo nation as they aligned with and resisted official nationalist rhetoric. While doing so, they also participated in international debates about the relationship between dance and politics in producing legitimate modern art.

Institutionalizing Postrevolutionary Mestizo Dancing Bodies: Hipólito Zybin's and Subsequent Dance Schools

The circulation of international dance artists across Mexico throughout its history enabled public and private efforts to train Mexican dancers and develop diverse dance practices.[5] International artists like Pavlova, Rouskaya, and

---

[5] See chapter 1 for a discussion of some teachers and dance practices during the eighteenth century in Mexico City. For other pedagogical efforts by national and international dance artists

Valencia, among others, stylized folkloric and indigenous dances that inspired many local teachers and dancers to follow their steps during the 1920s. This resurgent interest in a Mexican dance form, at a time of increased peace and prosperity after ten years of armed revolutionary struggles, led different cultural and political actors to promote dance as an art form worthy of joining official nation-building projects. The hope was that dance could join other arts in creating representations of the country's indigenous and mestizo history as part of the state's ideological governing apparatus.

Concerning state-sponsored dance schools, the press began to express what was at stake for people debating what constituted legitimate modern Mexican art. This desired art form would reflect the country's progress in a historical time when government officials aspired to inclusion in the League of Nations, an event seen as joining the "international concert . . . among all other nations of civilized humanity."[6] Writing for *Revista de revistas*, Pablo Leredo hoped that a dance school "could create a dance form with Mexican content but without cumbersome regionalism, a dance form that speaks to all men"; that is, not "a narrow ethnic dance but a universal ballet."[7] This idealized form of Mexican-based universalism illustrates the tension between conflicting desires. What would the most effective artistic approach be to creating a dance form with markers of its Mexicanness without falling into stereotypical representations? As had been the case in the past, Mexicans adopted dance techniques from Europe and the United States as embodied technologies for modernizing so-called traditional dances. These dances then could preserve their difference (their exotic allure) but in an aesthetically "refined" manifestation associated with dance consumption on international stages. For Leredo and others like him, a modernized Mexican dance form could preserve, through refined representations, the particularity of Mexican culture and history while having universal resonances with people in "all other nations of civilized humanity."

As this section demonstrates, debates about combining universalism and particularity, modernity and tradition, dance and politics were central to initial efforts to institutionalize professional dance training. In 1930, the new Escuela de Plástica Dinámica [School of Dynamic Plastic Art] initiated one of the most

teaching outside official government efforts, see, e.g., Patricia Aulestia, *Las "Chicas Bien" de Miss Carroll: Estudio y Ballet Carroll (1923–1964)*, INBAL; CENIDID-Danza (México DF: México, 2003).

[6] Juan Sánchez Azcona, president of the Mexican Chamber of Foreign Relations, reflected on Mexico's prospects for joining the "international concert" represented by the League of Nations. He thought this inclusion was, as he said, "of upmost importance, for this matter would profoundly impact our national life by determining the conditions in which our country will be placed among all other nations of civilized humanity" ("No hemos sufrido agravio: No es lo mismo no ser invitado, que ser excluido; México y la Liga de Naciones," *El universal*, March 24, 1919, 1).

[7] "Ballet" in this context can reference a "dance form," a "dance company," or a "dance piece." Pablo Leredo, "La escuela de danza," *Revista de revistas*, July 10, 1932, 33.

prominent government initiatives to train professional dancers and create mestizo choreographies. In the context of a dance school, the phrase "dynamic plastic art" seemed to assume dancers as artists creating meaning through their three-dimensional dancing bodies and their highly *dynamic* capacity to play with form as they move in space. Thus, the school's title functioned as a legitimizing strategy to place dance in official national discourse as equal in status to more *static* plastic arts like muralism and sculpture. According to Hipólito Zybin, who proposed the first educational curriculum, the School of Dynamic Plastic Art was to cultivate dance as art "made to personify all the manifestations in the animate and inanimate world by means of the expressively educated human machine."[8] Zybin was an accomplished Russian ballet dancer who decided to stay in Mexico City in 1930 after the company of dancers and singers with whom he was touring South America disbanded. His conceptualization of the nature of art relative to politics illuminates how national and international aesthetic discourses merged as part of the search for a Mexican universal dance form during the 1930s and 1940s. Zybin's case also begins to illuminate how debates over aesthetics and politics could be embodied in and manifested through dance techniques.

The success of the Ballets Russes in Europe as a new form of modern ballet at the turn of the twentieth century helped solidify the international status of ballet technique as an embodied modernizing technology foundational for professional dance training. Embracing this artistic ideological perspective, Zybin criticized dancers trained in techniques other than ballet. He associated what he called "invented ad hoc" techniques with emerging "free dance" forms that, for him, staged mere "fantasies inspired by psychological or social ideas with dancers who lacked proper physical training."[9] He viewed these techniques as promoting "contortions" and "radical and extreme" movements that distorted the body, causing the chest to sink, the extremities to slack, the legs to lose their jumping ability, and the back to develop exaggerated flexibility that weakened its alignment, thus hindering a good sense of equilibrium.[10]

In contrast, Zybin reasoned that ballet technique produced physically "perfect and beautiful bodies" through transformational qualities inherent in the "spiritual beauty of classical movement" (Figure 4.2).[11] He believed that ballet-trained dancers were able to physically detach from the terrestrial realm, to cultivate physical agility and precision, to execute almost supernatural jumps while conveying the exertion of minimal effort. The admission exam at the School of

---

[8] Zybin, quoted in César Delgado Martínez, "Escuela de Plástica Dinámica." *Cuadernos del CID DANZA No. 2* (México City: Centro de la Información y Documentación de la Danza [CID-Danza], 1985), 8.
[9] Ibid., 7–8.
[10] Ibid., 8.
[11] Ibid.

Figure 4.2 Hipólito Zybin teaching at the Escuela de Danza, 1932. Pablo Leredo, "La Escuela de Danza," *Revista de revistas*, July 10, 1932, unpaged. Public Domain, Courtesy of Biblioteca Miguel Lerdo de Tejada de la Secretaría de Hacienda y Crédito Público.

Dynamic Plastic Art required the presence of "a good arch and instep"[12] specifically to be able to point the feet down while jumping in the air, an ability that student Gloria Albert remembered as signaling applicants' "potential to become ballerinas."[13] The ballet training of these specialized dancers prepared them to perform "Oriental, tap, jazz, classical, [and] Spanish" dances—or, as student Raquel Gutierrez summarized—"we could do anything."[14] As Zybin helped institute ballet as the foundational training technique for professional dancers in Mexico, he and others believed that these new artistic bodies could dance any other dance style and content as embodiments of a dynamic plastic art form.

Through the performance of dance forms from around the world, this sense of cosmopolitanism produced a type of embodied modern *mestizaje*. However, Zybin's initial pedagogical proposal emphasized a local source already present in public murals, novels, and musical tunes: indigenous Mesoamerican cultures. In his proposed educational plan, sent to Franklin O. Westrup, director of the

---

[12] Josefina Lavalle, quoted in Roxana Guadalupe Ramos Villalobos, *Una mirada a la formación dancística mexicana (ca. 1919–1945)* (México: INBA/CENIDID-Danza, 2009), 110.
[13] Ibid., 12.
[14] Ibid., 83.

Department of Physical Education, Zybin expressed his desire to "discover" and "restore the ancient Aztec dances of the Mexican Republic," to study "their choreographic development" and reconstruct them for "their exhibition to the Mexican public."[15]

In subsequent revisions to his curricula, the class for Mexican dances, introduced alongside classical technique, comprised the first four of eight years of study.[16] However, his educational plan eventually began to marginalize Mexican dances, in contradistinction to his initially stated goal of "discovering" Aztec dances. Concurrently, dance forms from various parts of the world continued to be integral to a professional dance education founded on ballet technique.[17] By adopting this cosmopolitan ideology while establishing ballet as an embodied modernizing technology, people like Zybin developed a practice of embodying the world in ways that confirmed Mexico's capacity to join the concert of civilized humanity. This performance of danced cosmopolitanism reaffirmed ballet as the defining factor in choreographing the "universal" through dances of the world, thereby obscuring the racial and classist origins of ballet and casting it as culturally and racially "neutral."

Zybin's conceptualization of dance as a legitimate universal art form had a particular relationship to politics, specifically Mexico's revolutionary ideology. Zybin shunned what he called the psychological and social basis of "free dance" techniques that, in his estimation, lacked rigorous training standards. He also distrusted politicians and artists who wanted "to use art as a powerful propagandistic mechanism for their social ideas thus demanding forms of art that aroused more forcefully the benevolent, or ill, instincts of the multitudes."[18] For him, art and politics belonged to two different spheres of experience. Legitimate dance as art must concern itself with cultivating "perfect bodies" of "spiritual beauty." Politics could only serve the interests of populist opportunists invested in the ideological indoctrination of the masses. Zybin's efforts were short-lived, but his views about which dance techniques were conducive to the proper training of professional dancers and the creation of a legitimate dance form would continue for decades to come.

The School of Dynamic Plastic Art was soon replaced by the new Escuela de Danza (School of Dance) on April 16, 1932, under the directorship of Guatemala-born painter Carlos Mérida. The school's assistant director, Nellie Campobello, would take the reins of subsequent versions of the state-sponsored dance

---

[15] Quoted in Delgado Martínez, "Escuela de Plástica," 14. For a discussion about Rouskaya and her Mexican collaborators' interest in "resurrecting" dances of the "ancient Aztec race" in 1919, see chapter 3.
[16] Ramos Villalobos, *Una mirada*.
[17] Ibid.
[18] Quoted in Delgado Martínez, "Escuela de Plástica," 7.

educational institution from 1937 to 1984 after musician Francisco Domínguez had led it between 1935 and 1937. Campobello and her sister, Gloria, promoted ballet as the foundational training regimen for dancers who could perform Mexican dances and dance styles from other parts of the world.

While preparing dancers to embody these forms of modern *mestizajes*, the School of Dance and its precursor played an important cultural and ideological role in nation-building projects. As part of consolidating a culturally and racially mestizo state with modern aspirations, the dance schools served as a legitimate educational body producing modern dancing bodies and subjects. The Department of Fine Arts functioned as the state's regulatory body by overseeing the dance schools' day-to-day administration and the direction of debates over aesthetics and politics. The institutional organism, tasked with producing professional dancing bodies and dance as a legitimate art form, sought to advance Mexico's cultural modernization within a revolutionary ideological framework. At times, dancers aligned themselves with these official efforts. At other times, they resisted them, as Zybin's case illustrates.

Didactic Revolutionary Nationalism and Universalist Socialism: The Campobello Sisters' *Ballet Simbólico 30-30*

In the early 1930s, institutional efforts to train professional dance artists and teachers produced the first generations of dancers. These young artists would forge a modern mestizo dance form within the context of revolutionary nationalism. On November 20, 1931, Zybin's students danced *Fiesta del Fuego* [Feast of Fire] as part of a massive event celebrating the twentieth anniversary of the onset of the armed phase of the Mexican Revolution. In the same program, the Campobello sisters presented *Ballet Simbólico 30-30* [Symbolic Ballet 30-30], a mass dance that included thousands of performers.[19] The inclusion of dance in massive political and cultural events represented an extension of José Vasconcelos's earlier efforts to create a postrevolutionary national identity through mass spectacles, just as other countries have done in their nation-building projects.

While historicizing mass spectacles in Europe and Russia, performance and theater scholar Erika Fischer-Lichte rejects a recurrent suggestion that totalitarian governments created these events as instruments of populace manipulation.[20] Fischer-Lichte posits instead that massive performance events such as

---

[19] "30-30" refers to a popular rifle used by the federal army and revolutionary groups during the Mexican Revolution.

[20] Erika Fischer-Lichte, *Theater, Sacrifice, Ritual: Exploring Forms of Political Theater* (London: Routledge, 2005).

pageants "originated in a deep yearning for communal experience widespread in European culture at the turn of the [twentieth] century which stimulated the exploration of different kinds of fusion between theater and ritual."[21] I will suggest that the Campobello sisters' mass dances integrated both an ideological desire to create a cohesive sense of national belonging and an aesthetic interest in experimenting with different performance practices, primarily dance.[22] As their case illustrates, this combination of ideology and aesthetics emerged within Mexico's revolutionary idealism when the effects of the Great Depression prompted a resurgence of international socialist movements. While dancing within the nation-state in relation to the international stage in the early 1930s, the Campobello sisters' mass dances prompted quarrels about the most conducive choreographic approaches to creating a genuinely revolutionary dance form, aesthetically and politically.

The US stock market crash in 1929 reverberated around the world. Its effects impacted economic, political, and cultural discourse in Mexico. Dissatisfaction with capitalism as an inefficient economic system led some political and social factions within the country to reinvigorate a more socialist national environment. In this context, some nationalist factions distrusted foreign capitalist interventionism. In *El universal*, a 1932 editorial warned against a resurgence of antiforeign nationalism that could "excite the dormant hate of the *primitive* against the foreigner" (emphasis added).[23] Reproducing colonial racism implicitly in these categorizations of the local (primitive, brown, Indian) and the foreign (modern, white, European/"American"), the editorial advocated for a "well-understood" and "civilized" nationalism.[24] A more rational nationalist attitude was necessary to deal with the reality many factions resented: that "undesirable" capitalist foreigners exploited workers, propagandized a corrupt economic system, and enjoyed more privileges than national industrialists and business impresarios.[25]

Nationalist sentiments also informed political debates about who was more apt to continue the revolutionary project. Referring to militant youth, Mexican president Pascual Ortiz Rubio (1930–1932) declared that "we [the veterans of the Revolution] must take a step back and allow this vigorous youth to take a frank step forward as we yield to them the reins not only of the country but also of the Revolution. They shall then with their efforts, with their patriotism, and

---

[21] Ibid., 90.
[22] For a brief historical account of the role of dance and the body in mass spectacles and events in countries such as Italy, Germany, Russia, and the United States at the turn of the twentieth century, see Claire Warden, "Mass Dance," *Routledge Encyclopedia of Modernism*, 2016, accessed July 7, 2022, https://www.rem.routledge.com/articles/mass-dance.
[23] "Nacionalismo, no antiextranjerismo," *El universal*, Sección: Editorial, April 26, 1932, 3.
[24] Ibid.
[25] Ibid.

with their intelligence teach the Mexican people the path they must take among civilized nations."[26] Some of the *old guard* were more cautious about entrusting the fate of the country to younger generations. The influential politician Juan Sánchez Azcona favored keeping the more experienced and "capable vanguard [the] faithful rear battalion" in power to ensure that the country's "social and political development unfolds rhythmically, harmoniously, safely, and in a disciplined manner."[27]

Through dance practices, choreographers contributed to the production of these discursive debates. After leaving Letti Carroll's dance group Chicas Bien [Well-Off Girls] late in 1929, the Campobello sisters entered the 1930s with a renewed purpose during this critical period of social and political transformation.[28] While dancing with Carroll, Nellie's billing was "miss Nellie Campbell," "a rising star" among "a group of charming girls" drawn from the Mexican and foreign elites of the metropolitan society.[29] The sisters refashioned their identities after departing from this company, changing their last name from Campbell to Campobello and performing endearing popular dances, some of them en pointe, such as the *Jarabe Tapatío* (Figure 4.3) and *Fantasía Yucateca* (Figure 4.4) in a symbolic gesture of revolutionary patriotism.[30] Carroll trained them in ballet and other dance forms from around the world as a means to their social edification as upper-class "girls." However, they would create a nationalist dance practice in alignment with the working-class masses.

As if responding to the concerns of both President Ortiz Rubio and García Azcona, the Campobello sisters adopted a dynamism that seems to have aligned with Ortiz Rubio's call for the old vanguard to step aside so that the vigorous youth could take the reins of the revolution and propel the country forward. As the young dancers departed from Carroll's socially elitist sphere, they took frank (dancing) steps forward, backward, to the side, to the right, and far to the left. However, as they embraced nationalist ideology, their multitudinous performances were not always as "safe" or "disciplined" as Sánchez Azcona would have advised. Their mass dances were often praised by political ideologues

---

[26] Quoted in Sánchez Azcona, "Vanguardismo y retaguardias en el ciclo evolucionario," *El universal*, April 22, 1932, 3.

[27] Ibid.

[28] Carroll was a dancer from the United States who arrived in Mexico City in 1910. She devoted most of her life to training primarily young girls from the upper classes among Mexican elites and enclaves of immigrants from other countries. For a discussion of her contributions to the development of dance in Mexico, see Aulestia, *Las "Chicas Bien."* For analyses of racial, gender, and social class aspects in Carroll's work, see chapter 3 in Jose L. Reynoso, "Choreographing Politics, Dancing Modernity: Ballet and Modern Dance in the Construction of Modern Mexico (1919–1940)" (PhD diss., University of California Los Angeles, 2012.

[29] *El universal*, "Una estrella que surge," March 4, 1927, 4.

[30] For a discussion of the Campobello sisters' *Jarabe Tapatío* performances and their role as dance artists in Mexico's broader pedagogical agenda, see Manuel R. Cuellar, *Choreographing Mexico: Festive Performances and Dancing Histories of a Nation* (Austin: University of Texas Press, 2022).

MAKING A POSTREVOLUTIONARY MODERN DANCE FORM 179

Figure 4.3 Nellie and Gloria Campobello dancing the *Jarabe Tapatío*. Carlos del Rio, "Nelly y Gloria Campobello, creadora [sic] de danzas," *Revista de revistas*, October 12, 1930, 38. Public Domain, Courtesy of Biblioteca Miguel Lerdo de Tejada de la Secretaría de Hacienda y Crédito Público.

and criticized by art critics concerned with technical rigor or the extent to which aesthetics should combine with overt political content.

Active in these debates, the Campobello sisters' choreographies joined the state's efforts to "teach the Mexican people the *path* they must take among civilized nations."[31] Indeed, a militant Nellie, immersed in the Cultural Missions,

---

[31] Ortiz Rubio, quoted in Sánchez Azcona, "Vanguardismo y Retaguardias," 3.

Figure 4.4 Nellie and Gloria Campobello dancing *Fantasía Yucateca* en pointe. Carlos del Rio, "Nelly y Gloria Campobello, creadora [sic] de danzas," *Revista de revistas*, October 12, 1930, 39. Public Domain, Courtesy of Biblioteca Miguel Lerdo de Tejada de la Secretaría de Hacienda y Crédito Público.

effused that "to love the people is to teach them the alphabet, to orient them toward things of beauty . . . it is to teach them what are their rights and how to make those rights be granted and respected."[32] She envisioned the working class

[32] Quoted in Margarita Tortajada Quiroz, "Transgresoras-constructoras del cuerpo y las imágenes I. Las pioneras de la danza escénica mexicana del siglo XX-I: Nellie y Gloria Campobello," in *La danza en México. Visiones de cinco siglos*, Vol. I. *Ensayos históricos y analíticos*, ed. Maya Ramos y Patricia Cardona (México: CNCA-INBA-CENIDI-Danza-Escenologia, 2002), 702.

and the indigenous integrated into the political, social, and cultural spheres of a "civilized" revolutionary nation.

For the Campobello sisters, the path led toward a socialist revolution, yet not without tensions and contradictions. In collaboration with government authorities, they congregated thousands of people as performers and audiences for massive events as they embarked on a collective mission. Their mass dances mobilized choreographically national affectivities that could potentially "excite the dormant hate of the primitive against the foreigner," specifically the capitalist, a possibility that the 1932 editorialists for *El universal* warned against.[33] Nellie had long harbored anti-"gringa" (anti-US) sentiments, claiming while still in Carroll's troupe that "North Americans always humiliate[d] the Mexicans."[34] However, the Campobello sisters' intervention also embodied a "civilized" nationalism, like that desired by the same *El universal* editorial. That is, while the Campobello sisters' socialist critique appeared contained within the confines of a dance performance, they sparked debates about revolutionary politics and aesthetics beyond the symbolic space. Ineluctably, dancing bodies played a crucial role in defining the cultural context where competing social and political efforts contributed to restructuring Mexico as a modern nation in a historic time of global economic precarity and ideological shifts.

Choreographing the National Collective and International Socialism: *Ballet Simbólico 30-30*

Nellie Campobello's personal embodied memories of revolutionary armed fighting informed her words as an author and her movements as a choreographer.[35] As a child growing up in Northern Mexico before migrating to the relative safety of Mexico City, Nellie experienced firsthand images of bodies running, hiding, jumping, falling, dying. These images imprinted on her young mind and body scenes of executions, the sounds and odors of death. As an artist, her subjectivity was greatly affected by these corporeal experiences during her formative years. In 1931, those embodied experiences found expression through her

---

[33] *El universal*, "Nacionalismo, no antiextranjerismo," 3.

[34] Quoted in Felipe Segura, *Gloria Campobello: La primera ballerina de México*. Centro Nacional de Investigación, Documentación e Información de la Danza "José Limón" (México: INBA, 1991), 10.

[35] In addition to her work as a dancer, choreographer, and dance administrator, Nellie Campobello published several books, including *Yo* [I] (1929); *Cartucho* [Cartridge] (1931); *Las manos de mamá* [My mom's hands], illustrated by José Clemente Orozco (1937); *Apuntes sobre la vida militar de Francisco Villa* [Notes about the military life of Francisco Villa] (1940); *Tres poemas* [Three poems] (1957); and *Mis libros* [My books] (1960). She coauthored with her sister, Gloria, *Ritmos indigenas de México* [Indigenous rhythms of Mexico] (1940).

novella *Cartucho* and her choreography in *Ballet Simbólico 30-30*.[36] The book and the dance viscerally captured a sense of the ideals, goals, and consequences of the armed revolution.[37] If her literary work emphasized the bloody consequences of an armed insurrection, the choreographed mass dance produced class solidarity, including with those who could not read, that galvanized socialist affinities with international revolutionary movements.

Ballet Simbólico 30-30 became integral to official national celebrations for its ideological potency, its didactic potential, and its capacity to mobilize multitudes. After its 1931 premiere, one of many presentations of the mass dance was for President Lázaro Cárdenas on the 1935 Day of the Soldier at the National Stadium, celebrating the twentieth anniversary of the Mexican Revolution. Nearly 3,000 people, including female sowers, laborers, peasants, soldiers, police officers, choruses, music bands, and students from various schools, participated as performers.[38]

In three main sections, the work attempted to transform the working classes into active agents in the (choreographed) construction of their revolutionary redemption. According to the critic Armando de Maria y Campo, "Revolución" [Revolution], the first section of *Ballet Simbólico 30-30*, "was not far from classical precepts," and its rhythmic movement was "extraordinary."[39] Exalting what might have been Nellie Campobello's forceful performance qualities, the writer noted that the dance work was profoundly expressive but simple in its design so that the thousands of spectators could apprehend and feel the "symbolic uprising that burns and sweeps up everything as soon as it is touched by the human torch of the Revolution—Nellie Campobello" (Figure 4.5).[40]

Nellie's female body *was* revolution. Her dynamic body ran from place to place to mobilize the hundreds of performers on "stage" as thousands witnessed her embodied revolutionary leadership from the bleachers. In the writer's mind, Campobello's moving body was the burning force that fueled mobilization toward collective transformation. Evelia Beristain, who participated in the dance as a student, reminisced, "I will never forget the image of Nellie Campobello dressed in red, holding that torch while running across the whole stadium as she encouraged us to join her . . . and as we took our rifles, an authentic 30-30, to join the fight" (Figure 4.6).[41] This image of Nellie running with a torch

---

[36] "Cartucho" literally translates as "cartridge" and, in this context, refers to a device that carries bullets in a pistol or rifle.

[37] There is much scholarship and commentary on Nellie Campobello's literary work, but for a discussion of how her literary and choreographic work informed one another, see Sophie Bidault de la Calle, *Nellie Campobello: Una escritura salida del cuerpo* (México, INBAL/CENIDID-Danza, 2003).

[38] Tortajada Quiroz, "Transgresoras-constructoras . . . XX-I: Nellie y Gloria Campobello," 685–715.

[39] Quoted in Segura, *Gloria Campobello*, 23.

[40] Ibid.

[41] Ibid.

MAKING A POSTREVOLUTIONARY MODERN DANCE FORM   183

Figure 4.5 Nellie Campobello running with a torch while dancing in *Ballet Simbólico 30-30*, c. 1935. Courtesy of Archivo Histórico de la Escuela Nacional de Danza Nellie y Gloria Campobello. Fondo Nellie Campobello.

inciting hundreds of bodies to join the armed struggle spoke, at least in the realm of dance representations, to the dramatic conversion of women from docile exotic *chinas poblanas* and refined, highly moral ballerinas to determined revolutionary leaders. These emergent politicized female physical dynamos were to mobilize the masses toward a socialist revolution.

The mass dance's second section, "Siembra" [Sow], was, according to de Maria y Campo, the most "traditional and Mexican" as it included stylized

Figure 4.6 Nellie Campobello inciting women to join the revolutionary movement in *Ballet Simbólico 30-30*, c. 1935. Courtesy of Archivo Histórico de la Escuela Nacional de Danza Nellie y Gloria Campobello. Fondo Nellie Campobello.

versions of regional dances and costumes (Figure 4.7).[42] The combination of Mexican-derived dances with movement "not far from classical precepts" that de Maria y Campos noted, together with dance idioms based on emerging "free dance" techniques, constituted a form of experimental mestizo modernism. These new forms of modernist *mestizaje* resonated with the search for a Mexican universal.

"Liberación" [Liberation], the last section of *Ballet Simbólico 30-30*, pointed toward that possibility. It gathered workers, peasants, and soldiers in an idealized process of communist liberation. At either end of the stadium that served as the large stage, a group of women carrying small red flags marched in a circular formation (Figure 4.8).[43] An additional line of marching performers formed a human string running from one circle to the other, its movement generated by the constant rotation of the two groups. As a collective, the

---

[42] Quoted in Tortajada Quiroz, "Transgresoras-constructoras," 701.

[43] The basis for descriptions in this and the following paragraph is a photograph of the entire scenery, which I could not include in this book (see the image in Reynoso, "Choreographing Politics"). The image included here captures one of the referenced circular formations but not the rest of the elements in my description.

Figure 4.7 Women dancing traditional dances in *Ballet Simbólico 30-30*, c. 1935. Courtesy of Archivo Histórico de la Escuela Nacional de Danza Nellie y Gloria Campobello. Fondo Nellie Campobello.

performers represented two enormous rotating pulleys of a human machine in constant motion. They were the very bodies of modernity's industrialization—subject to exploitation but also unified as a class. These performing bodies were part of the machine/ry that exploited them through their physical labor. Yet, as willful performers, they constituted themselves as subjects united in the machine's de/construction in collective efforts toward their social emancipation.

Hundreds of female sowers formed a large square configuration at center stage, in between these rotating human pulleys that kept revolutionary aspirations in motion. Within this enormous human frame, groups of peasants and workers arranged themselves in a choreographed rendition of a hammer and sickle, a symbol referencing proletarian solidarity first adopted by socialists during the Russian Revolution of 1917.[44] All these bodies laboring

---

[44] For an analysis of the Moscow-based Communist International's early efforts to direct a revolutionary movement in Mexico between 1919 and 1929, see Daniela Spenser, *Stumbling Its Way through Mexico: The Early Years of the Communist International*, trans. Peter Gellert (Tuscaloosa: University of Alabama Press, in association with Centro de Investigaciones y Estudios Superiores en Antropología Social, 2011).

Figure 4.8 Performers forming a human pulley, carrying red flags in *Ballet Simbólico 30-30*, c. 1935. Courtesy of Archivo Histórico de la Escuela Nacional de Danza Nellie y Gloria Campobello. Fondo Nellie Campobello.

as performers activated the space by literally putting in motion symbols dear to communist efforts to replace capitalism with socialist alternatives. Deep emotions must have stirred among the thousands of people gathered on the stage and in the bleachers. In this mass dance, performers and the audience's bodies *were* revolution, whether they moved and ran across the performing stage or cheered from their seats around the stadium. At the grand finale, they all became one human mass as they vocalized in unison the *Internationale*. The vibrations of this international socialist anthem resonated loud and clear as a large Mexican flag in the background danced sinuously to the rhythms of the wind. Within a nationalist context, *Ballet Simbólico 30-30* provided audiences and performers an opportunity to join affectively and ideologically with one another as a unified national body politic. Simultaneously, the mestizo modernist mass dance also choreographed the audience's and performers' revolutionary Mexicanness within universalist aspirations of a global socialist revolution.

Debating the Aesthetic Merits of the Campobellos' Mass Dances: Performing Art and Political Ideology

According to one critic, *Ballet Simbólico 30-30* was "the most important and original choreographic work of our epoch."[45] In the context of aesthetic ideological debates, this characterization could mean different things for different factions. A note in the newspaper *El universal* acknowledged that the mass dance represented a type of "revolutionary conquest" due to its effectiveness in "putting art to the service of the people."[46] For its capacity to congregate multitudes as a collective national body, Campobello's mass choreography became part of the ideological state apparatus, in line with the government's efforts to appropriate the arts. Indeed, according to the press assessment, such mass events served as "powerful auxiliaries in efforts to improve the conditions of our people for they carry an educational component . . . especially those works with a clear vision toward social evolution."[47] This appreciation for the edifying component of art and mass dances under the state's management resonated with the revolutionary desire voiced by President Ortiz Rubio to "teach the Mexican people the path they must take among civilized nations."[48] It also echoed Nellie Campobello's own desire to orient people "toward things of beauty . . . [and] to teach them . . . their rights."[49] In other words, didactic revolutionary nationalism—circulating in the public sphere (through the press), in the political arena (through public policy), and on the artistic stage (through the Campobello sisters' mass dances)—provided a cultural context for identity formation processes in alignment and opposition to official nationalist ideology.

While de Maria y Campo exalted *Ballet Simbólico 30-30* as a profoundly expressive dance, he also noted its simple design, which unobtrusively facilitated access to the spirit of the revolution. It is precisely this simplicity in the service of propagating political ideology that bothered those like Zybin, who wanted a clearer demarcation between art and politics. These detractors distrusted both the appropriation of dance as a mechanism for stirring nationalist passion among the masses and the use of dancers who lacked "proper dance training."[50] Indeed, most performers in the Campobello sisters' mass dances, except students from the state-sponsored dance schools, were workers from non-dance related occupations. As was the case in other countries, mass dances within socialist contexts required neither that all performers have "rigorous" dance techniques

---

[45] Quoted in Tortajada Quiroz, "Transgresoras-constructoras," 700.
[46] *El universal*, "Buenos espectáculos a precios reducidos," May 8, 1932, 1.
[47] Ibid.
[48] Quoted in Sánchez Azcona, "Vanguardismo y Retaguardias," 3.
[49] Quoted in Tortajada Quiroz, "Transgresoras-constructoras," 702.
[50] Zybin quoted in Delgado Martínez, "Escuela de Plástica," 7–8.

nor the cultivation of aesthetic excellence as primary goals.[51] Instead, as *Ballet Simbólico 30-30* shows, the value given to performing bodies was simply their ability to walk and march, to unify employing synchronicity and uniformity in a (national) collective. One of the didactic purposes of this aesthetic of precision and sameness was to foster ideological identification and, perhaps, as Fischer-Lichte might suggest, a "deep yearning for communal experience,"[52] among people who organized, performed, and watched the dance. The Campobello sisters kept dancing and marching on as they continued garnering praise and scorn for their choreographic approach.

They gained the support of President Lázaro Cárdenas (1934–1940), whose socialist leanings led him to implement agrarian reform by expropriating land to be distributed among small collectives (*ejidos*) and nationalize the oil industry. With his backing, the Campobello sisters continued performing *Ballet Simbólico 30-30* and choreographing more revolutionary yet aesthetically controversial mass dances. *Barricada* [Barricade] premiered in 1935.[53] De Maria y Campos thought the production was a "generous attempt at creating an exponent of Mexican Revolutionary plastic theater."[54] Gerónimo Baqueiro Fóster noted in an affirmation that the show was not to "be considered a ballet of the ordinary type.... It breaks with all established tradition," and he condemned "ignorant" skeptics who could not see its value.[55]

However, Carlos Mérida, a painter and School of Dance director between 1932 and 1935 was less enthused. In a 1935 article, he discussed his ideas about developing "a modern choreographic practice with idiosyncratic character"[56] while also noting *Barricada*'s aesthetic failures. As if he could see inside audiences' minds, he claimed that the "divorce," the lack of "rhythm" among all parts of the production—dance, music, libretto, plastic art expression—was perceptible to the eye of the spectator. He faulted *Barricada* for including a group of "actors" of the "absolute folkloric type—a group of peasants wearing serapes."[57] Mérida's vision for a genuinely embodied mestizo modernism avoided overt cultural specificity that might border on the "picturesque" and therefore undermine art's

---

[51] Warden, "Mass Dance," 2016. Also, debates over proper technical dance proficiency and the relationship between aesthetics and politics had striking resemblance in Mexico City and New York City, mainly because international flows of bodies and ideas drove these debates. See Reynoso, "Choreographing Politics."
[52] *Theater, Sacrifice, Ritual*, 90.
[53] Another mass dance, *Tierra* [Land], premiered in 1936. It included 3,000 students from various schools as performers to represent "Mexico's agrarian revolution." Segura, quoted in Tortajada Quiroz, *Danza y poder* (México, DF: INBA/CENIDID-Danza, 1995), 104.
[54] Tortajada Quiroz, *Danza y poder*, 102.
[55] Ibid., 104.
[56] Mérida, "Danza y teatro," reprinted in Cristina Mendoza, *Escritos de Carlos Mérida sobre el arte: La danza*. (México: INBA/Centro Nacional de Investigación y Documentación de Artes Plásticas, 1990), 214.
[57] Ibid.

universal potential. Mérida sought to achieve the *right* synthesis of aesthetic revolutionary ideology and rigorous dance training to create the "precise conditions characteristic of all perfect theater."[58] Barros Sierra concurred that the project of creating a "genuinely national dance ... with international value" (a Mexican universal) would not be possible until Mexico produced "specialized bodies."[59] A new impetus for a truly modern dance practice and dancing bodies that could represent the country's character emerged.

Looking at the United States for a Modernist Formula to a "Truly" Revolutionary Dance: Merida, Sokolow, and Waldeen

In the latter half of the 1930s, debates began to take a new direction as people who disliked the Campobello sisters' populist choreographic approach looked for alternatives. New discussions focused on which embodied technologies were most appropriate to producing "specialized" dancing bodies and a dance form that could embody the *right* combination of revolutionary idealism and modernity's universalism. Mérida, much like Zybin before him, had initially advocated for ballet as a foundational dance technique for choreographing Mexican folkloric dances. In his 1932 essay "Danza y teatro" [Dance and theater] (published the same year that he took the helm of the School of Dance), Mérida disagreed with one of the foremost exponents of expressive modern dance at the time, the German Mary Wigman. He quoted the artist as saying that "the ballet dancer was no longer representative of an interior expression [and] has fallen into mere virtuosity ... only concerned with developing idealized agility and lightness."[60] It was precisely an emphasis on technical virtuosity, agility, and lightness that Mérida valued as central to developing a professional dance training regimen.

Shifting his views by 1937, Mérida seemed to have found a dancing body prototype that could fuse the expression of interiority and virtuosic physicality. In a time of fervent revolutionary nationalism under President Lázaro Cárdenas, Mérida (and many others who shared his artistic taste) wanted dancing bodies that could combine progressive politics with the rigor of modern aesthetics. He presented a revised version of his 1932 essay for the Congress of the Liga de Escritores y Artistas Revolucionarios (LEAR) [League of Revolutionary Artists and Writers] in 1937.[61] His talk, titled "Ponencia sobre problemas de la danza

---

[58] Ibid.
[59] Quoted in Tortajada Quiroz, *Danza y poder*, 103.
[60] Mérida 1932, quoted in Mendoza, *Escritos de Carlos Mérida*, 138.
[61] LEAR, instituted by a group of artists and intellectuals in 1933, encouraged the production of politically revolutionary art. Considered the Mexican branch of the International Union of

mexicana moderna" [Reflections on the problems of modern Mexican dance], was the only one about dance at this meeting. In it, Mérida seems to adopt Wigman's view, though he had refuted it five years earlier: "times change," "the old and endeared tradition begins to lag behind," and dance artists must return to "the human body and its rhythmic expression."[62] As he addressed his revolutionary comrades, Mérida's confidence rested on what for him was a new fact, that "the rhetoric" and technique of classical ballet represented a "system contradictory to the laws proper to the human body" and "its natural development."[63] He rebuked dance schools harshly, including what he called "ours" at the Palace of Fine Arts (his former school, then led by Nellie Campobello), for continuing to "anachronistically implement" ballet as foundational for dance training.[64]

Although Mérida concurred with Wigman's assessment of ballet at this time as an anachronistic expressive and training technique, he did not direct his eyes toward Wigman's German expressionist dance. Instead, he believed that a truly modern dance form was in "gestation" in the United States. He characterized the "extraordinary Martha Graham" as "the highest exponent of contemporary choreography" and lauded those artists who had followed her steps, such as "Anna Sokolow, Doris Humphrey, Lilian Shapero [sic], Charles Wiedmann [sic], [and] Tamiris, Lilian Holm [sic]."[65] Perhaps hoping to appeal to his audience's revolutionary ideological leanings, Mérida mentioned dances such as *Suite of Soviet Songs* (Anna Sokolow, 1936), *Speaker* (Anna Sokolow, 1935), *Two Songs about Lenin* (Sophie Maslow, 1934), *Inquisition ['36]* (Anna Sokolow, 1936), and *Histrionic[s]* (Anna Sokolow, 1933) whose contents addressed leftist interests. As he imagined a new training methodology and choreographic practice, Mérida, similar to Wigman, stated that "time does not stop," and thus a new form of expression required "new laws" so that its character could deepen, its form dramatize, and its content be socially conscious.[66] In order to embark on this new artistic modernizing venture, he urged his colleagues to consider the "profound, penetrating" dances "filled with a sense of social responsibility" created by dancers in the United States.[67]

During the 1930s, state-sponsored dance schools in the context of institutionalized socialist education in Mexico served as part of a governing apparatus invested in creating representational and affective national cohesiveness.

Revolutionary Writers, LEAR was established in 1930 by the Communist International organization in the Soviet Union.

[62] Quoted in Mendoza, *Escritos de Carlos Mérida*, 138.
[63] Mérida 1937, in ibid., 146.
[64] Ibid.
[65] Ibid., 147.
[66] Ibid., 146.
[67] Ibid., 147.

However, the national project of developing a form of embodied mestizo modernism, a Mexican universal dance form, implied diverse approaches to what people imagined a legitimate revolutionary modern artist should be. As the end of the decade drew near, dance artists, intellectuals, and government officials debated the *right* way to dance a modern *leftist* revolution. Their political and aesthetic ideologies collided as these different actors quarreled over what constituted dance as a legitimate form of modern art and, thus, to what extent overt cultural referents compromised its ostensibly universal potential. Modern dance choreographers from the United States would soon join these debates.

Contrasting Revolutionary Modern Dance Forms: Sokolow's and Waldeen's Distinctive Choreographic Approaches

The transnational circulation of leftist politics during the 1930s enabled the flow of artists and ideas across geopolitical borders, including between Mexico and the United States.[68] As the decade waned, Sokolow and Waldeen, two choreographers from Mexico's northern neighbor country, collaborated with local artists and government officials to form new ways of thinking about dance-making in Mexico. Though these two artists had much in common—they shared identity as US dancers and were both communist and Jewish—these women's individual histories of embodying aesthetics developed very differently. In Mexico, their distinctive choreographic approaches participated in debates over what role cultural particularity and political ideology could play in producing modern art with universal reach.

To understand these debates and the pivotal role these two artists played during this new phase in the search for a Mexican modern dance form, one needs to appreciate these dancers' different approaches to choreography, representation, and abstraction. For some observers, Sokolow turned more to Spain for source material, while Waldeen consistently embraced Mexican history for inspiration. As modernist artists, Sokolow and Waldeen relied on abstraction as a mode of representation, although Mexican nationalists valued Waldeen's explicit references to their country's cultural and political life. As her case illuminates below, Waldeen's work continued the Campobello sisters' tradition of staging representations of Mexican female revolutionary leaders. In so doing,

---

[68] For examples of cultural exchanges and the binational circulation of artists after the Mexican Revolution between the United States and Mexico, see Ellen G. Landau, *Mexico and American Modernism* (New Haven, CT: Yale University Press, 2013); Helen Delpar, *The Enormous Vogue of Things Mexican: Cultural Relations between the United States and Mexico, 1920-1935* (Tuscaloosa: University of Alabama Press, 1992); Laurence P. Hurlburt, *The Mexican Muralists in the United States* (Albuquerque: University of New Mexico Press, 1989).

this gesture defied men's dominance in representations of the revolution and in the production of the arts, including as dance administrators. Sokolow created abstracted representations of Mexican and Latin American motifs in some of her dances as well.[69] While her efforts did not always please some nationalist critics, her close collaborators, Mexican and Spanish exiles, continued to support and praise her work. Sokolow's and Waldeen's unique choreographic approaches and thematic choices seemed to have set them apart in the eyes of funders, critics, and audiences at different moments in their trajectories in Mexico.[70] While negotiating these tensions, Sokolow's and Waldeen's contributions were vital to producing professional dancers and modern Mexican dance practices.

The following section examines some of the factors that contextualized Sokolow's reception in Mexico as a model for a truly revolutionary modern artist. It accounts for how Sokolow's works with anti-fascist overtones garnered the support of Mexico City–based Spanish exiles who fled during the Spanish Civil War (1936–1939) as fascist general Francisco Franco rose to power. The discussion follows with an analysis of Waldeen's arrival in Mexico. Comparing Sokolow's and Waldeen's cases show how the two artists strived for resources while shaping debates over how politics and dance should coexist in a time of fervent nationalism in Mexico and the rise of fascism in Europe.

Mexican and Spanish Universalisms in a time of Rising Fascism: Sokolow's Ballet de Bellas Artes and La Paloma Azul Dance Companies

Before arriving in Mexico, Sokolow and her dancers had become known in New York City for successfully merging revolutionary political ideology and rigorous technical dance standards. Early in the 1930s, when debates about dance were along the lines of "bourgeois" and "revolutionary" practices, Sokolow's *right* synthesis of excellent technique and *leftist* political ideology made the art of

---

[69] Hannah Kosstrin, *Honest Bodies: Revolutionary Modernism in the Dances of Anna Sokolow* (New York: Oxford University Press, 2017).

[70] Both artists likely experienced forms of anti-Semitism in Mexico, which could have affected their relationships with some local factions. However, as argued in the following discussion, artistic collaborators and government officials often aligned with either Sokolow or Waldeen based on how these artists combined aesthetics and politics, especially relative to the Mexican nationalist ideology of *mexicanidad* (Mexicanness: something recognized and valued as Mexican). For an analysis of the implications of Sokolow's Jewishness in Mexico, see Kosstrin, *Honest Bodies*. For discussions of the history of the Jewish establishment in Mexico, including forms of anti-Semitism against them, see Daniela Gleizer Salzman, *Unwelcome Exiles: Mexico and the Jewish Refugees from Nazism, 1933–1945* (Leiden: Brill, 2014); Claudio Lomnitz, "Anti-Semitism and the Ideology of the Mexican Revolution," *Representations* 110, no. 1 (2010): 1–28; Korinne A. Krause, *Los judíos en México: Una historia con énfasis especial en el período de 1857 a 1930*, trans. Ariela Katz de Gugenheim (México: Universidad Iberoamericana, Departamento de Historia, 1987).

dance into "a weapon of propaganda."[71] This combination must have resonated with Mérida when he saw Sokolow's group dancing onstage at the New School for Social Research while he was visiting New York in 1939 to "study the rhythms of the city."[72]

Sokolow's modern dance bodies possessed a physical groundedness, a bodily strength that gave and took their weight as they negotiated their relationship to gravity. Propelled by a revolutionary ideological militancy, they corporealized timely calibrated movements conveying a sense of complete commitment as they pierced through clearly designed spatial formations.[73] This politicized forceful corporeality must have been what commanded audiences' attention and mobilized their emotions. As dance scholar Mark Franko has noted about the role of emotion in revolutionary dance at that time in New York City, "[w]ithout emotion, no revolution."[74]

One can imagine the emotional and ideological excitement that Mérida must have experienced while seeing such a powerful group of dancers. Their revolutionary dance practice combined proletarian and anti-fascist political militancy with rigorous technical proficiency in ways he had advocated for during his presentation to his comrades at the LEAR conference in 1937. Furthermore, Sokolow's refined technique was traceable to Martha Graham, whom Mérida had described as "extraordinary . . . the highest exponent of contemporary choreography," and with whom Sokolow had trained and danced.[75] That night, Mérida propelled himself backstage to invite Sokolow and her group to Mexico City. Forty years later, Sokolow reminisced about their encounter: "I thought he [Mérida] was kidding me [but] he was serious!" she exclaimed.[76] Shortly after their backstage meeting, she received a formal invitation from the Department of Fine Arts of the Mexican government to perform in Mexico City. As Sokolow and her group traveled down to the Mexican capital, a new direction was about to begin in making a national modern dance form in Mexico.

After some tribulations due to a lack of suitable organization for their trip south of the Mexico-US border, Sokolow and her Dance Unit arrived in Mexico City in

---

[71] For historical accounts of these debates in New York City, see Ellen Graff, *Stepping Left: Radical Dance in New York City, 1928–1942* (Durham, NC: Duke University Press, 1997); Mark Franko, *Dancing Modernism/Performing Politics* (Bloomington: Indiana University Press, 1995); Lynn Garafola, Russell Gold, and Barbara Melosh, eds., *Of, by, and for the People: Dancing on the Left in the 1930s* (Society of Dance History Scholars, Studies in Dance History vol. 5, no. 1, Spring 1994).

[72] Larry Warren, *Anna Sokolow: The Rebellious Spirit* (Amsterdam: Harwood Academic Publishers, 1998), 63.

[73] See Kosstrin, "Inevitable Designs: Embodied Ideology in Anna Sokolow's Proletarian Dances," *Dance Research Journal* 45, no. 2 (August 2013): 5–23.

[74] Mark Franko, *The Work of Dance: Labor, Movement, and Identity in the 1930s* (Middletown, CT: Wesleyan University Press, 2002), 8

[75] Mérida 1937, quoted in Mendoza, *Escritos de Carlos Mérida*, 147.

[76] Quoted in Warren, *Anna Sokolow*, 81–2.

early April 1939. They received the star treatment customarily shown to international artists. Perhaps to make them feel at home, their hosts accommodated them at the luxurious Hotel Imperial, where according to Frances Hellman, one of Sokolow's dancers, "they serve only American food. It's owned by Mexicans, of course, but only Americans stay here."[77] As happened to many international dancers and other tourists, their hosts took Sokolow's group to the most picturesque places in the Mexican capital (Figure 4.9). Sokolow remembered introductions to "all the great artists—[Diego] Rivera, [José Clemente] Orozco, [David Alfaro] Siqueiros," who accepted her as a "fellow artist."[78] So enthusiastic was their welcome that she declared, "for the first time in my life I knew what it felt like to be an artist [because Mexicans] have a tradition of respecting art and whoever is involved in art is respected there."[79] As Sokolow and her dancers came to feel at home in various ways, they integrated themselves into the class of cultural architects and social engineers—national and international artists, intellectuals, and government officials—shaping Mexican political and dance histories.[80]

Asserting Herself on Mexico City Stages: Sokolow's Dances as a "Truly" Revolutionary Art

Mérida's ideological and kinesthetic empathic resonances while watching Sokolow's dancing bodies in New York City indeed aligned with some of his colleagues' experiences when they saw the group performing *Poema Guerrero* [War Poem] in Mexico City at the cultural cathedral of Mexican high art, the Palacio de Bellas Artes [Palace of Fine Arts] (Figure 4.10).[81] Late in April 1939, dance critic César Ortiz lauded the performance as a "faithful reproduction of the rhythms of death" contextualized by war, which forcefully responded to fascism.[82] He described bodies moving with "strange contortions," expressions of

---

[77] Letter from Mexico City to her family in the Bronx, New York. "Frances Hellman's Diary: With Anna Sokolow in Mexico, 1939," *Sokolow Theater/Dance Ensemble*, dated near April 6, 1939, 18, accessed February 202, 2022, https://sokolowtheatredance.org/archives/frances-hellmans-diary-with-anna-sokolow-in-mexico-1939/.

[78] Sokolow, quoted in Warren, *Anna Sokolow*, 69.

[79] Ibid., 70.

[80] Sokolow would continue traveling between Mexico City and New York City, often living six months at a time in each place for decades.

[81] The program for Sokolow's show on April 22, 1939, at the Palace of Fine Arts lists dancers Aza Cefkin, Ruth Freeman, Frances Hellman, Rose Levy, Grusha Mark, Rebecca Rowen, Katherine Russell, Florence Schneider, Sasha Spector; musical director Alex North; and, as a guest artist, baritone singer Mordecai Bauman. "Frances Hellman's Diary," slides 47–49, accessed February 2, 2020, https://sokolowtheatredance.org/archives/frances-hellmans-diary-with-anna-sokolow-in-mexico-1939/.

[82] "La danza moderna," *El popular*, April 21, 1939, 3.

Figure 4.9 Anna Sokolow's dance group on a Mexican *trajinera* (Mexican gondola) at Xochimilco park, April 15, 1939. Anna Sokolow (*top right*) and Frances Hellman (*bottom right*) with other unidentified company members. Courtesy of the family of Edward J. and Frances H. Bauman.

agony as if on a battlefield where torsos were being torn apart by the fire of heavy artillery, legs and arms agitatedly dangling in the air as the "muted protest of humanity."[83] The critic likewise characterized Sokolow's *Exilio* [The exile] as having a "clear political message and defined anti-fascist stand."[84] Like Mérida, Ortiz

[83] Ibid.
[84] Ibid., 6.

Figure 4.10 Anna Sokolow on the front page of a printed program for a show by her company at the Palace of Fine Arts, Mexico City, April 22, 1939. Photograph of Anna Sokolow in "Slaughter of the Innocents" by Barbara Morgan. Courtesy of the family of Edward J. and Frances H. Bauman.

appreciated that such political militancy was not compromised by "gratuitous recourse" to such socialist-themed props and costumes as "the red flag and the overalls," as many Mexican dancers had done in the service of creating "'revolutionary' dance."[85] He assumed that Sokolow's right combination of ideology and artistic rigor awakened "pleasant sensations of superiority that only *real art* can elicit" and from which Mexican dancers could learn (emphasis added) (Figure 4.11).[86]

Writing for another leftist publication, *El popular*, on April 27, 1939, dance critic Lya Kostakowsky echoed Ortiz's praise for Sokolow's work vis-à-vis deficient dance efforts in the country. She also cherished the possibility of developing a more sophisticated form of Mexican dance. The commentator began her analysis, like Ortiz, by noting, in her opinion, the failed efforts the majority of Mexican dancers (and their advocates) had shown in the formation of a genuinely

[85] Ibid.
[86] Ibid., 3.

Figure 4.11 Anna Sokolow dancing. Roberto el Diablo, "Marginalias faranduleras," *Revista de revistas*, April 9, 1939, 31. Public Domain, Courtesy of Biblioteca Miguel Lerdo de Tejada de la Secretaría de Hacienda y Crédito Público.

artistic dance form. She critiqued the Campobello sisters' *Ballet Simbólico 30-30* for what she saw as its colorful unpleasantness, emotional and technical hollowness, and employment of groups of people who merely acted in a "revolutionary" manner while wearing overalls and carrying red flags.[87] Kostakowsky attributed the more than 200 performances of the mass dance in the preceding three years to the stubbornness of those desiring to create a "proletariat art"

---

[87] Kostakowsky, "La juventud de Anna Sokolow," *El popular*, April 27, 1939, unpaged.

without really knowing much about art.[88] Thus, the writer prescribed that an "authentically revolutionary artistic manifestation must be, before anything else, art."[89] She saw the right synthesis of aesthetics as revolution and anti-fascism in Sokolow's *La matanza de los inocentes* [Slaughter of the innocents], in which an archetypal Spanish mother carries her dead son in her arms while running beneath the strikes of fascist airplanes. So strong must have been the power of this highly stylized choreographic representation of war and human despair that Kostakowsky reported how one's hands would clench at the thought of the fascist barbarism that the regime of Francisco Franco represented in Spain.[90]

Taking the Reins of Mexican Modern Dance: Sokolow's Ballet de Bellas Artes

Mérida, Ortiz, and Kostakowsky, among others, called for sophisticated revolutionary art rather than mere proletariat agitprop.[91] Sokolow embodied the *right* synthesis of *leftist* political ideology and rigorous modernist aesthetics for these Mexican cultural arbiters.[92] For them, she was the perfect candidate to lay the foundation for developing a new Mexican modern dance practice.

A month after her debut, the press reported that the Casa del Artista [House of the Artist], funded by the Secretariat of Education, was forming its first "corps de ballet" and would soon start rehearsing four ballets by Mexican composers.[93] Carlos Mérida, who had invited Sokolow to Mexico, was the institution's director of the plastic arts department. On May 27, a newspaper announced that Sokolow had been hired for eight months to train the newly formed corps de ballet.[94] The note relayed that the group of fifteen girls, some of whom had recently graduated from the School of Dance, would work with modern techniques that the "Russian artist possesses."[95] The article clarified that "the goal is not that Mrs. Sokolow imprints in our dancers any particular foreign styles but instead that she enables them technically through the field of modernism so that they can, by themselves, face the problems posed by the creation of a Mexican Ballet that must arise from Mexico's folkloric sources."[96] Sokolow was to lead the first groups of graduates

---

[88] Ibid.
[89] Ibid.
[90] Ibid.
[91] Revolutionary dancers and critics had similar debates in the early 1930s in New York City. See Reynoso, "Choreographing Politics."
[92] For an excellent analysis of how Sokolow's works mobilized communist politics within a transnational leftist circuit, primarily in the United States, Mexico, and Israel, see Kosstrin, *Honest Bodies*.
[93] *El universal*, "Inauguración de la 'Casa del Artista,'" March 30, 1939, 14.
[94] *El universal*, "Permanecerá en México la danzarina Anna Sokolow," May 27, 1939, 5.
[95] Ibid.
[96] Ibid.

from the state-sponsored dance schools into creating a mestizo dance form that combined US modernism and Mexican folklorism.

After a few private presentations and a show at the Fábregas Theater, the Department of Fine Arts presented Sokolow's Ballet de Bellas Artes [Ballet of Fine Arts] dance company to the general public.[97] The program included *Don Lindo de Almería* (the title references a male figure from the Spanish city of Almería), *Los pies de pluma* [The feathered feet or Feet as light as a feather], and *Entre sombras anda el fuego* [The fire walks between shadows]. Contrary to the initial plan announced in the newspaper, which was to use music from four Mexican composers for the dances, only one composition was by Mexican artist Blas Galindo. This change in music choices led some audiences and government officials with nationalist sentiments to express disappointment. They had hoped for Mexican sources to serve as material for creating dances with broad appeal to diverse audiences at home and abroad. While critics such as César Ortiz and Lya Kostakowsky praised Sokolow's US group, the Dance Unit, for its use of rigorous dance technique and choreographic designs as an embodied response to fascism, others voiced resentment at Sokolow's emphasis on Spanish themes in works with her Ballet of Fine Arts Mexican dance company.

Strengthening Alliances with Anti-fascist Spanish Exiles in Mexico: Sokolow's La Paloma Azul

After Sokolow had completed her tenure at the state-sponsored dance company, she created a new group, La Paloma Azul [The Blue Dove], whose goal was to provide dancers with "modern and eclectic techniques" as part of producing culture and art that could serve as the basis for national spectacles.[98] This new group resulted as part of the cultural activities promoted by Spanish exiles residing in Mexico City. On September 6, 1940, a newspaper announced that Sokolow, the "dancer of supreme elegance," would open the fall season at the Palace of Fine Arts with this new dance company's inaugural presentation.[99] The program included dances previously presented with the Ballet of Fine Arts but also new pieces: *Antigona* [Antigone], *La madrugada del panadero* [The dawn of the baker], *El renacuajo paseador* [The wandering tadpole], and *Balcon de España* [Spanish balcony]. It was a collaborative production with Mexican and Spanish

[97] *El universal*, "Ballets—Jorge Sandor—Ángel Reyes," Sección: *Crónicas Musicales*, March 31, 1940, 11.
[98] *El universal*, "Anna Sokolow triunfa en su temporada de ballet," September 18, 1940, 8. The dance group initially formed under the name of Grupo Mexicano de Danzas Modernas y Clásicas [Mexican Group of Modern and Classical Dances].
[99] "La gran bailarina Anna Sokolow de la Paloma Azul," *El universal*, 2da sección, September 6, 1940, 6.

writers, musicians, and visual artists: José Bergamin, Carlos Chávez, Rodolfo Halffter, Carlos Mérida, Carlos Obregón Santacilia, and Silvestre Revueltas. Sokolow's roster of international collaborators destabilized essentialist notions of nationalist identity. In other words, who and what could be considered Mexican.

The tension created by those who supported a new flow of Spanish migration in the late 1930s, and those who harbored anti-Spanish sentiments since the colonization of Mexico, provided the context for debating Sokolow's work. As the renowned Mexican intellectual Carlos Monsiváis noted, "If Liberals in the XIX century made efforts to 'de-Hispanize' Mexico, the conservatives attempted to present the country as a branch office of the Gran Vía."[100] However, in 1939, the situation was more complex. President Lázaro Cárdenas's nationalism, one of the most radically revolutionary, included an anti-fascist stand in response to Hitler's rise to power in Germany and Francisco Franco in Spain. Members of the Spanish community already established in Mexico actively supported Cárdenas's efforts to receive Spaniards fleeing Franco's fascist dictatorship emerging during the Spanish Civil War (1936–1939).

Just a couple of weeks before the debut of Sokolow's US dance company in Mexico City, a newspaper reported that members of the Casa de España [House of Spain] were negotiating with French diplomats in Mexico. They requested the release of Spanish intellectuals held in concentration camps in France so that they could travel to Mexico.[101] Cárdenas's government had already received nearly 500 Spanish children in the summer of 1937,[102] and 599 additional Spanish exiles arrived in the port of Veracruz on the *Sinai* on June 13, 1939.[103] However, with xenophobic overtones, a newspaper editorial characterized the "unrestricted" opening of the country's doors to the Spanish migration as an "inconvenience" because Spaniards would take jobs from Mexicans and as an "error" because the immigrants could potentially meddle in events related to a series of upcoming elections.[104] Furthermore, the article generalized the identity of these exiles, characterizing them not as "workers" but as "professional political agitators expelled from their country."[105] Some of Sokolow's Spanish associates

---

[100] "Gran Vía" translates as "Great Way" and references a street, an urban esplanade serving as the cultural and commercial center in Madrid, Spain. Carlos Monsiváis, "García Lorca y México," in *Cuadernos hispanoamericanos: Homenaje a García Lorca* 1, no. 433–34 (July–August 1986): 249.

[101] *El universal*, "Más intelectuales españoles a México," March 9, 1939, 1.

[102] See Dolores Pla Brugat, *Los niños de Morelia: Un estudio sobre los primeros refugiados españoles en México* (México, DF: Instituto Nacional de Antropología e Historia, 1985).

[103] Archivo General de la Nación, "AGN Recuerda el Arribo del Sinai," June 12, 2017, accessed March 15, 2020, https://www.gob.mx/agn/articulos/agnrecuerda-el-arribo-del-sinaia?idiom=es.

[104] *El universal*, "El arribo de agitadores españoles," Sección Editorial, March 16, 1939, 3.

[105] Ibid. The welcoming attitude toward Spaniards became more ambivalent and less welcoming under President Manuel Ávila Camacho (1940–1946). Despite these tensions, the Mexican government favored Spanish political exiles, limiting refugee immigration for Jews fleeing the Holocaust.

in Mexico were born in the country to Spanish parents, and others arrived there from Spain within the previous few months and years.[106]

This influx of collaborators from Spain directly influenced Sokolow's dance work. Indeed, *Don Lindo de Almería*, a portrayal of life in the Andalusian region of Spain conceived by Bergamin and Halffter before they left Spain due to political turmoil, was one of Sokolow's most celebrated productions in Mexico.[107] Halffter learned that Sokolow spoke some Spanish and knew flamenco dancing, so he asked her to incorporate the Andalusian focus.[108] The critic Jesús Bal y Gay characterized the dance production as possessing a " 'shophisticate' [sic] Spanishism."[109] Barros Sierra experienced the work as a "masquerade of Andalusian customs,"[110] and dance historian Hannah Kosstrin concluded that part of its "dramatic action portrayed elite Spanishness."[111] Similarly, *Lluvia de Toros* [Rain of Bulls] inspired by the Spanish romantic painter Francisco José de Goya, and other dances in the program referenced Spanish life and political tribulations. Despite the cultural and geographical specificity of Spain as source material for these dances, the assumption was that they had a universal appeal within the historical context of the growth of fascism.[112] Still, many were disappointed because, as Nicholas Dorantes put it in the *Kenyon Review*, Sokolow "left untouched the enormous heritage from the Mexican dancing tradition."[113] Similarly, Carlos González Peña praised La Paloma Azul's young Mexican dancers for having accomplished a high degree of technical proficiency.[114] However, the critic noted that the group could pursue the "nationalization" of its repertoire by "imprinting it with Mexican profiles."[115] While some noticed Sokolow's work's proximity to Spanish influences, others highlighted its distance to Mexican sources.

---

[106] For historical accounts of the influx and influence of Spanish exiles in Mexico in and around 1939, see Mónica Jato, *El éxodo español de 1939: Una topología cultural del exilio* (Leiden: Brill Rodopi, 2020); Abdón Mateos, "Los republicanos españoles en el México cardenista," *Ayer*, No. 47, *Los exilios en la España contemporánea* (2002): 103–28.

[107] Both Bergamin and Halffter arrived in Mexico City at the invitation of President Cárdenas in May 1939 as part of a contingent of Spanish intellectuals to plan the reception of more Spanish exiles arriving in the country on the *Sinai* in June. See Nigel Dennis, "El baile en el exilio: La Paloma Azul (México, 1940)," in *El exilio republicano de 1939 y la segunda generación*, ed. Manuel Aznar Soler and José Ramón López García, Biblioteca del Exilio (Sevilla: Editorial Renacimiento, 2011): 865–76.

[108] Warren, *Anna Sokolow*, 1998.

[109] "'La Paloma Azul': Resumen de su primera temporada," *El universal*, Sección: *Cronicas Musicales*, October 20, 1940, 2.

[110] Quoted in Kosstrin, *Honest Bodies*, 107.

[111] Ibid., 108.

[112] These universalist assumptions resonated with Bergamin's ideas about "el idealismo andaluz" [Andalusian idealism] as a form of "andalucismo universal" [Andalusian universalism] that led to an "idealidad artística" [artistic ideality]. See Dennis, "El baile en el exilio."

[113] Quoted in Kosstrin, *Honest Bodies*, 117. As discussed later in this chapter, Sokolow embraced a more abstract approach to Mexican nationalism in the mid-1940s.

[114] "Los bailarines de 'La Paloma Azul,'" *El universal*, October 3, 1940, 3.

[115] "Queda una posibilidad más: la de nacionalizarlo imprimiéndole perfiles mexicanos." Ibid.

"Silent War" against La Paloma Azul's Spanishness: Toward Waldeen as an Alternative

Evidence suggests that La Paloma Azul's emphasis on Spain significantly contributed to Sokolow's shift from the state-sponsored Ballet de Bellas Artes to the privately funded dance company. The project received funding from Cárdenas's government via his personal secretary, Agustín Leñero. However, funding for the new group was money primarily acquired by the Junta de Cultura Española [Council of Spanish Culture] founded by Bergamin before arriving in Mexico City from Paris.[116] Adela Formoso de Obregón Santacilia, a philanthropist born in Mexico to Spanish parents,[117] and the wife of one of Sokolow's collaborators, was also a crucial financial supporter in the formation of Sokolow's new group.[118]

The phrase "La Paloma Azul" was associated with a traditional Mexican song, but the organization chose the expression because it was the name of a bar where people related to the new dance group gathered.[119] Despite these Mexican references, some critics highlighted what they perceived as the European lineage of the phrase. A writer identified as F. M. characterized Sokolow's company name as a "poetic one . . . and evocative of another group that was once famous in Europe," although he does not name the presumed precursor.[120] Bal y Gay thought La Paloma Azul was a "good title for a Mexican dance company, reminiscent of our European aesthetic affinities."[121] In this assessment, he may have been thinking of the song "La paloma azul," with its source in the colonial era (Spanish Basque composer Sebastián Iraider Salaverri composed "La paloma" in 1863. The song was later known as "La paloma azul"). Additionally, Bal y Gay may have been thinking of the dance group's slogan—"Las artes hice mágicas volando" [The arts magic I made flying]—a phrase from a 1624 poem written by Spanish poet Lope de Vega.[122] The European connotations that La Paloma Azul had for some enthusiasts endowed Sokolow's new Mexican dance company with

---

[116] Dennis, "El baile en el exilio."
[117] For a perspective of how Adela Formoso was seen as part of social and political life in Mexico City at the time, see Catalina D'Erzell, "Mujeres de México: Adela Formoso de Obregón S.," *Revista de revistas*, January 14, 1940, 2.
[118] Formoso married architect Carlos Obregón Santacilia, who designed decorations for Sokolow's *Antigone*.
[119] Dennis, "El baile en el exilio."
[120] "Teatros," *El universal*, September 22, 1940, 11.
[121] "Sandor—La Paloma Azul," *El universal*, Sección, *Crónicas Musicales*, September 22, 1940: 10.
[122] *Últimos amores de Lope de Vega Carpio, revelados por él mismo en cuarenta y ocho cartas inéditas y varias poesías* (Madrid: Imprenta de José María Ducazcal, 1876), 140. The poetic nature of the slogan invites distinctive interpretations. Kosstrin translates the phrase as "I transformed the arts into flying magic" (*Honest Bodies*, 113).

an added sense of prestige and legitimacy, but not everyone was enthusiastic. Nationalists saw these associations as too Eurocentric.

The focus on modern dances that emphasized Spanish themes, and the addition of dancers and dances from Spain as part of La Paloma Azul, worried some members of the artistic organization. Even some of Sokolow's closest supporters considered the move an unfortunate miscalculation with ideological and practical consequences. Responding to a program that included Sokolow's company alongside a Spanish group directed by renowned flamenco dancer Antonio Triana in September 1940, Bal y Gay complained that it was a "pity from the Mexican standpoint" that La Paloma Azul had offered an entire program of "imported dance" (Figure 4.12).[123] His disappointment lay in the fact that "the corporeal reality that animated the stage was a Spanish group" under Spanish direction, relegating the Mexican dancer Margo to performing in Spanish dances.[124] Like many others, Bal y Gay claimed that the company's goal should be to adapt modern techniques for the creation of a dance form that could evoke, not necessarily mimic, a presupposed essence of the Mexican character.[125] In his note titled "La Paloma Azul: Spanishized," the critic characterized La Paloma Azul's inclusion of Spanish artists and dances as a "lamentable mistake."[126]

Mérida, who had been a Sokolow ally all along, was well-versed in the era's political and aesthetic ideological debates. Since the early 1930s, he had actively advocated for creating a Mexican dance form and professionalizing dancers. As part of the close group of La Paloma Azul collaborators, he (like others who sensed potentially negative consequences) counseled against the group's expansion beyond its initial goal of forming a Mexican dance company with Sokolow. Like Bal y Gay, Mérida thought that the "grafting" of Sokolow's La Paloma Azul with Spanish dances by Spanish artists was a "capital error" resulting in "a very explicable antagonism between the two widely dissimilar parts" performing together in some of the same shows and being part of the same artistic organization.[127] He lamented that this mistake caused the project to be cut down from ten to only five performances, thereby hindering young Mexican dancers' opportunities to gain professional performing experience.[128]

---

[123] "La Paloma Azul: Españolizada," *El universal*, 2da Sección: *Cronicas Musicales*, September 29, 1940, 2.
[124] Ibid.
[125] Ibid.
[126] Ibid.
[127] "'La Paloma Azul . . .': Lo que el publico no ve," *El universal*, Sección: *El Ojo de la Llave*, December 3, 1940, 3.
[128] Ibid.

Figure 4.12 Ad for one of La Paloma Azul's shows, including Anna Sokolow and her Mexican dancers alongside Antonio Triana's Spanish Ballet and guest artists. *El universal*, October 4, 1940, 11. Public Domain, Courtesy of Biblioteca Miguel Lerdo de Tejada de la Secretaría de Hacienda y Crédito Público.

Knowledgeable about institutional bureaucracy, as he had been part of it, Mérida decried the lack of governmental support for La Paloma Azul and characterized the Department of Fine Arts' disinterest as a "guerra sorda" [silent war] waged against Sokolow's group.[129] He denounced the inadequate technical assistance and limited time given to the modern dance troupe at the Palace of Fine Arts for dress rehearsals and shows. For Lluvia de Toros, the dancers were allowed to rehearse in the performance space for only one hour the day before the show. To accommodate a presentation of The Wizard of Oz by a group of preschoolers for about 200 of their "mamás desmañanadas" [sleepy mothers who had gotten out of bed early], the theater canceled Sokolow's scheduled morning rehearsal.[130]

For El Renacuajo Paseador, Sokolow's La Paloma Azul was allowed to rehearse at the Palace of Fine Arts ninety minutes the day prior and only thirty minutes the day of the show. During the premiere, the staff refused to move a large duck, designed by Mérida, onto the stage, thereby preventing it from appearing as part of the work.[131] Similarly, stagehands were unwilling to pull the backstage ropes necessary to lift a set-designed pig carrying the eponymous protagonist of Don Lindo de Almería while he tried to escape a compromising situation in the dance's plot.[132] The lack of technical assistance and limited rehearsal time hindered the quality of works presented by Sokolow's dance group. Quarrels over the integration of Spanish dances by Spanish dancers, the lack of official production support, and decreased funding—including by Adela Formoso—contributed to the disbanding of La Paloma Azul.

When she arrived in Mexico City the previous year, Sokolow garnered the favor of the press as a model of a truly revolutionary artist who had mastered the combination of political ideology and modernist aesthetics in the United States. Her distrust of overt nationalist and revolutionary references aligned with critics who associated abstraction and universalism with notions of legitimate modern art.[133] Furthermore, her commitment to antifascism understandably led her to establish close alliances with Spanish artists and intellectuals who had fled the rise of fascism in Spain before arriving in Mexico. However, the perceived emphasis on Spanish themes in her dances caused disappointment among Mexicans who hoped that Sokolow would help them create a modern dance form that could reflect the country's character and have universal appeal. Despite critiques by nationalists, Sokolow changed how people thought about dance as she provided a model for young Mexican dancers to experience what it meant to

[129] Ibid.
[130] Ibid.
[131] Ibid.
[132] Ibid.
[133] For more on this topic, see the coda.

be a modern dancer in mid-twentieth century Mexico. Her contributions were vital for rethinking and rechoreographing new forms of mestizo modernisms. However, as private and state support became elusive for her company, a new alternative was already in the works.

The Emergence of a "Truly" Mexican Revolutionary Dance with Universal Appeal: Waldeen's *La Coronela*

As part of official efforts to create a dance form "of profound Mexican style and spirit," in early October 1940 government officials redirected resources to a different project for which rehearsals were underway: one under Waldeen.[134] Mérida was disappointed by what he saw as a narrow-minded initiative, finding it "absurd, penurious, and unintelligent" to grant exclusive institutional support to only one group.[135] The Department of Fine Arts under director Celestino Gorostiza (through an arts council that included artists Gabriel Fernández Ledesma and Seki Sano[136]) hired Waldeen to lead a reinvigorated Ballet of Fine Arts, the same group previously directed by Sokolow. According to the press, the Mexican group's new choreographic direction would focus on the "basic study of universal dance, contemporary as well as classical ballet techniques, and styles from foreign and folkloric dances."[137]

This artistic mission to adopt modernizing dance techniques to create dances with Mexican character was not much different from that initially expected of Sokolow. However, while some of Sokolow's dances relied on Spanish elements to choreograph universal themes, Waldeen's new group's Mexican universalism was marked more explicitly by brown bodies and their folkloric cultural repertoires. As her case shows, Waldeen's work, specifically *La Coronela*, relied on the particularity of Mexican culture and history as legitimate sources to create a nationalist dance form that was revolutionary and

---

[134] *El universal*, "Estudio básico de la danza universal: Ha comenzado el entrenamiento de un ballet mexicano, nueva técnica," October 8, 1940, 7.
[135] "'La Paloma Azul,'" 3.
[136] Seki Sano was a foundational figure in the development of modern Japanese theater in the 1920s and Latin America after the 1940s. As with many communist fellow travelers circulating within leftist transnational networks, he arrived in Mexico City from New York City as a political exile in 1939 after having built an international reputation as a theater artist. Like Sokolow and Waldeen, Sano soon began collaborating with the leftist Mexican intellectual and artistic elites. He played influential roles in shaping the ideological and artistic development of Waldeen's *La Coronela*, a dance work discussed below. See Sandra Pujals, "*Los Poputchiki*: Communist Fellow Travelers, Comintern Radical Networks, and the Forging of a Culture of Modernity in Latin America and the Caribbean," in *Left Transnationalism: The Communist International and the National, Colonial, and Racial Questions*, ed. Oleksa Drachewych and Ian McKay (Montreal: McGill-Queen's University Press, 2019), 155–82.
[137] *El universal*, "Estudio básico de la danza," 7.

universal. In so doing, the work advanced official racial and cultural discourses the government promoted as foundational to reconstructing the nation and the ideologies of *mestizaje* and *mexicanidad*.

A Different Type of Revolutionary Artist: Waldeen's Way to Mexico

Waldeen trained in ballet with the Russian dancer and actor Theodore Kosloff and had her first solo performance at age thirteen for the Los Angeles Opera Company in 1926. Five years later, she met Japanese American modern dance choreographer Michio Ito while he toured in California. She joined his company and performed with him nationally and internationally. Waldeen's visit to Mexico City in 1934 in Ito's dance company influenced her reception as an independent artist upon her return to the city in 1939.

On her first visit to Mexico City, she stood out among Ito's dancers. Critics described her dancing with tropes associating aesthetics with spirituality, not politics. A writer identified as Amendolla characterized her as "Terpsichore's masterful priestess" whose dancing "body and spirit," reflected in her temperament and expressive force, captivated audiences (Figure 4.13).[138] In a daring gesture, the commentator compared the dancer to one of the most revered religious figures in a primarily Catholic country: Waldeen was as "full of grace as the Ave María."[139] In casting Waldeen as the hybrid embodiment of an ancient Greek priestess (aligned to the Muse of dance) and the holy Virgin Mother, Amendolla attempted to establish the modern dancer's import as an aesthetic and spiritual artist of the highest order. Relying on similar assumptions about the inherent spirituality of high art and its ostensible capacity to transcend the mundane desires of the flesh, Arturo Rigel spoke of Waldeen's "spontaneous" rhythms, full of grace and emotion, as capable of ridding her body—a "palpitating sculpture"—of any "tempting sexual characteristics."[140] For Rigel, the desexualized dancer's body was simultaneously the result and the conduit of a spiritually transcendental aestheticism, an aesthetic discourse that emphasized the role high art

---

[138] "Una fiesta de plasticidad y belleza fue la presentación de Michio Ito el notable bailarín japones y sus solistas," *La prensa*, June 4, 1934, 4.

[139] This was a daring gesture because in 1919, another critic compared Anna Pavlova to the Virgin. This act led to public protests and demands from a Catholic organization for minor excommunication from the church for both the newspaper writer and Pavlova; *El pueblo*, "Han sido excomulgados un diario local y la Pavlowa," February 12, 1919, 3. For a more detailed discussion of this incident, see Reynoso, "Choreographing Politics," 66–7.

[140] "Waldeen: Artista y creadora," Fotos de Agustín Jiménez, *Revista de revistas*, July 15, 1934, 27.

Figure 4.13 Waldeen demonstrating her modernist movement lyricism. Roberto el Diablo, "La semana teatral," *Revista de revistas*, June 17, 1934, unpaged. Public Domain, Courtesy of Biblioteca Miguel Lerdo de Tejada de la Secretaría de Hacienda y Crédito Público.

played in producing a spirituality with civilizing effects on the base instincts of the flesh.[141]

After a successful engagement in Mexico City in 1934 as an extraordinary modern dancer with Ito's company, Waldeen returned to the United States. She worked in Hollywood performing various dance forms in films to make money

---

[141] For analyses of the relationship between dance aesthetics and spiritual discourse concerning the dancing body and the legitimization of dance as an art form in the works of Ruth St. Denis and Isadora Duncan, see Susan L. Foster, "Closets Full of Dances: Modern Dance's Performance of Masculinity and Sexuality," in *Dancing Desires: Choreographing Sexualities on and off the Stage*, ed. Jane C. Desmond (Madison: University of Wisconsin Press, 2001), 147–207; Jane C. Desmond, "Dancing Out the Difference: Cultural Imperialism and Ruth St. Denis's 'Radha' of 1906," *Signs* 17, no. 1 (Autumn 1991): 28–49.

to fund her independent productions.[142] In New York City, she taught modern dance, choreography, and dance history at the Nicholas Roerich Museum and the Neighborhood Playhouse, before finally debuting at the Guild Theater in February 1938.[143] John Martin, the influential modern dance theorist-critic, noted that the dance method Waldeen had developed revealed "the characteristic strengths of both styles, of the ballet and of the Japanese dancer [Ito]," and he explained that the "former gives her a brilliance that she uses well and the latter has enabled her to acquire attacking precision."[144]

However, writing for the *New York Herald-Tribune*, dance critic Jerome Bohm evaluated Waldeen's work in direct relation to the dance environment in New York at the time. He said, "Only here and there, as in the 'Dance for Regeneration,' . . . was there a suggestion in an occasional gesture or movement of a more modern [than Duncan's] approach, although at no time could her efforts be closely associated with the newer trends in her art."[145] For these and other writers, Waldeen's ballet training was as recognizable in her technique as was Ito's influence. Bohm seemed to suggest that Waldeen's eclectic modern dance style was not contemporary enough and thus did not align with either revolutionary or bourgeois approaches being debated in New York City in the early 1930s when Sokolow was rising as a star of the revolutionary dance.[146] Waldeen's experimentations with different dance idioms seemed to have rendered her a "misfit modernist" in this specific cultural and historical context.[147]

Indeed, Waldeen appears not to have identified with contemporary ("bourgeois") modern dance in New York City. While not favoring Graham's technique, she later remembered, "I did not have any intention of falling into the trap of a new formalism; for me, the majority of dance styles in New York had fallen into that."[148] Although she strove to develop a socially conscious movement practice expressive of the "inner world of the dancer" and the "external reality of life and society," she did not seem to have a place within New York City's revolutionary

---

[142] Jonathan Cohen, "Waldeen and the Americas: The Dance Has Many Faces," in *A Woman's Gaze: Latin American Women Artists*, ed. Marjorie Agosín (Fredonia, NY: White Pine Press, 1998), 224–42.

[143] Ibid.

[144] Quoted in Delgado Martínez, *Waldeen: La Coronela de la danza mexicana* (México: FONCA, Escenología, 2000), 24.

[145] Quoted in Cohen, "Waldeen and the Americas," 228.

[146] Early in the 1930s, some dancers and critics in New York used *revolutionary* and *bourgeois* to distinguish between what they perceived as an emphasis on political ideology or formal aesthetics, respectively, as if assuming these possibilities were always mutually exclusive.

[147] For a formulation of the concept of "misfit moderns" to describe the work of writers who did not conform to modernism's literary conventions, see Rob Hawke, *Ford Madox Ford and the Misfit Moderns: Edwardian Fiction and the First World War* (Basingstoke: Palgrave Macmillan, 2012).

[148] Quoted in Delgado Martínez, *Waldeen*, 23.

dance community either.[149] What Waldeen especially wanted was to avoid what she called "the coercive seal of the latest technological artifacts, with their anti-humanism and automatization of men and women."[150] By the end of the 1930s, Waldeen had cultivated embodied histories and aesthetic ideas that at times overlapped with those of Sokolow but that also differed, often significantly. These differences would become evident as Waldeen's second visit to Mexico City coincided with Sokolow's tour there.

Waldeen arrived in the Mexican capital in 1939 with two other soloists, Winifred Widener and Elizabeth Waters. Critics expressed contradictory opinions about her work. As in her first visit in 1934, some regarded her as among the modernist reformers of the art of dance. The critic F. M. declared that, aesthetically, Waldeen was doing in dance what some audacious painters had "merely begun to see" because she truly was "a modern, sober, innovator spirit" (Figure 4.14).[151] However, others saw Waldeen's work as antithetical to legitimate high art. The influential critic Carlos González Peña, who had chronicled Pavlova's visits during 1919 and 1925, distrusted Waldeen as one more of those stemming from a lineage of the "desatornillada" [unscrewed] Isadora Duncan.[152] He saw Waldeen as embodying a new understanding of dance arising from what he deemed Duncan's negative influence. Disapprovingly, he lamented that "what once we used to understand as dance, is no longer dance."[153] According to González Peña's aesthetic ideology and sensibilities, Waldeen's experimental movement vocabulary and music choices contributed to a desecration of the art of dance by dancers like her who created a "symbolic and abstract language" that the writer claimed nobody understood.[154]

Despite detractors like González Peña, the innovative modern dancer was fervently embraced by the artistic and intellectual community in Mexico City, like Sokolow. As Waldeen remembered, "Everything was opening up for Mexican artists and they just carried me with them. They were my teachers—they introduced me to Mexico . . . I was simply saturated with Mexico. I didn't want to go back to the United States."[155] Indeed, Waldeen became a Mexican citizen and stayed in the country for the rest of her life. Neither she nor González Peña—nor very many others—ever imagined that Waldeen would become one of the most

---

[149] By the mid-1930s, militant revolutionary dance had already begun to shift from a focus on the "worker" to the abstract construct of the "people," a focus that was shaped in part by events leading up to World War II (see Graff, *Stepping Left*).

[150] Quoted in Delgado Martínez, *Waldeen*, 23.

[151] "Granados y Waldeen en Bellas Artes," *El universal*, 3ra. Sección: *Teatros*, March 5, 1939, 1.

[152] "La farsa del baile," *El universal*, April 6, 1939, 3. *Desatornillada/o* suggests that a person, here related to a machine as a metaphor, thinks or functions erratically as if all the person's screws are not in place and properly tightened. Being "crazy" is a common negative connotation of the word.

[153] Ibid.

[154] Ibid.

[155] Quoted in Cohen, "Waldeen and the Americas," 229.

Figure 4.14 Waldeen performing embodied geometric, architectural designs, valued characteristics of dance modernism. Arturo Rigel, "Waldeen, artista creadora," *Revista de revistas*, July 22, 1934, unpaged. Photographer, Agustín Jiménez. Public Domain, Courtesy of Biblioteca Miguel Lerdo de Tejada de la Secretaría de Hacienda y Crédito Público.

influential figures in the development of Mexican nationalist dance. As Waldeen and Sokolow emphasized different aspects of cultural and revolutionary content in dance-making, dance artists, critics, government officials, and audiences continued debating what constituted dance as a legitimate form of universal modern art.

Choreographing Mexican Universalism: *La Coronela*'s Embodied Politics

In March 1939, while concluding a series of her shows at the Palace of Fine Arts, Waldeen taught her "difficult postures" to advanced students at the School of Dance.[156] She then took the reins of the state-sponsored Ballet of Fine Arts dance company that Sokolow had led months earlier. With her new company, Waldeen premiered four works at the Palace of Fine Arts on November 23, 1940. By relying on Mexican history and culture as sources of inspiration, these works represented an alternative to what some nationalists perceived as Sokolow's emphasis on Spanish themes. While Waldeen's works followed the Campobello sisters' approach to staging representations of female revolutionary leaders, she introduced innovative combinations of (modernizing) dance techniques.

The four pieces in Waldeen's premiere were sequenced in a way that they created different meanings individually and as a collective. *Seis Danzas Clasicas: Variaciones* [Six classical dances: Variations], which opened the night of performances, was a short series of dances to music by Johann Sebastian Bach. Critic Horacio Quiñones declared that the piece evinced Mexico's "comprehension of what is universally human."[157] Indeed, these dance variations may have been an attempt to begin the evening by stating that Mexican dancing bodies could be modern subjects. Only one year earlier, the Mexican critic González Peña had critiqued Waldeen for her "predilection for certain moderns," including Bach.[158] With this piece, and contra this criticism, the modernist dance artist employed the composer's music just as Isadora Duncan, one of Waldeen's inspirations, had used it in the past. The softness of classically trained dancers who strove to move gracefully in space characterized the dance movement vocabulary.

With this first dance of the night, Waldeen's Mexican dancers demonstrated their ability to *be* both modern and universal. They did so by employing aesthetic elements associated with notions of (white) Western culture as the highest

---

[156] *El universal*, "Teatros: Danzas y danzarines," March 28, 1939, 10.
[157] "El ballet mexicano," *Hoy*, dibujos de Germán Horacio, December 7, 1940, 72.
[158] "La farsa del baile," 3.

standard of human civilization and the representative of a universal human experience. However, through the three subsequent dances, the program seemed to say something different, something like, "look, we can dance to the (Western) rhythms of human civilization, but we can also choose to construct universal dances out of our own cultural and historical idiosyncrasies." Waldeen and her collaborators were determined to choreograph a form of Mexican universalism.

According to one newspaper, *Procesional* [Processional], the program's second dance represented "the Spanish domination in Mexico."[159] As state-sponsored muralism had done through visual imagery on public buildings since the 1920s, Waldeen's *Procesional*, through dancing bodies, reminded people of their colonial history as integral to forging a dominant racial discourse of *mestizaje*. In its contemporary moment, the piece also seemed to critique what some nationalists viewed with suspicion: the strong cultural influence that exiled Spanish artists and intellectuals had in the country during the 1930s. Indeed, a writer identified as Roberto El Diablo noted, with a tone of resentment, how the influence of these "so-called 'refuges' [sic]" "had a manifested meddling in our theatrical activities."[160]

As if choreographing an anticolonial stand, *Procesional* embodied sentiments against both historical colonialism and the current Spanish-centrism of specific artistic productions in the city, including those by Sokolow's Ballet of Fine Arts and later La Paloma Azul. Like other fellow artists, Waldeen and her dancers wanted Mexico's new forces—peasants, working classes, indigenous communities, and their cultural and political histories—to represent a legitimate source for a new mestizo modern dance form. The third dance in the program, *Danza de las Fuerzas Nuevas* [Dance of the new forces], not only "expressed the agitated life of modern Mexico"[161] but also conveyed a sense of the country's faith in its future.[162]

La Coronela, the concluding work, choreographed these new forces onstage as mobilized by a female colonel who led the transition from the Porfiriato to a revolutionary state. This dance was conceived almost as an ideological "homage" to President Cárdenas's further institutionalization of the Mexican Revolution.[163] As the president shared in a speech to university students early in May 1940, "a culture lacking a concrete sense of solidarity with the pain of common people is not fecund; it is limited culture, a mere ornament of parasites who obstruct

---

[159] *El universal*, "Gran temporada en el Palacio de Bellas Artes," Segunda Sección, October 25, 1940, 8.
[160] "Ballet y revista," *Revista de revistas*, Sección: *El Año Teatral*, December 29, 1940, 22.
[161] *El universal*, "Gran temporada," 8.
[162] Quiñones, "El ballet mexicano," 72.
[163] Lavalle, quoted in Tortajada Quiroz, "La Coronela de Waldeen: Una danza revolucionaria," *Casa del tiempo* 1, no. 8 (June 2008): 57.

collectivism as a project."[164] Cárdenas highlighted the role cultural practices must play in fulfilling his government's revolutionary populist mandate.

La Coronela, arranged in four parts, physically represented the trajectory of these common people, the disinherited ones, from oppression to liberation. The opening piece, "Damitas de Aquellos Tiempos" [Ladies of Those Past Times], parodied the frivolities and banalities of the female bourgeoisie inspired by French culture under Porfirio Díaz's regime.[165] Highly mimetic yet stylized movement vocabulary characterized by lightness and delicacy portrayed aristocratic ladies going about various activities, from dancing and leisurely strolling to having tea while gossiping. Props, sets, and costumes supported this physicalized sense of cultural elitism and class privilege.[166]

Employing a more abstract, modernist movement style and music by composers Silvestre Revueltas and Blas Galindo, "Danza de los Desheredados" [Dance of the Disinherited] represented the other side of the social and economic (if not racial) spectrum. Through women's bodies, it staged the plight of the dispossessed who had endured centuries of economic, social, and political struggles (Figures 4.15 and 4.16).[167] Their physical heaviness, almost lethargic being, as they sat and knelt on the ground with backs and heads bending forward as if depleted of energy, their torsos slowly rocking from side to side, gradually rising, signaled the dense atmosphere of marginalization that contained their bodies during the Porfiriato. Their bodies physicalized their historical inner turmoil as their arms hammered forward and down into the air in forceful punctuations that transformed into effortful energy. The women's emotional and physical energies flowing through their limbs seemed to burst out through the tips of their fully stretched and outspread fingers. As if searching within their bodies for the force of their resilience, their heads and upper backs bending backward created elastic counterpoint tension, while their fisted hands pulled down in the opposite direction in front of their standing and kneeling bodies. These expressions of bodily tension and effortful energies corporealized some of the emotional, affective, and visceral sensations that a body might experience while forging through immediate and historical time and space.

Music critic Sonia Verbitzty, like many others, found this dance deeply moving. The sense of expectation was high before hearing the first musical notes,

---

[164] Cárdenas, quoted in ibid., 54.

[165] See figure 2.1 of David Alfaro Siqueiros's "From the Dictatorship of Porfirio Díaz to the Revolution," a section of his mural *The People in Arms* (1957), in chapter 2.

[166] Unless otherwise noted, descriptions of sections in *La Coronela* are based on my viewing of a reconstruction of the work in 1986. I am grateful to Dr. Margarita Tortajada Quiroz for facilitating a DVD copy of this production: *La Coronela*. Dirección Artística, Ana Mérida; Montaje Coreográfico, Evelia Beristain y Josefina Lavalle. Producido por la Unidad de Televisión Educativa y Cultura (UTEC) en colaboración con el Instituto Nacional de Bellas Artes (INBA), 1986, DVD.

[167] Thanks to Dr. Tortajada Quiroz for helping me identify dancers in Figures 4.15–4.17.

Figure 4.15 *From left*: Edmée Pérez, Gloria Mestre, Ana Mérida, and Evelia Beristaín in the "Dance of the Disinherited," a section of *La Coronela*, Mexico City, c. 1950. Photographer, Simón Flechine SEMO. Courtesy of Instituto Nacional de Antropología e Historia.

and the curtain began to rise. "I waited," she said, "with anguish, with shortness of breath, my throat was dry."[168] She elaborated:

> A group of disinherited female silhouettes began to emerge from the Shadows. With remarkably slow and profound lines, with a sharp F in the lower tonalities, Revueltas sings [and the women dance] pain . . . an implacable pain . . . the pain of a whole race, of the people of a country. The Mexican woman moans, she bends down due to her torment as the music expresses her agony. There are accents of supplication, accents of revelry, of cries and grumbles. Pain and more pain. It seems as though all that Mexico has suffered for centuries has been accumulated in its son Silvestre Revueltas [and in the dancers' moving bodies].[169]

---

[168] Sonia Verbitzty, "'La Coronela' de Silvestre Revueltas," *El universal*, Suplemento Dominical: *Magazine Para Todos*, December 8, 1940, 2.

[169] Ibid. Revueltas was an accomplished Mexican musician who composed the music for the dance.

Figure 4.16 *From left*: Edmée Pérez, Ana Mérida, and Guillermina Bravo in the "Dance of the Disinherited," a section of *La Coronela*, Mexico City, c. 1950. Photographer, Simón Flechine SEMO. Courtesy of Instituto Nacional de Antropología e Historia.

For the critic, the music and the dance activated bodily and affective sensations through the combined effect of aural stimuli and a kinesthetic empathy that enabled her and others to *feel* the historical pain of a national collective.[170]

Verbitzty saw female dancers as universal proxies for all Mexicans who had endured centuries of colonization under the Spanish and the French, subjugation under Díaz, and capitalist exploitation from Europe and the United States. However, they also stood for archetypes of womanhood. The dancers wore a simple blouse and wide dark-blue skirt, with an undecorated shawl around their heads. The plain costumes and austere colors effectively portrayed these women as universal mothers, daughters, wives, and lovers. Their abstracted movement vocabulary embodied human suffering and struggle amid sociopolitical turmoil, conveying the loss of their children, siblings, spouses, and partners.

As the dance continued, the women witnessed the arrest of the (indigenous) man, who stood for all other men, by representatives of the two pillars of

---

[170] For analyses of scientific, sociopolitical, and cultural contexts within which different formulations of the concept of kinesthetic empathy (as the capacity to experience the movement one sees in others, including dance) have developed, see Foster, *Choreographing Empathy: Kinesthesia in Performance* (London: Routledge, 2011).

MAKING A POSTREVOLUTIONARY MODERN DANCE FORM 217

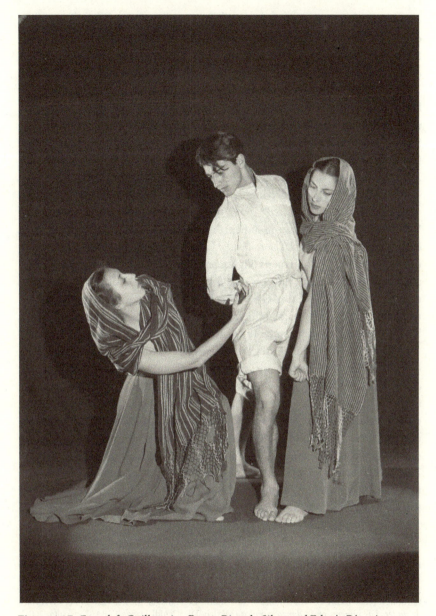

Figure 4.17 *From left*: Guillermina Bravo, Ricardo Silva, and Edmée Pérez in the "Dance of the Disinherited," a section of *La Coronela*, Mexico City, c. 1950. Photographer, Simón Flechine SEMO. Courtesy of Instituto Nacional de Antropología e Historia.

colonialist power, the church, and the military (Figure 4.17). Then the *coronela* emerges, the dance's namesake, wearing bandoliers of ammunition across her torso, brandishing her 30-30 rifle at her current and historical enemies. Her recognizably revolutionary attire contextualized the *mestizaje* of her movement vocabulary—a combination of mimetic gestures (i.e., pointing rifle forward) and leg extensions evocative of ballet technique. Her firm bodily demeanor projected resolute bravery as she forcefully advanced, surveying the space around her. She embodied the capacity of women to fight and lead the revolution. Within the discursive constraints of the masculinist, if not patriarchal, character of the Mexican Revolution, *La Coronela* followed a female empowerment tradition the Campobello sisters had staged in mass dances since the early 1930s.[171]

"Dance of the Disinherited" spoke so strongly to people in rural areas that Waldeen once recalled how the audience asked that the piece be performed again before the next section of *La Coronela*.[172] In the work's third section, "La Pesadilla de Don Ferruco" [Mr. Ferruco's Nightmare], the masses in the process of liberation celebrate the fall of the powerful *ferrucos* [elegant, affluent male members of the economic and political elites] who had helped sustain systems of domination. This section drew some critiques; critic Víctor Moya suggested editing its length and synchronizing better the dancing between man-and-woman pairs.[173]

El Juicio Final [The Final Judgment] represented the damnation, despite political standing and connections, of all the exploiters.[174] This section included colorful costumes and sets evocative of José Guadalupe Posada's Porfirian-era artistic imagery, which became iconic in the repertoire of popular Mexican culture before and after the revolution. A *calavera* [skeleton] played a large violin as if tuning sounds of the ultimate punishment, death, while a high-energy *diablito* [little devil] roamed around the space, tempting whoever came his way. The *diablito* had emerged from the jaws of a large portrait set of a dragon-like figure in the background, as flames from the monster's mouth waited to devour those who had been on the wrong side of social justice.[175] *La Coronela* relied on

---

[171] For historical accounts of the influence of national and international women in the development of Mexican modern dance, see Tortajada Quiroz, "Transgresoras-constructoras . . . XX-I: Nellie y Gloria Campobello," 685–715; "Transgresoras-constructoras del cuerpo y las imágenes II. Las pioneras de la danza escénica del siglo XX-II: Anna Sokolow y Waldeen," in *La danza en México. Visiones de cinco siglos*, Vol. I: *Ensayos Históricos y Analíticos*, ed. Maya Ramos and Patricia Cardona CNCA-INBA-CENIDI Danza "José Limón—Escenología, México (2002): 717–39; *Frutos de mujer: Las mujeres en la danza escénica* (México, DF: Cenidi Danza/INBA/Conaculta, 2001); *Mujeres de danza combativa* (México, DF: Cenidi Danza/INBA/Conaculta, 1998).

[172] Quoted in *La Coronela (1940) Punto de Partida*. Investigación: Josefina Lavalle; Realización, Guión y Edición: Lourdes Roca, Eugenio Cobo y Josefina Lavalle; Producción: Eugenio Cobo y Josefina Lavalle. CONACULTA, FONCA, INBA, CENART, México DF: México, 2001. VHS Documental.

[173] Quoted in Tortajada Quiroz, "La Coronela de Waldeen," 57.

[174] Delgado Martínez, *Guillermina Bravo: Historia Oral* (México City: Instituto Nacional de Bellas Artes; Cenidi-Danza "José Limón": 1994).

[175] An image of this scene is included in Tortajada Quiroz, "La Coronela de Waldeen," 55.

a linear narrative characteristic of revolutionary ideology: oppressive forces, a phase of struggle, class consciousness-raising, and ultimate liberation. However, in Waldeen's work, what would otherwise be a typical narrative included a punishment phase for those who had oppressed the indigenous, the proletariat, the worker, and the people.

La Coronela's Universal Potential as Modern Art and Its Capital Sin as Political Propaganda: Quiñones, Bal y Gay, and other Dance Critics

Through its choreographic composition (i.e., dynamic tensions among characters through specific spatial configurations, abstracted and codified movement vocabularies) and thematic choices (i.e., overt Mexican referents such as revolutionary figures, images from Posada's work), *La Coronela* made a statement on the direct relationship that dance and revolutionary politics should have. It is necessary to analyze responses the work elicited to appreciate the extent to which this embodied statement was influential in fueling related debates at the time. As analysis of previous cases has suggested, critics, audiences, and government officials were also active agents in producing the knowledge that dance generated.

Despite its historical, political, and cultural specificity—its Mexicanness—*La Coronela* drew strong praise from the press as an instance of universal modern art that could situate Mexico on equal standing with other "civilized" nations. According to Quiñones, this dance represented the "beginning of a vigorous Mexican renaissance . . . what is ours expressed to such human heights that it is universally valid . . . a Mexican thing with universal essence."[176] He further clarified that the group of artists involved in producing Waldeen's *La Coronela* "managed to extract from our very inner core the elements to create a superior expression of Mexican characteristics. Not Spanish. Not Indigenous. Mexican."[177] Quiñones might have been responding to a perceived Spanish-centrism in many of Sokolow's works in Mexico while also alluding to the prevalent paternalistic indigenism promoted by the state. The critic combined these racial and cultural polarities—Spanish and indigenous—into the dominant ideology of *mestizaje* as characteristic of what it meant to be a mid-twentieth-century postrevolutionary Mexican. For him and others, this culturally specific Mexican embodied mestizo modernism had the capacity to speak of a universal human experience.[178]

---

[176] "El Ballet Mexicano," 72.
[177] Ibid.
[178] Quiñones's characterization of a Mexican artistic expression as "Not Spanish. Not indigenous. Mexican" responded to what some commentators at the time viewed as "otro racismo" [another racism]. An unidentified writer for *El universal* suggested that the implicit whiteness in the label

Accordingly, dance historian Cesar Delgado Martínez has suggested that *La Coronela* was "an expression of the victory of a group of people who fight for their freedom."[179] Like Quiñones in 1940, Delgado Martínez decades later relied on a discourse of universalism, suggesting that the work centered the Mexican nationalist revolutionary struggle as a universal model. In other words, framing *La Coronela* as a universally appealing work assumed that it could inspire people in other countries to pursue freedom, demand rights, and engage in revolutionary action. If Sokolow's representation of a Spanish mother in *Slaughter of the Innocents* could stand for other women's struggles under fascism and similar dire circumstances, Waldeen's Mexican disinherited women had a similar universal representational value. If Sokolow, wrapped in a shawl, finally understood the "despair she inferred in [Mexican] women's lives" when she embodied it in her *Mexican Retablo*, performed in New York City in 1946,[180] Waldeen seems to have realized that despair six years earlier while choreographing *La Coronela*'s female brown bodies in Mexico City. Both Sokolow's and Waldeen's choreographic representations operated within distinctive, somewhat picturesque (if not exoticizing) contexts. However, these artists hoped that their gendered characters could stand for other humans beyond the specifics of their life conditions and particular cultural environments.

For Mauricio Muñoz, a League of Revolutionary Writers and Artists member, *La Coronela* was a superior form of Mexican artistic expression with universal reach, one that could also unify Mexicans nationally. With a conciliatory tone, he lauded the School of Dance under Nellie Campobello's directorship for producing the generation of professional dancers who helped modernize Mexican dance.[181] He acknowledged the House of the Artist for hiring Sokolow to lead the first Mexican modern dance company. He applauded the artistic contributions of Spanish artists like Halffter and the financial support that Mrs. Adela Formoso de Obregón y Santacilia provided to subsidize Sokolow's La Paloma Azul. Muñoz concluded that the only way to continue creating "authentically national" dances that could speak to people in Mexico and beyond would be to overcome institutional and private antagonisms in what should have been

"la hispanidad" (Hispanicity) to refer to nations and people in "América hispano-india" (Hispano-indigenous America) was racist. Similar to Quiñones, the article claimed that "[n]uestros pueblos son de ascendencia española, pero también india" [our nations are of Spanish ancestry but also indigenous] (*El universal*, "Dia de la raza, el otro racismo." Primera Sección, Por el Ojo de la Llave, October 15, 1940, 3). Neither Quiñones nor the unidentified author of the article noted possible complicity in *another* form of racism: the omission and erasure of people of African and Asian descent in constructing countries across the Americas, including Mexico.

[179] *Guillermina Bravo*, 23.
[180] Kosstrin, *Honest Bodies*, 148.
[181] Muñoz, "Nuestro primer cuerpo de ballet: La danza moderna," *El universal*, October 16, 1940, 11.

a collective effort.[182] For him, the newly invigorated Ballet of Fine Arts and its *La Coronela* represented the hope for a national reunification of its fractured sociopolitical and cultural factions, an unlikely possibility.

Assuming different notions of taste, many continued the debates about what constituted dance as a legitimate form of universal modern art. Some commentators objected to *La Coronela*'s overt referents to lower-class Mexican life. Others reiterated objections to merging art and politics in ways perceived as too explicit and thereby not legitimately artistic. Whereas in 1919, Pavlova had not faced much resistance for using a Mexican *rebozo* [shawl], at the time already established as a beloved (albeit exoticized) marker of indigenous and rural Mexican women, Waldeen faced criticism for including the distinctive garment in the premiere of *La Coronela* twenty-one years later.[183] Gabriel Fernández Ledesma, who was part of the National Institute of Fine Art's artistic council that hired Waldeen and participated in writing the work's libretto, told the choreographer that she could not use *rebozos* at the prestigious Palace of Fine Arts. Waldeen did so regardless, noting, "yo como soy muy terca" [because I am so stubborn].[184] Although *La Coronela*'s producing team intended to stylize Mexican folkloric and popular sources to depart from "todo falso 'folclorismo'" [all false "folklorism"] of the 1930s,[185] some critics still noted the work's "picturesque" nature. Víctor Moya recommended that in future performances, the *coronela* should be dressed differently, for her chosen "costume of calendar-colonel could only enthrall tourists."[186] Moya found the character too stereotypically Mexican and revolutionary.

Bal y Gay wrote two articles employing a clever performative writing strategy to express what constituted legitimate art for him and some of his contemporaries. The first was about the work's artistic elements and the second on its revolutionary politics, respectively categorized as merits and faults. On December 3, 1940, Bal y Gay published his first article, which celebrated the dance as an "obra de arte" [work of art] while alerting his readership to the forthcoming piece questioning

---

[182] Ibid.

[183] Pavlova confessed to a Mexican critic, "as far as I am concerned, I marveled at myself wearing a *rebozo* [shawl] or any other thing that has this traditional [Mexican] stamp! That is the reason why I staged 'Fantasía Mexicana'" (quoted in Buffalmacco, "Lo que dijeron a la Señora Pavlova en el extranjero, respecto a México, y lo que ella ha venido a encontrar: Palabras de sinceridad y entusiasmo," *El pueblo*, March 27, 1919, 3, 5). Like Waldeen, but six years later, Sokolow used a *rebozo* in *Mexican Retablo* as a stereotypical symbol of a representational (if not ideological) affinity with disinherited Mexican women whose plight may resonate with diverse human beings in other contexts (Kosstrin, *Honest Bodies*, 147).

[184] Quoted in *La Coronela (1940)*, 2001.

[185] Lavalle, quoted in Tortajada Quiroz, "La Coronela de Waldeen," 58.

[186] Quoted in ibid., 57. "Calendar-colonel" references paper calendars displaying postcard-like images of characters such as indigenous people and revolutionary figures (including *coronelas*). These images circulated within national and international tourist industries that valued stereotyped representations marketed as Mexican "authenticity."

the "legitimacy" of some dubious aspirations evident in the work.[187] In this first installment, he noted an "excess" of mimetic movement but, in general, exalted Waldeen's signature dance vocabulary. He said, "Mexicanness penetrates softly but efficiently the repertoire of movements that constitute Waldeen's dance language."[188] The critic recognized the work of the young dancers who ably executed the choreography, including Dina Torregrosa, who danced the role of the *coronela*. Furthermore, he praised the use of *Procesional*'s "subtle musical and plastic allusion" to create an atmosphere that truly felt as if one had traveled back in time to Mexico's viceregal epoch.[189] The writer also expressed delight at Revueltas's music and the costumes, lighting, and other theatrical elements. Without noting any potential political critique embodied in the piece, Bal y Gay described the dance's movements as arranged in an orderly fashion and asserted that the "noble" music "of good taste" did not have unnecessary effects but rather a "profound efficacy" in supporting the dance.[190] In sum, Bal y Gay praised the formal and production aspects of the works in the program. He characterized *La Coronela* specifically as an artistic success marking a possible direction toward a Mexican ballet.[191]

Five days later, on December 8, Bal y Gay published his promised second article, "El arte y la política. Un ejemplo cubano" [Art and politics. A Cuban example].[192] If *La Coronela* resonated with President Cárdenas's left-wing cultural politics, Bal y Gay's article offered a contrasting view on the role of art. Vocalizing the social and aesthetic values of many readers whom he represented in his authority as a legitimized expert, the critic suggested that he could neither condone illegitimate forms of art nor could he "feel the pain" of the common citizen. In his "Art and politics," Bal y Gay focused on questioning the legitimacy of certain sources of inspiration when it came to creating art, discussing what he called the work's "original sin: its political sentiments."[193] He noted that the explicit intention of the dance was to exalt the Mexican Revolution, and therefore he refused to use his position as a writer to disseminate more "political propaganda," to avoid committing the same "sin" he was condemning.[194] In other words, while he characterized *La Coronela*'s politics as (sinful) ideological propaganda, he did

---

[187] "Julián Carrillo, compositor. Coros y ballet en Bellas Artes," *El universal*, December 3, 1940, 8.
[188] Ibid.
[189] Ibid.
[190] Ibid.
[191] Ibid.
[192] *El universal*, 3ra Sección, *Crónicas Musicales*, December 8, 1940, 2, 12. In the last paragraph of this article, the writer offered a "'positive'" example of legitimate art—a Cuban music event—that served to contrast the "negative" example he criticized, *La Coronela* (thus the "Cuban" reference in his article's title).
[193] Ibid., 2.
[194] Ibid.

not see his conceptualization of art as a form of aesthetic ideology with profound political implications.

Bal y Gay certainly saw how *La Coronela*'s dancing bodies mobilized politics onstage as much as muralists did on walls. He equated this dance work with political murals that some people had threatened to destroy. The critic assured his readers that those works were "conceived by politics not *Art*" (added emphasis).[195] His opinion implied that the murals' political genesis made them deserving of destruction, and perhaps for the same reasons, he wanted to destroy *La Coronela* in his critique. He rationalized that true art belonged to the "dominion of the spirit."[196] His spiritualized aestheticism tacitly relied on racist and classist assumptions characteristic of some civilizing projects. Thus, he concluded that the "salvation of the Art of the future resides in a eugenics that refutes all parasitic or deleterious elements to artistic creation and delectation."[197] Bal y Gay's response to *La Coronela*'s embodied politico-aesthetic enunciations illustrates how ideological perspectives by critics, legitimized as cultural experts, contribute to naturalizing notions of what art should be.

Bal y Gay reproduced a spiritualized aesthetic discourse that historically had informed conceptualizations of politics as belonging to the quotidian realm of the mundane while art functioned as a conduit to a higher plane of existence.[198] As he put it, politics must be left where they belonged, "in newspapers, books, and conferences," for combining art with politics would "prostitute" art.[199] The publication pattern of his two articles, separated by a few days, maintained the opposition that his characterization of these two forms of knowledge production, art and politics, must have held. His article emphasizing *La Coronela*'s aesthetic elements and his sequel condemning the work's politicized intentions literally and figuratively created the two separate spheres where the critic and those his voice represented believed art and politics should exist.

[195] Ibid.
[196] Ibid.
[197] Ibid. Bal y Gay was not the only critic who suggested that Waldeen and her collaborators used art for the "illegitimate" purpose of instilling revolutionary ideology among the populace. Roberto El Diablo celebrated the artistic promise of the Ballet of Fine Arts' young Mexican dancers. However, he declared that the technique "imposed" on them by their teacher, Waldeen, had deviated from classical precepts in favor of a prevalent "political opportunism" and concluded that the modern dance group "did not satisfy the general public's taste" (Roberto El Diablo, "Ballet y Revista," 23). These critics' views resonated with other critics, dancers, choreographer, and dance administrators such as Arturo Rigel, Carlos González Peña, and Hipólito Zybin in the 1930s.

[198] In reality, the relationship between art and politics could take many forms. In other words, both expressed and implied definitions of art and politics depend on what political and aesthetic ideologies artists, writers, and producers embrace. Thus, the discussion here attempts to reflect the arbitrary schism that people like Bal y Gay created between arts and politics to formulate their ideas about the relationship between arts and spirituality and their assumed opposition to the *mundane* political realm.

[199] Bal y Gay, "Art and Politics," 2.

To some extent, Bal y Gay's different responses to Waldeen's and Sokolow's ways of articulating politics and aesthetics reflected aspects of his positionality as a Spanish exile. While he had objected to Sokolow's work with La Paloma Azul for its Spanish-centrism, as discussed earlier, he did not seem to have an issue with its political intent, perhaps because he found it less "picturesque," just as Sokolow had intended with her work. Perhaps he appreciated the anti-fascist undertones in Sokolow's work because he had been affected by fascism. It could be the case that Bal y Gay's desire for a more Mexicanized yet politically neutral and aesthetically refined dance form was part of the process of negotiating his recent arrival in Mexico. The writer had fled Spain during the Civil War (1936–1939) and was already a prestigious musician and musicologist[200] when he arrived in Mexico as part of President Cárdenas's program to host Spanish artists and intellectuals. Based at the newly inaugurated Casa de España [House of Spain], these refugees had a space to continue developing their work as they actively immersed themselves in the Mexican capital's cultural life.[201] Although these Spanish compatriots held affinities as exiles, they also had political differences among themselves. While Bal y Gay, a moderate Republican liberalist, critiqued La Paloma Azul's Spanish-centrism, Halffter, a committed communist like Sokolow, collaborated closely with the choreographer's group.[202] Bal y Gay's political and artistic background influenced his assessment of both Sokolow's La Paloma Azul and Waldeen's *La Coronela* as he was still adjusting to Mexico's nationalist and revolutionary effervescence under President Cárdenas.

In his review condemning *La Coronela*'s "capital sin" of a political bent, the writer confessed, "many Mexicans would tell me that I cannot feel the Mexican Revolution. It is true for I have not experienced it. But what nobody can take away from me is the possibility that I can feel what is Art."[203] While Bal y Gay was responding to *La Coronela* merely two years after he arrived in the country and thereby could not relate to the country's revolutionary history, he asserted his authority on matters of legitimate modern art. He associated artistic production

---

[200] Carlos Villanueva, "Jesús Bal y Gay: La biografía (¿definitiva?) de Don Manuel que nunca llegó a publicarse," in *Manuel de Falla en el Imaginario de dos Músicos exiliados: Adolfo Salazar y Jesús Bal y Gay*, ed. Consuelo Carredano and Carlos Villanueva (Ciudad de México: El Colegio de México, 2017), 132.

[201] The Casa de España became the Colegio de México [College of Mexico], an institution of higher education, in 1940. For a history of this cultural and educational space, including the crucial role that Spanish exiles played in its initial institutionalization, see Clara Eugenia Lida, José Antonio Matesanz, and Josefina Zoraida Vázquez, *La Casa de España y el Colegio de México: Memoria, 1938–2000* (México, DF: El Colegio, 2000).

[202] Consuelo Carredano, "La crítica musical en México: Carlos Chávez y los músicos del exilio español," in *Manuel de Falla*, 40–41. For an analysis of the diversity of aesthetic and political views and their shifting nature over time among Spanish composers and musicians before and after exile and upon their return to Spain under Franco, see Eva Moreda Rodríguez, *Music and Exile in Francoist Spain* (Farnham, Surrey: Ashgate, 2016).

[203] Bal y Gay, "Art and Politics," 2.

with a morally edifying spirituality belonging to a realm autonomous from politics. For him, like other writers—Mexican and foreign—engaged in these debates, his *feelings,* and aesthetic ideologies constituted the discursive bases for evaluating what legitimate Art must be.

La Coronela made a choreographic statement about the direct relationship that artists like Waldeen and her collaborators thought art and politics should have. It did so by relying on the specificity of Mexican history and culture while aspiring to have universal appeal. Like the Campobello sisters' *Ballet Symbólico 30-30, La Coronela* aspired to mobilize revolutionary politics nationally while resonating with socialist movements internationally. As it integrated a combination of dance techniques while creating a form of embodied mestizo modernism, Waldeen's dance offered an alternative to the perceived "Spanishness" of Sokolow's work. Contradicting responses by the press animated debates that extended beyond the dance stage, thereby demonstrating how dance played a vital role constructing national, racial, and cultural identities.

Dancing Gender, Nationalism, and Exoticism: *La Coronela*'s Contradictions and Its Potential Pluriversalism

Some writers, artists, government officials, and audiences considered Waldeen's *La Coronela* "a new point of departure"[204] in creating a modern dance form that was authentically Mexican, aesthetically and politically revolutionary, and universal in appeal. Certainly, the process of its creation and performance at the prestigious Palace of Fine Arts and in outdoor settings in rural areas enacted multiple meanings simultaneously. At the time of its premiere on November 23, 1940, the dance work paid homage to the Mexican Revolution, marking the thirtieth anniversary of Francisco I. Madero's uprising against Díaz's dictatorial regime on November 20, 1910.[205] *La Coronela* also represented an embodied politico-aesthetic affirmation of the fervent revolutionary government led by President Cárdenas. At the same time, the dance functioned as a farewell to his presidency, just a few weeks before Manuel Ávila Camacho took up the country's reins. *La Coronela* might have been an attempt to choreographically enunciate the revolutionary impetus that its creators and like-minded allies wished for the new government to continue cultivating.

At this transitional moment, *La Coronela* also embodied contradictory progressive gender politics and tensile relations to exoticism. The work continued

---

[204] *La Coronela* (1940).
[205] November 20 is celebrated in Mexico as the Día de la Revolución Mexicana (Day of the Mexican Revolution).

a tradition where dance as a primarily feminized space enabled representations of female figures as revolutionary agents and leaders of the movement. Ten years earlier, the Campobello sisters' mass dances, such as *Ballet Simbólico 30-30*, portrayed women as central to the mobilization of radical politics through (danced) armed struggle. These performances—the mass dances and *La Coronela* alike—constructed a new woman who played a central role in socialist nation-building projects.[206]

These politically progressive female representations provided an alternative to the seemingly docile *china poblana* performed in the postcolonial era and into the twentieth century by highly regarded national and international dancers such as María de Jesús Moctezuma, Felipa López, and Anna Pavlova. Female revolutionary leaders in dance representations could also translate as indicative of women's capacity for political transformation in the private and public spheres. They choreographed crucial interventions at a time of relegation for Mexican women to second-class citizenship (they would not gain suffrage until 1953).[207] The subversive zeal of these *coronelas, adelitas, and soldaderas* represented a symbolic gesture of progressiveness in a feminized field of cultural production that was at odds with the official policy toward women who fought and danced for their rights.

As a central protagonist in the dance, the *coronela* embodied a recognizable female revolutionary figure mythologized within the national popular culture as the *adelita*, an archetype that stood for *soldaderas* (female soldiers) who joined the armed revolution.[208] The masculinist and patriarchal thrust of the

---

[206] For analyses of the relationship between dance, performance, and the formation of socialist and communist states, see Christina Ezrahi, *Swans of the Kremlin: Ballet and Power in Soviet Russia* (Pittsburgh: University of Pittsburgh Press, 2012); Jens Richard Giersdorf, *The Body of the People: East German Dance since 1945* (Madison: University of Wisconsin Press, 2013); Angela Marino, *Populism and Performance in the Bolivarian Revolution of Venezuela* (Evanston, IL: Northwestern University Press, 2018); Emily Wilcox, *Revolutionary Bodies: Chinese Dance and the Socialist Legacy* (Oakland: University of California Press, 2019); Elizabeth B. Schwall, *Dancing with the Revolution: Power, Politics, and Privilege in Cuba* (Chapel Hill: University of North Carolina Press, 2021).

[207] For an account of the struggles of women's suffrage in Mexico after the revolution, see Gloria Luz Alejandre Ramírez and Eduardo Torres Alonso, "El Primer Congreso Feminista de Yucatán 1916. El camino a la legislación del sufragio y reconocimiento de ciudadanía a las mujeres. Construcción y tropiezos," *Estudios políticos* 39 (September–December 2016): 59–89, accessed May 6, 2019, https://www.sciencedirect.com/science/article/pii/S0185161616300166. For other developments of feminist movements in postrevolutionary Mexico, see Jocelyn H. Olcott, *Revolutionary Women in Postrevolutionary Mexico* (Durham, NC: Duke University Press, 2005); Jocelyn H. Olcott, Mary K. Vaughan, and Gabriela Cano, ed., *Sex in Revolution: Gender, Politics, and Power in Modern Mexico* (Durham, NC: Duke University Press, 2006).

[208] The *corrido* [ballad song] "La adelita" played an influential role in the consolidation of this figure in the national revolutionary imaginary. For a history and critical analysis of the song and the figures of *adelitas, soldaderas,* and *coronelas*, see Christine B. Arce, *México's Nobodies: The Cultural Legacy of the Soldadera and Afro-Mexican Women* (Albany: State University of New York Press, 2017); Elena Poniatowska, *Las Soldaderas: Women of the Mexican Revolution*, trans. David Dorado Romo (El Paso: Cinco Puntos Press, 2006; orig. ed. 1999]); Alicia Arrizón, "'Soldaderas' and the

institutionalized Mexican Revolution created representations of these female fighters as eroticized objects of heterosexual desire.[209] Against this cultural backdrop, Waldeen's *coronela* decidedly embodied a female subject who attempted to transcend the eroticizing gaze by calling attention to herself as a capable revolutionary catalyst. However, this woman fighter coexisted within an imaginary that exoticized female revolutionaries as stereotypical representations of the nation.

The figure of the *coronela* existed within a machinery of exoticization that mobilized legacies of colonialism within transnational webs of cultural, political, and economic relations. Early in 1940, several months before *La Coronela*'s premiere, journalist Xavier Sorondo decried the fact that foreign capitalists, primarily from the United States, owned Mexico's tourist industry, which produced ostensibly "authentic" yet exotic representations of Mexicanness. According to the writer, so strong was their desire for the exotic and so strong was their influence on the "meticulous" creation of a Mexican imaginary for tourists that he declared, "México nunca a sido nuestro" [Mexico has never been ours].[210] This powerful statement suggests that Mexico had been an idea manufactured partly by foreign capitalists invested in the tourist industry. One among many implications of Mexico's transnational nationalisms was often the country's own auto/exoticization.[211]

Such was the context behind critic Víctor Moya's suggestion that the *coronela*'s costume rendered her an exotic, stereotyped figure that "could only enthrall tourists."[212] It was this potentially picturesque exoticism associated with touristic consumption that Sokolow was "afraid of," for it could undermine dance's legitimacy as a modern art with universal import.[213] However, within this historical time of revolutionary fervor and political transition, Waldeen and her collaborators engaged the particularity of local culture. They did so even when the operation of exoticism as a colonial mechanism risked rendering (nonwhite) Mexicanness, including representations of the Mexican revolution, as a tourist attraction and commodity.

One of many implications of *La Coronela* was its potential exoticization due to the visible markers of its cultural and racial specificity. However, as exotic as it might have been, the work yet exerted itself in the political register, as Bal y Gay's condemnation, among others, made evident. *La Coronela*, like other forms

---

Staging of the Mexican Revolution," *Drama Review* 42, no. 1 (Spring 1998): 90–112; Elizabeth Salas, *Soldaderas in the Mexican Military: Myth and History* (Austin: University of Texas Press, 1990).

[209] Arrizón, "'Soldaderas.'"
[210] Sorondo, "La única industria," *Revista de revistas*, February 4, 1940, unpaged.
[211] For the relationship between tango and the concepts of exoticism and autoexoticism, see Marta E. Savigliano, *Tango and the Political Economy of Passion* (Boulder, CO: Westview Press, 1995).
[212] Quoted in Tortajada Quiroz, "La Coronela de Waldeen."
[213] Sokolow, quoted in Kosstrin, *Honest Bodies*, 141.

of embodied mestizo modernisms, was not totally depoliticized by the colonial logic that historically had imagined nonwhite others as culturally and racially exotic bodies and subjects.[214] *La Coronela*'s strategic marking of cultural *mestizaje* existed in tension with the colonial presupposition that a "nonracialized," acultural white body assumed neutrality that could transcend markers of difference and achieve universality—an ostensible neutral body that could never be racially and culturally exotic.

Assuredly, *La Coronela* "marked" the invisible whiteness of Western cultural modernity—embodied in the dance techniques and universalist ideology it adopted—while potentially remaining entangled in a web of exoticization. This enabling auto/exoticism, as a form of politicized cultural *mestizaje*, strategically adopted neocolonial "modernizing" technologies for training dancers and making dances starting in the 1930s. It did so as part of intercultural practices that inevitably impact the transnational formation of nation-states, nationalist cultural imaginaries, power relations, and individual and collective identities. In other words, the exercise of some forms of anticolonial and decolonial agency has taken place as part of negotiating one's existence as an individual and a nation within a "colonial matrix of power."[215] That is, people debating the relationship between aesthetics and politics during the 1930s and 1940s did so as they also negotiated national and international power dynamics. In this context, dancers and other artists with diverse racial and national backgrounds produced *La Coronela* (and other such works) to construct Mexican transnational nationalisms.

Embodied mestizo modernisms such as *La Coronela* challenged the ostensible racial and cultural neutrality with which whiteness had historically established itself as the universal organizing principle for human relations and art production. These danced modernist *mestizajes*, which unapologetically represented aspects of Mexicanness, eschewed archetypal desires of cultural and racial transcendence embodied in ostensibly unmarked ballet and modern dance practices. Thus, the visible cultural markings of dances such as *La Coronela* functioned as a decolonial challenge to the discursive invisibility of whiteness and its colonialist assumptions that "legitimate" art must transcend any markers of difference. That is, as a precursor of color-blind ideologies, the desire to transcend constructs such as race and culture risks reproducing the rhetoric of neutrality, invisibility, and universality with which whiteness has established its presumed supremacy.[216] In contrast, the strategic markings of cultural production, including dance, can have the opposite

---

[214] As Savigliano has asserted, exoticism has been part of the machinery of colonialism (*Tango and the Political*, 1995).

[215] For theorizing the "colonial matrix of power," see Walter D. Mignolo, *The Darker Side of Western Modernity: Global Futures, Decolonial Options* (Durham, NC: Duke University Press, 2011).

[216] Echoes of these transcendental aspirations would inform post-racial and color-blind ideologies in Mexico and other countries decades later.

effect: the validation and valuation of diverse ways of being human, thus creating a *pluri*versality, "a world in which many worlds [can] coexist."[217] Marked embodied mestizo modernisms offered *other* modernities as practices that can create a pluriversal world. That is, dancing mestizo modernisms engenders and models a world in which diverse ways of being, thinking, feeling, doing, and making are equally valuable to Western forms of modernism that assumed or strived for an ostensible racial and cultural neutrality.

---

[217] Mignolo, *The Darker Side of Western Modernity*, 54. For more on the concept of the pluriversal, see the introduction to this book.

Coda
Contemporary Mestizo Modernisms and Transnational Nationalisms in the United States

Between September 12 and 14, 2007, I attended the most exciting dance studies conference I had ever participated in as a graduate student. The collective Grupo Danzateórica organized the event at the National Autonomous University of Mexico (UNAM) in Mexico City. Dance scholars, dancers, visual artists, and cultural promoters from the United States, Canada, Italy, Mexico, and other countries in Latin America led master classes and workshops. They presented papers, performances, photographic exhibitions, films, and collaboration opportunities. Each participant could choose simultaneous translation in English, French, Italian, and Spanish via individual remote headphones. National and international scholars such as Andrée Martin (UQAM), Ana María Martínez de la Escalera (UNAM), John Wesley Days (UCLA), Margarita Baz (UAM), and the late Randy Martin (NYU) delivered keynote addresses. For three days, all participants attended as a collective the same sequence of presentations at the UNAM's Carlos Lazo Theater, with a capacity of 422 people. Although there were empty seats at the dance studies conference, the venue "was packed" for each presentation, and the audience applauded with palpable appreciation.[1]

I particularly remember this experience because the response to my presentation made evident the eagerness to talk, or hear, about subjects that were still difficult to discuss in conversations about dance in Mexico and other countries (c. 2007). I presented a paper on how social class, race, ethnicity, and gender intersected in the work of Manuel Ballesteros, a dancer and choreographer from the northern (norteño) city of Hermosillo. In "NorteArte," the performance I analyzed, Ballesteros combined contemporary dance and norteño culture—dance, music, and fashion often considered *corriente* or *naco* (think "tacky" or "ghetto") by people with upper-class sensibilities.[2] I highlighted some of the classist and racial prejudices coded in Mexican contemporary dance practices

---

[1] For general information, see https://cimacnoticias.com.mx/noticia/encuentro-internacional-mirar-adentro-y-por-fuera-de-la-danza/, accessed May 6, 2022.

[2] In the paper, I used the colloquial terms "fresas" (strawberries) and "nacos" relative to upper-class and lower-class people and sensibilities, respectively.

Dancing Mestizo Modernisms. José Luis Reynoso, Oxford University Press. © Oxford University Press 2024.
DOI: 10.1093/oso/9780197622551.003.0006

and aesthetic discourses. To contextualize my argument, I shared the following paragraph:

> Mexico continues to be a country in which racism is still embedded in the Mexican collective conscious and unconscious. Take for example the precarious living conditions to which indigenous communities of Mesoamerican and African descent are relegated. Or the many derogatory jokes and characters in Mexican popular culture that portray people from these communities as ignorant "primitives" incapable of being "civilized" (i.e., La India María, Memín Pinguín). Or the role of servitude dark-skin Mexicans are given in *telenovelas* (soap operas), TV melodramas whose embedded disciplinary lessons function to preserve the status quo in the formation of privileged identities and the distribution of power and resources along social class (for the affluent), race (for whites), gender (for men), and sexuality (for heterosexuals). But what about the often most familiar? The selective expressions we ourselves, our *tias/tios* (aunts/ uncles), *abuelitas/abuelitos* (grandparents), *vecinas/vecinos* (neighbors) tend to utter when we come to see a newly born: if the baby is *morenito/a* (dark-skinned, dark-eyed, dark-haired), he or she *esta bien "curiosito/a y simpatico/a"* (is cute, cute, cute); if the baby is *medio guerito/a or "moreno/a claro"* (light-skinned), he or she *"esta muy bonito/a"* (very pretty); but if the baby is *guerito/a, blanco/ a, de ojos azules/verdes, y rubio/a* (light-skinned/white, blue/green-eyed, and blond), ¡Ay Dios mío! the baby *esta bien precioso/a, adorable, y hermosisimo/ a* (Oh my God! The baby is so precious, adorable, and stunningly beautiful), *parece muñequito/a de porcelana* (he/she looks like a porcelain doll).[3]

As I was finishing uttering the last word of this paragraph in my presentation, I was interrupted by a thunderous noise. Audience members were raucously stomping their feet on the floor. It was loud. I could feel the vibrations of the resonant sound in my body. It was as though these vibrations manifested a collective affect, released by bodies who felt the need to be in sync, even if for a moment of intimate connection through shared embodied memories. I realized that merely naming some of these topics struck a chord among audience members for whom my memories resonated at the level of their individual life experiences. *Our* collective (colonial) racial/ized unconscious manifested itself in this brief moment of shared affective identification. Like many among the audience, as a working-class, brown body, I grew up in Mexico witnessing, perpetuating, and being subjected to some of the quotidian racialized social dynamics I evoked in my paper.

---

[3] I added some words in this version for even more accuracy in these colloquial expressions while still using the gender binary prevalent at the time.

A decade and a half later, in this book, I traced some of these racialization and socialization processes to colonial Mexico (1521–1821). I focused on how dance practices have reproduced and resisted these colonialist legacies stemming from a *sistema de castas* (caste system) that organized social and power relation in New Spain and whose logic resonated with racialization processes in Europe and the United States. The book theorized the concepts of *embodied mestizo modernisms* and *transnational nationalisms* as analytical methods. I used them to analyze how national and international dancers negotiated transnational aesthetic, political, economic, and cultural forces that contributed to the formation of Mexico at different historical moments. The story began in the years immediately after the official declaration of independence (1821) and extended to postrevolutionary Mexico when, in 1940, a new form of Mexican modern dance emerged.

The concept of embodied mestizo modernisms illustrated the complex ways in which dances choreographed and performed by people with diverse aesthetic, social, racial, and national backgrounds perpetuated and challenged colonial legacies of racialization and socialization. Case studies in each chapter traced the shifts from forms of post/colonial ambivalence toward *mestizaje* and indigeneity in nation formation to embracing these categories of difference as official racial and cultural ideology in constructing a postrevolutionary state. On the one hand, embodied mestizo modernisms illuminated the selective inclusion, marginalization, and erasure to which the rhetoric of *mestizaje* subjected Asian, Black, and indigenous Mesoamerican communities. On the other hand, it facilitated an understanding of how mestizo dance practices—those including visible cultural markers of indigeneity and Mexicanness—represented an anticolonial alternative to the assumed cultural and racial neutrality associated with notions of European and Euromerican modernity. Mestizo modernist practices then challenged notions of whiteness as a foundational ideology for ostensibly superior cultural, racial, and social identities forged during and after colonial Mexico. The analysis also accounted for how these efforts existed within colonial practices of exoticization by which non-white others have been stereotyped, commodified, and consumed by imperial powers. In this context, the state-sponsored production of mestizo modernist practices highlighting cultural and ethnoracial elements simultaneously risked auto/exoticization while attempting to "elevate" Mexican culture and history.

The book called special attention to national and international dancers' collaborations in creating these complex embodied mestizo modernisms as central to the ongoing construction of Mexico as a nation, a process I termed "transnational nationalisms." Chapters traced how embodied mestizo modernisms changed relative to how they looked and functioned in nation-building processes. In sum, the book traced diverse embodied mestizo modernisms from French choreographer Andrés Susano Pautret Chapalber's ballet *Allusion to the*

Cry of Dolores—performed in 1825, just four years after Mexico's official declaration of Independence—to North American dancer Waldeen's *La Coronela*, premiered in 1940 as Lázaro Cárdenas, one of the most revolutionary presidents, was leaving office. This trajectory elucidated how national and international dancers believed that Mexican "traditions," "modernized" by European and Euro-American dance techniques, could be as valuable and "universal" as cultural practices in Europe and the United States. Ultimately, the book analyzed the different ways mestizo modernist dance practices contributed to Mexico's formation as a post/colonial and postrevolutionary nation. It suggested that national and international dancers experienced a sense of agency as they created, negotiated, and resisted individual and collective identities within an interconnected network of colonial histories.

Dancing Mestizo Modernisms: Choreographing Postcolonial and Postrevolutionary Mexico traced these histories to illustrate how dance practices recreated and combated legacies of racialization and socialization stemming from colonial Mexico. While focusing on the post/colonial period after the Mexican Independence, the Porfirian dictatorship, and the first three decades of postrevolutionary Mexico, the book also aimed to open space for subsequent studies on the impact these histories had in Mexico during the rest of the twentieth century, and in the United States in the twenty-first century. In the remainder of this coda, I offer some preliminary thoughts about how embodied mestizo modernisms impacted the development of Mexico's dance, political, and cultural histories after 1940 when the world order shifted from World War II to the Cold War. This short history seeks to lay the groundwork for continued explorations of how transnational nationalisms apply not only to national and international dancers shaping Mexican history, as I have discussed in this book, but also to the role dancers and other people of Mexican descent play in re/creating the sociopolitical, economic, and cultural landscape in the United States. To do so, I will contextualize migration histories, gesturing toward the fact that flows of people and ideas between Mexico and the United States have contributed to constructing the two nations. I will end by situating the work of a group of first-generation Mexican American dancers who produce contemporary forms of embodied *mestizaje*, as part of a significant Latina/o/x/e force shaping the United States in the twenty-first century.

Clashing Modernities: The Emergence of Mexican Nationalist Dance between World War II and the Cold War

Anna Sokolow's and Waldeen's distinctive modernist dance practices between 1939 and 1940 (chapter 4) shaped decades-long debates over what constituted a much-sought-after Mexican dance form with national character and universal appeal.[4] As a more conservative president, Manuel Ávila Camacho, took the reins of the nation at the close of 1940, classical ballet had a short-lived resurgence. Nellie and Gloria Campobello (chapter 4) continued their commitment to a revolutionary nationalist dance practice by adopting ballet technique and aesthetics as the foundation for their dance company Ballet de la Ciudad de México, founded in 1943.[5] However, many dance artists, audiences, and government officials had already determined that ballet was "anachronistic," as Carlos Mérida had noted in 1937 when he also suggested looking to the United States for a modernist dance formula that could help develop a distinctively Mexican dance form.

In 1946, a new president, Miguel Alemán Valdéz, inaugurated the Instituto Nacional de Bellas Artes (INBA) (National Institute of Fine Arts) to create and administer official cultural policy in the production of nationalist Mexican art. Carlos Chávez, the renowned music composer who experimented with classical music and indigenous sounds and themes, became the INBA's director. He instituted the Academia de Danza Mexicana (ADM) (Academy of Mexican Dance), a professional dance company charged with researching, creating, and performing modern nationalist dances. Debates engendered by Sokolow's and Waldeen's work took new yet resonant forms as their Mexican disciples and collaborators, Ana Mérida (daughter of Carlos Mérida) and Guillermina Bravo, respectively, served as the ADM's initial co-directors.

The attempt to bring together representatives of two aesthetically antagonistic factions—by then known as *Sokolovas* (after Sokolow) and *Waldeenas* (after Waldeen)—was short-lived. Merida's preference for abstraction contrasted with Bravo's interest in socially conscious (and thus more accessible) dance practice. As the world transitioned from World War II to the Cold War, Merida's approach reflected not only her mentor Sokolow's and her father's aesthetic preferences but also the fact that had abstraction gained more momentum as an aesthetic practice and ideological discourse in Western countries. In that context, as a *Waldeena*, Bravo's interests in a socially conscious dance form represented an aesthetic and ideological Other (there were even accusations of her running a communist cell within the ADM).[6] The friction was such between the two camps

---

[4] This section focuses on discursive debates for the purposes of this coda. I will historicize and analyze specific dances more closely in a future work.

[5] They published their book, *Ritmos Indígenas*, in 1940, which reflected their ethnographic research findings among indigenous and rural communities and served as a resource for modern nationalist choreographies. For an analysis of the Campobello sisters' ballet company within President Ávila Camacho's political and cultural context, see chapter 4 of Margarita Tortajada Quiroz, *Danza y poder* (México, DF: INBA/CENIDID-Danza, 1995), and concerning visual artist José Clemente Orozco, see chapter 8 in K. Mitchell Snow, *A Revolution in Movement: Dancers, Painters, and the Image of Modern Mexico* (Gainesville: University Press of Florida, 2020).

[6] For in-depth insight into the development of nationalist Mexican dance within the Cold War context by dancers who lived through the experience, see Margarita Tortajada Quiroz and Rosa

that at some point members of one group refused to dance in a work created by a member of the opposite group.[7] As a result, Mérida created her Grupo Experimental (Experimental Group) in 1949. Bravo also departed and formed the Ballet Nacional de México (National Ballet of Mexico) as an organization founded on the premise that "the art of choreography does not constitute a mere abstract cultural expression [instead, it] must fulfill its mission to contribute to Mexico's national, cultural, and social development and integration."[8]

These contrasting views reflected ongoing frictions between Sokolow's and Waldeen's approaches to modernist dance practices. While Sokolow criticized *Waldeenas* for creating "welcome-to-sunny-Mexico" dances,[9] an allusion to what she considered picturesque representations of Mexico, Waldeen accused Sokolow of "not being Mexican enough and for her dismissiveness of dance rooted in *Mexicanidad* [Mexicanness]."[10] In the mid-1950s, Sokolow spoke openly in public forums about "her beliefs that because Mexican dance was too concerned with nationalism, patriotism, and marking itself with indigenous and folkloric elements, it lacked individualism and potential for growth."[11] It seemed that Sokolow believed that Mexican specificity hindered the "universal" potential associated with abstract art (art often assumed as culturally and racially "neutral" in its overt visual representations). Waldeen characterized such statements "as a racist, antinationalist series of attacks against patriotism in Mexican art."[12] Miguel Covarrubias, an influential visual artist, and director of INBA's Dance Department, advised that Sokolow not treat the themes of nationalism and patriotism lightly.[13]

Covarrubias's appointment as dance director in 1950 to ease the tensions between *Sokolovas* and *Waldeenas* carried on the mandate to create a nationalist modern dance form with universalist aspirations. He hired people without direct associations with the two antagonistic factions: the painter Santos Balmori as ADM director and Xavier Francis, a dancer from New York City, as the person in charge of Mexican dancers' technical professionalization. Covarrubias also invited José Limón, a Mexican American dancer and choreographer who built his artistic reputation in the United States. In 1950 and 1951, the Mexican-born

---

Reyna, *Entre aplausos y críticas detrás del muro: Alcances y transformaciones de la danza moderna nacionalista mexicana en la gira de 1957* (México, DF: CONACULTA, INBA, Cenidi Danza, 2012).

[7] Miguel Cobarruvias, quoted in Tortajada Quiroz, *Danza y poder*, 186.
[8] The company's declaration reproduced by Raquel Tibol, quoted in ibid., 187.
[9] Larry Warren, *Anna Sokolow: The Rebellious Spirit* (Amsterdam: Harwood Academic Publishers, 1998), 75.
[10] Hanna Kosstrin, *Honest Bodies: Revolutionary Modernism in the Dances of Anna Sokolow* (New York: Oxford University Press, 2017), 117.
[11] Ibid., 155.
[12] Ibid.
[13] Ibid.

Limón and his company presented his modern dance works (e.g., *The Moor's Pavane*) and some mestizo modernist dances. Works such as *Los Cuatro Soles* (The Four Suns), *Tonantzintla*,[14] *Diálogos* (Dialogues), and *La Malinche*[15] combined indigenous Mesoamerican themes and a modern dance technique Limón had developed with principles he learned while training under Doris Humphrey's mentorship.

Limón's embodied mestizo modernisms provoked mixed reactions that resonated with debates between Sokolow and Waldeen as well as their collaborators and advocates in Mexico. A music critic identified as Wanderer assured readers that Limón's Mexicanized works reflected the "unavoidable power of his ancestry"[16] and his dancing projected that "his temper, his nerve, his passion [had] an unmistakably Mexican flavor."[17] The writer Manlio S. Fuentes noted that Limón's performances conveyed a "message of choreographic modern art" and could serve to inspire other Mexican dancers "to create a new form of expression of our artistic personality, taking advantage of the musical folkloric themes and modes of indigenous dances, as painters have done."[18] While many in the press highlighted Limón's Mexicanness in his works and persona as an inspiration for a renewed Mexican dance form, Limón clarified that "Mexican art could be achieved by 'being simply Mexican' in the spirit, without having to fall into an 'irrational nationalism.'"[19] He predicted that the "indigenism" and "professionally exploited Mexicanism" prevalent in forming a nationalist art form at the time would fail.[20]

Although Limón's mestizo modernist dances were visibly "Mexican" to many among his audiences (e.g., *La Malinche*'s recognizably costumed three characters of the Indian, the Conquistador, and La Malinche), he seemed to advocate, like Sokolow and Ana Mérida, for a more abstract approach to making "universal" dances with Mexican themes. Most commentators praised Limón's dances. However, some observers found them troubling. The writer Sánchez Flores evaluated *La Malinche* as an "unfinished experiment."[21] Another critic said that a "childish mind" conceived the work.[22] Similarly, Covarrubias himself noted that

[14] *Tonantzintla* is a Nahuatl word meaning "place of our beloved mother (or goddess)." It is the name of a small town in the state of Puebla, near Mexico City, and the location of a colonial-era church whose architectural decorations inspired Limón's dance.
[15] La Malinche was a Nahuatl woman who became a translator and lover to conquistador Hernán Cortés during the Spanish conquest of the Aztec Empire. For analyses of different aspects of Limón's *La Malinche*, see *José Limón and La Malinche: The Dancer and the Dance*, ed. Patricia Seed (Austin: University of Texas Press, 2008).
[16] Quoted in Tortajada Quiroz, "José Limón and La Malinche in Mexico: A Chicano Artist Returns Home," in *José Limón and La Malinche*, 123.
[17] Ibid., 124.
[18] Quoted in ibid., 127.
[19] Limón quoted in ibid., 124.
[20] Ibid., 140.
[21] Quoted in ibid., 131.
[22] Ibid., 129.

Limón's *La Malinche* was "a kind of pastoral about the Conquest seen through the naive eyes of a Mexican boy from the other side of the Río Bravo; in other words, José Limón's *blurred memories of Mexico*" (emphasis added).[23] It is precisely Limón's experience as a Mexican immigrant that I will take up now to illustrate the impact that flows of Mexican migration to the United States had before, during, and after the Mexican Revolution (1910–1920).[24]

The Construction of US Mestizo Modernities: Mexican Immigrant and Mexican American Laboring Bodies

Like many other Mexicans during the revolution, José Limón's family immigrated to the United States in 1915 when he was seven years old. He built his reputation as a modern dance "pioneer" in New York City starting in the late 1920s, mentored by Charles Weidman and Doris Humphrey. He became a US citizen in 1946; in 1954, he and his company became the first dancers to represent the United States as cultural ambassadors through the State Department's inaugural Cultural Exchange Program. Limón represented his adopted country as a choreographer and dancer multiple times in various parts of the world in the context of the Cold War and cultural diplomacy efforts.

It is not surprising, then, that Limón's return to Mexico as a consolidated dance artist made an indelible mark on the development of what became known as the Golden Age of Mexican dance under Covarrubias's leadership in the early 1950s. In addition to his contributions in the aesthetic realm, Limón's Mexican background stirred his admirers' nationalist sentiments. As I have suggested elsewhere, "he could be seen as a heroic Mexican who crossed the border to a perceived and/or real imperial center and became there, against many odds, a sort of artistic Mexican conqueror."[25] The boy who left Mexico escaping the tribulations caused by the Mexican Revolution "returned home"[26] to visit as a heroic figure, making many of *his* people proud after he became an influential artist shaping modern dance histories in the United States.

---

[23] Ibid., 133.

[24] See, e.g., Kelly Lytle Hernández, *Bad Mexicans: Race, Empire, and Revolution* (New York: W. W. Norton, 2022), and *Migra: A History of the U.S. Border Patrol* (Berkeley: University of California Press, 2010); Lawrence A. Cardoso, *Mexican Emigration to the United States, 1897–1931* (Tucson: University of Arizona, 2019); Jaime Marroquín, Adela Pineda, and Magdalena Mieri, eds., *Open Borders to a Revolution: Culture, Politics, and Migration* (Washington, DC: Smithsonian Institution Scholarly Press, 2013); Rodolfo F. Acuña, *Corridors of Migration: The Odyssey of Mexican Laborers, 1600–1933* (Tucson: University of Arizona Press, 2007).

[25] Jose L. Reynoso, "Towards a Critical Globalized Humanities: Dance Research in Mexico City at the CENIDID," in *The Futures of Dance Studies*, ed. Susan Manning, Janice Ross, and Rebecca Schneider (Madison: University of Wisconsin Press, 2020), 533.

[26] Tortajada Quiroz, "José Limón and La Malinche in Mexico: A *Chicano Artist Returns Home*."

Like Limón, through diverse dance practices and other forms of labor, Mexicans who immigrated to the United States during and after the Mexican Revolution have shaped their adopted country's sociopolitical, economic, and cultural landscape. Although Limón choreographed a few modern dances inspired by his Mexican heritage, he built his artistic reputation by embracing a universalist modernist formula that influenced aesthetic discourse within a primarily white modern dance community. These modern choreographers' dances framed "bodies as forms in motion, not necessarily as people [who] share movements from specific historical, cultural, or geographical contexts."[27] Other Mexican immigrants, not at all famous as Limón, have re/created unique mestizo modernist formulas. These highlight their historical, cultural, and geographical backgrounds as they transform their local communities, the cities where they live, and the trans/national networks they have created.

These Mexican immigrant communities have readapted and created new mestizo cultural practices while refashioning their identities and world-making strategies in a country that often sees them as perpetual foreigners. Diasporic Mexican groups[28] have invariably included diverse dance traditions as they form tight-knit communities to advocate for the betterment of their living conditions, through the politicization of different forms of leisure,[29] through hometown associations,[30] and through the annual production of the Guelaguetza Festival.[31] Many have done so while negotiating dual cultural citizenships; that is, maintaining and cultivating cultural, economic, and affective connections between *their* two countries (whether or not documented in the United States).[32] Since the 1930s, some Mexican immigrants and US-born Mexican Americans[33] embraced the iconic figure of the *charro*, the cowboy-like character of the *Jarabe Tapatío* dance discussed in this book, to coalesce their communities' forces toward social justice while reshaping notions of race and identity in the United States.[34]

---

[27] Clare Croft, *Dancers as Diplomats: American Choreography in Cultural Exchange* (Oxford: Oxford University Press, 2015), 66.

[28] I am thinking here of Mexican immigrants, their children born in the United States, and Mexicans who had lived for generations in what became part of the US Southwest after the 1848 annexation of Mexican territory.

[29] José M. Alamillo, *Making Lemonade Out of Lemons: Mexican American Labor and Leisure in a California Town, 1880–1960* (Urbana: University of Illinois Press, 2006).

[30] Xóchitl Bada, *Mexican Hometown Associations in Chicagoacán: From Local to Transnational Civic Engagement* (Piscataway, NJ: Rutgers University Press, 2014).

[31] Xóchitl C. Chávez, *The Guelaguetza: Performative Crossroads, Ethnicity, and Greater Oaxaca* (New York: Oxford University Press, forthcoming).

[32] Adrián Félix, *Specters of Belonging: The Political Life Cycle of Mexican Migrants* (New York: Oxford University Press, 2018).

[33] George J. Sánchez, *Becoming Mexican American: Ethnicity, Culture, and Identity in Chicano Los Angeles, 1900–1945* (New York: Oxford University Press, 1993).

[34] Laura R. Barraclough, *Charros: How Mexican Cowboys Are Remapping Race and American Identity* (Oakland: University of California Press, 2019); Adrián Félix, "'Vivitos y Coleando': The

All along, many of these communities have integrated Mexican folklórico dance, indigenous Mesoamerican dances, and social dance practices—often in combination with elements from the United States—into their cultural activities and political activism.[35] The back-and-forth of these dances, their constant migration within and between Mexico and the United States, has been part of reimagining geopolitical cartographies within a broader cultural landscape that some scholars have identified as Greater Mexico.[36] Decades after the flow of migration spurred by the Mexican Revolution and subsequent transnational economic arrangements such as the *bracero* program (1942–1964)[37] and the North American Free Trade Agreement (NAFTA, 1994),[38] people of Mexican descent, dancers and other laborers, contributed to shaping twentieth-century notions of cultural and material modernity in the United States. I endeavor to emphasize here that unlike Limón's documented influence on modern dance histories in the United States as a famous individual artist, millions of anonymous Mexican immigrants—dancers and non-dancers—have impacted the country's development in the twentieth and twentieth-first centuries.[39] In other words, this analysis highlights the cumulative effect that relatively anonymous individuals and collectives, including dancers in community settings and contemporary dance circles, have in shaping the spaces they inhabit and affective bonds they cultivate.

Cultural Politics of Paisa Periphery," *Boom California*, September 16, 2020, accessed May 17, 2022, https://boomcalifornia.org/2020/09/16/vivitos-y-coleando-the-cultural-politics-of-the-paisa-periphery/.

[35] See, e.g., Manuel R. Cuellar, "Epilogue," in *Choreographing Mexico: Festive Performances and Dancing Histories of a Nation* (Austin: University of Texas Press, 2022); the expansive anthology edited by Olga Nájera-Ramírez, Norma E. Cantú, and Brenda M. Romero, *Dancing across Borders: Danza y Bailes Mexicanos* (Urbana: University of Illinois Press, 2009); and Sydney Hutchinson, *From Quebradita to Duranguense: Dance in Mexican American Youth Culture* (Tucson: University of Arizona Press, 2007).

[36] See Nájera-Ramírez, Cantú, and Romero's introduction to *Dancing across Borders*. Folklorist and Chicano Studies scholar Américo Paredes theorized "Greater Mexico" as "cultural rather than political . . . areas inhabited by people of Mexican culture" that extend between Mexico and the United States (Paredes, quoted in footnote 1 in Nájera-Ramírez et al., *Dancing across Borders*, xxii).

[37] "Bracero" refers to a manual laborer. The program allowed "guestworkers" from Mexico to work in the agricultural and railroad industries in the United States during World War II. The program extended from 1942 to 1964. See, e.g., Erasmo Gamboa, *Bracero Railroaders: The Forgotten World War II Story of Mexican Workers in the U.S.* (Seattle: University of Washington Press, 2016); Mireya Loza, *Defiant Braceros: How Migrant Workers Fought for Racial, Sexual, and Political Freedom* (Chapel Hill: University of North Carolina Press, 2016).

[38] Roland L. Mize, *Consuming Mexican Labor: From the Bracero Program to NAFTA* (Toronto: University of Toronto Press, 2010).

[39] For an analysis of the construction of the "illegal alien" as a "problem" in the formation of US modernity relative to Mexican and other immigrants from different nationalities, see Mae M. Ngai, *Impossible Subjects: Illegal Aliens and the Making of Modern America* (Princeton, NJ: Princeton University Press, 2004). For a discussion of the role of Mexican migration in the development of US capitalist modernization, see Cardoso, *Mexican Emigration*.

The Emergence of Post/Modern Mexicans in America Tropical: Mestizo Contemporary Dance Practices

As a brown, working-class, young-adult Mexican immigrant, I have personally been part of these migratory flows of anonymous bodies and their diaspora building.[40] I lived for over two decades in the working-class neighborhood of Boyle Heights, just right on the other side across the bridge that separates this primarily Mexican immigrant and Mexican American barrio from downtown Los Angeles, California.[41] I was an active member of my community. I navigated a strong commitment to volunteer work through various community programs while working in construction for fourteen years (I constructed and repaired living and commercial spaces in and around Los Angeles County). During the evenings, I attended an English as a Second Language program, then a high school program for adults, community college, and eventually California State University Los Angeles to complete my undergraduate work and first graduate degree. I received my *education* in East Los Angeles. I learned to enjoy the affective bonds of my community; to survive gang violence and police harassment; to confront historical nativist xenophobia exacerbated in the mid-1990s by developments before, during, and after Proposition 187.[42] My most formative years in the United States were influenced primarily by the experience of a vibrant Mexican American and Mexican immigrant community, its struggles, resilience, and embodied histories.[43]

---

[40] My level of anonymity changes because the privileges inherent in my subsequent roles as a choreographer who shows work, a professor who works with students, and an academic who publishes expose me (i.e., my work) to a broader audience.

[41] For an in-depth history of Boyle Heights as a home for subsequent enclaves of Native peoples and Spanish colonizers, Jewish and Japanese communities, and people of Mexican and other Latina/o/x/e descent for more than a century, see George J. Sánchez, *Boyle Heights: How a Los Angeles Neighborhood Became the Future of American Democracy* (Oakland: University of California Press, 2021).

[42] Proposition 187 was a ballot initiative (also known as the "Save our State [SOS] initiative") proposed by anti-immigrant organizations and championed by California Republican governor Pete Wilson. The measure sought to prevent undocumented immigrants from accessing state public services such as education and health care. It was passed by voters on November 9, 1994, prompting massive pro-immigrant mobilizations, and eventually ruled unconstitutional by the courts.

[43] My experience was also greatly influenced by Japanese Americans such as Harry and Katz, who had deep roots in the barrio and profoundly inspiring personal histories. My beloved father-figure, Harry Okamoto (a retired grocery store clerk in Los Angeles), had traveled across the Hawaiian Islands entertaining military personnel as a musician and magician during World War II. He continued teaching on the side under his artistic name, the Great "Kiku, the Oriental Mystifier" (1922–2019). He lived with his wife Lily in the same building as me. I loved him deeply for nearly thirty years until he transitioned at age ninety-six, just a few months after I took him back home to Oʻahu, where he wanted to return. And my dear construction boss of fourteen years, Katsumi "Katz" Imoto, was born in an internment camp where the US government forcibly detained Japanese and Japanese American people during World War II. He grew up just a block away from my apartment, where his father, Mr. Yoshio (1915–2009), lived until his passing. Katz's flexibility as a boss enabled me to miss work when I needed to attend to school homework after starting my ESL program.

Almost a decade after I had stopped playing soccer (due to knee injuries) and discovered modern dance in community college, I began exploring the Mexican immigrant experience through dance as part of my research for an MFA degree at UCLA. I began working on ideas under the title "The Emergent Postmodern Mexicano in America Tropical."[44] For this conceptual framework, I combined two sources: Mexican American anthropologist and cultural critic José E. Limón's interchapter titled "Emergent Postmodern Mexicano"[45] and Mexican muralist David Alfaro Siqueiros's mural "America Tropical." From a Mexican American perspective, Limón articulates a racial and class critique of postmodern discourse arising in the 1970s. He concerns himself with the emergence of an alternative postmodernism that accounts for cultural practices by people from "below." Limón contextualizes these "contemporary folkloric practices— indebted to tradition—among marginalized working-class Mexican-Americans in south Texas and possibly beyond" as part of a continuous "war with a late-capitalist urbanized 'Anglo' culture of postmodernity."[46]

Siqueiros, an artist associated with an artistic renaissance emerging from the Mexican Revolution, also focused on marginalized sectors among people of Mexican and Latin American descent while visiting the United States. In 1932, the artist painted the commissioned "America Tropical" on a building in Olvera Street, a historic district refashioned in the 1930s as a Mexican tourist attraction in downtown Los Angeles, less than a five-minute drive from where I lived in Boyle Heights.[47] His patrons requested a rendition of (their colonialist fantasies about) Latin America as a land of tropical abundance and exotic allure. Instead, the night before the mural's unveiling on October 9, Siqueiros painted the work's central figure: a brown peon crucified on a cross on whose top rested an eagle representing US imperialism. Dried, thorny branches, not lush tropical vegetation, surrounded the laborer crucified in front of a Mesoamerican pyramid.[48] Siqueiros's politics resonated with the historical recurrence of xenophobic anti-immigrant sentiments and policies, in this case, prompted by the Great Depression of 1929, which led to the so-called repatriation of Mexicans and Mexican Americans to Mexico during the 1930s.[49] The controversial mural

---

[44] A year later, I presented the development of this research under the title of "The Mex... UNTITLED" as part of "Border Zones," a series of four solo and group works I choreographed and performed on March 3–4, 2006, at UCLA's Glorya Kaufman Dance Theater.

[45] Not to be confused with José Limón, the dancer. See José E. Limón, *Dancing with the Devil: Society and Cultural Poetics in Mexican-American South Texas* (Madison: University of Wisconsin Press, 1994).

[46] Ibid., 116.

[47] La Placita Olvera, as it is known in Spanish, dates to the 1820s, before the US annexation of Mexican territory.

[48] See a brief contextualization at https://www.olvera-street.com/siqueiros-mural.

[49] See, e.g., Francisco E. Balderrama, *Decade of Betrayal: Mexican Repatriation in the 1930s*, rev. ed. (Albuquerque: University of New Mexico, 2006).

prompted Siqueiros' expulsion from the United States and the whitewashing of his mural within a year.[50]

In a section of my solo performance, I projected footage of the actual whitewashing of Siqueiros's mural while I lay on the floor in front of the video projection. As soon as the image of the crucified brown peon disappeared, I stood up as a symbolic gesture of surrogation. In what preceded and followed this section, I attempted to embody the histories that Siqueiros's brown peon represented, the negation and erasure of his body, a metonym for communities among Mexican Americans, Mexican immigrants, and other brown people of Latin American ancestry. By combining the politics of Siqueiros's modernist mural and Limón's critique of "Anglo" postmodernism, I began to explore possibilities for the emergence of a post/modern Mexican body and community resisting the fragmentation of their collective political identities and the systematic negation of their rights and existence. Far from claiming the formulation of a (utopic) *master plan* for social change through dance, my efforts represented a framework to orient my research, develop tools for different forms of survival, and cultivate alliances with students, colleagues, and my community (I commuted from the Eastside to the Westside while I completed MFA and PhD degrees at UCLA).

My soccer player and construction worker's physicality never left me.[51] It prepared me for, and was recultivated by, intense training in release, modern dance, and ballet techniques. I also reconstituted my body by training and dancing with South Korean American choreographer Hae Kyung Lee for a few years. Her "modern-postmodern fusion" movement system combined various Western dance idioms and Korean spiritual, aesthetic, and breathing principles.[52] For "The Emergent Postmodern Mexicano in America Tropical," I combined these dance and non-dance embodied knowledges with music by Terrestre of the Tijuana-based collective Nortec, a group of artists who mix electronic sounds with norteño banda music.

As a form of *mestizaje*, this embodied research furthered my interests in the ideological aspects of aesthetic discourses, and the relationship between different manifestations of politics and contemporary dance-making in the United States. These interests prompt questions as I reflect on connections between the contexts

---

[50] For an overview of the multimillion-dollar project of reconstruction and preservation of Siqueiros's mural between 1988 and 2012, see https://www.getty.edu/conservation/our_projects/field_projects/siqueiros/siqueiros_overview.html.

[51] Neither did my laborer physicality cultivated as a teenage worker at the textile factory where three generations from both sides of my family had worked in Mexico.

[52] My work with Lee emphasized more metaphysical and transcendental interests rather than any explicit social and political concerns (e.g., the last work I performed with her company was titled "Healing the Wounded Galaxies"). For a nuanced discussion of ethical implications in Lee's work, see Judith Hamera, "Dancing Other-Wise: Ethics, Difference, and Transcendence in Hae Kyung Lee and Dancers," chapter 4 in *Dancing Communities: Performance, Difference, and Connection in the Global City* (Basingstoke: Palgrave Macmillan, 2011), quote on p. 9.

of nineteenth- and twentieth-century Mexico and the twenty-first-century United States, especially for dancers of Mexican descent whose work embodies diverse forms of *mestizaje*. Specifically, to what extent do dance practices intentionally highlighting racial, ethnic, class, and cultural elements resist expectations of "neutrality" as an implicit hallmark of legitimate contemporary dance as art?[53] To what extent must the performance of difference be abstracted enough for artists of color to access historically white contemporary, experimental dance-performance spaces? To what extent do dance artists of color who gain this access render such spaces "democratically inclusive"? What are the potential risks of performing one's difference in these and other spaces? More important, how does dancers' work relate intentionally and unintentionally to their unique position in daily life as human beings with specific backgrounds (i.e., gender, social, racial)? A short overview of Primera Generación, a dance collective of dance-makers born to Mexican immigrant families, begins to illuminate how contemporary dance artists of Mexican descent grapple with the complexities these questions raise.

Mestizo Contemporary Dance Practices: The *Desmadre* of *Rascuache Mestizaje*

On September 16, 2016, I saw "Ni Fú Ni Fá,"[54] a dance choreographed and performed by Primera Generación Dance Collective as part of the BlakTina 4 Dance Festival at the Bootleg Theater in Los Angeles, California.[55] In the dance opening, Irvin Manuel González, Alfonso (Fonzy) Cervera, and Rosa Rodríguez-Frazier stand still upstage left in a triangle configuration facing diagonally downstage right where Patricia (Patty) Huerta, also standing, looks back at them. Rodríguez-Frazier stomps on the floor twice, and the four bodies explode in dynamic motion. They go up and down as they lift one another momentarily while others quickly move as if they want to fill in or pass-through spaces created between themselves. At different moments, they spin on their vertical

---

[53] Discussing the ideological aspects and multiple meanings of "contemporary" as an aesthetic category, not merely a temporal reference, related to dance and performance is beyond the scope of this coda. However, to contextualize these specific questions, I conceptualize "contemporary" *dance as art* as a set of codes and conventions constituting an aesthetic discourse and dance-performance tradition known as "contemporary" or "experimental," and which can be traced to the Judson Dance Theater lineage starting in New York City in the early 1960s. I have begun to explore these questions in Jose L. Reynoso, "Democracy's Body, Neoliberalism's Body: The Ambivalent Search for Egalitarianism within the Contemporary Post/Modern Dance Tradition," *Dance Research Journal* 51, no. 1 (2019): 47–65. See also SanSan Kwan, "When Is Contemporary Dance?," *Dance Research Journal* 49, no. 3 (2017): 38–52.

[54] An idiomatic expression that suggests with some indifference, "neither one thing nor the other."

[55] Currently, "BlakTinx."

axis in multiple forms. They shift and share weight. They fleetingly lean on one another. They do so in ways that highlight the tension and release of physical energy necessary to execute all these bodily inter/actions. Occasionally, a leg extends straight out while a dancer stands on their opposite leg, or while lifted in the air. Other dancers propel their bodies in space with abandon, following the momentum initiated by a bent knee thrown forward. My eyes are constantly moving from place to place, prompted by arms fully swinging here and there, bodies slightly and lightly hopping and skipping across the space, always in relation to one another. Brief moments of unison between two dancers quickly morph into more dynamic motion, creating ever-evolving spatial visual textures. There is no music, only the sound of bodies moving efficiently yet emitting the inevitable aural traces of their physical effort. They inhale and exhale effortfully. The sound score created by their bare feet rubbing against the surface of the Marley covering the dance floor resists any coherent harmony. The combination of bodily sounds complements the physical exuberance of this group of contemporary dance artists at work.

Only a short time into this dance about physical dynamics, spatial configurations, and shifting forms, the four performers began to clap and sing along in unison, *dale dale dale, no pierdas el tino, por que si lo pierdes, pierdes el camino* (at Mexican parties, the song is typically longer, and its length measures the time a person must take for their turn to attempt breaking a piñata by hitting it with a stick). The quartet immediately resumes its formalist dancing, continuing the brief opening section. I experienced the piñata song "interruption" as a statement that marked and framed this contemporary dance work as Mexican American and Latina/o/x/e more broadly. Indeed, sombreros appeared, staging a satire of stereotypes related to Cinco de Mayo celebrations. The final section of this nine-minute work included techno cumbia music by the iconic, Tejana Tex-Mex singer-dancer, Selena Quintanilla. Her song provided the space and rhythms to create a dance *mestizaje* that combined cumbia dancing and evocations of the formalist contemporary dance vocabulary seen in previous sections. It is this mestizo combination of explicit cultural and ethnic references one finds in Primera Generación's other works.[56]

Primera Generación is an up-and-coming dance collective based in Los Angeles and Riverside, California, since December 2015.[57] Conceptually,

---

[56] Many of their ideas have informed the production of "Nepantla," one of their most recent works, both in film and live versions.

[57] They formed the group at the University of California, Riverside, where its members completed undergraduate and graduate work. I was a member of Fonzy's, Patty's, and Rosa's MFA committees, and I chaired Irvin's doctoral dissertation committee. I have followed their work closely ever since. I acknowledge the tensions that my proximity to the group might create relative to "academic critical distance." However, such proximity also illuminates the point I am trying to make about generational collaborations among people of Mexican and other Latin American descent, dancers and

the collective's *mestizaje* comes about and manifests itself in multiple ways through the individual work of its members and as a collective. Under the rubric of "Poc-chuc," Cervera combines both Mexican folklórico and postmodern dance techniques. His works examine "what it means to be a queer bicultural body that negotiates the relationship between ballet folklórico communities, family histories, labor, homoeroticism, and the Mexican-American identity."[58] In addition to her interests in contemporary experimental performance, Huerta foregrounds her expertise in Latin American social dances in her performance and choreographic collaborations, teaching pedagogy, and club dancing. While working on a project exploring biographical stories of cultural transmission and assimilation, Rodríguez-Frazier combined contemporary and *banda/Norteño* social dance aesthetics to formulate the concept of *desmadre* (messiness). She uses it to think about the generative potential of messy tensions and contradictions "that exist . . . in the multi-dimensional nature of cultural identity, its relationship to contemporary art, and the risks of auto/stereotyping (strategically)."[59] In his doctoral work, González reworked the concept of *rascuache mestizaje* to emphasize the affective aspects of a working-class-inspired aesthetic sensibility and community-building efforts among *quebradita* dancers moving between Mexico and the United States, including himself.[60]

Individual collective members' intersecting work animates Primera Generación's aesthetic and sociopolitical interests. Their aesthetic *mestizaje* embodies a *rascuache* "(resourcefully tacky) play, used to reflect, generate, question, and re-imagine the Mexican American experience"[61] as well as the adverse effects anti-immigrant rhetoric and laws have on Mexican immigrant families.[62] Stemming from the specificity of their first-generation Mexican American experience, the group resignifies the sociocultural construct of "Latinidad" to create

non-dancers, who share cultural and political affinities as they transform their communities and the spaces they inhabit in the United States.

[58] https://acerv002.wixsite.com/alfonsocerveradance/poc-chuc, accessed June 6, 2022.

[59] "Border *Ocurrencias*/'Occurrences' *Fronterizas*" (Unpublished MFA thesis, University of California Riverside, 2015), 2.

[60] *Rascuachismo* (crummy; an attitude, a taste, an "underdog perspective," a working-class sensibility) was theorized by Chicano Studies scholar Tomás Ybarra Frausto in 1989; see *Rasquachismo: A Chicano Sensibility* (San Antonio, TX: School by the River Press). For González's emphasis on the affective aspects of what he calls *rascuache mestizaje*, see his doctoral dissertation, "Dancing Quebradita: Transnational Belonging and Mexicanidades across the U.S.-Mexico Border" (University of California, Riverside, 2021). Hutchinson also adapts ideas of *rascuachismo* and *mestizaje*; see "Breaking Borders/Quebrando Fronteras: Dancing in the Borderscape," in *Transnational Encounters: Music and Performance at the U.S.-Mexico Border*, ed. Alejandro L. Madrid (New York: Oxford University Press, 2011), 41–66; and *From Quebradita to Duranguense*.

[61] From marketing materials for their "Nepantla" performance on June 17–19, 2022.

[62] See, e.g., Jeff Slayton, "Mixed Results for Week Two of Redcat's Virtual Now Festival 2020," *LA Dance Chronicle*, November 7, 2020, accessed November 15, 2020, https://www.ladancechronicle.com/mixed-results-for-week-two-of-redcats-virtual-now-festival-2020/.

alliances with other people of color, including queer, indigenous, Asian, Pacific Islanders, and Black communities.[63] In so doing, their creative, activist, and educational efforts are but one example of "the work Latinxs do to create communal healing among the traumas that have especially plagued us" historically.[64]

The group's work extends beyond the dancing floor by creating opportunities for and supporting communities with whom they identify. As producers, Primera Generación creates platforms and spaces to foster communal bonds, most recently as directors of Show Box L.A., a nonprofit organization devoted to "hosting and fostering artists at different stages of their career" while "centering QTBIPOC [Queer, Trans, Black, Indigenous, People of Color] artmakers."[65] Through various activities, the dance collective often organizes fundraisers to make donations to LGBT and immigrant rights organizations. As tenure-track professors and visiting lecturers in various universities across the United States, they contribute to educating the next generations of artists, scholars, and other world-makers. In all their endeavors, Primera Generación embodies a group of young *desmadre*-makers who aspire to unsettle "the bounds of 'experimental' art"[66] while joining forces with other constituencies working toward the betterment of their communities.

However, like dancers discussed in this book's chapters, Primera Generación's work embodies tensions as it exists within complex political and ideological frameworks. In this book, I have situated the work of primarily renowned dancers within complex transnational histories of colonization and power dynamics in Mexico. The book illustrated how both Mexican and foreign dancers reproduced and challenged systems of domination and normative social values. In other words, it was not only their work as dancers embodying numerous contradictions, but also their work's existence within a network of artistic, political, cultural, and economic dynamics working together that shaped the spaces they inhabited. In that way, national and international dancers contributed to the formation of ideas about Mexico during the nineteeth and twentieth centuries.

Similarly, but in the era of neoliberalism, dancers like Primera Generación strategically highlight their (ethnoracial and class) differences to resist forms of

---

[63] "Latinidad" is a construct with a complicated history. For discussions about some of its enabling and contradictory aspects, see Cindy García, *Salsa Crossings: Dancing Latinidad in Los Angeles* (Durham, NC: Duke University Press, 2013); Ramón H. Rivera-Servera, *Performing Queer Latinidad: Dance, Sexuality, Politics* (Ann Arbor: University of Michigan Press, 2012); Frances R. Aparicio, "Jennifer as Selena: Rethinking Latinidad in Media and Popular Culture," *Latino Studies* 1 (2003): 90–105.

[64] José Alfaro, "Tiempos Desmadrosos: Dancing Latinidad to the Beat of Grief (FLACC 2019)," Dance Is Not a Metaphor, December 17, 2019, accessed January 10, 2021, https://danceisnotametaphor.wordpress.com/2019/12/17/tiempos-desmadrosos-dancing-latinidad-to-the-beat-of-grief-flacc-2019/.

[65] https://showboxla.wordpress.com/about-2/, accessed June 10, 2022.

[66] Ibid.

a color-blind ideology within the contemporary experimental dance tradition. However, they often do so while replicating capitalist modes of production, just like many other contemporary dancers do inadvertently.[67] Furthermore, as they perform their difference for varied audiences, their work might satisfy neoliberal notions of diversity that "celebrates cultural differences," even within "democratically inclusive" experimental dance spaces. Thus, Primera Generación's work might risk auto/exoticization, even while doing it as a strategic act of agency, as Rodríguez-Frazier suggested while thinking about her work. That is, working within the limits of representation and identity politics while attempting to problematize the politics of identity has both enabling and contradicting implications.

While embracing these risks, as many of the dancers discussed in this book did within their specific historical contexts, Primera Generación's work contributes to creating enabling forms of sociality in historically volatile times. As the mother of one of many students who had seen Primera Generación's "Nepantla" reportedly expressed, she felt connected to the dance "even though she thought she wouldn't understand dance."[68] Her sense of connection was likely a response to the dance's sounds and imagery evoking Mexican immigrant and Mexican American life. These opportunities to connect and reaffirm one's existence become vitally important in a time when anti-Mexican immigrant rhetoric continues to take multiple forms—from micro- and macro-aggressions in daily life by ordinary people and politicians to a mass killing motivated by white supremacist ideology.[69] The importance of connection is a lesson I learned firsthand while living in the barrio and working closely with children and adults in East Los Angeles through different community programs as a volunteer.

The sociality Primera Generación's work cultivates reflects how they situate themselves as people who are also dance artists. That is, from their unique positionalities, they intentionally place themselves as people with specific backgrounds while addressing questions about "contemporary" aesthetic discourse relative to the complexities of contemporary life in the United States. While doing so, their work as dancers, producers, activists, and professors joins other efforts by many people of Mexican and other Latin American descent, dancers, and non-dancers. Together, their distinctive forms of labor collectively create opportunities for affective connections and potential political alliances geared toward the ongoing forging of a Latina/o/x/e futurity.

---

[67] See Reynoso, "Democracy's Body, Neoliberalism's Body."

[68] Steven Vargas, "How Primera Generación Dance Collective Brought 'Nepantla' from Screen to Stage," *Los Angeles Times*, June 23, 2022, accessed June 24, 2022, https://www.latimes.com/entertainment-arts/story/2022-06-23/primera-generacion-dance-collective-takes-nepantla-from-screen-to-stage-at-the-odyssey-theater.

[69] See, e.g., "Police: El Paso Shooting Suspect Said He Targeted Mexicans," *PA News*, August 9, 2019, accessed June 28, 2022, https://apnews.com/article/shootings-el-paso-texas-mass-shooting-us-news-ap-top-news-immigration-456c0154218a4d378e2fb36cd40b709d.

LatinMex: Past-Present-Future

In many ways, histories of Mexican migration contextualize the emergence of Primera Generación's work as first-generation Mexican Americans who identify and collaborate with other people of Latin American identification. The collusion between Mexican dictator Porfirio Díaz and US investors who owned considerable amounts of land and industry in Mexico displaced agricultural workers who migrated across the US-Mexico border in the last two decades of the nineteenth century. The tumultuous 1910 Mexican Revolution that removed Díaz from power promoted further migration across the border to the extent that "it changed who we are as people" in the United States.[70] The Bracero Program continued promoting Mexican migrant flows between the 1940s and 1960s. By 1980, Mexican migration was such that it ended the United States' migration story dominated by Europeans, and by 2010, Mexican immigrants constituted the largest immigrant group in US history.[71] Today, with Mexican Americans and Mexican immigrants leading the numbers, "Latinos[/as/xs . . .] are the largest non-white population in the Unites States."[72] Projections say that by 2045, the United States will be "a 'minority white' nation, with Mexican Americans and Mexican immigrants driving the shift."[73]

I see these ongoing nation-building processes as the context in which Primera Generación's efforts join forces with many groups of anonymous dancers and non-dancers of Mexican and other Latin American backgrounds. All these groups' distinctive forms of labor, differences, and internal quarrels transform their communities within the specificity of their unique localities across the United States. This book's chapters focused on how national and international forces and people reproducing and combating colonial legacies of racialization contributed to the formation of post/colonial and postrevolutionary Mexico. This coda gestures toward the multidirectional impact of people moving between Mexico and the United States, in continuously forming the two nations from the nineteenth century to today.

Retaining the idea of *mestizaje*, I think of Primera Generación as a *LatinMex* group whose work navigates contradicting forces implicated in diaspora formations in the United States. The collective highlights the specificity of its members' Mexican American experience, and their Mexican parents' and ancestors', while simultaneously identifying as and establishing alliances with diverse communities of Latin American ancestry (queer, Black, Asian, indigenous, and mestizo). Like many other first-generation Mexican Americans, Mexican

---

[70] Lytle Hernández, *Bad Mexicans*, 8.
[71] Ibid., 7.
[72] Ibid., 8.
[73] Ibid.

immigrants, and other Latina/o/x/e people with unique transnational histories, their individual and collective work embodies the legacies of colonialism, independence, and revolution; the histories of migration and xenophobia; the politics that shape the transnational flows of people, cultural practices, and aesthetic discourses; and the complexities of forming diasporas. Through different forms of labor in the diverse spaces they inhabit—including dancing folklórico, quebradita, danza Azteca, pasito duranguense, danza de los matachines, banda, salsa, merengue, cumbia, bachata, contemporary dance, and new dance practices—all these groups of people, relatively anonymous, including Primera Generación, constitute a broader Latina/o/x/e community. From their specific localities, they all contribute to shaping the United States' sociopolitical, cultural, and economic landscape while navigating the country's violent histories of racialization and social stratification in the twenty-first century.

Bibliography

(References for additional primary sources are included in footnotes throughout the book)

1910, el arte en un año decisivo: La exposición de artistas mexicanos. México City: Museo Nacional de Arte, 1991.

Acuña, Rodolfo F. *Corridors of Migration: The Odyssey of Mexican Laborers, 1600–1933*. Tucson: University of Arizona Press, 2007.

Agostoni, Claudia. *Monuments of Progress: Modernization in Mexico City, 1876–1910*. Calgary: Univeristy of Calgary, 2003.

Aguilar Camín, Héctor, and Lorenzo Meyer. *In the Shadow of the Mexican Revolution: Contemporary Mexican History, 1910, 1989*. Translated by Luis Alberto Fierro. Austin: University of Texas Press, 1993.

Alamillo, José M. *Making Lemonade out of Lemons: Mexican American Labor and Leisure in a California Town, 1880–1960*. Urbana: University of Illinois Press, 2006.

Alejandre Ramírez, Gloria Luz, and Eduardo Torres Alonso. "El Primer Congreso Feminista de Yucatán 1916. El camino a la legislación del sufragio y reconocimiento de ciudadanía a las mujeres. Construcción y tropiezos." *Estudios políticos* 39 (September–December 2016): 59–89.

Anderson, Benedict. *Imagined Communities: Reflections on the Origin and Spread of Nationalism*. London: Verso, 2006.

Anzaldúa, Gloria. *Borderlands/La Frontera: The New Mestiza*. San Francisco: Aunt Little Books, 1987.

Aparicio, Frances R. "Jennifer as Selena: Rethinking Latinidad in Media and Popular Culture." *Latino Studies* 1 (2003): 90–105.

Arce, Christine B. *México's Nobodies: The Cultural Legacy of the Soldadera and Afro-Mexican Women*. Albany: State University of New York Press, 2017.

Arrizón, Alicia. *Queering Mestizaje: Transculturation and Performance*. Ann Arbor: University of Michigan Press, 2006.

Arrizón, Alicia. "'Soldaderas' and the Staging of the Mexican Revolution." *Drama Review* 42, no. 1 (Spring 1998): 90–112.

Arzubide, Germán List. *El movimiento estridentista*. Jalapa: Ediciones de Horizonte, 1927.

Aulestia, Patricia. *Las "Chicas Bien" de Miss Carroll: Estudio y Ballet Carroll (1923–1964)*. México, DF: INBA/CENIDID-Danza, 2003.

Bada, Xóchitl. *Mexican Hometown Associations in Chicagoacán: From Local to Transnational Civic Engagement*. Piscataway, NJ: Rutgers University Press, 2014.

Balderrama, Francisco E. *Decade of Betrayal: Mexican Repatriation in the 1930s*. Rev. ed. Albuquerque: University of New Mexico, 2006.

Banerji, Anurima. *Dancing Odissi: Paratopic Performances of Gender and State*. London: Seagull Books, 2019.

Bargalió Sánchez, Isabel, and Monserrat Bargalió Sánchez. "¿Colección o inspiración? Los textiles americanos de Carmen Tórtola Valencia/Collection or Inspiration? Carmen Tórtola Valencia's Latin American Textiles." *Datatèxtil*, no. 22 (2010): 30–50.

Barraclough, Laura R. *Charros: How Mexican Cowboys Are Remapping Race and American Identity*. Oakland: University of California Press, 2019.

Benessaieh, Afef. "Boas Goes to Americas: The Emergence of Transamerican Perspectives on 'Culture.'" In *Mobile and Entangled Americas*, edited by Maryemma Graham and Wilfried Raussert, 301–20. London: Routledge, 2016.

Best Maugard, Adolfo. *Manuales y tratados: Método de dibujo: Tradición, resurgimiento y evolución del arte mexicano*. México: Ediciones la Rana; Departamento de la Secretaria de Educación Pública, 1923; Secretaria de Educación Pública, 1964.

Bidault de la Calle, Sophie. *La escenificación del cuerpo en la crónicas modernistas de José Juan Tablada*. México, DF: Amate Editorial, CENIDID-Danza, INBA, CONACULTA, 2010.

Bidault de la Calle, Sophie. *Nellie Campobello: Una escritura salida del cuerpo*. México, DF: INBAL/CENIDID-Danza, 2003.

Blanco Borelli, Melissa. "'¿Y ahora qué vas a hacer, mulata?': Hip Choreographies in the Mexican *Cabaretera* Film *Mulata* (1954)." *Women & Performance: A Journal of Feminist Theory* 18, no. 3 (2008): 215–33.

Briggs, Laura, Gladys McCormick, and J. T. Way. "Transnationalism: A Category of Analysis." *American Quarterly* 60, no. 3 (September 2008): 625–48.

Bristol, Joan C. *Christians, Blasphemers, and Witches: Afro-Mexican Ritual Practice in the Seventeenth Century*. Albuquerque: University of New Mexico Press, 2007.

Bristol, Joan C. "Health Food and Diabolic Vice: Pulque Discourse in New Spain." In *Substance and Seduction: Ingested Commodities in Colonial Mesoamerica, the Atlantic World, and Beyond*, edited by Stacy Schwarzkopf and Kathryn Sampeck, 128–46. Austin: University of Texas Press, 2017.

Bunker, Steven B. *Creating Mexican Consumer Culture in the Age of Porfirio Díaz*. Albuquerque: University of New Mexico Press, 2012.

Campobello, Nellie. *Cartucho*. México: Ediciones Integrales, 1931.

Cardoso, Lawrence A. *Mexican Emigration to the United States, 1897–1931*, Tucson: University of Arizona Press, 2019.

Carredano, Consuelo. "La crítica musical en México: Carlos Chávez y los músicos del exilio español." In *Manuel de Falla en el imaginario de dos músicos exiliados: Adolfo Salazar y Jesús Bal y Gay*, edited by Consuelo Carredano and Carlos Villanueva, 33–52. Ciudad de México: El Colegio de México, 2017.

Carreño King, Tania. *El charro: La construcción de un estereotipo nacional (1920–1940)*. México: INEHRM, Federación Mexicana de la Charrería, 2000.

Carrera, Magali M. *Imagining Identity in New Spain: Race, Lineage and the Colonial Body in Portraiture and Casta Paintings*. Austin: University of Texas Press, 2003.

Carrillo, Rubén. "Asia llega a América: Migración e influencia cultural asiática en Nueva España (1565–1815)." *Asiadémica*, no. 3 (January 2014): 81–98.

Carroll, Patrick J. "Mandinga: The Evolution of a Mexican Runaway Slave Community, 1735–1827." *Comparative Studies in Society and History* 19, no. 4 (October 1977): 488–505.

Castro-Gómez, Santiago, and Ramón Grosfoguel, eds. *El giro decolonial: Reflexiones para una diversidad epistemica más alla del capitalismo global*. Bogotá: Siglo del Hombre Editores, 2007.

Chávez, Xóchitl C. *The Guelaguetza: Performative Crossroads, Ethnicity, and Greater Oaxaca*. New York: Oxford University Press, Forthcoming.
Chávez-Hita, Adriana Naveda. "De San Lorenzo de los negros a los morenos de Amapa: Cimarrones veracruzanos, 1609–1735." In *Rutas de la esclavitud en África y América Latina*, edited by Rina Cáceres Gómez, 157–74. San José: De la Universidad de Costa Rica, 2001.
Cherniavsky, Eva. *Incorporations: Race, Nation, and the Body Politics of Capital*. Minneapolis: University of Minnesota Press, 2006.
Ciccariello-Maher, George. *Decolonizing Dialectics*. Durham, NC: Duke University Press, 2017.
Cinco Basurto, Monica Georgina. "La expulsión de chinos de los años treinta y la repatriación de chino mexicanos de 1960." Master's thesis, Centro de Estudios de Asia y África, Colegio de México, 2009.
Clayton, Michelle. "Modernism's Moving Bodies." *Modernist Cultures* 9, no. 1 (May 2014): 27–45.
Clayton, Michelle. "Touring History: Tórtola Valencia between Europe and the Americas." *Dance Research Journal* 44, no. 1 (Summer 2012): 28–49.
Coffey, Mary K. *How a Revolutionary Art Became Official Culture: Murals, Museums, and the Mexican State*. Durham, NC: Duke University Press, 2012.
Cohen, Jonathan. "Waldeen and the Americas: The Dance Has Many Faces." In *A Woman's Gaze: Latin American Women Artists*, edited by Marjorie Agosín, 224–42. Fredonia, NY: White Pine Press, 1998.
Cohen, Theodore W. *Finding Afro-Mexico: Race and Nation after the Revolution*. Cambridge: Cambridge University Press, 2020.
Conway, Christopher. "Ignacio Altamirano and the Contradictions of Autobiographical Indianism." *Latin American Literary Review* 34, no. 67 (January–June 2006): 34–49.
Coons, Lorraine. "Artiste or Coquette? *Les Petits Rats* of the Paris Opera Ballet." *French Cultural Studies* 25, no. 2 (2014): 140–64.
Cope, R. Douglas. *The Limits of Racial Domination: Plebeian Society in Colonial Mexico City, 1660–1720*. Madison: University of Wisconsin Press, 1994.
Craven, David. *Art and Revolution in Latin America, 1910–1990*. New Haven, CT: Yale University Press, 2002.
Creelman, James. *Díaz Master of Mexico*. New York: D. Appleton & Co., 1911.
Creelman, James. "President Díaz: Hero of the Americas." *Pearson's Magazine* 19 (March 1908): 231–77.
Croft, Clare. *Dancers as Diplomats: American Choreography in Cultural Exchange*. Oxford: Oxford University Press, 2015.
Crónica Oficial de las Fiestas del Primer Centenario de la Independencia de México, Genaro García (director de publicación). Ciudad de México: Secretaría de Gobernación, Talleres del Museo Nacional, 1911.
Cuellar, Manuel R. *Choreographing Mexico: Festive Performances and Dancing Histories of a Nation*. Austin: University of Texas Press, 2022.
Dallal, Alberto. "Loie Fuller en México." *Anales del Instituto de Investigaciones Estéticas* 13, no. 50 (México: UNAM, 1982): 2:297–307.
Dalton, David S. *Mestizo Modernity: Race, Technology, and the Body in Postrevolutionary Mexico*. Gainesville: University of Florida Press, 2018.
Daly, Ann. *Done into Dance: Isadora Duncan in America*. Middletown, CT: Wesleyan University Press, 2002; orig. ed. Bloomington: Indiana University Press, 1995).

DeFrantz, Thomas F. *Dancing Revelations: Alvin Ailey's Embodiment of African American Culture*. Oxford: Oxford University Press, 2004.
Delgado Martínez, César. "Escuela de Plástica Dinámica." *Cuadernos del CID DANZA No. 2*, 8. México City, Centro de la Información y Documentación de la Danza (CID-Danza), 1985.
Delgado Martínez, César. *Guillermina Bravo: Historia Oral*. México: Instituto Nacional de Bellas Artes; Cenidi-Danza "José Limón," 1994.
Delpar, Helen. *The Enormous Vogue of Things Mexican: Cultural Relations between the United States and Mexico, 1920–1935*. Tuscaloosa: University of Alabama Press, 1992.
Dennis, Nigel. "El baile en el exilio: La Paloma Azul (México, 1940)." In *El exilio republicano de 1939 y la segunda generación*, edited by Manuel Aznar Soler and José Ramón López García, 865–76. Biblioteca del Exilio. Sevilla: Editorial Renacimiento, 2011.
Desmond, Jane C. "Dancing Out the Difference: Cultural Imperialism and Ruth St. Denis's 'Radha' of 1906." *Signs* 17, no. 1 (Autumn 1991): 28–49.
Echeverría, Bolívar. *Modernidad y blanquitud*. Mexico, DF: Era, 2010.
Echeverría, Bolívar, ed. *La americanización de la modernidad*. México, DF: Era, Universidad Nacional Autónoma de México, 2008.
Escobar, Arturo. *Designs for the Pluriverse: Radical Interdependence, Autonomy, and the Making of Worlds*. Durham, NC: Duke University Press, 2018.
Ezrahi, Christina. *Swans of the Kremlin: Ballet and Power in Soviet Russia*. Pittsburgh: University of Pittsburgh Press, 2012.
Félix, Adrián. *Specters of Belonging: The Political Life Cycle of Mexican Migrants*. New York: Oxford University Press, 2018.
Firmino-Castillo, María Regina. "Dancing the Pluriverse: Indigenous Performance as Ontological Praxis." *Dance Research Journal* 48, no. 1 (April 2016): 55–73.
Fojas, Camilla. *Cosmopolitanism in the Americas*. West Lafayette, IN: Purdue University Press, 2005.
Fortuna, Victoria. *Moving Otherwise: Dance, Violence, and Memory in Buenos Aires*. New York: Oxford University Press, 2019.
Foster, Susan L. *Choreographing Empathy: Kinesthesia in Performance*. London: Routledge, 2011.
Foster, Susan L. "Choreographing History." In *Choreographing History*, edited by Susan L. Foster, 3–21. Bloomington: University of Indiana Press, 1995.
Foster, Susan L. *Choreography and Narrative: Ballet's Staging of Story and Desire*. Bloomington: Indiana University Press, 1996.
Foster, Susan L. "Closets Full of Dances: Modern Dance's Performance of Masculinity and Sexuality." In *Dancing Desires: Choreographing Sexualities on and off the Stage*, edited by Jance C. Desmond, 147–207. Madison: University of Wisconsin Press, 2001.
Foster, Susan L. "Dance Theory?" In *Teaching Dance Studies*, edited by Judith Chazin-Bennahum, 19–34. New York: Routledge, 2005.
Foster, Susan L. "Dancing Bodies." In *Meaning in Motion: New Cultural Studies of Dance*, edited by Jane C. Desmond, 235–57. Durham, NC: Duke University Press, 1997.
Foster, Susan L. *Reading Dancing: Bodies and Subjects in Contemporary American Dance*. Berkeley: University of California Press, 1986.
Foster, Susan L., et al. "Introduction." In *Corporealities: Dancing, Knowledge, Culture, and Power*, edited by Susan L. Foster, xi–xvii. London: Routledge, 1996.
Foucault, Michael, and Jay Miskowiec. "Of Other Spaces." *Diacritics* 16, no. 1 (Spring 1986): 22–27.

Franko, Mark. *Dancing Modernism/Performing* Politics. Bloomington: Indiana University Press, 1995.
Franko, Mark. *The Work of Dance: Labor, Movement, and Identity in the 1930s*. Middletown, CT: Wesleyan University Press, 2002.
Gallo, Rubén. *Mexican Modernity: The Avant-Garde and the Technological Revolution*. Cambridge, MA: MIT Press, 2005.
Gamboa, Erasmo. *Bracero Railroaders: The Forgotten World War II Story of Mexican Workers in the U.S.* Seattle: University of Washington Press, 2016.
Gamio, Manuel. *Forjando patria: Pro-nacionalismo*. México: Librería de Porrúa Hermanos, 1916.
Garafola, Lynn. *Diaghilev's Ballets Russes*. New York: Oxford University Press, 1989.
Garafola, Lynn, Russell Gold, and Barbara Melosh, eds. *Of, by, and for the People: Dancing on the Left in the 1930s*. Society of Dance History Scholars. *Studies in Dance History* 5, no. 1 (Spring 1994): entire issue.
García, Cindy. *Salsa Crossings: Dancing Latinidad in Los Angeles*. Durham, NC: Duke University Press, 2013.
García Canclini, Néstor. *Hybrid Cultures: Strategies for Entering and Leaving Modernity*. Translated by Christopher L. Chiappari and Silvia L. López. Minneapolis: University of Minnesota Press, 1995.
García Sáiz, María Concepción. *Las castas mexicanas: Un género pictórico americano*. s.l.: Olivetti, 1989.
García y Santisteban, Rafael. *El potosí submarino: Zarzuela cómico-fantástica de gran espectáculo en tres actos y en verso*. Music by Emilio Arrieta. Madrid: Imprenta de José Rodríguez, 1870.
Garland, Iris. "Early Modern Dance in Spain: Tórtola Valencia, Dancer of the Historical Intuition." *Dance Research Journal* 29, no. 2 (Autumn 1997): 1–22.
Giersdorf, Jens Richard. *The Body of the People: East German Dance since 1945*. Madison: University of Wisconsin Press, 2013.
Gleizer Salzman, Daniela. *Unwelcome Exiles: Mexico and the Jewish Refugees from Nazism, 1933–1945*. Leiden: Brill, 2014.
González, Anita. *Afro-Mexico: Dancing between Myth and Reality*. Austin: University of Texas Press, 2010.
González, Anita. *Jarocho's Soul: Cultural Identity and Afro-Mexican Dance*. Lanham, MD: University Press of America, 2004.
González, Irvin M. "Dancing Quebradita: Transnational Belonging and Mexicanidades across the U.S.-Mexico Border." PhD diss., University of California, Riverside, 2021.
González Navarro, Moisés. "Las ideas raciales de los científicos." *Historia mexicana* 37, no. 4 (April–June 1988): 565–83.
Gottschild, Brenda Dixon. *Digging the Africanist Presence in American Performance: Dance and Other Contexts*. Westport, CT: Greenwood Press, 1996.
Graff, Ellen. *Stepping Left: Radical Dance in New York City, 1928–1942*. Durham, NC: Duke University Press, 1997.
Grewal, Inderpal. "On the New Global Feminism and the Family of Nations: Dilemmas of Transnational Feminist Practice." In *Talking Visions: Multicultural Feminism in a Transnational Age*, edited by Ella Shohat, 501–30. Cambridge, MA: MIT Press, 1998.
Guerrero, Ellie. *Dance and the Arts in Mexico, 1920–1950*. Cham, Switzerland: Palgrave Macmillan, 2018.

Guevara Meza, Carlos. *Conciencia periférica y modernidades alternativas en América Latina*. Ciudad de México: CONACULTA/INBA, Cenidiap, 2011.
Hamera, Judith. *Dancing Communities: Performance, Difference, and Connection in the Global City*. Basingstoke: Palgrave Macmillan, 2011.
Hassig, Ross. *Aztec Warfare: Imperial Expansion and Political Control*. Norman: University of Oklahoma Press, 1988.
Hawke, Rob. *Ford Madox Ford and the Misfit Moderns: Edwardian Fiction and the First World War*. Basingstoke: Palgrave Macmillan, 2012.
Hedrick, Tace. *Mestizo Modernism: Race, Nation, and Identity in Latin American Culture, 1900–1940*. New Brunswick, NJ: Rutgers University Press, 2003.
Hellerman, M. Kasey. "The Coatlicue-Malinche Conflict: A Mother and Son Identity Crisis in the Writings of Carlos Fuentes." *Hispania* 57, no. 4 (December 1974): 868–75.
Hellier-Tinoco, Ruth. *Embodying Mexico: Tourism, Nationalism & Performance*. New York: Oxford University Press, 2011.
Hernández Araico, Susana. "Espectacularidad musical indígena: Desde cronistas y ritos novohispanos a Sor Juana." *Romance Notes* 59, no. 1 (2019): 41–49.
Lytle Hernández, Kelly. *Bad Mexicans: Race, Empire, and Revolution*. New York: W. W. Norton, 2022.
Lytle Hernández, Kelly. *Migra: A History of the U.S. Border Patrol*. Berkeley: University of California Press, 2010.
Höfling, Ana Paula. *Staging Brazil: Choreographies of Capoeira*. Middletown, CT: Wesleyan University Press, 2019.
Hooker, Juliet. *Theorizing Race in the Americas: Douglass, Sarmiento, Du Bois, and Vaconcelos*. New York: Oxford University Press, 2017.
Hurlburt, Laurence P. *The Mexican Muralists in the United States*. Albuquerque: University of New Mexico Press, 1989.
Hutchinson, Sidney. "Breaking Borders/Quebrando Fronteras: Dancing in the Borderscape." In *Transnational Encounters: Music and Performance at the U.S.-Mexico Border*, edited by Alejandro L. Madrid, 41–66. New York: Oxford University Press, 2011.
Hutchinson, Sidney. *From Quebradita to Duranguense: Dance in Mexican American Youth Culture*. Tucson: University of Arizona Press, 2007.
Irwin, Robert McKee, Edward J. McCaughan, and Michelle Rocío Nasser. "Sexuality and Social Control in Mexico, 1901." In *The Famous 41: Sexuality and Social Control in Mexico, 1901*, edited by Robert McKee Irwin, Edward J. McCaughan, and Michelle Rocío Nasser, 1–18. New York: Palgrave Macmillan, 2003.
Jato, Mónica. *El éxodo español de 1939: Una topología cultural del exilio*. Leiden: Brill Rodopi, 2020.
Johns, Michael. *The City of Mexico in the Age of Díaz*. Austin: University of Texas Press, 1997.
Joseph, Gilbert M., and Jürgen Buchenau. "Porfirian Modernization and Its Costs." In *Mexico's Once and Future Revolution: Social Upheaval and the Challenge of Rule since the Nineteenth Century*, 15–36. Durham, NC: Duke University Press Books, 2013.
Katzew, Ilona. *Casta Painting: Images of Race in Eighteenth-Century Mexico*. New Haven, CT: Yale University Press, 2004.
Kendi, Ibram X. *Stamped from the Beginning: The Definitive History of Racist Ideas in America*. New York: Nation Books, 2016.

Klein, Gabriele. "Toward a Theory of Cultural Translation in Dance." In *New German Dance Studies*, edited by Susan Manning and Lucia Ruprecht, 247–58. Urbana: University of Illinois Press, 2012.

Kosstrin, Hanna. *Honest Bodies: Revolutionary Modernism in the Dances of Anna Sokolow.* New York: Oxford University Press, 2017.

Kosstrin, Hanna. "Inevitable Designs: Embodied Ideology in Anna Sokolow's Proletarian Dances." *Dance Research Journal* 45, no. 2 (August 2013): 5–23.

Krause, Korinne A. *Los judíos en México: Una historia con énfasis especial en el período de 1857 a 1930.* Translated by Ariela Katz de Gugenheim. México: Universidad Iberoamericana, Departamento de Historia, 1987.

Kraut, Anthea. *Choreographing Copyright: Race, Gender, and Intellectual Property Rights in American Dance.* New York: Oxford University Press, 2016.

Kraut, Anthea. "White Womanhood, Property Rights, and the Campaign for Choreographic Copyright: Loie Fuller's *Serpentine Dance*." *Dance Research Journal* 43, no. 1 (Summer 2011): 3–26.

Kwan, SanSan. *Kinesthetic City: Dance and Movement in Chinese Urban Spaces.* Oxford: Oxford University Press, 2013.

Kwan, SanSan. "When Is Contemporary Dance?" *Dance Research Journal* 49, no. 3 (2017): 38–52.

Landau, Ellen G. *Mexico and American Modernism.* New Haven, CT: Yale University Press, 2013.

Lavalle, Josefina. "Anna Pavlova y El Jarabe Tapatío." In *La danza en México: Visiones de cinco siglos*, edited by Maya Ramos Smith and Patricia Cardona Lang, Vol. I, 641–642. Antología: Cinco Siglos de Crónicas, Crítica y Documentos (1521–2002). México: CENIDID, INBA, CONACULTA, Escenología, 2002.

Lavalle, Josefina. *El Jarabe . . . El Jarabe Ranchero o Jarabe de Jalisco.* México, DF: Cenidi Danza/INBA, 1988.

Lepecki, André. *Singularities: Dance in the Age of Performance.* Abingdon: Routledge, 2016.

Lida, Clara Eugenia, José Antonio Matesanz, and Josefina Zoraida Vázquez. *La Casa de España y el Colegio de México: Memoria, 1938–2000.* México, D.F.: El Colegio, 2000.

Limón, José E. *Dancing with the Devil: Society and Cultural Poetics in Mexican-American South Texas.* Madison: University of Wisconsin Press, 1994.

Lisbona Guillén, Miguel. "Danzas como tradición y como disputa: La ilusión comunitaria china en el soconusco chiapaneco." *Península* 10, no. 1 (January–June 2015): 9–28.

Lomnitz, Claudio. "Anti-Semitism and the Ideology of the Mexican Revolution." *Representations* 110, no. 1 (2010): 1–28.

López, Rick A. "The Noche Mexicana and the Exhibition of Popular Arts: Two Ways of Exalting Indianness." In *The Eagle and the Virgin: Nation and Cultural Revolution in Mexico 1920–1940*, edited by. Mary K. Vaughan and Stephen Lewis, 23–42. Durham, NC: Duke University Press, 2006.

López Chávez, América Nicte-Ha. "La movilización etnopolítica afromexicana de la Costa Chica de Guerrero y Oaxaca: Logros, limitaciones y desafíos." *Perfiles latinoamericanos* 26, no. 52 (2018): 1–33.

Lott, Eric. "Love and Theft: The Racial Unconscious of Blackface Minstrelsy." *Representations*, no. 39 (Summer 1992): 23–50.

Loza, Mireya. *Defiant Braceros: How Migrant Workers Fought for Racial, Sexual, and Political Freedom.* Chapel Hill: University of North Carolina Press, 2016.

Macías González, Víctor. "The *Lagartijo* at *the High Life*: Masculine Consumption, Race, Nation, and Homosexuality in Porfirian Mexico." In *The Famous 41: Sexuality and Social Control in Mexico, 1901*, edited by Robert McKee Irwin, Edward J. McCaughan, and Michelle Rocío Nasser, 227–49. New York: Palgrave Macmillan, 2003.

Madrid, Alejandro L. *Music in Mexico: Experiencing Music, Expressing Culture*. New York: Oxford University Press, 2013.

Madrid, Alejandro L. *Sounds of the Modern Nation: Music, Culture, and Ideas in Post-Revolutionary Mexico*. Philadelphia: Temple University Press, 2008.

Mallon, Florencia R. *Peasant and Nation: The Making of Postcolonial Mexico and Peru*. Berkeley: University of California Press, 1995.

Manning, Susan. "Modern Dance in the Third Reich: Six Positions and a Coda." In *Choreographing History*, edited by Susan L. Foster, 164–76. Indianapolis: Indiana University Press, 1995.

Manning, Susan. *Modern Dance, Negro Dance: Race in Motion*. Minneapolis: University of Minnesota Press, 2004.

Manning, Susan, et al. "Inside/Beside Dance Studies: A Conversation, Mellon Dance Studies in/and the Humanities." *Dance Research Journal* 45, no. 3 (December 2013): 5–28.

Margheritis, Ana, and Anthony W. Pereira. "The Neoliberal Turn in Latin America: The Cycle of Ideas and the Search for an Alternative." *Latin American Perspectives* 34, no. 3 (May 2007): 25–48.

Mariátegui, José Carlos. *Siete ensayos de interpretación de la realidad peruana*. Santiago de Chile: Editorial Universitaria, 1955; orig. ed. 1928.

Marino, Angela. *Populism and Performance in the Bolivarian Revolution of Venezuela*. Evanston, IL: Northwestern University Press, 2018.

Marroquín, Jaime, Adela Pineda, and Magdalena Mieri, eds. *Open Borders to a Revolution: Culture, Politics, and Migration*. Washington, DC: Smithsonian Institution Scholarly Press, 2013.

Martin, Randy. *Critical Moves: Dance Studies in Theory and Politics*. Durham, NC: Duke University Press, 1998.

Martínez, Ana. *Performance in the Zócalo: Constructing History, Race, and Identity in Mexico's Central Square from the Colonial Era to the Present*. Ann Arbor: University of Michigan Press, 2020.

Martínez, María Elena. *Genealogical Fictions:* Limpieza de Sangre, *Religion and Gender in Colonial Mexico*. Stanford, CA: Stanford University Press, 2008.

Mateos, Abdón. "Los republicanos españoles en el México cardenista." *Ayer*, no. 47, *Los exilios en la España contemporánea* (2002): 103–28.

Matthews, Michael. *The Civilizing Machine: A Cultural History of Mexican Railroads, 1876–1910*. Lincoln: University of Nebraska Press, 2014.

Mendoza, Cristina. *Escritos de Carlos Mérida sobre el arte: La danza*. México: INBA/Centro Nacional de Investigación y Documentación de Artes Plásticas, 1990.

Messinger Cypress, Sandra. *La Malinche in Mexican Literature from History to Myth*. Austin: University of Texas Press, 1991.

Meyer, Michael C. *The Course of Mexican History*. 7th ed. New York: Oxford University Press, 2003.

Mignolo, Walter D. *The Darker Side of Western Modernity: Global Futures, Decolonial Options*. Durham, NC: Duke University Press, 2011.

Miranda, Gloria E. "Racial and Cultural Dimensions of 'Gente de Razón' Status in Spanish and Mexican California." *Southern California Quarterly* 70, no. 3 (Fall 1998): 265-78.

Mize, Roland L. *Consuming Mexican Labor: From the Bracero Program to NAFTA*. Toronto: University of Toronto Press, 2010.

Money, Keith. *Anna Pavlova: Her Life and Art*. New York: Knopf, 1982.

Monsiváis, Carlos. "The 41 and the *Gran Redada*." Translated by Aaron Walker. In *The Famous 41: Sexuality and Social Control in Mexico, 1901*, edited by Robert McKee Irwin, Edward J. McCaughan, and Michelle Rocío Nasser, 139-67. New York: Palgrave Macmillan, 2003.

Monsiváis, Carlos. "García Lorca y México." *Cuadernos hispanoamericanos: Homenaje a García Lorca* 1, no. 433-434 (July-August 1986): 249-256.

Montag, Warren. "The Universalization of Whiteness: Racism and Enlightenment." In *Whiteness: A Critical Reader*, edited by Mike Hill, 281-93. New York: New York University Press, 1997.

Nájera-Ramírez, Olga, Norma E. Cantú, and Brenda M. Romero. *Dancing across Borders: Danza y Bailes Mexicanos*. Urbana: University of Illinois Press, 2009.

Navarro, Héctor. "Creating Masculinity and Homophobia: Oppression and Backlash under Mexico's Porfiriato." *Historical Perspectives: Santa Clara University Undergraduate Journal of History*, Series II, 22, Article 8 (2017): 30-48.

Ngai, Mae M. *Impossible Subjects: Illegal Aliens and the Making of Modern America*. Princeton, NJ: Princeton University Press, 2004.

Olcott, Jocelyn H. *Revolutionary Women in Postrevolutionary Mexico*. Durham, NC: Duke University Press, 2005.

Olcott, Jocelyn H., Mary K. Vaughan, and Cano Gabriela, eds. *Sex in Revolution: Gender, Politics, and Power in Modern Mexico*. Durham, NC: Duke University Press, 2006.

Palmer, Colin A. *Slaves of the White God: Blacks in Mexico, 1570-1650*. Cambridge, MA: Harvard University Press, 1976.

Paz, Octavio. *El laberinto de la soledad*. 5th ed. México: Fondo de Cultura Económica, 1967.

Paz, Octavio. *México en la obra de Octavio Paz*. México, DF: Fondo de Cultura Económica, 1987.

Piccato, Pablo. *City of Suspects: Crime in Mexico City, 1900-1931*. Durham, NC: Duke University Press, 2001.

Pla Brugat, Dolores. *Los niños de Morelia: Un estudio sobre los primeros refugiados españoles en México*. México, DF: Instituto Nacional de Antropología e Historia, 1985.

Poniatowska, Elena. *Las soldaderas: Women of the Mexican Revolution*. Translated by David Dorado Romo. El Paso: Cinco Puntos Press, 2006 (orig. ed. Mexico, 1999).

Proctor, Frank T. "Slave Rebellion and Liberty in Colonial Mexico." In *Black Mexico: Race and Society from Colonial to Modern Times*, edited by Ben Vinson III and Matthew Restall, 21-50. Albuquerque: University of New Mexico Press, 2009.

Pujals, Sandra. "*Los Poputchiki*: Communist Fellow Travelers, Comintern Radical Networks, and the Forging of a Culture of Modernity in Latin America and the Caribbean." In *Left Transnationalism: The Communist International and the National, Colonial, and Racial Questions*, edited by Oleksa Drachewych and Ian McKay, 155-82. Montreal: McGill-Queen's University Press, 2019.

Quijano, Aníbal. "Coloniality of Power, Eurocentrism, and Latin America." *Nepantla: Views from South* 1, no. 3 (2000): 533-80.

Ramírez Domínguez, Silvia. *Alusión al grito de dolores: El ballet se Suma a las fiestas que celebran la independencia de México*. Ciudad de México: CENIDID, Forthcoming.

Ramos, Maya, and Patricia Cardona, comps. *La danza en México. Visiones de cinco siglos. Tomo II: Antología, cinco siglos de crónicas, crítica y documentos (1521–2002)*. México, DF: Cenidi Danza/INBA/CONACULTA/Escenología, 2002.

Ramos Smith, Maya. *El ballet en México en el siglo XIX: De la independencia al segundo imperio (1825–1867)*. Ciudad de México: Alianza, CONACULTA, 1991.

Ramos Smith, Maya. *La danza en México durante la época colonial*. México: Alianza Editorial Mexicana: CONACULTA, 1990.

Ramos Smith, Maya. *La danza teatral en México durante el Virreinato (1521–1821)*. México, DF: Escenologia Ediciones, 2013.

Ramos Smith, Maya. *María de Jesús Moctezuma*. Cuadernos del CID Danza No. 18. México, DF: CID Danza/INBA, 1987.

Ramos Smith, Maya. *Teatro musical y danza en el México de la Belle Époque: 1867–1910*. México, DF: Universidad Autonoma Metropolitana, Grupo Editorial Gaceta, 1995.

Ramos Villalobos, Roxana Guadalupe. *Una mirada a la formación dancística mexicana (ca. 1919–1945)*. México: INBA/CENIDID-Danza, 2009.

Rastovac-Akbarzadeth, Heather. "Do Iranian Dancers Need Saving?: Savior Spectatorship and the Production of Iranian Dancing Bodies as 'Objects of Rescue.'" In *Futures of Dance Studies*, edited by Susan Manning, Janice Ross, and Rebecca Schneider, 453–70. Madison: University of Wisconsin Press, 2020.

Reiter, Bernd, ed. *Constructing the Pluriverse: The Geopolitics of Knowledge*. Durham, NC: Duke University Press, 2018.

Reynoso, Jose L. "Choreographing Modern Mexico: Anna Pavlova in Mexico City (1919)." *Modernist Cultures* 9, no. 1, edited by Carrie J. Preston (May 2014): 80–98.

Reynoso, Jose L. "Choreographing Politics, Dancing Modernity: Ballet and Modern Dance in the Construction of Modern Mexico (1919–1940)." Doctoral Dissertation, University of California Los Angeles, 2012.

Reynoso, Jose L. "Democracy's Body, Neoliberalism's Body: The Ambivalent Search for Egalitarianism within the Contemporary Post/Modern Dance Tradition." *Dance Research Journal* 51, no. 1 (2019): 47–65.

Reynoso, Jose L. "Racialized Dance Modernisms in Lusophone and Spanish-Speaking Latin America." In *The Modernist World*, edited by Stephen Ross and Allana C. Lindgren, 392–400. London: Routledge, 2015.

Reynoso, Jose L. "Towards a Critical Globalized Humanities: Dance Research in Mexico City at the CENIDID." In *The Futures of Dance Studies*, edited by Susan Manning, Janice Ross, and Rebecca Schneider, 523–40 Madison: University of Wisconsin Press, 2020.

Rivera Cusicanqui, Silvia. *Sociología de la imagen: Miradas Ch'ixi desde la historia andina*. Buenos Aires: Tinta Limon, 2015; repr. 2018.

Rivera-Servera, Ramón H. *Performing Queer Latinidad: Dance, Sexuality, Politics*. Ann Arbor: University of Michigan Press, 2012.

Robinson Wright, Marie. *Mexico: A History of Its Progress and Development in One Hundred Years*. Philadelphia: George Barrie & Sons, 1911.

Rochfort, Desmond. *Mexican Muralists*. San Francisco: Chronicle Books, 1998.

Rodríguez, Moreda Eva. *Music and Exile in Francoist Spain*. Farnham, Surrey: Ashgate, 2016.

Rodríguez-Frazier, Rosa. "Border *Ocurrencias*/'Occurrences' *Fronterizas*." Unpublished MFA thesis, University of California, Riverside, 2015.

Romero, Robert Chao. *The Chinese in Mexico, 1882–1940*. Tucson: University of Arizona Press, 2010.

Rosa, Cristina F. *Brazilian Bodies and their Choreographies of Identification: Swing Nation.* Houndmills: Palgrave Macmillan, 2015.
Saavedra, Leonora. "Carlos Chávez's Polysemic Style: Constructing the National, Seeking the Cosmopolitan." *Journal of the American Musicological Society* 68, no. 1 (2015): 99–149.
Saavedra, Leonora, ed. *Carlos Chávez and His World.* Princeton, NJ: Princeton University Press, 2015.
Said, Edward. *Orientalism.* New York: Pantheon Books, 1978.
Salas, Elizabeth. *Soldaderas in the Mexican Military: Myth and History.* Austin: University of Texas Press, 1990.
Saldívar, Gabriel. *El Jarabe: Baile Popular Mexicano.* México: Talleres Gráficos de la Nación, 1937.
Salinas Álvarez, Manuel. *Los Caminos de México, History of the Roads of México.* México: Banco Nacional de Obras y Servicios Públicos, 1994.
Sánchez, George J. *Becoming Mexican American: Ethnicity, Culture, and Identity in Chicano Los Angeles, 1900–1945.* New York: Oxford University Press, 1993.
Sánchez, George J. *Boyle Heights: How a Los Angeles Neighborhood Became the Future of American Democracy.* Oakland: University of California Press, 2021.
Santos, Boaventura de Sousa. *The End of the Cognitive Empire: The Coming of Age of Epistemologies of the South.* Durham, NC: Duke University Press, 2018.
Sasportes, José. "Grand Opera and the Decline of Ballet in the Latter Nineteenth Century: A Discursive Essay." *Dance Research: The Journal of the Society for Dance Research* 33, no. 2 (Winter 2015): 258–68.
Savigliano, Marta E. *Tango and the Political Economy of Passion.* Boulder, CO: Westview Press, 1995.
Seed, Patricia, ed. *José Limón and La Malinche: The Dancer and the Dance.* Austin: University of Texas Press, 2008.
Seijas, Tatiana. *Asian Slaves in Colonia Mexico: From Chinos to Indians.* New York: Cambridge University Press, 2014.
Serur, Raquel. "La barbarie del Imperio y la 'barbarie' de los bárbaros." In *La americanización de la modernidad,* edited by Bolívar Echeverría, 269–87. México, DF: Universidad Nacional Autónoma de México, 2008.
Schneider, Luis Mario. *El estridentismo: México 1921–1927.* México, DF: Universidad Autónoma de México, 1985.
Schwall, Elizabeth B. *Dancing with the Revolution: Power, Politics, and Privilege in Cuba.* Chapel Hill: University of North Carolina Press, 2021.
Scolieri. Paul A. *Dancing the New World: Aztecs, Spaniards, and the Choreography of Conquest.* Austin: University of Texas Press, 2013.
Shea Murphy, Jacqueline. *The People Have Never Stopped Dancing: Native American Modern Dance Histories.* Minneapolis: University of Minnesota Press, 2007.
Sheridan, Guillermo. *Los contemporáneos ayer.* México, DF: Fondo de Cultura Económica, 2015.
Siu, Lok C. D. *Memories of a Future Home: Diasporic Citizenship of Chinese in Panama.* Stanford, CA: Stanford University Press, 2005.
Snow, K. Mitchell. "Orientalized Aztecs: Observations on the Americanization of Theatrical Dance." *Dance Research Journal* 51, no. 2 (August 2019): 35–50.
Snow, K. Mitchell. *A Revolution in Movement: Dancers, Painters, and the Image of Modern Mexico.* Gainesville: University Press of Florida, 2020.

Spenser, Daniela. *Stumbling Its Way through Mexico: The Early Years of the Communist International*. Translated by Peter Gellert. Tuscaloosa: University of Alabama Press, in Association with Centro de Investigaciones y Estudios Superiores and Anthropología Social, 2011.

Srinivasan, Priya. "The Bodies beneath the Smoke or What's behind the Cigarette Poster: Unearthing Kinesthetic Connections in American Dance History." *Discourses in Dance* 4, no. 1 (Summer 2007): 7–47.

Stein, William W. *Dance in the Cemetery: José Carlos Mariátegui and the Lima Scandal of 1917*. Lanham, MD: University Press of America, 1997.

Tally, Robert T., Jr. *Spatiality*. London: Routledge, 2013.

Tauro, Alberto. "'Colónida' en el modernismo peruano." *Revista iberoamericana* 1, no. 1 (May 1939): 77–82.

Taylor, Diana. *The Archive and the Repertoire: Performing Cultural Memory in the Americas*. Durham, NC: Duke University, 2003.

Tenenbaum, Barbara A. "Streetwise History: The Paseo de la Reforma and the Porfirian State, 1876–1910." In *Rituals of Rule, Rituals of Resistance: Public Celebrations and Popular Culture in Mexico*, edited by William H. Beezley, Cheryl English Martin, and William E. French, 127–50. Wilmington, DE: Scholarly Resources Press, 1994.

Tenorio-Trillo, Mauricio. *Mexico at the World's Fair: Crafting a Modern Nation*. Berkeley: University of California Press, 1996.

Thompson, Alvin O. *Flight to Freedom: African Runaways and Maroons in the Americas*. Jamaica: University of the West Indies Press, 2006.

Torgovnick, Marianna. *Gone Primitive: Savage Intellect, Modern Lives*. Chicago: University of Chicago Press, 1990.

Tortajada Quiroz, Margarita. "La Coronela de Waldeen: Una danza revolucionaria." *Casa del tiempo* 1, no. 8 (June 2008): 54–60.

Tortajada Quiroz, Margarita. *Danza y poder*. México, DF: Instituto Nacional de Bellas Artes; Centro Nacional de Investigación, Documentación e Información de la Danza José Limón, 1995.

Tortajada Quiroz, Margarita. *Frutos de mujer: Las mujeres en la danza escenica*. México, DF: Cenidi Danza/INBA/Conaculta, 2001.

Tortajada Quiroz, Margarita. "José Limón and La Malinche in Mexico: A Chicano Artist Returns Home." In *José Limón and La Malinche: The Dancer and the Dance*, edited by Patricia Seed, 119–53. Austin: University of Texas Press, 2008.

Tortajada Quiroz, Margarita. *Mujeres de danza combativa*. México, DF: Cenidi Danza/INBA/Conaculta, 1998.

Tortajada Quiroz, Margarita. "Transgresoras-constructoras del cuerpo y las imágenes I. Las pioneras de la danza escénica mexicana del siglo XX: Nellie y Gloria Campobello." In *La danza en México. Visiones de cinco siglos*, Vol. I: *Ensayos históricos y analíticos*, edited by Maya Ramos y Patricia Cardona, 685–715. México: CNCA-INBA-CENIDI Danza-Escenologia, 2002.

Tortajada Quiroz, Margarita, and Rosa Reyna. *Entre aplausos y críticas detrás del muro: Alcances y transformaciones de la danza moderna nacionalista mexicana en la gira de 1957*. México, DF: CONACULTA, INBA, Cenidi Danza, 2012.

Twinam, Ann. "Pedro de Ayarza: The Purchase of Whiteness." In *The Human Tradition in Colonial Latin America*, 2nd ed., edited by Kenneth J. Andrien, 221–36. Lanham, MD: Rowman & Littlefield, 2013.

Twinam, Ann. *Purchasing Whiteness: Pardos, Mulattos, and the Quest for Social Mobility in the Spanish Indies*. Stanford, CA: Stanford University Press, 2015.

Twinam, Ann. "Racial Passing: Informal and Official 'Whiteness' in Colonial Spanish America." In *New World Orders: Violence, Sanction, and Authority in the Colonial Americas*, edited by John Smolenski and Thomas J. Humphrey, 249–72. Philadelphia: University of Pennsylvania Press, 2007.

Urías Horcasitas, Beatriz. "Ethnología y filantropía: Las propuestas de 'Regeneración' para los indios de la Sociedad Indianista Mexicana, 1910–1914." Serie de *Historia Moderna y Contemporánea—Instituto de Investigaciones Históricas, UNAM*, no. 37, edited by Claudia Agostoni and Elisa Speckman, 223–39. México, DF: Universidad Autónoma de México, 2001.

Urías Horcasitas, Beatriz. *Historias secretas del racismo en México (1920–1950)*. México, DF: Tusquests Editores, 2007.

Vasconcelos, José. *La raza cosmica: Misión de la raza iberoamericana*. México: Agencia Mundial de Librería, 1925.

Vázquez Mantecón, María del Carmen. "La china mexicana, mejor conocida como china poblana." *Anales del Instituto de Investigaciones Estéticas* 22, no. 77 (2000): 123–50.

Velazquez, Marco, and Mary Kay Vaughan. "Mestizaje and Musical Nationalism in Mexico." In *The Eagle and the Virgin: Nation and Cultural Revolution in Mexico 1920–1940*, edited by Mary Kay Vaughan and Stephen E. Lewis, 95–118. Durham, NC: Duke University Press, 2006.

Villanueva, Carlos. "Jesús Bal y Gay: La biografía (¿definitiva?) de Don Manuel que nunca llegó a publicarse." In *Manuel de Falla en el imaginario de dos músicos exiliados: Adolfo Salazar y Jesús Bal y Gay*, edited by Consuelo Carredano and Carlos Villanueva, 127–205. Ciudad de México: El Colegio de México, 2017.

Vinson, Ben, III. *Bearing Arms for His Majesty: The Free-Colored Militia in Colonial Mexico*. Stanford, CA: Stanford University Press, 2001.

Vinson, Ben, III. *Before Mestizaje: The Frontiers of Race and Caste in Colonial Mexico*. New York: Cambridge University Press, 2018.

Vinson, Ben, III, and Matthew Restall, eds. *Black Mexico: Race and Society from Colonial Modern Times*. Albuquerque: University of New Mexico Press, 2009.

Warden, Claire "Mass Dance." In *Routledge Encyclopedia of Modernism*, 2016, accessed July 7, 2022. https://www.rem.routledge.com/articles/mass-dance#.

Warren, Larry. *Anna Sokolow: The Rebellious Spirit*. Amsterdam: Harwood Academic Publishers, 1998.

Wasserman, Mark. *Pesos and Politics: Business, Elites, Foreigners, and Government in Mexico, 1854–1940*. Stanford, CA: Stanford University Press, 2015.

Wilcox, Emily. *Revolutionary Bodies: Chinese Dance and the Socialist Legacy*. Oakland: University of California Press, 2019.

Williams, Raymond. *Marxism and Literature*. Oxford: Oxford University Press, 1977.

Wright, Amie. "'La bebida nacional': Pulque and mexicanidad, 1920–46," *Canadian Journal of History* 44, no. 1 (2009): 1–24.

Wylie, Lesley. *Colonial Tropes and Postcolonial Tricks: Rewriting the Tropics in the Novela de la Selva*. Liverpool: Liverpool University Press, 2009.

Ybarra-Frausto, Tomás. *Rasquachismo: A Chicano Sensibility*. San Antonio, TX: School by the River Press, 1989.

Zárate Toscano, Verónica. "'Los pobres en el Centenario' in Bi-Centenario: La fiesta interrumpida." *Revista proceso*, no. 6 (September 2009): 4–19.

Zavala, Adriana. *Becoming Modern, Becoming Tradition: Women, Gender, and Representation in Mexican Art*. University Park: Pennsylvania State University Press, 2010.

Index

For the benefit of digital users, indexed terms that span two pages (e.g., 52–53) may, on occasion, appear on only one of those pages.
Figures are indicated by *f* following the page number

Academia de Danza Mexicana (ADM), 234
Acuña, Rodolfo F., 237n.24
agency, 16, 26, 27, 30, 228, 246–47
Agostoni, Claudia, 45n.30
El águila y el olivo (The eagle and the olive tree), 97–104, 98*f*
Alamillo, José M., 238n.29
Alcalde, Carlos, 93–94
Alcaraz y Chopitea, Luis and Pedro, 68
Alegoría de "La Paz" (Allegory of Peace), 93–94, 94*f*, 105–6
Alejandre Ramírez, Gloria Luz, 226n.207
Alemán Valdéz, Miguel, 234
Alfaro, José, 246n.64
allegorical floats, 104–6, 105*f*
allegorical posters (*caratualas alegóricas*), 93
Allegory of Peace (*Alegoría de "La Paz"*), 93–94, 94*f*, 105–6
Allusion to the Cry of Dolores ballet, 38–41
Alonso de Ortigosa, José Gregorio, 69–70, 70n.132
Altamirano, Ignacio Manuel, 47–50, 49n.50
ambivalent spatial *mestizaje*, 34–79
  dancing race and social class, 50–54
  debating aesthetics of social and racial formations, 72–74
  marked and unmarked bodies choreographing, 64–72
  Mexico City kinesthetics, 35–36
  Pautret and Moctezuma choreographies, 38–43
  performing desire to be white, 74–79
  Plateros Boulevard and Altamirano choreographies, 43–50
  post/colonial, 36–37
  from post/colonial wars to dictatorship, 43–45
  un/lawful bodies performing choreographies of gender and sexuality, 54–64
ambivalence toward mestizaje and indigeneity, 30–31, 36–37, 38–43, 48, 74–79, 80, 82, 232

América Septentrional, 39n.14
"America Tropical" (Siqueiros), 241–42
"Anahuac" (Enciso), 102–4
Andalusian idealism, 201n.112
Anderson, Benedict, 3n.7
Angel of Independence monument, 84
anti-Semitism, 192n.70
Anzaldúa, Gloria, 4n.8
Aparicio, Frances R., 246n.63
Apolodoro, 154n.128
Arce, Christine B., 226–27n.208
Army of the Three Guarantees, 113n.113
Aroche, Eduardo, 127
Arrieta, Emilio, 58n.81
Arrizón, Alicia, 4n.8, 226–27n.208
arts, democratizing access to, 137–42
Ateneo of Madrid, 156–57
Aulestia, Patricia, 171–72n.5, 178n.28
auto/exoticism, 32, 227n.211, 228
Ávila Camacho, Manuel, 200n.105, 233–34
Aztec Palace, 103n.79
Aztec race, 130–31, 142–53
  Greco-Roman-Aztecized modernity, 147–52
  Rouskaya as mestizo body, 145–47
  transnational life of, 152–53
Azuela, Mariano, 5n.11

Bada, Xóchitl, 238n.30
Badel, Amelia Marguerite (Rigolboche), 49
Balanchine, George, 20n.60
Balderrama, Francisco E., 241n.49
ballet, 41n.20, 50–54
  Moctezuma, María de Jesús, 41–43
  modernized *Jarabe Mexicano*, 70–72
  Pautret's *Allusion to the Cry of Dolores*, 38–41
Ballet de Bellas Artes, 198–99
Ballet Nacional de México (National Ballet of Mexico), 234–35
Ballet Simbólico 30-30, 181–86, 187–89
Ballets Russes, 125
Bal y Gay, Jesús, 201, 202–3, 219–25

Banerji, Anurima, 29n.84
Bargalió Sánchez, Isabel, 158n.146, 158n.147, 162n.165, 162n.167
Bargalió Sánchez, Monserrat, 158n.146, 158n.147, 162n.165, 162n.167
Barraclough, Laura R., 238–39n.34
Barricada, 188–89
Battle of Puebla, 44–45
Bauman, Mordecai, 194n.81
belle époque, 51n.53
beneficence, Centenario, 89–92
Benessaieh, Afef, 90n.39
Berenguer de Marquina, Felix, 70n.134
Bernardelli, Oscar, 41–42
Bernis, Alberto, 51
Bernis-Burón company, 51
Best Maugard, Adolfo, 132–34
Bidault de la Calle, Sophie, 99n.62, 182n.37
blackface, 52–53
Blanco Borelli, Melissa, 53n.62
Bloch, Gabrielle (Gab Sorère), 66n.118
blood cleansing (*limpieza de sangre*) system, 12–17
The Blue Bird (*El pájaro azul*), 89
Boas, Franz, 90, 90n.39, 132–33
bodies and space, 35–36, 46–47, 54–64, 74, 104–13, 135, 140–42, 155–56, 185–86, 239, 242–43
bodies-for-hire, 72
Bohm, Jerome, 209
Bosco, 71
el boulevard (Plateros Boulevard), 46–47
Bourne, Matthew, 66n.116
bracero program, 239, 248
Brahman, 51–52
Briggs, Laura, 10n.24
Bristol, Joan, 16n.45, 131n.41
Buchenau, Jürgen, 45n.30
Buffalmacco, 130–31, 131n.46, 137n.72, 139n.78
Bunker, Steven B., 45
Burón, Leopoldo, 51

cakewalk dances, 51–54
Calderón, Felipe, 107n.89
calendar-colonel, 221
Campobello, Gloria, 175–89, 181n.35
 Ballet Simbólico 30-30, 181–86
 debating aesthetic merits of mass dances, 187–89
Campobello, Nellie, 5n.11, 175–89, 181n.35
 Ballet Simbólico 30-30, 181–86
 debating aesthetic merits of mass dances, 187–89

cancan
 Altamirano's civilizing view of, 47–50
 choreographies of gender and sexuality, 54–55
Cano, Gabriela, 226n.207
Cantú, Norma E., 239n.35
caratualas alegóricas (allegorical posters, Porfiriato drawing contest), 93
Cardona, Patricia, 18n.49, 42n.22, 49n.50, 65n.111, 65n.114, 67n.121, 69n.130
Cardoso, Lawrence A., 237n.24, 239n.39
Carnegie, Andrew, 82–83
Carreño King, Tania, 1n.1
Carrera, Magali M., 13n.32
Carrillo, Julián, 4–5
Carrillo, Rubén, 20n.62
Carroll, Letti, 178, 178n.28
Carroll, Patrick J., 16n.45
caste system, New Spain (Colonial Mexico), 12–17
Castillo Villasana, Heriberto, 127
Castrejón, Eduardo, 63n.108
Castro-Gómez, Santiago, 26n.78
Cecchetti Method, 51
Cefkin, Aza, 194n.81
Centenario, 80–117, 124
 beneficence and scientific discourse, 89–92
 Cry of Dolores ceremony, 114–17
 dance and theater during month of, 87–89
 Díaz, Porfirio, 82–87
 drawing and painting indigenous modern into national imaginaries, 93–104
 parades of indigeneity in national public sphere, 104–13
Centro Mercantil (Mercantile Center), 104–5
charro, 1n.1, 4. See also *Jarabe Mexicano* and *Jarabe Tapatío*
Chávarri Juvenal, Enrique, 56, 69
Chávez, Carlos, 4–5, 234
Chávez, Xóchitl C., 238n.31
Chávez-Hita, Adriana Naveda, 16n.45
Cherniavsky, Eva, 23n.69
china poblana, 4, 17–20, 71, 73. See also *Jarabe Mexicano* and *Jarabe Tapatío*
choreographic analysis, 29, 32, 82, 84, 109
choreographies, 38–43
 dancing Spanish and Mexican mestizo modernities, 68–69
 of gender and sexuality, 54–64
 Moctezuma's integrative *mestizaje*, 41–43
 Pautret's *Allusion to the Cry of Dolores*, 38–41
 Pavlova's *Fantasía Mexicana*, 125–42

INDEX 267

from post/colonial wars to
    dictatorship, 43–45
Public Procession, 104–13
Serpentine Dance, 64–67
taming *Jarabe Mexicano*, 69–72
Ciccariello-Maher, George, 26n.78
Cinco Basurto, Monica Georgina, 20n.62
Civic Parade (Desfile Cívico), 106–7
civil war, 43–44
Clayton, Michelle, 121n.5, 154n.130, 156n.135, 156n.137, 157–58n.144, 159nn.150–51, 160n.153, 161n.161, 163n.169
Clitandro, 125n.15, 146n.100, 146n.103, 146n.105, 158n.145
Coffey, Mary K., 4n.9, 96n.57, 102n.77, 170n.4
Cohen, Jonathan, 209n.142
Cohen, Theodore W., 20n.62
Cold War, 234–35
colonial affectivity, 154–64
colonial matrix of power, 26, 27, 228
colonial racial unconscious, 23, 31–32, 122–23, 231
Colónida, 143–44
contemporary dance, 243n.53
contemporary mestizo modernisms, 230–49
    construction of US mestizo modernities, 237–43
    Desmadre of Rascuache Mestizaje (Primera Generación Dance Collective), 243–49
    emergence of Mexican nationalist dance, 233–37
Conway, Christopher, 48n.40, 48n.43
Coons, Lorraine, 56n.67
Cope, R. Douglas, 16n.45
La Coronela, 168–70, 206–29
corporeality of multiplicity, 6–7n.15, 8–9, 35, 78
    embodied *mestizaje*, 122–23
    marginalizing and invisibilizing indigenous, 21
    Pavlova, Anna, 17–18, 131–32
    Valencia, Carmen Tórtola, 161–62
Corro Ramos, Octaviano, 16n.45
Cortés, Hernán, 108–13, 109n.96
Covarrubias, Miguel, 235–36
Craven, David, 133n.57
Creelman, James, 79n.160, 82–83, 85n.13, 86nn.18–20
critics, dance, 219–25
Croft, Clare, 67n.122, 238n.27
cross viewing, 56n.69
Cry of Dolores, 38–41, 106–7, 114–17
"Cuadro de Castas," 14*f*

Cuellar, Manuel R., 6n.14, 89n.36, 103n.79, 152n.121, 178n.30, 239n.35
"La Cuenca" (Trinidad Huertas), 68
cuerpos coreográficos, 87
cultural architects, 128–30
cultural extractivism, 158–59
cultural globalization, 90
cultural missions, 128, 179–81
Cunningham, Merce, 66n.116
Cypress, Sandra Messinger, 109n.96

Dallal, Alberto, 68n.124
Dalton, David S., 8n.18
Daly, Ann, 157n.141
Damitas de Aquellos Tiempos (Ladies of Those Past Times in *La Coronela*), 214
Dance of the Disinherited (Danza de los Desheredados en *La Coronela*), 214, 218
Dance of the new forces (*Danza de las Fuerzas Nuevas, en La Coronela*), 213
dance schools, 171–76, 189–91
dancing
    embodied legacies of colonial racial and social formations, 11–26
    Jarabe Tapatío, 1–4
    key concepts of, 6–11
    race and social class, 50–54
Danza de las Fuerzas Nuevas (Dance of the new forces in *La Coronela*), 213
Danza de los Desheredados (Dance of the Disinherited in *La Coronela*), 214, 218
La Danza Incaica Guerrera (Inca War Dance), 160–64
Darwinian evolutionary principles, 89n.37
dead Indians, 27–28, 92, 104, 122, 142–53
decolonial, 23–24, 24n.71, 26–28, 26n.78, 228–29, 228n.215
de-essentialized mestizaje, 9, 9n.22, 24–25, 43, 120n.2
DeFrantz, Thomas F., 22n.68
Delgado Martínez, César, 173n.8, 175n.15, 175n.18, 187n.50
Delia Franciscus (Rouskaya, Norka), 121–22, 142–53, 142n.82
Delpar, Helen, 152n.122, 153n.125, 191n.68
democratizing access to arts, 137–42
Dennis, Nigel, 201n.107
D'Erzell, Catalina, 202n.117
Desfile Cívico (Civic Parade), 106–7
Desfile Histórico (History Parade), 106–7, 110*f*, 114*f*, 146–47
Desmadre of Rascuache Mestizaje (Primera Generación Dance Collective), 243–49

Desmond, Jane, 157n.141, 208n.141
Desmond, Jane C., 25n.72
Diario del Hogar, 34
Díaz, Porfirio, 10n.26, *See also* Porfiriato
　ancestry of, 79, 83n.2
　creator and hero of modern Mexico, 82–87
　government periods of, 44n.29
　overthrowing Lerdo de Tejada, 44–45
　Wright's dedication to, 116n.125
Díaz Master of Mexico (Creelman), 86
dictatorship
　from independence to, 34–79
　to revolution from, 80–117
Ducazcal, José María, 202n.122
Duncan, Isadora, 65–66, 143n.88, 145n.94, 157n.141, 208n.141

The eagle and the olive tree (El águila y el olivo), 97–104, 98f
Echeverría, Bolívar, 22n.66, 26n.78
embodied mestizo modernisms, 1–33, 118–67
　coloniality of modernist mestizo artistic practices, 122–23
　embodied legacies of colonial racial and social formations, 11–26
　establishing national dance repertoire, 164–67
　forging new nations, 121–22
　Jarabe Tapatío, 1–4
　key concepts of, 6–11
　mestizaje contradicting multiplicity and decolonial potential, 6–11
　Pavlova's *Fantasía Mexicana*, 125–42
　revalorizing indigenous, 123–25
　Rouskaya resurrecting Aztec race, 142–53
　Valencia's Inca-inspired Latin American pan-indigeneity, 154–64
　value of racial and cultural markings, 24–26
"Encarnación de Francia en México," 34
Enciso, Jorge, 97–104
En el Japón, 51–52
Escamon, 58–59
Escobar, Arturo, 25n.74
Escuela de Danza (School of Dance), 175–76
Escuela de Plástica Dinámica (School of Dynamic Plastic Art), 172–76
Europeans, 4n.8
exoticism, 32, 52n.56, 130–31, 146, 153, 155, 155n.132, 225–29
Experimental Group (Grupo Experimental), 234–35
Exposición de Artistas Mexicanos, 102–4
Ezrahi, Christina, 226n.206

Fantasía Mexicana, 125–42
　crossing social and ideological boundaries, 130–36
　cultural architects and social engineers, 128–30
　democratizing access to arts, 137–42
　heterosexual and queer Pavlovians, 126–28
Fantasía Yucateca, 178, 180f
fascism, 192–206
Féeries, 51–54
Félix, Adrián, 126n.20, 238n.32
Fernández Ledesma, Gabriel, 2n.4
The Final Judgment (*El Juicio Final*), 218–19
Firmino-Castillo, María Regina, 25n.74
First Mexican Empire, 38
Fischer-Lichte, Erika, 176–77, 176n.20
Flachebba, Alberto, 147
Flores Magón brothers, 117n.127, 124n.11
fluid gender expressions
　forty-one *maricones*, 60–64
　Fregoli and *Potosí submarino*, 58–59
Fojas, Camilla, 27n.80
Follet, Stella, 65
Formoso, Adela, 202
Fortuna, Victoria, 8n.20
Foster, Susan L., 2n.6, 6–7n.15, 8–9n.21, 29n.85, 35n.5, 52n.57, 65–66, 66n.116, 67n.123, 72n.142, 147n.106, 157n.141, 208n.141, 216n.170
Foucault, Michel, 35n.4
Franko, Mark, 193n.71, 193n.74
free elections (Mexican Revolution), 123–24
Freeman, Ruth, 194n.81
Fregoli, Leopoldo, 58–59, 65
French culture, 34, 38–41, 44–45
　Altamirano, Ignacio Manuel, 47–50
　Plateros Boulevard, 46–47
From the Dictatorship of Porfirio Díaz to Revolution (Siqueiros), 81f
Fuentes, Manlio S., 236
Fuller, Loïe, 65n.110, 66n.118
　performance reports, 68
　Serpentine Dance, 64–67

Gab Sorère (Bloch, Gabrielle), 66n.118
Gallo, Rubén, 170n.4
Gamboa, Erasmo, 239n.37
Gamio, Manuel, 90n.39, 92n.52, 147–52, 148n.111, 151n.118
Garafola, Lynn, 125n.14, 193n.71
García, Cindy, 246n.63
García Canclini, Néstor, 26n.76, 26n.78

García Sáiz, María Concepción, 13n.32, 19n.59
García y Santisteban, Rafael, 58n.81
Garland, Iris, 154n.128, 154–55n.131, 156n.134, 156n.136, 157n.139, 157n.142, 160n.154, 161n.162
gender
  fluid gender expressions, 58–64
  La Coronela, 225–29
Genealogies (racial and social), 17–21
Giersdorf, Jens Richard, 226n.206
Gleizer Salzman, Daniela, 192n.70
Gloria (Glory), 95–97, 95*f*
Gold, Russell, 193n.71
González, Anita, 7n.17, 20n.61
González, Carlos E., 146–47, 146n.103, 158n.145
González, Macías, 76–78
González de Mendoza, José María, 99n.62
González Navarro, Moisés, 89n.37
González Peña, Carlos, 126n.18, 130–31, 130n.39, 131n.47, 132, 134, 134n.65, 138, 138n.74, 165n.171, 210
Gottschild, Brenda Dixon, 20n.60
Graff, Ellen, 193n.71
Greco-Roman arts, 40–41
  Rouskaya as mestizo body, 145–47
  Rouskaya's Greco-Roman-Aztecized modernity, 147–52
Greenwood, Grace, 4n.9
Greenwood, Marion, 4n.9
Grewal, Inderpal, 89–90n.38
Grosfoguel, Ramón, 26n.78
Grupo Experimental (Experimental Group), 234–35
Guelaguetza Festival, 238
Guerrero, Ellie, 6n.12, 8n.19
Guerrero, Vicente, 38
Guerrero Saldaña, Vicente Ramón, 16–17
Guevara Meza, Carlos, 22n.66, 26–27, 26n.78, 26n.79, 89n.37, 90n.39
Gutiérrez Nájera, Manuel, 48–49, 73, 73n.144
Guzmán, Martín Luis, 5n.11

Hamera, Judith, 242n.52
Hassig, Ross, 100n.66
Hawke, Rob, 209n.147
Hedrick, Tace, 8n.18, 128n.30, 129n.32
Heinly Page, Marian, 138–39
Hellerman, M. Kasey, 109n.96
Hellier-Tinoco, Ruth, 7n.17
Hellman, Frances, 194n.81
Hernández Araico, Susana, 12n.27
heterosexual dancers and audiences

Fantasía Mexicana, 126–28
  scandalizing Mexico City, 55–57
heterotopia, 35–36
Hidalgo y Costilla, Miguel, 39, 39n.13, 81, 114–16
History Parade (Desfile Histórico), 106–7, 110*f*, 114*f*, 146–47
Höfling, Ana Paula, 8n.20
Hooker, Juliet, 27n.82
Horacio, Germán, 168–69
Hoyos y Vinent, Antonio de, 162n.167
Huerta, Victoriano, 124n.11, 124n.12
Hurlburt, Laurence P., 191n.68
Hutchinson, Sydney, 36n.7, 239n.35, 245n.60

Idilios en la sombra (Idylls in the shadow), 88
Imoto, Katsumi "Katz," 240n.43
Imperial Russian Ballet, 125
INBA (Instituto Nacional de Bellas Artes), 214n.166, 234
Inca-inspired dance, 154–64
  artistic and ideological aspects in construction of modernist artist, 156–57
  colonial logic of cultural and material extractivism, 158–59
  performing "soul of indigenous America," 162–64
  reconstructing Inca indigenous soul, 159–62
Incas, 130–31
Inca War Dance (*La Danza Incaica Guerrera*), 160–64
Independence Centennial. *See* Centenario
Indianist Society (Sociedad Iñdianista), 91–92, 101–2
indiano, 147n.108
indigenous Mesoamerican, 4n.8, 18, 29–30, 31, 124
  beneficence and scientific discourse, 89–92
  castes system, 12–13, 15–16, 19, 21–22
  defined, 12n.29
  drawing and painting into national imaginaries, 93–104
  parades of indigeneity in national public sphere, 104–13
  point of view of Díaz, 86–87
  revalorizing, 123–25
Instituto Nacional de Bellas Artes (INBA), 214n.166, 234
International Americanist Congress, 90
Iron Palace (Palacio de Hierro), 45, 106
Irwin, Robert McKee, 60n.91, 60–61nn.96–98, 61nn.100–3, 62n.105, 63n.109
Izquierdo, María, 4n.9

270 INDEX

jacalones, 52–53, 56–57
Jarabe Gatuno, 17–18, 69–70
Jarabe Mexicano
   Moctezuma, María de Jesús, 41–42, 43
   taming, 69–72
Jarabe Tapatío, 1–4, 139–42
   Campobello Sisters, 178, 179*f*
   Fantasía Mexicana featuring, 131–32
   half-finished drawing of, 118–19,
      119*f*, 165–67
Jato, Mónica, 201n.106
Johns, Michael, 46
José Limón (choreographer), 235–37, 236n.15,
   236n.16, 238
José E. Limón (anthropologist), 241, 241n.45
Joseph, Gilbert M., 45n.30
jota, 62–63, 73
Juárez, Benito, 43–44
Judson Dance Theater, 243n.53
El Juicio Final (The Final Judgment in *La
   Coronela*), 218–19
"Jura del Pendón" (Oath of
   Allegiance), 109–11

Kahlo, Frida, 4n.9
Kendi, Ibram X., 16n.44
kinesthetic empathy, 216n.170
Klein, Gabriele, 10n.24
Konetzke, 15n.42
Kosstrin, Hanna, 7n.17, 8n.19, 10n.24, 192n.69,
   192n.70, 193n.73, 198n.92, 227n.213,
   235n.10
Kostakowsky, 197n.87
Krause, Korinne A., 192n.70
Kraut, Anthea, 21n.63, 23n.69, 29n.85, 65–66,
   65n.110
Kwan, SanSan, 36n.6

La Bella, Augusta, 70–71
Ladies of Those Past Times (Damitas de
   Aquellos Tiempos en *La Coronela*), 214
Land (*Tierra*), 188n.53
Landau, Ellen G., 191n.68
Larroder, Luis de, 162n.165
La Scala of Milan, 51–52
Latinidad, 245–46
LatinMex, 248–49
Latinidad, 245–46, 246n.63, 246n.64
Latina/o/x/e, 233, 240n.41, 244, 247, 248–49
Latinos/as/xs, 248
Latinx, 245–46
Lavalle, Josefina, 17n.48, 131n.47, 165n.172,
   166n.176, 174n.12

LEAR (Liga de Escritores y Artistas
   Revolucionarios), 189–90
Lee, Hae Kyung, 242
Leff, Enrique, 25n.73
Lepecki, André, 155n.133
Lepri, Amalia, 71
Lepri, Giovanni, 51
Lerdo de Tejada, Sebastián, 44–45
Leredo, Pablo, 172n.7
Levy, Rose, 194n.81
Lewis, Stephen E., 4n.9
Lida, Clara Eugenia, 224n.201
Liga de Escritores y Artistas Revolucionarios
   (LEAR), 189–90
Lilly Clay's Colossal Gaiety Company, 56
Lima, Peru, 121, 142–43, 159–60
Limón, José, 235–38
Limón, José E., 241
limpieza de sangre (blood cleansing)
   system, 12–17
Lindsay, Jossie, 65
Lisbona Guillén, Miguel, 20n.61
List Arzubide, Germán, 5n.11
live Indians, 27–28, 92, 104, 111–12,
   122, 142–53
Lomnitz, Claudio, 192n.70
López, Felipa, 71, 71n.139
López, Rick A., 130n.34, 132n.56
López, Ursula and Laura, 68
López Chávez, América Nicte-Ha, 20n.62
López Obrador, Andrés Manuel, 20n.62
Lott, Eric, 23n.70, 53n.62
Lowe, Sarah M., 4n.9
Loza, Mireya, 239n.37
Lytle Hernández, Kelly, 117n.127, 237n.24,
   248n.70

Macías González, Víctor, 59n.89, 76n.151,
   78n.158, 85n.12
Madero, Francisco I., 124n.12
Madero González, Francisco Ignacio, 123–24
Madrid, Alejandro L., 5n.10
magical tricks (*Féerie*), 52
Magón, Enrique, 124n.11
Magón, Jesús Flores, 124n.11
Magón, Ricardo, 124n.11
La Malinche, 108–9, 109n.96, 236–37
malinchista, 109n.96
Mallon, Florencia R., 121n.7
Mangrove, 66n.116
Manning, Susan, 2n.6, 23n.69, 30n.86, 53n.61,
   56n.69, 60n.90
Marcos, subcomandante, 25n.73

Margheritis, Ana, 126n.18
Mariátegui, José-Carlos (father), 142–43n.83, 143n.85
Mariátegui, José-Carlos (son), 142–43n.83, 144n.89, 144n.92, 159n.152
Maricones (the dance of the 41), 58–59, 60–64
Marino, Angela, 226n.206
Mark, Grusha, 194n.81
Marroquín, Jaime, 237n.24
Martin, John, 208–9
Martin, Randy, 8–9n.21, 36n.8
Martínez, Ambrosio, 73–74
Martínez, Ana, 108n.92
Martínez, Conchita, 68
Martínez, Delgado, 218n.174, 220
Martínez, Francisca (Paca), 68, 70–71, 73
Martínez, María Elena, 12n.30, 13n.33, 13n.35
mass dances, 187–89
La matanza de los inocentes (Slaughter of the innocents), 196–98, 220
Mateos, Abdón, 201n.106
material extractivism, 158–59
Matesanz, José Antonio, 224n.201
Matthews, Michael, 45n.31
Maximilian of Habsburg, 43–44
McCaughan, Edward J., 63n.109
McCormick, Gladys, 10n.24
McEvoy, Carmen, 143–44, 143n.84, 143n.87
Melosh, Barbara, 193n.71
Mendoza, Cristina, 188n.56, 189n.60, 190n.62, 193n.75
Mercantile Center (Centro Mercantil), 104–5
Mérida, Carlos, 188–92, 188n.56, 189n.60, 190n.63, 193n.75
mestiza docile femininity, 1n.1
mestizaje, 4
  ambivalent spatial *mestizaje*, 34–79
  contradicting multiplicity and decolonial potential, 26–28
  defined, 4n.8
  establishing national dance repertoire, 164–67
mestizo modernist dances, 68–69
mestizo modernity, 118–67
  coloniality of modernist mestizo artistic practices, 122–23
  establishing national dance repertoire, 164–67
  forging new nations, 121–22
  Mexican immigrant and Mexican American laboring bodies, 237–43
  Pavlova's *Fantasía Mexicana*, 125–42
  revalorizing indigenous, 123–25

Rouskaya resurrecting Aztec race, 142–53
Valencia's Inca-inspired Latin American pan-indigeneity, 154–64
metaphorical minstrelsy, 52–53
methodologies, 28–30
Mexican Hat Dance, 1n.1
Mexican immigrants, 237–43, 245–46, 247, 248–49
  anti-immigrant (xenophobia), 240, 240n.42, 241–42, 241n.49, 245–46, 247, 248–49
  neutrality (racial/ cultural), 64–65, 78, 79, 175, 227–29, 232, 235, 242–43, 247, 248–49
  politically, 224
Mexican modernity, 6
Mexican Revolution, 3–4, 120–21, 248
Mexican universalism, 212–19
Mexico City, 34–79
  dancing race and social class, 50–54
  debating aesthetics of social and racial formations, 72–74
  kinesthetics and spatial *mestizaje*, 35–36
  marked and unmarked bodies choreographing, 64–72
  Pautret and Moctezuma choreographies, 38–43
  performing desire to be white, 74–79
  Plateros Boulevard and Altamirano choreographies, 43–50
  post/colonial ambivalence toward mestizaje and indigeneity, 36–37
  from post/colonial wars to dictatorship, 43–45
  un/lawful bodies performing choreographies of gender and sexuality, 54–64
Meyer, Michael C., 45n.30
Mieri, Magdalena, 237n.24
Mignolo, Walter, 23–24, 24n.71, 25n.73, 25n.74, 26n.75, 26nn.77–78, 52n.56, 76n.157, 116n.126, 122n.8, 228n.215
Miramontes, Arnulfo, 147
Miranda, Gloria E., 13n.36
misfit moderns, 209n.147
Miskowiec, Jay, 35n.4
Mize, Roland L., 239n.38
Moctezuma, María de Jesús, 41–43, 71, 73–74
Moguel, Sánchez, 91
Money, Keith, 2n.3, 125n.17, 140n.80
Monplaisir, Adèle, 41–42
Monplaisir, Hippolyte, 41–42
Monsiváis, Carlos, 60, 60n.91, 60n.94, 60n.95, 61n.104, 63n.106, 200n.100
Montag, Warren, 22n.67
morality, 55–57, 66–67

Moreda Rodríguez, Eva, 224n.202
Mr. Ferruco's Nightmare (La Pesadilla de Don Ferruco), 218
Muñoz, Mauricio, 220–21

Nacho de la Torre, 76
NAFTA (North American Free Trade Agreement), 239
Nájera-Ramírez, Olga, 239n.35, 239n.36
Napoleon III, Emperor, 43–44
Narvaez, Conchita, 68
Nasser, Michelle Rocío, 63n.109
National Autonomous University of Mexico (UNAM), 230
National Ballet of Mexico (Ballet Nacional de México), 234–35
national imaginaries, 93–104
  assimilating indigenous into national organism, 95–97
  centering indigenous body as figure of national representation, 102–4
  ornamental indigeneity, 93–94
  reimagining indigenous barbarian, 97–102
Navarro, Héctor, 60n.93
neo/colonialism, 51–54
A new life (La nueva vida), 88
Ngai, Mae M., 239n.39
"Ni Fú Ni Fá" dance (Primera Generación Dance Collective), 243–44
Nijinsky, Vaslav, 121n.5
North, Alex, 194n.81
North American Free Trade Agreement (NAFTA), 239
La nueva vida (A new life), 88

Oath of Allegiance ("Jura del Pendón"), 109–11
object of rescue (indigenous), 89–90
Ocampo, Javier, 40n.19
Offenbach, Jacques, 49
Okamoto, Harry, 240n.43
Olavarría y Ferrari, Enrique de, 57n.77, 71n.138
Olcott, Jocelyn H., 226n.207
Oles, James, 4n.9
opera performances, 87–88
Orion, 146n.102, 146n.104, 147n.107, 150n.115
ornamental indigeneity, 93–94
Orozco, José Clemente, 4–5, 181n.35
Ortiz Rubio, Pascual, 177–78

Paca (Martínez, Francisca), 68, 70–71, 73
El pájaro azul (The Blue Bird), 89
Palacio de Hierro (Iron Palace), 45, 106
Palmer, Colin A., 16n.45

La Paloma Azul, 199–201
pan-indigeneity, 154–64
Paredes, Américo, 239n.36
Paul III, Pope, 13
Pautret, Andrés, 38–41, 39n.14
Pavlova, Anna, 2n.6, 121–22, 130n.40
  Fantasía Mexicana, 125–42
  Jarabe Tapatío, 1–5
  popularization of shows, 137n.70
  seasons in Mexico City, 121n.6
  on wearing shawls, 221n.183
Paz, Octavio, 109n.96, 120–21, 120n.3
Peña Nieto, Enrique, 107n.89
Peninsulares, 38
Pereira, Anthony W., 126n.20
Pérez Claro, Eva, 135
Peruvian avant-garde, 159–62
La Pesadilla de Don Ferruco (Mr. Ferruco's Nightmare), 218
Pianowsky, Mieczyslaw, 3f
Piccato, Pablo, 57n.76
Pineda, Adela, 237n.24
Pla Brugat, Dolores, 200n.102
Plan de Tuxtepec, 44–45
Plateros Boulevard (el boulevard), 46–47
Plaza el Toreo, 1, 137–39, 139f
pluriversal, 25–26, 25n.73, 25n.74, 28, 171, 225–29
pluriversalism, 25–26, 225–29
Poema Guerrero (War Poem), 194–96
Politics of dance, 6
Ponce, Manuel M., 4–5
Poniatowska, Elena, 226–27n.208
Porfiriato. See also Centenario; Díaz, Porfirio
  defined, 10n.26
  homophobia, 60–64
  to revolution from, 123–25
  systematic criminalization, 57n.76
Posada, José Guadalupe, 60–61, 62f
positivist Darwinian scientism, 89–90, 116–17
post/colonial nation
  ambivalence toward mestizaje and indigeneity, 36–37
  ornamental indigeneity in construction of, 93–94
  from wars to dictatorship, 43–45
post/colonial Mexico, 5, 11–26, 35–37, 38–43, 44–45, 69–72, 91n.46, 108, 114–15, 121n.7, 122, 232
postrevolutionary modern dance form, 168–229
  Campobello sisters, 176–89
  contradictions and pluriversalism of La Coronela, 225–29

looking at United States for, 189–92
Sokolow, Anna, 192–206
Waldeen, 206–25
Zybin and dance schools, 171–76
Potosí submarino, 58–59
Primera Generación Dance
  Collective, 243–47
primitivism, 52–53
Procesional (Processional in Waldeen), 213
Proctor, Frank, III, 16n.45
Proposition 187, 240
Public Procession (Porfiriato), 104–13
Puig, Magdalena, 70–71
pulque, 130–31

Quecha Reyna, Citlali, 20n.62
queer Pavlovians, 126–28
Quijano, Aníbal, 13n.34, 22n.66
Quiñones, Horacio, 168n.2, 219–25
Quiroz, Tortajada, 214n.166, 218n.171,
  227n.212, 237n.26

Rabinoff, Marie La Salle, 87
Rabinoff company, 87
racialization, 11–26
  ballet and emergence of new artists, theater,
    and dance genres, 50–54
  debating aesthetics of formations for, 72–74
  excavating racial and social
    genealogies, 17–21
  mechanisms of racial and social distinction
    in new Spain caste system, 12–17
  racial ideologies in production of marked
    and unmarked bodies, 21–24
  value of embodied mestizo modernisms'
    racial and cultural markings, 24–26
  visibilizing and racializing whiteness, 21
racialized interclass colonization, 122, 125–42
  crossing social and ideological
    boundaries, 130–36
  cultural architects and social
    engineers, 128–30
  democratizing access to arts, 137–42
  heterosexual and queer Pavlovians, 126–28
railroad system, 45
Ramírez Domínguez, Silvia, 39n.9, 39n.14, 40
Ramos Smith, Maya, 12n.27, 18n.49, 41n.20,
  41–42nn.21–22, 42n.23, 44n.26, 49n.50,
  52n.54, 53n.58, 54n.64, 55n.65, 55n.66,
  56n.68, 56n.70, 57n.75, 57n.77, 58n.80,
  65nn.111–12, 65nn.113–14, 66n.119,
  67nn.120–21, 68n.127, 69n.130, 70n.135,
  73n.143, 73n.146, 75n.149

belle époque of Mexico, 51n.53
  dances of Felipa López, 71n.139
  on *tiples*, 54
Ramos Villalobos, Roxana Guadalupe, 174n.12,
  175n.16
rascuache mestizaje, 245n.60
Rastovac-Akbarzadeth, Heather, 89–90n.38
Restall, Matthew, 20n.62
revolution
  from dictatorship to, 80–117
  from Porfiriato to, 123–25
revolutionary nationalism, 176–89
Revueltas, Silvestre, 4–5
Reyna, Rosa, 234–35n.6
Reynoso, Jose Luis, 2n.6, 10n.24, 121nn.5–6,
  126n.21, 135n.67, 178n.28, 188n.51,
  198n.91, 237n.25, 243n.53, 247n.67
Rigolboche (Badel, Amelia Marguerite), 49
Rivera, Diego, 4–5
Rivera Cusicanqui, Silvia, 26n.78
Rivera-Servera, Ramón H., 246n.63
Robinson Wright, Marie, 111n.103, 111n.106,
  113, 113n.112, 115n.121, 116, 116n.124,
  116n.125, 123n.10
Rochfort, Desmond, 4n.9
Rodríguez, Luis A., 9n.23, 132n.48
Romero, Brenda M., 239n.35, 239n.36
Romero, Robert Chao, 20n.62
Romero Rubio de Díaz, Carmen, 111–12
Romo, David Dorado, 226–27n.208
Root, Elihu, 82–83
Rosa, Cristina F., 8n.20
Rouskaya, Norka (Delia Franciscus), 121–22,
  142–53, 142n.82
Rowen, Rebecca, 194n.81
Rubio, Ortiz, 179n.31
Ruiz, Luis Bruno, 140n.81
Ruiz de Molina, Bernardo, 69n.130, 70n.133
Russell, Katherine, 194n.81

Saavedra, Leonora, 5n.10, 170n.4
Said, Edward, 52n.56
St. Denis, Ruth, 66n.116, 157n.141
Salas, Elizabeth, 226–27n.208
Saldívar, Gabriel, 2n.5
Salinas Álvarez, Manuel, 106n.82
Sánchez, George J., 238n.33, 240n.41
Sánchez Azcona, Juan, 172n.6, 178n.26,
  179n.31, 187n.48
Sano, Seki, 206n.136
Santa María, Javier, 56, 57n.75
Santos, Boaventura de Sousa, 26n.78
Sasportes, José, 44n.27

Savigliano, Marta E., 2n.6, 28n.83, 52n.56, 130, 130n.35, 132n.55, 134n.64, 155n.132, 227n.211
savior spectatorship, 89–90n.38
scenarios of discovery, 108n.91
Schneider, Florence, 194n.81
Schneider, Luis Mario, 5n.11
Schneider, Rebecca, 30n.86
School of Dance (Escuela de Danza), 175–76
School of Dynamic Plastic Art (Escuela de Plástica Dinámica), 172–76
Schwall, Elizabeth B., 8n.20, 226n.206
scientific discourse, 89–92
Scolieri, Paul A., 7n.17
Second Mexican Empire, 43–44, 53–54
Segura, Felipe, 181n.34, 182n.39, 188n.53
Seijas, Tatiana, 18n.53, 20n.62
Seis Danzas Clasicas (Six classical dances, Waldeen), 212
Serpentine Dance, 64–67
Serur, Raquel, 101n.75
sexual identities
  forty-one *maricones*, 60–64
  staging acceptable expressions of, 58–59
Shawn, Ted, 66n.116, 153
Shea Murphy, Jacqueline, 113, 153n.126
Sheridan, Guillermo, 5n.11
"Silent War" (against Sokolow) 202–6
Siqueiros, David Alfaro, 4–5, 81*f*, 214n.165, 241–42
Siu, Lok C. D., 10n.24
Six classical dances (*Seis Danzas Clasicas* en Waldeen), 212
Slaughter of the innocents (*La matanza de los inocentes*), 196–98, 220
slavery, 16–17, 16n.44
Slayton, Jeff, 245n.62
Snow, Mitchell K., 6n.13, 153n.123, 234n.5
social engineers, 128–30
socialization, 11–26
  ballet and emergence of new artists, theater, and dance genres, 50–54
  debating aesthetics of formations for, 72–74
  excavating racial and social genealogies, 17–21
  mechanisms of racial and social distinction in new Spain caste system, 12–17
  Pavlova's *Fantasía Mexicana*, 130–36
  racial ideologies in production of marked and unmarked bodies, 21–24
  value of embodied mestizo modernisms' racial and cultural markings, 24–26
  visibilizing and racializing whiteness, 21
social values, 6

Sociedad Indianista (Indianist Society), 91–92, 101–2
Sokolovas, 234–35
Sokolow, Anna, 7n.17, 10n.24, 189–206, 194n.78
  anti-Semitism in Mexico, 192n.70
  Ballet de Bellas Artes, 198–99
  contrasting views between Waldeen and, 233–37
  dances as revolutionary art, 194–98
  La Paloma Azul, 199–201
  "Silent War" against, 202–6
Sorel, P., 159n.149
Sorondo, Xavier, 227
spatial *mestizaje*, 12–17, 35–36
Spector, Sasha, 194n.81
Spenser, Daniela, 185n.44
Srinivasan, Priya, 2n.6
stage effects, 52
St. Denis, Ruth, 208n.141
Stein, William W., 145n.93
Strangeness (in dance), 155

Tablada, José Juan, 46, 58, 99n.63, 99n.65, 100n.67
Tally, Robert T., Jr., 35n.3
tandas, 88
Tarazona brothers, 95–97
Tauro, Alberto, 143n.85
Taylor, Diana, 91n.46, 108n.91, 120n.4, 162n.164
Teatro Arbeu, 53–54, 87–88, 126, 137–38
Teatro Granat, 137–38
Teatro Romea, 156–57
Tehuanas, 89
Tenenbaum, Barbara A., 96n.56
Tenorio-Trillo, Mauricio, 152n.121
Thierry, Celestina, 41–42
Thompson, Alvin O., 16n.45
Thompson, David A., 82–83
Tibol, Raquel, 235n.8
Tierra (Land), 188n.53
tiples, 54, 88, 132
Torgovnick, Marianna, 53n.59
Torres Alonso, Eduardo, 226n.207
Torres Quintero, Gregorio, 48n.42
Tortajada Quiroz, Margarita, 166n.175, 166n.177, 180n.32, 182n.38, 184n.42, 187n.45, 187n.49, 188nn.53–54, 189n.59, 234n.5, 234–35n.6
Tórtola Valencia, Carmen, 121n.5, 154n.128, 154–55n.131, 157–58n.144, 159n.151
transnational elite alliances, 126n.20
transnational feminism, 89–90n.38

INDEX   275

transnational nationalisms, 1–33, 118–67, 230–49
   coloniality of modernist mestizo artistic practices, 122–23
   construction of US mestizo modernities, 237–43
   Desmadre of Rascuache Mestizaje (Primera Generación Dance Collective), 243–49
   emergence of Mexican nationalist dance, 233–37
   establishing national dance repertoire, 164–67
   forging new nations, 121–22
   Pavlova's *Fantasía Mexicana*, 125–42
   revalorizing indigenous, 123–25
   Rouskaya resurrecting Aztec race, 142–53
   Valencia's Inca-inspired Latin American pan-indigeneity, 154–64
Trinidad Huertas ("La Cuenca"), 68
Trio Lara, 88
Twinam, Ann, 15nn.39–41, 15n.42, 22n.64

UNAM (National Autonomous University of Mexico), 230
United States, 189–92, 230–49
   construction of US mestizo modernities, 237–43
   Desmadre of Rascuache Mestizaje (Primera Generación Dance Collective), 243–49
   emergence of Mexican nationalist dance, 233–37
   investment in Mexico, 34–35n.2
   looking at for modernist formula to revolutionary dance, 189–92
universalism, 25–26, 172–73, 212–19
universalist socialism, 176–89
Urías Horcasitas, Beatriz, 91n.48, 168n.1

Valdelomar, Abraham, 142–43
Valencia, Carmen Tórtola, 121–22, 154–64
Vargas, Steven, 247n.68
Vasconcelos, José, 27n.82, 128, 166n.175, 166n.177, 167n.178
Vaughan, Mary Kay, 4n.9, 5n.10, 226n.207
Vázquez Mantecón, María Del Carmen, 1n.1, 18n.50, 19n.57
Vega, Lope de, 202–3
Velazquez, Marco, 5n.10
Verbitzty, Sonia, 214–16
Villanueva, Carlos, 224n.200
Vinson, Ben, III, 13n.32, 20n.62, 27n.82
Viva México phrase, 2nn.4–5

Waldeen (Waldeen Falkenstein), 168–69, 189–92, 206–25
   anti-Semitism in Mexico, 192n.70
   contrasting views between Sokolow and, 233–37
   dance critics, 219–25
   La Coronela, 212–19
   way to Mexico, 207–12
Waldeenas, 234–35
Wanderer, 236
Warden, Claire, 177n.22, 188n.51
War Poem (*Poema Guerrero*), 194–96
Warren, Larry, 193n.72, 193n.76, 194n.78, 235n.9
wars of the flowers, 99–100
Wasserman, Mark, 34–35n.2, 86n.17
Waters, Elizabeth, 210
Way, J. T., 10n.24
Weeks, William Earl, 153n.123
Wentink, Andrew, 139n.79
Western expansion, 42
white and whiteness, 36–37, 89, 99, 101–2, 116–17, 119–22, 127, 129, 135–36, 140, 145, 146–47, 149–50, 151–52, 165, 177, 212–13, 219–20n.178
   caste system, 12–17
   as dominant ideology in post/colonial Mexico, 38
   La Coronela, 228
   performing desire to be, 74–79
   products to whiten skin, 76, 77*f*, 85
   racial ideologies in production of marked and unmarked bodies, 21–24
   Serpentine Dance, 64–67
   visibilizing and racializing, 21
Widener, Winifred, 210
Wilcox, Emily, 226n.206
Williams, Raymond, 12n.28
Wilson, Woodrow, 124n.12
World War I, 3–4, 121
World War II, 126n.20, 234–35
Wright, Amie, 131n.41
Wylie, Lesley, 164n.170

Ybarra Frausto, Tomás, 245n.60

Zamora, Francisco, 130n.34, 132n.56
Zanini, Ester, 87
Zárate Toscano, Verónica, 27n.81, 111n.107
zarzuela cómico-fantástica de gran espectáculo, 58
zarzuelas, 51–54
Zavala, Adriana, 4n.9, 129n.31
Zócalo plaza, 107, 108
Zoraida Vázquez, Josefina, 224n.201
Zybin, Hipólito, 171–76, 173n.8, 187n.50